*Accounting as social and institutional practice* is the first major collection of critical and socio-historical analyses of accounting. It gathers together work by scholars of international renown to address the conditions and consequences of accounting practice. Challenging conventional views that accounting is a technical practice, and that it comprises little more than bookkeeping, this collection demonstrates the importance of analysing the multiple arenas in which accounting emerges and operates. As accounting continues to gain in importance in so many spheres of social life, an understanding of this calculative technology is vital. Its relevance extends far beyond the discipline of accounting. This book will be of considerable interest not only to accountants, but to specialists in organizational analysis, sociologists, and political scientists, as well as the general reader interested in understanding the increasing significance of accounting in contemporary society.

*Cambridge Studies in Management* 24

# Accounting as social and institutional practice

*Cambridge Studies in Management*

Formerly Management and Industrial Relations series

*Editors*
WILLIAM BROWN, *University of Cambridge*
ANTHONY HOPWOOD, *London School of Economics*
and PAUL WILLMAN, *London Business School*

*Cambridge Studies in Management* focuses on the human and organizational aspects of management. It covers the areas of organization theory and behaviour, strategy and business policy, the organizational and social aspects of accounting, personnel, and human resource management, industrial relations and industrial sociology.

The series aims for high standards of scholarship and seeks to publish the best among original theoretical and empirical research; innovative contributions to advancing understanding in the area; and books which synthesize and/or review the best of current research, and aim to make the work published in specialist journals more widely accessible.

The books are intended for an international audience among specialists in university and business schools, undergraduate, graduate and MBA students, and also for a wider readership among business practitioners and trade unionists.

*For a list of titles in this series, see end of book.*

# Accounting as social and institutional practice

*Edited by*

## Anthony G. Hopwood

*London School of Economics and Political Science*

## Peter Miller

*London School of Economics and Political Science*

CAMBRIDGE
UNIVERSITY PRESS

Published by the Press Syndicate of the University of Cambridge
The Pitt Building, Trumpington Street, Cambridge CB2 1RP
40 West 20th Street, New York, NY 10011-4211, USA
10 Stamford Road, Oakleigh, Melbourne 3166, Australia

First published 1994

Printed in Great Britain at the University Press, Cambridge

*A catalogue record for this book is available from the British Library*

*Library of Congress cataloguing in publication data*

Accounting as social and institutional practice / Anthony G. Hopwood,
Peter Miller, [editors].
   p.    cm. – (Cambridge studies in management; 24)
Includes index.
ISBN 0 521 39092 3 (hc)    0 521 46965 1 (pb)
1. Accounting–Social aspects.   2. Managerial accounting.
I. Hopwood, Anthony G.   II. Miller, Peter, 1954–  .   III. Series.
HF5657.A2568   1994
657–dc20   93-45992   CIP

ISBN 0 521 39092 3 hardback
ISBN 0 521 46965 1 paperback

SE

# Contents

# Contributors

PETER ARMSTRONG is Senior Lecturer at Sheffield University Management School, where he has been since 1991.

PHILIP BOUGEN is Professor of Accounting, Madrid Business School, where he has been since 1990.

STUART BURCHELL is the European Adviser to the Special Engineering Contractors Group in London.

COLIN CLUBB is Lecturer in Accounting at the Management School, Imperial College of Science, Technology and Medicine.

DAVID COOPER is Professor of Accounting at the University of Alberta, Edmonton, where he has been since 1989.

ANTHONY HOPWOOD is Professor of International Accounting and Financial Management at the London School of Economics and Political Science, where he has been since 1985.

KEITH HOSKIN is Lecturer in Accounting and Finance at the University of Warwick, where he has been since 1989.

ANNE LOFT completed her PhD at the London Business School in 1986, and is now Associate Professor of Accounting at the Copenhagen Business School.

BRENDAN MCSWEENEY is Lecturer in Accounting and Finance at the University of Warwick, where he has been since 1987.

RICHARD MACVE is Julian Hodge Professor of Accounting, University of Wales, Aberystwyth, where he has been since 1979.

PETER MILLER is a Senior Lecturer in Accounting at the London School of Economics and Political Science, where he has been since 1987.

TED O'LEARY is Associate Professor of Accounting, National University of Ireland (University College, Cork), where he has been since 1991.

MICHAEL POWER is a Lecturer in Accounting at the London School of Economics and Political Science, where he has been since 1987.

TONY PUXTY is Professor of Accounting and Finance at the University of Strathclyde, where he has been since 1987.

KEITH ROBSON is a Lecturer in Accounting at the School of Management, UMIST, where he has been since 1988.

GRAHAME THOMPSON is Senior Lecturer in Economics at the Open University, where he has been since 1972.

JIM TOMLINSON is Reader in Economic History at Brunel University, where he has been since 1977.

HUGH WILLMOTT is a Reader in the School of Management at UMIST, where he has been since 1988.

# Acknowledgements

The editors and publishers acknowledge with thanks permission from the following to reproduce copyright material.

University of North Carolina Press, for figures 2.2 and 2.7, from R.E. Taylor, *No Royal Road: Luca Pacioli and His Times* (1942).

T.C. & E.C. Jack, for figure 2.3, from R. Brown, *History of Accounting and Accountants* (1905).

Kraus Reprint Co., for figure 2.4, from S. Morison, *Fra Luca de Pacioli of Borgo San Sepolcro* (1969).

Scholar Book Co., for figures 2.5 and 2.6, from J.B. Geijsbeek, *Ancient Double-Entry Bookkeeping* (1914).

# 1 Accounting as social and institutional practice: an introduction

*Peter Miller*

In the space of little more than a decade, there has been a profound transformation in the understanding of accounting. Accounting has come to be regarded as a *social and institutional practice*, one that is intrinsic to, and constitutive of social relations, rather than derivative or secondary. This concern with the social and institutional aspects of accounting has entailed a move by researchers beyond organizations as the exclusive level of research. Attention has been directed to the ways in which accounting exerts an influence on, and in turn is influenced by, a multiplicity of agents, agencies, institutions, and processes. Particular accounting events have been analysed in terms of their conditions of possibility, as well as their consequences. The manner in which accounting has become embedded in so many areas of social and economic life has been a continuing concern. And the focus throughout has been on accounting as a *practice*, a view that accounting is, above all, an attempt to intervene, to act upon individuals, entities and processes to transform them and to achieve specific ends. From such a perspective, accounting is no longer to be regarded as a neutral device that merely documents and reports 'the facts' of economic activity. Accounting can now be seen as a set of practices that affects the type of world we live in, the type of social reality we inhabit, the way in which we understand the choices open to business undertakings and individuals, the way in which we manage and organize activities and processes of diverse types, and the way in which we administer the lives of others and ourselves.

To view accounting in this way is to attend to the complex interplay between ways of calculating and ways of managing social and organizational life. For accounting techniques, ranging from double-entry bookkeeping to costing, invent a particular way of understanding and acting upon events and processes. There are complex linkages between the calculative practices of accounting and other managerial practices. These calculative practices are more than imperfect mirrors of economic reality. They do more than distort or modify results after the event. Accounting practices create the costs and the returns whose reality actors and agents are asked to acknowledge and respond to. Accounting practices define the profits and

1

the losses to which various parties react. Accounting practices make up the realm of financial flows to which certain Western societies have come to accord such vital significance. And, as a body of expertise, accounting competes with and intrudes onto the terrains occupied by other bodies of expertise, whether these terrains be those of the engineer, the lawyer, the economist, or the business strategist. In all these different ways, the calculative devices of accountancy have shaped and formed the possibilities for action in many organizations. It is in these multiple respects that accounting can be analysed as a social and institutional practice. The emergence, distribution, location, and intensity of accounting practices are thus research issues that promise to tell us something about the type of social relations that obtain in different national settings, and at different points in time.

At least three distinctive aspects of this view of accounting as social and institutional practice can be identified.

First, there is an emphasis on accounting as a *technology*, a way of intervening, a device for acting upon activities, individuals and objects in such a way that the world may be transformed. As one of the pre-eminent means of quantification in certain Western societies, accounting accords a particular form of visibility to events and processes, and in so doing helps to change them. It is this transformative capacity that is emphasized here. For to calculate and record the costs of an activity is to alter the way in which it can be thought about and acted upon. To reconfigure an organization into profit centres, cost centres, investment centres, strategic business units, or whatever is to change lines of responsibility and the possibilities of action by a change in the form of visibility. To evaluate performance by reference to normalized returns on investment, or by benchmarking costs against those of competitors, is to change incentive structures and impose the requirement that actions conform to the calculations that will be made of them. To insist that investment opportunities be quantified by the use of discounting techniques is to alter the ways in which the options open to managers are represented and assessed. Even if individuals seek to avoid or subvert the calculations made of and by them, the economic norm installed by such calculations remains in place and provides a more or less enduring reference point.

It is a singular capacity of accounting to be able to change the world in these different ways. Whilst accounting shares with other means of quantification such as statistics the ability to translate qualities into quantities, it does so largely by translating these qualitative differences into financial values which seek no further referent. In those Western societies that have given such elevated status to these financial summaries, this capacity of accounting has had far-reaching effects. By reducing diverse activities and processes to the end point of the single figure, accounting makes comparable the entities of which it produces calculations. In the process, accounting helps make possible a particular way of governing individuals and activities. For such numbers can be used to evaluate and compare individuals, departments or divisions. And they can also be used by individuals themselves to compare where they are with where they should be, what they have achieved with what they should have achieved. Whether this single figure takes the form of a Return on Investment, a Net Present Value of an investment opportunity, Earnings Per Share, Profit, or the labour efficiency variance of a department, accounting draws much of its social authority from the objectivity and neutrality accorded to the single financial figure in certain Western societies. By this device, accounting can claim a legitimacy that is set above the fray, apart from political interests and intrigue. Even if this objectivity and neutrality is questionable and always open to dispute, the elegance of the single figure provides a legitimacy that, at least in certain Western societies, seems difficult to disrupt or disturb.

Secondly, there is a focus on the complex language and meanings intrinsic to accounting. The term *rationales* can be used to designate this aspect of accounting as a social and institutional practice. For accounting practices are more than the numerical computations of costs, profits, losses, and returns. Accounting practices include particular discursive representations and vocabularies. These are assembled at various collective levels, articulated in diverse locales, and in relation to disparate concerns. It is these rationales, often borrowed from other bodies of expertise, that mobilize the calculative technologies of accounting. It is through such meanings that accounting practices are endowed with a significance that extends beyond the task to which they are applied, yet without determining the consequences or outcomes of their deployment in any particular setting.

For instance, calculations of costs are inextricably linked with the language of costliness and efficiency. Evaluations of investment opportunities are reciprocally related to the value of choice, embodied in the notion of managerial decision-making. And the selection of cost and profit centres as ways of organizing activities is mutually related to the vocabulary of responsibility. Reciprocally, notions such as efficiency and competitiveness often come to be translated into, and held to require, the calculative apparatus of accounting. Through such means, abstract notions of economic discourse are made calculable and knowable.

An understanding of accounting as a social and institutional practice suggests a need to attend to these rationales, as well as to the calculative practices that make up accountancy. For it is these rationales, rather than ones specific to the activities and processes in question, that come to articulate ways of knowing and managing organizations. And it is these rationales that provide the basis for a wider elaboration and diffusion of the calculative devices that make up accounting. Rationales of costliness and efficiency, of decision-making, of responsibility, of competitiveness, and much more besides come to constitute truths in the name of which organizations are to be remade, processes reconfigured, and attempts made to redefine the identity of individuals. Once established, these truths come to be taken as essential for the proper government of economic and social life.

Thirdly, in referring to accounting as a social and institutional practice, we seek to draw attention to the ways in which the 'economic' domain is *constituted and reconstituted* by the changing calculative practices that provide a knowledge of it.[1] For it is through the calculative machinery of accountancy that highly disparate ways of producing and providing things are made knowable in economic terms. The calculative technologies of accountancy make operable at the levels of firms, organizations, departments, divisions, and persons the abstract images of economic theory. Such entities can be construed as streams of discounted cash flows, costs of varying types, income defined in differing ways, collections of assets and claims, choices construed as decisions, and much else besides. Rather than begin from the assumption that there exists an irreducible sphere of economic events forever distinct from social practice, the perspective is inverted if one understands accounting as a social and institutional practice. The domain of economic processes is itself seen to be in important part the outcome of calculative practices and rationales. It is accounting that renders such processes visible in financial terms. It is accounting that 'makes up' the financial flows into which organizations come to be transformed.

By transforming the physical flows of organizations into financial flows, accounting creates a particular realm of economic calculation of which judgements can be made, actions taken or justified, policies devised, and disputes generated and adjudicated. This calculative expertise changes over time. In emphasizing the constitutive and changing nature of these calculations, attention is drawn to the reciprocal relations between the technical practices of accounting and the social relations they form and seek to manage. It is the historically specific assemblages, the fragile relations formed between a multiplicity of practices, and the tensions that traverse such complexes, that enable accounting to achieve such heightened significance at particular moments. The technical practice of accounting is intrinsically and irredeemably social.

These three dimensions of accounting are complementary. Technologies depend on rationales as a way of setting out the ends and objectives of particular ways of calculating. Specific rationales can entail appeals for more accounting, or a new way of accounting. And, at different points in time, or in different settings, a particular calculative technology can be linked up to different rationales. The combined effect of calculative technologies together with the rationales that give them their wider significance can be to constitute and reconstitute the realm of financial flows into which organizations can be transformed. To identify these three dimensions of accounting is in part to formulate working hypotheses, in part to offer an empirical description of what accountancy is and does. To address all three dimensions together is to address the conditions, capacities and consequences of accounting. It is to the formation of this distinctive and still developing agenda that we now turn.

## The contexts of accounting

The concern with accounting as a social and institutional practice emerged in large part within the discipline of accounting itself. It was principally management accounting practices that provided the reference point for this new research agenda. The starting point here was a concern with the *contexts* of accounting.

Accounting practices had been studied by a number of social scientists since at least the early 1950s.[2] But these pioneering studies remained relatively neglected by researchers interested in analysing how accounting operated in particular organizational settings. As late as 1978, Hopwood (1978: 4) could argue[3] that:

Even in cases where accounting has been studied in its organizational context, emphasis still has been placed on gaining a comparatively static understanding of the more individual, or at the most group, aspects of the process.

Budgeting, a key focus of accounting research during the 1970s, tended to be examined without consideration of its social and organizational aspects, according to Hopwood (1978). Studies of participation in the budgeting process, one of the principal objects of research in this area, had a largely static conception of the relationship between participation and managerial attitudes and styles (Hopwood, 1978). There was little attempt to analyse the organizational dynamics by which budgeting was interrelated with other organizational control structures and strategies.

This appeal for a more dynamic appreciation of accounting in its organizational context was to be one of many. But, by 1980, the appeal to study accounting in the contexts in which it was located was given a wider social science setting. By this date, a view was emerging that a much bolder step was required. It was important that accounting be situated in its *social* as well as its *organizational* contexts. It was not sufficient simply to develop and extend the analyses of accounting in its organizational contexts. It was necessary to look beyond the boundaries of organizations, and to address the interrelations between particular calculative practices and other managerial practices.[4] Moreover, a changed concept of organizations, and of the ways in which they were linked to their 'environments', was in the process of being formulated.[5] A further, and hitherto neglected, dimension was thus to be added to the study of accounting. The study of the organizational and social roles of accounting was declared, portentously but accurately, to be 'an area of enormous and largely uncharted complexity' (Burchell *et al.*, 1980: 22).

As accounting had come to occupy an ever more significant position in the functioning of modern industrial societies, it had become one of the most influential modes of management of organizational and social arrangements (Burchell *et al.*, 1980). Whether within private sector firms, the public sector, or in the management of financial resources more generally, accounting had become a dominant feature of social and economic life. Accounting research, it was argued, should recognize these broader aspects of the operation of the accounting craft. And to do so, such research needed to draw upon a much wider range of social science tools, and to deploy these across a more extensive terrain.

This appeal to study the roles of accounting in their organizational and social contexts entailed a distinctive understanding of the conditions and consequences of accounting technologies. These were to be understood as devices that constituted and shaped particular organizational and social arrangements, often in concert with other practices. Accounting was held to be central to the creation of specific patterns of organizational visibility, the articulation of certain forms of organizational structure and segmentation, and the formation and reinforcement of relations of power (Burchell *et al.*, 1980). It was these broader social roles of accounting that were to be brought into the picture. The mundane calculative routines of accounting were to be accorded the significance their social role merited. If accounting was a central and influential mechanism of economic and social management, then it should be studied as such. It was no longer sufficient to study accounting more or less wholly within the boundaries of organizations.

The call to study accounting in its organizational and social contexts took as its starting point accounting as it operated within organizations. But it added a rider which may now appear self-evident: organizations do not exist in a vacuum. Organizations, and accounting practices within them, are intrinsically dynamic and social entities. Organizations are reciprocally linked to a multiplicity of interests. Some of these interests are located primarily within organizations, some of them are located in the environment within which organizations operate, and some of them straddle the boundaries between organizations and their environments.

The dynamics of agency relationships, a research topic with its own distinct traditions and concerns, was identified as a key example of such processes (Hopwood, 1983). A focus on agency relationships should, or so it was argued, make possible an analysis of the ways in which the relevance of accounting information was determined within the contexts within which it was used, rather than limiting research to the formal and declared property of accounting systems. The operation of regulatory institutions was seen to offer another opportunity for the analysis of accounting as an organizational and social practice. In this case, one might investigate the political dimensions of accounting policy formulation. The technical components of accounting regulation, and the search for technical 'solutions', could be studied as key aspects of a complex pattern of institutional and political influences. In these different ways, an appreciation could be gained of the manner in which the roles of accounting were shaped by the pressures and demands for accounting innovation, rather than by having recourse to a presumed essence or purely technical function of accounting.

The issue of interests, and their influence on accounting practices, provided a focal point for researchers concerned with financial accounting. This gave further support to the view that accounting research should move beyond the boundaries of organizations. There was a concern with the rise of the notion of 'economic consequences'.[6] This referred to the impact of accounting reports on the decision-making behaviour of business, government, unions, investors and creditors. A concern with 'economic consequences' entailed a questioning of the assumption that accounting policy-making was neutral in its effects, or at least that it was not responsible for any such effects. Accounting standard-setting thus came to be seen as a practice that transcended traditional questions of accounting measurement and fair presentation. It came instead to be viewed as a process fundamentally imbued with 'economic consequences'.

The issue of 'interests' was made a key feature of a related research agenda that has come to be called 'positive accounting'.[7] The model here was drawn from an economic theory of the political process, one that views politics as consisting of a competition among individuals for wealth transfers. Within such a model, politicians and bureaucrats, like all other individuals, are held to have incentives to seek wealth transfers via the political process. Numbers in accounting reports can thus be seen as used by politicians in creating or resolving 'crises', reported earnings receiving particular attention. Price- and rate-setting by government regulatory agencies is held to provide further opportunities for interests to impact on accounting policy. For, in those cases where the rates or prices are set on the basis of formulae that use accounting-determined costs, incentives are held to be created for corporate managers to lobby regulatory agencies and standard-setting bodies for accounting procedures that yield the most favourable rates.[8]

But despite these developments, the research agenda at the beginning of the 1980s still tended to be weighted in favour of the organizational aspects of accounting practices. A conference held at the Graduate School of Management of the University of California at Los Angeles in July 1981, under the auspices of the journal *Accounting, Organizations and Society*, signalled the still nascent nature of research into the social contexts of accounting practices.[9] Indeed, the theme of this conference was 'Accounting in its Organizational Context'. Papers were presented that drew upon a wide range of approaches, including contingency theory, analyses of intraorganizational power relations, studies of the implication of accounting within other organizational processes, and historical analyses of the ways in which accounting had contributed to the emergence of the modern business enterprise.[10]

However, a wider agenda was present also, one which drew attention firmly and explicitly to the social and institutional contexts in which accounting operated.[11] There were suggestions that research should focus on the symbolic as distinct from the technical uses of accounting. To the extent that the symbolic roles of accounting help to define the real, and to give legitimacy to existing practices, then organizational life can in turn be modified in the name of the symbolic roles. And there were calls more generally for a greater appreciation of the broader social and ideological factors that had contributed to the rise of accounting.

These calls to address the social and institutional contexts of accounting practice were in part the result of an empirical observation: in so far as the agencies of the modern world increasingly appeal to accounting as a way of demonstrating the rational nature of organizational processes, then accounting research should address such institutional pressures. These pressures arose from bodies such as the State, the media and professional institutions. They arose also in a much more diffuse manner from appeals to notions such as 'efficiency', 'effectiveness', 'value for money' and much else besides. Accounting was, and still is, often held out as the means by which such ideals could be made operable.

The proposals to study the social and institutional dimensions of accounting were also in part the result of intellectual agendas from disciplines such as sociology and political science permeating accounting research. These disciplines started from the presumption that the study of discrete practices, events and processes needed to be conducted in relation to the changing nature of social institutions, structures, roles, and processes. As accounting sought to establish itself increasingly as a broadly based social discipline, so it came to take note of such intellectual agendas.

Reflecting on the complementary nature of the distinct agendas present at the 1981 UCLA conference, Hopwood spoke of 'the external origins of internal accounts'. Accounting, he argued, 'can never be seen in purely organizational terms' (Hopwood, 1983: 302). The paradox of this conclusion to a conference dedicated to exploring the organizational nature of accounting was not accidental. Rather, it was a way of highlighting the complex of pressures, demands and influences that operated on accounting practices. It was a way of signalling how much further accounting research needed to develop if it was to address such factors. And it was a way of registering the severe limitations that would result from continuing with an exclusively intraorganizational approach to the study of accounting. For to restrict the study of accounting to that which took place within organizations was to limit arbitrarily and mistakenly the terrain of accounting research. The factors influencing accounting change and innovation, the dynamics of accounting in its relations with other organizational processes, and the broader consequences of accounting, did not respect organizational boundaries. Whether one was interested in conducting field studies of accounting in action, historical analyses of the changing forms of accounting practices, or even conventional analyses based on contingency theory, the conclusion was the same. Accounting could not and should not be studied as an organizational practice in isolation from the wider social and institutional context in which it operated.

### Accounting and institutional environments

A concern with the social and institutional aspects of accounting emerged also in disciplines beyond accounting. Most notably, and with enduring effects, this occurred at a particular juncture between sociology and organization theory. Here, institutional theorists depicted accounting as a key element in the 'myth structure' of rationalized societies (Meyer and Rowan, 1977). Quite apart from its possible efficacy, the myths of accountants were held to have become part of the taken-for-granted means to accomplish organizational ends. The myths of the accountant – whether with respect to particular categories of costs, or the more general ceremonial value attached to financial values in a rationalized society – were placed on a similar footing to the myths of the doctor and other rationalized professions.

Institutional theorists argued that formal organizations are driven to incorporate the practices and procedures defined by prevailing concepts of what is rational (Meyer and Rowan, 1977). The labels of the organization chart, the conventions of modern accounting, and the vocabularies of personnel experts were identified as key mechanisms for isomorphism between environmental institutions and organizational practices. Institutional theorists argued that to the extent that organizations incorporate such practices and procedures, they increase their legitimacy and their survival prospects. In the process, they transform the formal structures of organizations in line with powerful institutional rules. These rules can then come to be binding on particular organizations. The formal structures of organizations can thus reflect the myths of their institutional environments, rather than the demands of their work activities.

This process by which formal organizations come to take on more and more of the rationalized aspects of their environments was held to be a general one. Professions were identified as one aspect of this process. Individually, the professions provide rules and procedures for taking activities out of the realm of 'moral mysteries', and bringing them within the realm of impersonal techniques. Taken as a system, the professions were also seen to be highly institutionalized. Legal obligations, the delegation of activities, and squabbles over jurisdictions, all demonstrated the importance of allocating activities to the appropriate professional domain. Various programmes for formalized organizations were also identified as highly influential in institutionalizing conceptions of the appropriate ways of conducting various functions. These ranged from programmes deemed appropriate to a business, to programmes deemed appropriate to a university. Such programmes tended to be ready-made formulae, held to be relevant to any organization of a given type. Institutionalized techniques were also seen as a key part of the process by which organizations take on the rationalized aspects of their environments. Technical procedures of production, accounting, personnel selection and much else besides were part of this process. Aside from their possible efficiency, such institutionalized techniques helped establish a conception of an organization as rational, responsible, and modern.

From an institutional perspective, accounting was seen as just one of the ways in which organizations come to incorporate rational conceptions of ways of organizing. Accounting was not unique. But it was nonetheless an increasingly central aspect of the institutionalization process of modern societies. Accounting provided a set of techniques for organizing and monitoring certain activities. Accounting also provided a language or a vocabulary by which to delineate organizational goals, procedures and policies. These vocabularies of motive were held to be analogous to the vocabularies of motive used to account for the activities of individuals. As Meyer and Rowan (1977: 31) commented:

Just as jealousy, anger, altruism, and love are myths that interpret and explain the actions of individuals, the myths of doctors, of accountants, or of the assembly line explain organizational activities.

This irreverent view of a practice that had long claimed the title 'profession' was much more than mere cynicism. It was the opening up of a substantial new research agenda. Accounting could henceforth be studied with much the same tools, and in a similar fashion, to the way in which organization theorists and sociologists had so fruitfully studied other professionalized practices such as law, medicine, and psychiatry. One could study modern accounting as a ceremonial function that legitimates organizations with the mythical 'users' of accounting information: internal participants, stockholders, the public, and with agencies such as the Securities Exchange Commission. One could study the origins of particular accounting practices in relation to their roles as rational institutional myths. One could study the impact of particular forms of accounting on organizations as an institutional process, rather than being limited to asking questions of their presumed efficiency effects. One could seek to explain organizational change in terms of isomorphic tendencies with collectively valued elements. And one could study the ways in which different environments determine the amount of accounting done in a particular society or organization, rather than tacitly accepting that this derives from intrinsically necessary technical work processes (Meyer, 1986).

The notion that accounting was a part of the institutionalized and rationalized myth structure of a society contributed to a significant broadening of the agenda of accounting research.[12] It helped reinforce and elaborate the already emerging shift in focus away from accounting viewed as a functional and neutral response to organizational imperatives.

More recently, a number of studies have demonstrated that accounting can be understood in this way as part of the cultural apparatus of a society. Covaleski and Dirsmith (1988a, 1988b) examined how, by whom, and for what purposes, societal expectations of acceptable budgetary practices were articulated, enforced, and modified during a period of organizational decline. The emphasis here was on the active political agency involved in the process of institutionalizing budgeting within a particular university's administrative apparatus. Fligstein (1987, 1990) studied the increasing dominance of finance personnel in the control of large corporations by pointing to changes in the strategy and structure of organizations, changes in anti-trust laws, and a process of mimicking of firms in similar environments. In this instance, a structural theory of power illustrated how key actors gain power both as a result of events outside their organizations and as a result of their definition of key problems within them. This institutional process was, Fligstein argued, one of the key ways in which a shift in intra-organizational power in favour of finance professionals was brought about. In a similar vein, Mezias (1990) studied the factors that explain the financial reporting practices used by large for-profit enterprises, and sought to explain these by adopting an interorganizational level of analysis. A study of financial reporting practices should, Mezias argued, focus primarily on entities in the institutional environment of firms, rather than on the focal firms themselves.

Other studies drew more loosely on the institutional perspective, whilst reinforcing the importance of analysing the effects of institutional environments on accounting systems and other organizational practices. Berry *et al.* (1985), in a study that drew in part on an institutional frame of reference, demonstrated that management control in an area of the National Coal Board could be used to enhance ambiguity and to provide legitimacy in and about the organization. In such a context, accounting statements were ambiguous documents with well known uncertainties about the reliability of the data and the extent of the controllability. But the ambiguity of such documents permitted management to cope with conflicting and often inconsistent demands from trades unions and government. Espeland and Hirsch (1990) also addressed the roles of accounting in legitimating and facilitating certain ways of organizing. The focus here was the conglomerate movement in American business during the 1960s. A proliferation of conglomerate mergers contributed, Espeland and Hirsch argued, to a reconceptualization of the nature of the corporation that emphasized its financial rather than its productive capacities. And the notion that accounting systems can help provide external legitimacy was further supported in Ansari and Euske's (1987) longitudinal field study of the patterns of information use in a military organization. The introduction of a particular costing system was argued to be a way of demonstrating to Congress and other external constituencies the rationality of internal control processes.

In their different ways, these studies reinforced the move towards analysing accounting as a social and institutional practice. For institutional theorists, the point was to address those pressures within the environment that led organizations to incorporate institutionalized activities, and thereby to establish or enhance legitimacy. To understand accounting practices from this perspective, one needed to trace the causal processes that linked accounting with its institutional environment. The nature and direction of these causal processes was to be the object of research. But the implications of this research agenda were more far-reaching than simply the demonstration that institutional factors needed to be addressed in seeking to explain the emergence, persistence and transformation of accounting practices. Institutional theorists substantially strengthened the intellectual case for accounting research moving beyond the confines of the firm and the organization, to address all aspects of accounting understood as a social and institutional practice.

## Economic calculation, economic policy, and economic discourse

Developments on the borders between economics and sociology gave further support to the concern with culturally specific forms of economic calculation (Cutler *et al.*, 1978). Yet the debates here were more localized, and tended to develop in parallel to research within the discipline of accounting, rather than in a close interrelationship with it. Nonetheless, the concern in this literature with the constitutive capacity of particular ways of calculating was remarkably similar to that which began to emerge within accounting in the late 1970s.

Enterprise calculation, it was argued, needed to be analysed in the concrete conditions of specific capitalist national economies, rather than by reference to general laws or tendencies of capitalist economies (Cutler *et al.*, 1978). Attention needed to be directed at the forms of organization and the conditions of operation of enterprises. For the criteria of calculation and the forms they took were shaped within particular institutional and social arenas. The measurement of returns, the calculation of costs, the manner in which the magnitude of the capital involved was determined, the mode of assessment of the enterprise's assets, and the overall evaluation of the performance of an enterprise in terms of 'profit' were all potentially variable. Different ways of calculating would produce different results. The category of profit was seen to be an outcome of particular forms of measurement, in conjunction with the choice of particular time periods for its application. Norms of calculation were thus seen as always potentially threatened by the existence of alternative and competing norms.

This concern with the formative effects of particular techniques of calculation was linked to a concern with economic policy, a concern that was again paralleled in the work of accounting researchers.[13] 'Policy' here was defined as much broader than simply State or governmental policy. Policy was taken to include the objectives and practices of any agent in the economic sphere. It was taken also to include the means and instruments through which these objectives were to be realized. This focus on the means and instruments of policy gave particular significance to techniques of economic calculation. For, if policies are articulated and made operable through particular calculative practices, and if those calculative practices define the costs, the revenues and the profits of enterprises, then it is difficult to disentangle economic policy and economic calculation. Moreover, policy and calculation require some agent or agency that calculates. Since such agents are always institutionally located, it was argued that the study of accounting as a particular form of economic calculation should be similarly located as an institutional practice. Analyses of accounting practices should address the dispersed organizational matrix within which they operate (Thompson, 1986: 9).

In a distinct, yet related vein, attention was focused on the historical nature of the categories of economic discourse. The point here was that it is not only the practices of economic calculation and measurement that change over time. The categories, concepts and meanings of economic discourse themselves change also, and these changes are linked to attempts to govern the domains in question in different ways. In so far as the management of a domain such as the economy is dependent on particular ways of conceptualizing the processes and entities to be included within it, then attention to the categories of economic discourse can have major implications for understanding changing forms of economic calculation.

The analysis of such apparently immutable categories as 'land' and 'labour' demonstrated the links between categories of economic discourse, and particular forms of economic calculation. For instance, in place of the moral or theological principles concerning the good performance of husbandry prevalent in the seventeenth century, there emerged around the middle of the eighteenth century a conception of the farm as a process (Tribe, 1978). In this new discursive formation, 'profit' was held to result from the good management of the farming process, rather than from the diligence of individuals who tended the resources provided by God. The farmer was understood as part of a series of exchanges in the economy which combined to effect the circulation of the product. The farm was understood as a unit of production, and could be compared with other units.

Within this new discursive formation, accounting came to occupy a number of important roles: it was the means by which texts were validated; it was the means by which the farmer organized and recorded his activities; and it was the means by which a landlord might control the actions of his estate manager. More generally, a numerical principle provided a means of 'discursive validation' (Tribe, 1978: 71). Calculation was the means by which the texts on farm management were validated. And once the farm had come to be regarded as a production unit, arguments could be advanced concerning the most appropriate size of such enterprises. Detailed records could be kept of items such as labour costs and working capital per acre. One could calculate the most profitable proportions for grass and arable farms, with differing capitals available. And one could construct 'ideal farms'. A plethora of calculations could be made, which would have significance and meaning only through the discursive formation within which they emerged.

In these different ways, and in disciplines at the margins of accounting, there emerged a concern with accounting as a social and institutional practice. A number of new research agendas were opened up. Accounting could now be studied with the same variety of social science tools as were available to other established disciplines.

### Multiple agendas

The concern to analyse accounting as a social and institutional practice has taken many forms. Thus far, the aim has been to set out some of the coordinates that helped shape the type of research present in this volume. But there has emerged in recent years a multiplicity of approaches to the study of accounting in its social and organizational contexts. The present volume presents just a selection of some of the key studies from this literature. Before proceeding to consider some of the issues raised by the chapters in this volume, it may be useful to identify briefly some of the related research agendas which have emerged in the accounting literature over the past decade or so. Of course, any review of this wider literature is inevitably selective. It is necessary to characterize broad themes or agendas to avoid simply listing all that has been said or done in the area. But if one is careful not to regard such themes or agendas as mutually exclusive categories, such a review can be of value as a way of indicating the multiplicity of ways in which accounting may be analysed.

One agenda in this literature can be termed an *ethnography* of accounting practices, to indicate a concern with accounting research that pays particular attention to the meanings and perceptions of those actors who develop and use accounting techniques or systems in particular settings.[14] Early research in this mode identified the importance of empirical research of the actual operation of accounting systems, and the need to commence from specific, real-world situations.[15] Such research would go beyond descriptive accounts of accounting systems, and would study the conditions and consequences of actual accounting practices in specific organizations. Case analyses should address accounting as a 'lived experience' for individual actors, and should recognize the symbolic use of accounting for individuals, whilst taking a critical view of the actor's definition of the situation (Boland and Pondy, 1983). Research of this type would, or so it was hoped, make possible an understanding of the way accounting practices contribute to the production and reproduction of organizational life (Roberts and Scapens, 1985).

This broad injunction to understand and explain accounting practices in concrete situations that have actually occurred, to focus on what was said and done in such situations, can be deployed in a wide variety of settings. It can be utilized when seeking to understand the apparently technical question of the changing relations between volumes and costs in the context of advanced manufacturing systems (Jonsson and Gronlund, 1988). For in such settings, practices and procedures are worked out in local settings. It is these local settings that need to be analysed and researched. Equally, a concern with the meanings people attach to their social world can prove valuable if one is seeking to understand accounting change within a particular organization, as Nahapiet (1988) has demonstrated. New ways of accounting have to be understood and made sense of. Even if resource allocation is thought of as an essentially routine activity, when new calculative practices are introduced, existing understandings can become problematic. In a similar manner, the emergence of a new organizational culture, one based on accounting rather than engineering, can be analysed in an interpretive frame (Dent, 1991).

An ethnography of accounting practices opens up new possibilities for accounting research. An allegorical tale of learning can convey the point that, in financial accounting, the communication of reality is also the construction of reality (Hines, 1988, 1989). A drama in five acts can convey the processes by which clinical budgeting practices are elaborated and articulated (Pinch *et al.*, 1989). The process of fabricating budgets can be traced by examining the chains of reasoning and mechanisms of influence involved in the building of a new budgeting system (Preston *et al.*, 1992). Internal accounting processes can be understood as powerfully influenced by the inspection and review processes of the British Inland Revenue (Preston, 1989).[16] And an *ex post* ethnography of the professional examination system of a professional accounting body can indicate some of the conditions and consequences of 'becoming' a professional accountant (Power, 1991).

A second agenda can be termed a *political economy* of accounting practices. As with the ethnography of accounting, this is a diverse agenda, rather than a unitary approach or method. At its most general level, a political economy of accounting means drawing attention to the conflicting political and economic interests at stake in accounting. It means emphasizing the fundamental interrelationship between political and economic forces in society. In place of a view of accounting as the provision of neutral technical information for decision-making, a political economy approach insists that accounting systems are often a mechanism through which power is exercised. In place of an image of accounting as the objective depiction of reality, it substitutes the view that accounting is a partial and interested language, one that furthers the interests of particular classes and occupational groups. And in place of an abstract notion of market equilibrium, a political economy approach highlights issues of social welfare and distribution.[17]

Political economy approaches in accounting have consisted in important part in a critique of other positions, in particular marginalist economics. There have also been a number of substantive studies conducted using such a framework. *Annual Reports* have been held to change in form and content in relation to strategies of capital accumulation (Neimark and Tinker, 1986). Modes of regulation of accounting practices have been held to vary according to the institutional and political structures in particular countries (Puxty *et al.*, 1987). The interrelations between accounting and industrial relations in a particular local context have been studied, via an analysis of the linkages formed between accounting and a variety of organizational priorities, structures and processes (Bougen, 1989). There has been a call to give greater attention to the conflicts of interest that divide the negotiating parties in contexts such as wage determination negotiations, illustrated by the example of British coalfield industrial relations (Bougen, Ogden and Outram, 1990).[18] The relative prominence of accounting controls over the labour process in British capitalism has been addressed in terms of the 'collective mobility project' of the accounting profession in the UK (Armstrong, 1985). This mobility project has, in turn, been analysed in terms of the key problems confronting British capitalism, and how these enabled the accounting profession to attain such a dominant position within the 'economic functions' of the global function of capital (Armstrong, 1987). And an historical–comparative method has been used to analyse the differential spread of practices of standard costing, budgeting, and the use of performance reports in the United States and Great Britain (Wardell and Weisenfeld, 1991).

Other studies have been conducted in a related mode. There has been an analysis of the interaction between State actions and the distributional consequences of accounting policies adopted by the US Medicare health insurance programme (Arnold, 1991). The links between cost accounting techniques and historically varying attempts to control the labour process have been addressed (Hopper and Armstrong, 1991). Laughlin (1987) has argued for the use of the critical theory of Habermas in the analysis of accounting change more generally.[19] Accounting has been held to play an active part in enhancing social conflict, particularly in a crisis context (Gallhofer and Haslam, 1991). And, more specifically, the political issues involved in economic calculation have been addressed in relation to the issue of transfer pricing (Picciotto, 1992). Transfer pricing is, according to this analysis, a political issue within the firm in relation to the strategic factors that affect pricing; and it is a political issue externally, in relation to State regulation and international taxation.

A third agenda entails a concern with issues of *organizational design and environments*, and their relations to accounting systems. Cast in the particular terms of contingency theory, this has of course been a long-standing concern of researchers in accounting. Contingency theory demonstrated the importance of bringing factors such as technology, environment, and managerial structures within the field of research.[20] But contingency theory tended to have a restrictive and static understanding of the ways in which accounting systems were affected by a number of factors (Hopwood, 1983). Contingency theory gave little attention to the processes through which accounting and ways of organizing were *reciprocally* related.

A distinct research tradition, one associated most notably with the work of James March, helped to give a new and fruitful direction to the concern in accounting with issues of organizational design and environments.[21] This research had demonstrated its value in the fields of organization theory and analysis for a decade or more before it was deployed in the accounting literature. Starting from models of rational decision-making, March weakened the rationality assumptions of such models, but did so by retaining a notion of the purposive action of individuals. Individuals might not conform to the idealized and naive models of rational behaviour. But their actions could nonetheless be understood by means of concepts such as limited rationality, contextual rationality, game rationality, and process rationality (March, 1978).

Such concepts have considerable implications for accounting. For accounting texts are adorned with images of rational individuals who search for complete information, evaluate it rationally, and then make decisions (Miller and O'Leary, 1990). March demonstrated conclusively that individuals and organizations do not operate in this manner. Individuals are much more constrained and much more uncertain of their preferences than the dreams of accounting textbook writers suggest. The notion of 'organized anarchies' conveys this sense of organizations as characterized by problematic preferences, unclear technology, and fluid participation (Cohen, March and Olsen, 1972).[22] Understood by means of such concepts, decisions can be viewed as outcomes or interpretations of several relatively independent streams or processes in organizations. Solutions do not follow from problems in a simple one-to-one manner. Solutions and problems are relatively uncoupled from one another. Problems, solutions and participants move from one choice opportunity to another. Decisions are only made when a shifting combination of problems, solutions and decision-makers happens to make action possible.

These ideas have much relevance for accounting researchers. March himself, in an address to the American Accounting Association in 1986, set out the implications for accounting of his research on the ambiguities surrounding individual and organizational decision-making (March, 1987). Arguing that the concepts of 'limited rationality' and 'conflict of interests' are an incomplete representation of the problems of decision-making, March identified four ambiguities of organizational decision-making: ambiguities of preferences; ambiguities of relevance; ambiguities of intelligence; and ambiguities of meaning. In terms similar to those of institutional theorists, March argued that theories of rational choice, and decision processes, are ways of celebrating central values of a society, in particular the idea that life is under intentional human control, and that control is exercised through individual and collective choices based on an explicit anticipation of alternatives and their probable consequences (March, 1987). To the extent that decision-making in organizations is surrounded by the four ambiguities identified, March argued that the design of information systems must be attentive to such characteristics, even when they are disconcerting.

Within accounting, others developed related ideas. Swieringa and Weick (1987) addressed the role of a technique such as Return on Investment in terms of its effects on action, rather than as an aid to decision-making. Accounting systems and techniques are so powerful, they argued, because they can initiate and sustain forceful action. This distinction between action-generating processes and decision-making processes was made by others. Brunsson (1982) suggested that an effective decision process that facilitates action generation breaks nearly all the rules for rational decision-making: few alternatives are analysed; only positive consequences are considered; and objectives are not formulated in advance. In a similar vein, Hedberg and Jonsson (1978) argued that accounting systems tend to stabilize organizations, by establishing fixed and standard repertoires over time. But organizations in changing environments, they argued, need information systems which destabilize. Organizations need information systems that are flexible enough to cope with unexpected developments. Accounting systems are needed that can be used to stimulate organizational curiosity, facilitate novel decision processes, and increase the ability to cope with variety and change in environments. And the notion of 'organized anarchies' was used as a way of understanding how budgets in particular, and accounting systems in general, can provide a basis for the rationalization of behaviour rather than as an input into decisions.

In their different ways, and to varying extents, all three of these research agendas indicate a concern with accounting as a social and institutional practice. However, they also highlight concerns or issues in a manner that is distinctive. The ethnographic approach suggests the importance of treating accounting practices as 'alien'. To this extent, accounting practices need to be explained in much the same ways, and possibly with some of the same tools, as those used by anthropologists and others to understand unfamiliar cultures and practices. The political economy approach places considerable emphasis on overt interests and conflicts, and on the links between such factors and accounting systems. This aspect of accounting continues to remain relatively undeveloped in accounting research. And a focus on questions of organizational design and environments highlights the importance of attending to the actual processes occurring within and between organizations, environments, and accounting systems. Questions of organizational design and accounting systems should no longer be subordinated to abstract and idealized images of rationality. In their respective ways, these three research agendas point to different possibilities for developing and extending the concern with accounting as a social and institutional practice.

### Analysing the emergence of calculative practices

The analyses of accounting as a social and institutional practice in this volume are primarily historical. But they are historical in a particular sense. Moving beyond earlier analyses of accounting in its organizational contexts, the studies collected here emphasize the social and institutional emergence of accounting. This is not to suggest that analyses of accounting within organizations are unimportant. But it is to suggest that if we are to understand fully how particular ways of accounting have emerged, and why such significance is accorded them, we have to move beyond the boundaries of the organization and examine the social and institutional practice of accounting. What links the chapters in this volume is this concern to analyse the relations between particular calculative practices and other practices of management and organization. It is the emergence of such practices in particular, localized historical settings, the 'how' of such processes, that is the focus of attention. For accounting is often formed out of an ensemble of diverse techniques that only come to be called 'accounting' after the event. It is the analyses of this process of emergence, that elsewhere has been termed 'genealogies of calculation',[23] that is one of the principle concerns of the studies collected here.

A concern with the multiple sites of emergence of accounting suggests that accounting has no 'essence'. For what we call 'accounting' is an entity that has been made up out of techniques and practices drawn from diverse disciplines and domains. Accounting changes in both content and form over time, only ever achieving a temporary stability. Such arguments are most persuasively illustrated by the contribution of Hoskin and Macve (chapter 3). Hoskin and Macve focus on the invention of that practice which is so often taken to be the core or essence of accounting: double-entry bookkeeping. They argue that we need to look to the apparently marginal field of education if we are to understand the emergence of double-entry bookkeeping.And it is, they suggest, one practice in particular that should be addressed: the examination. They focus first on the oral and ungraded examination of the twelfth century. They then address the written graded examination of the late eighteenth century. Drawing on the 'disciplinary' perspective of Foucault, they argue that a focus on educational institutions makes it possible to understand the emergence of accounting, and its role as a disciplinary mechanism. Accounting needs to be understood in this institutional sense as a powerful new way of 'writing the world', not as a means of recording data for rational economic decisions.

A focus on the institutional matrix within which particular accounting practices emerged is present also in the chapter by Thompson (chapter 2). But it is the early sixteenth century to which he directs his attention. He addresses three contingent and historically specific institutions: the church, the pedagogic apparatuses, and the publishing house. Together, Thompson argues, these institutions provided the conditions of possibility of accounting in its particular 'modern' form. Understood in these terms, double-entry bookkeeping is an effect of particular institutional and organizational configurations. Accounting takes its place alongside other political and economic discourses. Accounting is rhetorical, but rhetoric in this context is institutionally grounded.[24]

The emergence of cost accounting is the concern of the chapter by Loft (chapter 5). Addressing the rise of cost accounting during the First World War, Loft gives further support to the view that it is important to attend to the local conditions under which particular accounting techniques emerge and spread. Loft terms this process the 'coming into the light' of cost accounting. The decisive event here was the adding by the government of a clause to the Defence of the Realm Act in 1916. This clause was added in response to accusations of profiteering on the part of manufacturers of munitions and other supplies for the war. The new clause concerned the price which the war ministries would pay manufacturers for war supplies it purchased from them. That price was to be the cost of making the items in question, plus an allowance for profit. Rather than let the market set the price, costs were henceforth to be the arbiter. Through this route, accountancy was to gain a social status and a degree of acceptance which had been absent before the War. Knowledge about cost accounting, and expertise in using its techniques was to spread via technical books and journals, as well as by the few courses in cost accounting available at universities at the time.

Cost accounting remains the focus in the contribution by Miller and O'Leary (chapter 4), but in this case it is standard costing and budgeting that is the object of attention. It is the period between 1900 and 1930 that is of concern to Miller and O'Leary. For it is across this period that cost accounting was transformed and its domain massively expanded by the emergence of standard costing. Henceforth, cost accounting was to be concerned with the future as well as with the past. With standard costing it was possible routinely to calculate variances at the level of the firm as a whole, and at the level of every accountable person with the firm. This was more than a technical modification to accounting. As a way of rendering visible the inefficiencies of the person within the enterprise, standard costing made possible a new way of governing individuals within the firm, a new way of governing economic life within the enterprise. But standard costing was not an isolated phenomenon. Within the firm, it was closely allied to that vast project of standardization and normalization that has been called 'scientific management'. Beyond the firm, it was linked to a number of other normalizing initiatives, including a programme of 'national efficiency' and intelligence testing. Together, these diverse strategies helped to articulate the ideal of a rationally administered social order in which efficiency would be made visible at both an individual and a collective level.

The linkage between particular calculative techniques and broader rationales and policies is addressed by Tomlinson (chapter 7). The concern here is with techniques for measuring labour productivity, and the more general rise of the 'productivity problem' in the UK in the late 1940s. As argued above, attempts to change accounting practices, or to invent new ones, are typically linked to particular meanings or rationales. And these processes of invention are often faltering and uncertain, they involve experimentation and the discarding of one half-formed technique in favour of another. Tomlinson demonstrates the complexity of such processes with respect to the attempts to develop techniques for measuring labour productivity in the late 1940s in the UK. The setting here is the rise to prominence at this time of the concept of 'productivity'. This was a dual concern: at the macroeconomic level, there was an increasing preoccupation with the measurement of the national economy as part of the growth of national economic measurement; at the level of the enterprise, there was a rapid escalation in attempts to regulate the enterprise in the name of increased output and efficiency. Enterprises were to be encouraged to account for themselves in a new way, to measure labour productivity as part of their everyday management activity. By this period in the UK, techniques such as standard costing were still only weakly developed within enterprises. But attempts to transform the accounting practices of enterprises by arm's-length means are not always wholly successful. Notwithstanding the rise of the 'productivity problem' in the late 1940s, the reform of the management accounting practices of enterprises by governments was to remain an elusive goal.

The links between the macroeconomic concerns of governments and particular calculative techniques are addressed also in the chapter by Hopwood, Burchell and Clubb (chapter 9). These authors address the sudden upsurge of interest in value-added that occurred in the UK in the late 1970s. The concept 'value-added' appears as an indicator of the value created by the activities of an enterprise in a number of different sites, including private companies, newspapers, government bodies, trade unions, employer associations, and professional accountancy bodies. The concept was given form in a number of different practices, including financial reporting, payment systems, profit sharing schemes, economic analyses, and information disclosure to employees and trade unions. Hopwood and his colleagues address this sudden interest in the calculation of value-added by identifying three arenas: standard-setting for corporate financial reporting, macroeconomic management, and the system of industrial relations. In each of these three arenas, they chart the shifting patterns of relations between the various agencies functioning in the respective fields – the accounting profession, the government, and trade unions – and the changes in their modes of operation and objects of concern. Taken together, it is argued, these three distinct arenas can be addressed as an 'accounting constellation', a specific ensemble of actors and agencies pursuing interests and producing unintended consequences. The historical specificity of the value-added event is further demonstrated by the sudden decline in interest in value-added in the early 1980s. As each of the three arenas within which value-added emerged were transformed, the significance which had been attached to the idea no longer seemed salient. The concept of value-added declined almost as suddenly as it had emerged.

But a focus on the broader arenas within which particular calculative techniques emerge should not obscure the firm-specific conditions which can bring about accounting change. Also, an emphasis on the 'constructive' or constitutive capacities of accounting should not lead to a neglect of its 'destructive' potential. Bougen (chapter 6) examines the profit sharing scheme that emerged in one particular firm during the 1920s. He examines how and why accounting became integrated with industrial relations issues such as wage levels, bonus payments, managerial surveillance and control of work practices, changes in work practices and redundancies. He discusses how accounting became entangled in a web of heterogeneous elements, including the practices and procedures of scientific management, a paternalist managerial philosophy, the dictates of financial markets, and managerial discourses of business science. And he considers the clashes of truths and knowledges that accounting can become enmeshed within, ways of defining what accounting is to do, and what it is not to do, its legitimacies and illegitimacies, its continuities and discontinuities. As Bougen demonstrates, accounting is able not only to integrate at a technical level various organizational activities and resources. Accounting is also able to silence the voice of labour or confine it to the margins of interest and validity. However, the success of such strategies is not guaranteed. Such an ensemble can only be temporarily stabilized. The downfall of the profit sharing scheme studied by Bougen can thus be understood in much the same way as its emergence: by reference to the multiple linkages it made explicit between various organizational processes and structures, and by reference to the tactic of allowing labour voices and knowledges to be articulated.

The linkages between accounting and industrial relations are addressed also in the contribution by Armstrong (chapter 8). The concern here is with corporate control in large British companies, in particular the intersection of management accounting and industrial relations in the postwar period. Armstrong analyses the changes in company structure and accounting control systems that provide the context for postwar British industrial relations. He addresses the increased influence of accounting control systems on the managerial conduct of industrial relations from the mid-1970s onwards. What has developed, he argues, is a dual linkage of establishment level industrial relations with corporate policy: on the one hand, corporate industrial relations policy is enacted through local personnel management; on the other, accounting indicators of performance, in particular budgetary targets, connect local line managers with a corporate planning process that largely excludes industrial relations considerations. The policy trend during the 1980s and 1990s, Armstrong suggests, has been towards a devolution of collective bargaining, accompanied by a reliance on budgetary constraint as a means of retaining headquarters control. Local management initiative is thus increasingly likely to take place under the aegis of budgetary pressure, rather than under the broad framework of industrial relations policy.

One of the most consistent observations that emerges from the studies gathered here is that accounting has attained an increasing ascendancy over other managerial practices in the UK in the twentieth century. Nowhere is this more clearly demonstrated than in the recent changes in the UK public sector. As McSweeney (chapter 10) demonstrates, the notion of good management in the UK public sector has become synonymous with 'management by accounting'. Whether in Civil Service departments, or an increasing number of public sector organizations, accounting has come to be seen as the unquestioned cornerstone of 'good management'. McSweeney examines the stages in accounting's rise to such a dominant position. He begins by addressing the Financial Management Initiative launched in May 1982. For this initiative made accounting the central mechanism in attempts to identify and allocate responsibilities between managers, to define objectives, and to assess clearly costs and outputs. But McSweeney warns against the dangers of locating the emergence of management by accounting solely in relation to the rise of the entity that has been called 'Thatcherism'. As he shows, management by accounting predates the coming to power of Margaret Thatcher. The trajectory of management by accounting can be traced to the 1968 Fulton Committee Report, and the subsequent attempts to 'modernize' the Civil Service. Management by accounting can be traced also in the post-Fulton era of 'programmatic analysis', and its intensified concern with efficiency in the Civil Service. In so far as the public sector was identified as at 'the heart of Britain's economic difficulties' by the Conservative Government that came to power in 1979, the strategy of management by accounting was further reinforced by programmes such as the 'Rayner scrutinies', a 'Management Information System for Ministers' (MINIS), an inquiry by the Treasury and Civil Service Committee and, most recently, the Next Steps initiative. Notwithstanding the diversity of such schemes, there is, McSweeney argues, a common theme present in all these programmes. This common theme is that of 'performativity', the imperative to reduce diverse activities and services into a series of input–output relationships.

The accounting profession has not gone uncriticized. As Cooper *et al.* demonstrate in chapter 11, the legitimacy of those accounting practitioners who claim the status of 'professional' has been challenged repeatedly in recent years. In the UK, there have been changes in the legal framework, an increase in competition between the major players in the industry, and a series of scandals. Together, these events have cast doubt upon existing claims to independence and objectivity. Cooper *et al.* examine the dynamics of these processes by analysing three episodes in the regulation of accountancy: the negotiations over the scope and impact of the EC 8th Directive; the reactions of the accountancy bodies to the Financial Services Act 1986; and the continuing efforts of the professionalized accounting bodies to secure the powers of self-regulation conferred upon them by the State. The localized historical conditions of each of these issues are addressed. They are also taken as exemplars of the changing relationship between the accountancy 'profession' and the 'State'. This changing relationship, they argue, is at the heart of accounting regulation. Each of the three episodes examined indicates the tensions associated with the movement of accountants into new markets. For instance, in different ways, the EC 8th Directive and the Financial Services Act had the unintended consequence of raising the visibility of accountants' operation in areas such as consultancy and the selling of financial services, areas from which they had previously been absent. Such moves can unsettle or compromise existing claims to legitimacy. The claim to neutrality and objectivity so characteristic of bodies of expertise has to be re-established, and in relation to new tasks and self-images. In the process this self-image undergoes a transformation. The three episodes addressed by Cooper *et al.* inadvertently expose the extent to which accountancy has become a major industry. Cooper *et al.* analyse the ways in which accountants have sought to neutralize the diverse threats to their self-image as responsible, independent professionals. Whilst the accounting 'industry' has sought to reaffirm the concept of professional self-regulation, the accountancy bodies have had in turn to accept new regulatory structures that threaten to erode the ideals of neutrality and independence.

Yet, accountancy increasingly comes to appear as the image in which organizations and activities are fashioned in certain Western economies. As Power argues in chapter 12, this has developed to such an extent that we can speak now of the 'audit society' as a constitutive principle of social organization. The word 'audit' is no longer the prerogative of financial audit. We now hear of environmental audits, value for money audits, management audits, quality audits, forensic audits, data audits, intellectual property audits, medical audits, and many others besides. There is more at stake here than the adoption in diverse arenas of a fashionable label. Even though 'audit' practices are heterogeneous, and even though the descriptive utility of the concept itself is doubted by practitioners, the concept of audit has become a generalizable social practice. The variability of audit practices is less important than the ways in which the idea of audit is appropriated and mobilized. Audit, Power argues, can be understood as the 'control of control', for audits function at a temporal and often spatial distance from the organizational processes to which they are applied. As a distinctive administrative rationality, audit embodies three principles. Firstly, the invisibility of audit; for despite the rhetoric of transparency which has accompanied the growth of audit, the audit process itself remains publicly invisible. Secondly, the politics of 'regulatory failures'; for audit practices are constantly seeking to reproduce and intensify themselves. Thirdly, and perhaps most importantly, the construction of auditees; for the audit society is one characterized by an incessant desire to make environments auditable, an endeavour to structure organizations, activities and processes in such a way that they conform to the imperative of monitoring rather than to their own intrinsic agendas. In these different ways, Power demonstrates that audit is as much a distinctive principle of social and economic organization as it is a technical practice.

The studies gathered together in this volume share a concern to examine accounting as a social and institutional practice. In their differing ways, they address the conditions and consequences of accounting. They demonstrate the multiple, and often marginal fields in which accounting practices emerge. They analyse the frequently *ad hoc* ways in which accounting develops. They illustrate the extent to which the calculative technologies of accounting have become so central to diverse attempts to govern organizations, individuals and social relations more generally. They explore the tensions and clashes that are intrinsic to such processes, as they take shape within particular organizations and in relation to diverse agendas. And they document the growth and diffusion of accounting across the twentieth century in a particular national context. The social authority of accounting has not gone unchallenged in the process. But the skirmishes concerning the objectivity and legitimacy of accounting have not prevented it from becoming one of the pre-eminent devices for governing social and economic life in certain Western nations.

### Accomplishments and agendas

As the chapters in this volume demonstrate, a distinctive research agenda has recently emerged within accounting. This novel agenda, based as it is on the study of accounting as a social and institutional practice, broadens and extends existing concerns with accounting in its organizational and social context. The numerous appeals to study accounting in action in specific organizational settings are reinforced. But there is a further injunction: to move beyond organizations to include the social and institutional matrix within which individual organizations seek to innovate.[25] Accounting innovation is to be understood by analysing the complex interplay between the multiple arenas within which new ways of accounting emerge. Rather than making a clear-cut distinction between the 'inside' and the 'outside' of firms, attention is to be directed at the reciprocal relations formed between distinct locales.

But research that is novel soon comes to be regarded as routine. To this extent, it is worth registering the important accomplishments of the research traditions sketched here. Less than 20 years ago, the research gathered together in this volume would not have been possible.[26] New ways of posing questions about accounting have transformed the terrain of accounting research. As has been suggested above, this is more than a matter of importing methodologies from neighbouring disciplines, whether from anthropology, sociology, organization theory, history, or cultural analyses more generally. In large part, the achievements have been the result of innovations within the discipline of accounting itself. The novel ways of understanding the emergence and functioning of accounting that are now available were developed in important part out of analyses of specific calculative devices, and out of a concern to understand how particular ways of calculating, in alliance with other practices and processes, helped transform the world. The study of accounting has thus taken its place within the social sciences in a manner not dissimilar to early twentieth-century social science: out of the analysis of a practice.[27]

New topics are beginning to appear within accounting research. The rhetoric of accounting knowledge is becoming an important domain of analysis.[28] For accounting is as rich in meaning, as imbued with values and cultural significance as any other social practice. But it is more than the meanings of accounting that are to be addressed. The intrinsic links between accounting and 'economic reason' are being addressed.[29] For in so far as economics presupposes a capacity to calculate, and in so far as such calculations have consequences, accounting may well contribute to the eclipsing or obscuring of explicit value judgements. To this extent, accounting may be a key part of a self-fulfilling process in which economic reason becomes calculable, and thereby validates its own terms of reference. As it becomes increasingly possible to make social relations conform to the models of economic rationality, then the models themselves are declared as vindicated. And in so far as accounting knowledge depends on inscriptions, the quantitative orientation of accounting can be understood in relation to attempts to act upon and transform social relations by 'acting at a distance'.[30]

The borders between accounting and other bodies of expertise, in particular law, are being given increasing attention of late.[31] This can be attributed in part to the shifting institutional territory of these two professionalized practices, their changing claims to competence, and the growing interdisciplinarity between them at the level of their knowledge bases. The phenomenon of 'multi-disciplinary partnerships' and the opening up of new international markets gives rise to new territorial battles that are more than zero-sum games, since they have the potential to transform the practice of both accountancy and law.

Other topics gain a relevance within accounting, once it is understood in social and institutional terms. The issue of gender, so long marginalized in accounting, comes to the fore.[32] For if accounting helps to construct and make governable particular forms of subjectivity, analyses in terms of gender help to expand the account we currently have of accounting. Feminist scholarship focused initially on those social practices and institutionalized knowledges – medicine, biology, psychoanalysis – that are most overtly and intimately related to the condition and experience of the gendered individual. But accounting is now beginning to be studied in related terms. The position of women in the whole of the accountancy function, rather than just in professional accountancy, is being addressed. This means analysing historically the development of a situation where women are predominant in the lower levels of function (bookkeeping), and in a minority in the higher levels (accountancy). It also means analysing the different forms of discrimination against women that occur in the specific setting of accountancy. For whilst one might expect comparable patterns of discrimination to those that exist in other occupations, the particular images and norms that serve to discriminate against women in the field of accountancy need to be analysed. More generally, the roles of accounting in making possible gender-specific modes of governing individuals is an important topic for further study.

Accounting can be regarded as an intrinsic and constitutive component of the government of economic life.[33] The growth and deployment of accounting, that is to say, can be understood in relation to the emergence of particular political systems, and particular ways of seeking to govern the conduct of individuals. For accounting is one of the key ways in which attempts have been made to exert influence on individuals through indirect means. Such modes of government can be regarded as characteristic of liberal democratic societies. In so far as such societies mark out the economy as a distinct sphere with its own laws and regularities, and make the individual a fundamental locus of responsibility, accounting has a central place. Understood as a mode of government of economic life, accounting can be appealed to as a way of seeking to act upon the conduct of individuals to remedy deficits of rationality and responsibility. Accounting makes possible actions on the actions of others, by recourse to the single figure that is the end product of so many of the calculative technologies of accounting. In the single figure is located the neutrality and objectivity claimed for expertise. By this device, accounting seeks to accord itself a legitimacy based on a claim that it is above the fray, apart from the realm of politics and intrigue.

Understood in such terms, the studies gathered together in this volume have potential implications beyond the discipline of accounting. They have a particular relevance for the related fields of management and organization studies. For despite recent theoretical developments,[34] much of the research within these allied disciplines continues to retain an intraorganizational focus. When it moves beyond the organization, as in the writings of the neoinstitutionalists for example, such research tends to invoke conventional distinctions such as those between the macro and micro level, and between organizations and environments.[35] However, as the chapters in this volume indicate, there is much scope for extending and developing research agendas in the management area, through a dialogue between different research traditions and approaches.

And if accounting is understood as a social and institutional practice, then this has implications for the way in which policy is understood and operationalized. For from such a perspective, issues such as accounting harmonization within the EC can no longer be divorced from the distinct institutional and cultural histories of the member states. Attempts to put in place new ways of accounting for advanced manufacturing systems need to be understood in relation to the profound changes that are taking place in wider conceptions of economic citizenship in advanced industrial societies. Debates concerning the boundaries of a practice such as management accounting need to recognize the ways in which this boundary has been redefined over time. And the regulation of accountancy needs to be understood in terms of the historically specific ways in which attempts have been made by government agencies to act indirectly upon individuals, organizations, and bodies of expertise.

But this is not a question merely of extrapolating from the analyses presented here and elsewhere to policy implications. This would be to trivialize the policy process, and to mistake what it means to analyse accounting as a social and institutional practice. The matrix of actors, agencies, objectives, and aspirations in any individual policy issue is of such a complexity that simple recipes for action are unlikely to be contained in any particular study. Moreover, one of the principal implications of the material gathered together in this volume is that the past is not likely to be a reliable guide to the future. The multiple conditions of emergence of a particular calculative practice are institutionally localized and historically specific. Patterns may emerge as further studies are conducted, and particular classes of factors may come to be identified, but this does not amount to a prediction as to how they may operate under different conditions.

One final observation may be appropriate. The study of accounting as a social and institutional practice is only in its early stages. Much has already been accomplished. But the material discussed here, notwithstanding its achievements, has so far only begun to open up new possibilities for the study of accounting. There has been a burgeoning of topics, issues and methodologies. Each of these is worthy of development and further exploration. Single studies of particular events should be the starting point for new literatures, rather than a sign that the issues are now settled. The deployment of new methodologies, and the extension of existing ones, need to be further encouraged, with the proviso that this should be experimental rather than canonical or exegetical. And the implications of research on accounting for other social sciences need to be more explicitly registered. For there is little doubt that accounting is increasingly one of the most influential bodies of expertise in a number of Western nations. It is only by analysing the multiplicity of practices that make it up that we will be able to understand how it has come to assume such a dominant position. This is of profound sociological and institutional significance, rather than a matter of concern only to technical specialists and those within the discipline of accounting. To develop an understanding of such practices, the achievements of the research presented here need to be consolidated and supplemented, if the promise which these initial steps hold is to be fulfilled.

NOTES

I am grateful to Keith Hoskin, Anthony Hopwood, Ted O'Leary, Brendan McSweeney and Michael Power for comments on an earlier draft of this Introduction.

1. See Hopwood (1986, 1992).
2. See for instance the studies of Argyris (1952); Bower (1970); Roy (1969); Simon, Guetzkow and Tyndall (1954); Whyte (1955); Wildavsky (1964). See Birnberg, Turopolec and Young (1983) for a useful overview.
3. These reflections were in the context of an introductory essay to a collection of papers, most of which were initially presented at the Workshop on 'Designing Management Accounting Systems for Organizations in a Changing Environment', held in San Francisco in 1976, under the auspices of *Accounting, Organizations and Society*. The papers are published in *Accounting, Organizations and Society* 3(1) (1978).
4. A parallel, and related development occurred around the same time in relation to the multi-disciplinary concept of 'management control'. The Management Control Workshop Group in the UK, and the Management Information and Control System Workshop in Europe more generally, provided a focus for work in this area. On this, see Lowe and Machin (1983). For an example of work in this vein, see Lowe, Puxty and Laughlin (1983).
5. On this point, see Miller and O'Leary (1993).
6. Cf. Zeff (1978).
7. The most accessible collection of this material is to be found in Watts and Zimmerman (1986).
8. These research agendas centring on the question of interests, and typically invoking an economic model of political processes, provide an exception to the generalization that a concern with accounting as a social and institutional practice developed in relation to management accounting. However, to date there has not developed a body of research on financial accounting comparable to that featured in this volume. This is curious, for financial accounting would seem to be just as suitable a target for such research as management accounting.
9. See *Accounting, Organizations and Society* 8(2/3) (1983) for the published papers arising from this conference.
10. See, for example: Birnberg, Turopolec and Young (1983); Boland and Pondy (1983); Johnson (1983); Markus and Pfeffer (1983).
11. See in particular the papers by Cooper (1983) and Meyer (1983).
12. In a related case, Gambling (1977, 1987) suggested that accounting could be understood as a ritualistic activity. In so far as Gambling argued, following Cleverley (1973), that such rituals were part of the 'age-old responses of man to uncertainty' (Gambling, 1977), his concerns are distinct from those of institutional theorists to analyse the influence of historically specific practices.

13. Cf. Thompson (1986, 1987) and Burchell, Clubb and Hopwood (1985). It is worth noting that the latter was circulating in manuscript form in the early 1980s.

14. Sometimes this type of research is termed 'naturalistic'. For the purposes of exposition here, 'naturalistic' and 'ethnographic' research are taken to be equivalent. See for instance Tomkins and Groves (1983), and the commentaries on this paper by Abdel-Khalik and Ajinkya (1983); Morgan (1983); Willmott (1983). The term 'ethnographic' is used to refer here to a wider literature than that conventionally defined as ethnography. The term 'interpretive' also provides a label for designating this strand of research; cf. Chua (1988).

15. See for instance: Boland and Pondy (1983, 1986); Colville (1981); Roberts and Scapens (1985); Tomkins and Groves (1983).

16. Preston (1989) draws explicitly on the notion of discipline as set out in the work of Foucault. But the detailed attention to the meanings and significance attached by individuals to their actions justifies the use of the term 'ethnography' to characterize this study.

17. For arguments in favour of a political economy of accounting, see, for instance: Cooper and Hopper (1987); Cooper and Sherer (1984); Hopper, Storey and Willmott (1987); Tinker (1980, 1984, 1985); Tinker, Merino and Neimark (1982).

18. See also Ogden and Bougen (1985). For a different perspective on the issue of 'adversary accounting' see McBarnet, Weston and Whelan (1993).

19. See also Dillard (1991) on the use of critical theory in accounting research.

20. See for example Waterhouse and Tiessen (1978) for a classic statement of this research. See Cooper (1981) and Otley (1980) for useful overviews and assessments of this literature.

21. Of course, many other researchers have contributed, often in association with March, to this research. See March (1988) for a useful collection of some of the key pieces of this literature.

22. In accounting, cf.: Cooper, Hayes and Wolf (1981); Hedberg and Jonsson (1978).

23. Cf. Miller and Napier (1993) on this notion.

24. For a different approach to analysing the rhetoric of accounting, see Arrington and Francis (1989).

25. The 'Interdisciplinary Perspectives on Accounting' Conferences held in 1985, 1988 and 1991 have provided an ongoing international forum for research of this type. See Miller, Hopper and Laughlin (1991) for an introduction to some of the papers from the 1988 Conference.

26. Although the intellectual tools to carry out such research are now widely available, outside the UK the institutional preconditions are not equally widely available within departments of accounting.

27. There are analogies here between the development of studies of accounting, and studies of a number of other bodies of expertise such as statistics, psychiatry and the natural sciences. On the history of statistics, see: Hacking (1990); Porter (1986). See Power (1992a) on the use of statistical techniques in accounting. On the history of psychiatry, see Castel (1976); Foucault (1972); Miller and Rose (1986). On the sociology of science and technology, see Bijker *et al.* (1987); Latour (1988); Pickering (1992).

28. See for instance Arrington and Schweiker (1992).
29. See Gorz (1989); Hopwood (1992); Power (1992b).
30. See Robson (1992) and Miller (1991, 1992).
31. See, for instance, Freedman and Power (1991) and Dezalay (1991, 1992).
32. See the collection of essays on 'Accounting and Gender' in *Accounting, Organizations and Society* 12(1) (1987). See also the collection of essays on 'Feminist Perspectives on Accounting Research' in *Accounting, Organizations and Society* 17(3/4) (1992). See also Hammond and Preston (1992); Shearer and Arrington (1993); Kirkham and Loft (1993); and the collection of papers in *Accounting, Auditing & Accountability Journal* 5(3) (1992).
33. Cf. Miller and Rose (1990). See also Miller and O'Leary (1993).
34. See for instance: Burrell (1988); Clegg (1989, 1990); Cooper and Burrell (1988).
35. The most accessible collection of this material is Powell and DiMaggio (1991). For an assessment of ways in which the neoinstitutional tradition may be extended and developed, see Miller and O'Leary (1993).

REFERENCES

Abdel-Khalik, A.R. and Ajinkya, B.B., 1983. 'An Evaluation of "The Everyday Accountant and Researching his Reality"', *Accounting, Organizations and Society* 8(4): 375–84

Ansari, S. and Euske, K.J., 1987. 'Rational, Rationalizing, and Reifying Uses of Accounting Data in Organizations', *Accounting, Organizations and Society* 12(6): 549–70

Argyris, C., 1952. *The Impact of Budgets on People*, School of Business and Public Administration, Cornell University

Armstrong, P., 1985. 'Changing Management Control Strategies: The Role of Competition Between Accountancy and Other Organisational Professions', *Accounting, Organizations and Society* 10(2): 129–48

1987. 'The Rise of Accounting Controls in British Capitalist Enterprises', *Accounting, Organizations and Society* 12(5): 415–36

Arnold, P.J., 1991. 'Accounting and the State: Consequences of Merger and Acquisition Accounting in the US Hospital Industry', *Accounting, Organizations and Society* 16(2): 121–40

Arrington, C.E. and Francis, J.R., 1989. 'Letting the Chat out of the Bag: Deconstructionism, Privilege and Accounting Research', *Accounting, Organizations and Society* 14(1/2): 1–28

Arrington, C.E. and Schweiker, W., 1992. 'The Rhetoric and Rationality of Accounting Research', *Accounting, Organizations and Society* 17(6): 511–33

Berry, A.J., Capps, T., Cooper, D., Ferguson, P., Hopper, T. and Lowe, E. A., 1985. 'Management Accounting in an Area of the NCB: Rationales of Accounting Practices in a Public Enterprise', *Accounting, Organizations and Society* 10(1): 3–28

Bijker, W.E., Hughes, T.P. and Pinch, T.J. (eds.), 1987. *The Social Construction of Technological Systems: New Directions in the Sociology and History of Technology*, Cambridge, MA: MIT Press

Birnberg, J.G., Turopolec, L. and Young, M.S., 1983. 'The Organizational Context of Accounting', *Accounting, Organizations and Society* 8(2/3): 111–29

Boland, R.J. and Pondy, L.R., 1983. 'Accounting in Organizations: A Union of Natural and Rational Perspectives', *Accounting, Organizations and Society* 8(2/3): 223–34

1986. 'The Micro Dynamics of a Budget-Cutting Process: Modes, Models and Structure', *Accounting, Organizations and Society* 11(2/3): 403–22

Bougen, P.D., 1989. 'The Emergence, Roles and Consequences of an Accounting–Industrial Relations Interaction', *Accounting, Organizations and Society* 14(3): 203–34

Bougen, P.D., Ogden, S.G. and Outram, Q., 1990. 'The Appearance and Disappearance of Accounting: Wage Determination in the UK Coal Industry', *Accounting, Organizations and Society* 15(3): 149–70

Bower, J.L., 1970. *Managing the Resource Allocation Process*, Division of Research, Graduate School of Business Administration, Harvard University

Brunsson, N., 1982. 'The Irrationality of Action and Action Rationality: Decisions, Ideologies and Organizational Actions', *Journal of Management Studies* 19(1): 29–44

Burchell, S., Clubb, C., Hopwood, A. and Hughes, J., 1980. 'The Roles of Accounting in Organizations and Society', *Accounting, Organizations and Society* 5(1): 5–27

Burchell, S., Clubb, C. and Hopwood, A.G., 1985. 'Accounting in its Social Context: Towards a History of Value Added in the United Kingdom', *Accounting, Organizations and Society* 10(4): 381–413

Burrell, G., 1988. 'Modernism, Post Modernism and Organizational Analysis 2: The Contribution of Michel Foucault', *Organization Studies* 9: 221–35

Castel, R., 1976. *L'ordre psychiatrique*, Paris: Editions de Minuit

Chua, W.F., 1988. 'Interpretive Sociology and Management Accounting Research – A Critical Review', *Accounting, Auditing & Accountability Journal* 1(2): 59–79

Clegg, S.R., 1989. *Frameworks of Power*, London: Sage

1990. *Modern Organizations: Organization Studies in the Postmodern World*, London: Sage

Cleverley, G., 1973. *Managers and Magic*, Harmondsworth: Pelican

Cohen, M.D., March, J.G. and Olsen, J.P., 1972. 'A Garbage Can Model of Organizational Life', *Administrative Science Quarterly* 17(1), March, republished in J.G. March, *Decisions and Organizations* (1988)

Colville, I., 1981. 'Reconstructing "Behavioural Accounting"', *Accounting, Organizations and Society* 6(2): 119–32

Cooper, D., 1981. 'A Social and Organizational View of Management Accounting', in M. Bromwich and A. Hopwood (eds.), *Essays in British Accounting Research*, London: Pitman

1983. 'Tidiness, Muddle and Things: Commonalities and Divergencies in Two Approaches to Management Accounting Research', *Accounting, Organizations and Society* 8(2/3): 269–86

Cooper, R. and Burrell, G., 1988. 'Modernism, Postmodernism and Organizational Analysis: An Introduction', *Organization Studies* 9: 91–112

Cooper, D.J. and Hopper, T.M., 1987. 'Critical Studies in Accounting', *Accounting, Organizations and Society* 12(5): 407–14

Cooper, D.J. and Sherer, M.J., 1984. 'The Value of Corporate Accounting Reports:

Arguments for a Political Economy of Accounting', *Accounting, Organizations and Society* 9(3/4): 207–32

Cooper, D.J., Hayes, D. and Wolf, F., 1981. 'Accounting in Organized Anarchies: Understanding and Designing Accounting Systems in Ambiguous Situations', *Accounting, Organizations and Society* 6(3): 175–91

Covaleski, M.A. and Dirsmith, M.W., 1988a. 'An Institutional Perspective on the Rise, Social Transformation, and Fall of a University Budget Category', *Administrative Science Quarterly* 33: 562–87

1988b. 'The Use of Budgetary Symbols in the Political Arena: An Historically Informed Field Study', *Accounting, Organizations and Society* 13(1): 1–24

Cutler, A., Hindess, B., Hirst, P. and Hussain, A., 1978. *Marx's 'Capital' and Capitalism Today: Volume Two*, London: Routledge & Kegan Paul

Dent, J., 1991. 'Accounting and Organizational Cultures: A Field Study of the Emergence of a New Organizational Reality', *Accounting, Organizations and Society* 16(8): 705–32

Dezalay, Y., 1991. 'Territorial Battles and Tribal Disputes', *The Modern Law Review* 54: 792–809

1992. *Marchands de droit: La restructuration de l'ordre juridique international par les multinationales du droit*, Paris: Fayard

Dillard, J.F., 1991. 'Accounting as a Critical Social Science', *Accounting, Auditing & Accountability Journal* 4(1): 8–28

Espeland, W.N. and Hirsch, P.M., 1990. 'Ownership Changes, Accounting Practice and the Redefinition of the Corporation', *Accounting, Organizations and Society* 15(1/2): 77–96

Fligstein, N., 1987. 'The Intraorganizational Power Struggle: Rise of Finance Personnel to Top Leadership in Large Corporations, 1919–1979', *American Sociological Review* 52: 44–58

1990. *The Transformation of Corporate Control*, Cambridge, MA: Harvard University Press

Foucault, M., 1972. *Histoire de la folie*, Paris: Gallimard

Freedman, J. and Power, M., 1991. 'Law and Accounting: Transition and Transformation', *The Modern Law Review* 54: 769–91

Gallhofer, S. and Haslam, J., 1991. 'The Aura of Accounting in the Context of a Crisis: Germany and the First World War', *Accounting, Organizations and Society* 16(5/6): 487–520

Gambling, T., 1977. 'Magic, Accounting and Morale', *Accounting, Organizations and Society* 2(2): 141–51

1987. 'Accounting for Rituals', *Accounting, Organizations and Society* 12(4): 319–29

Gorz, A., 1989. *Critique of Economic Reason*, trans. G. Handyside and C. Turner, London: Verso

Hacking, I., 1990. *The Taming of Chance*, Cambridge: Cambridge University Press

Hammond, T. and Preston, A., 1992. 'Culture, Gender and Corporate Control: Japan as "Other"', *Accounting, Organizations and Society* 17(8): 795–808

Hedberg, B. and Jonsson, S., 1978. 'Designing Semi-Confusing Information Systems for Organizations in Changing Environments', *Accounting, Organizations and Society* 3(1): 47–64

Hines, R., 1988. 'Financial Accounting: In Communicating Reality, We Construct

Reality', *Accounting, Organizations and Society* 13(3): 251–61

1989. 'The Sociopolitical Paradigm in Financial Accounting Research', *Accounting, Auditing & Accountability Journal* 2(1): 52–76

Hopper, T. and Armstrong, P., 1991. 'Cost Accounting, Controlling Labour and the Rise of Conglomerates', *Accounting, Organizations and Society* 16(5/6): 405–38

Hopper, T., Storey, J. and Willmott, H., 1987. 'Accounting for Accounting: Towards the Development of a Dialectical View', *Accounting, Organizations and Society* 12(5): 437–56

Hopwood, A.G., 1978. 'Towards an Organizational Perspective for the Study of Accounting and Information Systems', *Accounting, Organizations and Society* 3(1): 3–13

1983. 'On Trying to Study Accounting in the Contexts in Which it Operates', *Accounting, Organizations and Society* 8(2/3): 287–305

1986. 'Management Accounting and Organizational Action: An Introduction', in M. Bromwich and A.G. Hopwood (eds.), *Research and Current Issues in Management Accounting*, London: Pitman

1992. 'Accounting Calculation and the Shifting Sphere of the Economic', *European Accounting Review* 1(1): 125–43

Johnson, H.T., 1983. 'The Search for Gain in Markets and Firms: A Review of the Historical Emergence of Management Accounting Systems', *Accounting, Organizations and Society* 8(2/3): 139–46

Jonsson, S. and Gronlund, A., 1988. 'Life With a Sub-Contractor: New Technology and Management Accounting', *Accounting, Organizations and Society* 13(5): 512–32

Kirkham, L. and Loft, A., 1993. 'Gender and the Construction of the Professional Accountant', *Accounting, Organizations and Society* 18(6): 507–58

Latour, B., 1988. *The Pasteurization of France*, Cambridge, MA: Harvard University Press

Laughlin, R.C., 1987. 'Accounting Systems in Organizational Contexts: A Case for Critical Theory', *Accounting, Organizations and Society* 12(5): 479–502

Lowe, T. and Machin, J.L.J., 1983. *New Perspectives in Management Control*, London: Macmillan

Lowe, E.A., Puxty, A.G. and Laughlin, R.C., 1983. 'Simple Theories for Complex Processes: Accounting Policy and the Market for Myopia', *Journal of Accounting and Public Policy* 2: 19–42

McBarnet, D., Weston, S. and Whelan, C.J., 1993. 'Adversary Accounting: Strategic Uses of Financial Information by Capital and Labour', *Accounting, Organizations and Society* 18(1): 81–100

March, J.G., 1978. 'Bounded Rationality, Ambiguity, and the Engineering of Choice', *Bell Journal of Economics* 9(2), Autumn; reprinted in J.G. March, *Decisions and Organizations* (1988)

1987. 'Ambiguity and Accounting: The Elusive Link between Information and Decision Making', *Accounting, Organizations and Society* 12(2): 153–68

1988. *Decisions and Organizations*, Oxford: Basil Blackwell

Markus, M.L. and Pfeffer, J., 1983. 'Power and the Design and Implementation of Accounting and Control Systems', *Accounting, Organizations and Society* 8(2/3): 205–18

Meyer, J.W., 1983. 'On the Celebration of Rationality: Some Comments on Boland and Pondy', *Accounting, Organizations and Society* 8(2/3): 235–40

1986. 'Social Environments and Organizational Accounting', *Accounting, Organizations and Society* 11(4/5): 345–56

Meyer, J.W. and Rowan, B., 1977. 'Institutionalized Organizations: Formal Structure as Myth and Ceremony', *American Journal of Sociology* 83(2): 340–63, reprinted in J.W. Meyer and W.R. Scott, *Organizational Environments: Ritual and Rationality*, Beverly Hills, CA: Sage (1983) (page references are to the latter)

Mezias, S.J., 1990. 'An Institutional Model of Organizational Practice: Financial Reporting at the Fortune 200', *Administrative Science Quarterly* 35: 431–57

Miller, P., 1991. 'Accounting Innovation Beyond the Enterprise: Problematizing Investment Decisions and Programming Economic Growth in the UK in the 1960s', *Accounting, Organizations and Society* 16(8): 733–62

1992. 'Accounting and Objectivity: The Invention of Calculating Selves and Calculable Spaces', *Annals of Scholarship* 9(1/2): 61–86

Miller, P. and Napier, C., 1993. 'Genealogies of Calculation', *Accounting, Organizations and Society* 18(7/8): 631–74

Miller, P. and O'Leary, T., 1990. 'Making Accountancy Practical', *Accounting, Organizations and Society* 15(3): 479–98

1993. 'Neoinstitutionalism and Practices of Government', *Working Paper*, LSE

1994. 'Accounting "Economic Citizenship" and the Spatial Reordering of Manufacture', *Accounting, Organizations and Society* 19(1): 15–43

Miller, P. and Rose, N. (eds.), 1986. *The Power of Psychiatry*, Cambridge: Polity Press

1990. 'Governing Economic Life', *Economy and Society* 19(1): 1–31

Miller, P., Hopper, T. and Laughlin, R., 1991. 'The New Accounting History: An Introduction', *Accounting, Organizations and Society* 16(5/6): 395–403

Morgan, G., 1983. 'Social Science and Accounting Research: A Commentary on Tomkins and Groves', *Accounting, Organizations and Society* 8(4): 385–8

Nahapiet, J., 1988. 'The Rhetoric and Reality of an Accounting Change: A Study of Resource Allocation', *Accounting, Organizations and Society* 13(4): 333–58

Neimark, M. and Tinker, T., 1986. 'The Social Construction of Management Control Systems', *Accounting, Organizations and Society* 11(4/5): 369–95

Ogden, S. and Bougen, P., 1985. 'A Radical Perspective on the Disclosure of Accounting Information to Trade Unions', *Accounting, Organizations and Society* 10(2): 211–24

Otley, D., 1980. 'The Contingency Theory of Management Accounting: Achievements and Prognosis', *Accounting, Organizations and Society* 5(4): 413–28

Picciotto, S., 1992. 'International Taxation and Intrafirm Pricing in Transnational Corporate Groups', *Accounting, Organizations and Society* 17(8): 759–92

Pickering, A., 1992. *Science as Practice and Culture*, Chicago: University of Chicago Press

Pinch, T., Mulkay, M. and Ashmore, M., 1989. 'Clinical Budgeting: Experimentation in the Social Sciences: A Drama in Five Acts', *Accounting, Organizations and Society* 14(3): 271–301

Porter, T.M., 1986. *The Rise of Statistical Thinking*, Princeton: Princeton University Press

Powell, W.W. and DiMaggio, P.J. (eds.), 1991. *The New Institutionalism in Organizational Analysis*, Chicago: University of Chicago Press

Power, M., 1991. 'Educating Accountants: Towards a Critical Ethnography', *Accounting, Organizations and Society* 16(4): 333–53

1992a. 'From Common Sense to Expertise: Reflections on the Prehistory of Audit Sampling', *Accounting, Organizations and Society* 17(1): 37–62

1992b. 'After Calculation? Reflections on "Critique of Economic Reason" by Andre Gorz', *Accounting, Organizations and Society* 17(5): 477–99

Preston, A.M., 1989. 'The Taxman Cometh: Some observations on the Interrelationship Between Accounting and Inland Revenue Practice', *Accounting, Organizations and Society* 11(4/5): 398–413

Preston, A.M., Cooper, D.J. and Coombs, R.W., 1992. 'Fabricating Budgets: A Study of the Production of Management Budgeting in the National Health Service', *Accounting, Organizations and Society* 17(6): 561–93

Puxty, A.G., Willmott, H.C., Cooper, D.J. and Lowe, T., 1987. 'Modes of Regulation in Advanced Capitalism: Locating Accountancy in Four Countries', *Accounting, Organizations and Society* 12(3): 273–91

Roberts, J. and Scapens, R., 1985. 'Accounting Systems and Systems of Accountability – Understanding Accounting Practices in their Organizational Contexts', *Accounting, Organizations and Society* 10(4): 443–56

Robson, K., 1992. 'Accounting Numbers as "Inscription": Action at a Distance and the Development of Accounting', *Accounting, Organizations and Society* 17(7): 685–708

Roy, D., 1969. 'Making Out: A Counter-System of Workers' Control of Work Situation and Relationships', in T. Burns (ed.), *Industrial Man*, Harmondsworth: Penguin

Shearer, T.L. and Arrington, C.E., 1993. 'Accounting in other Wor(l)ds: A Feminism Without Reserve', *Accounting, Organizations and Society* 18(2/3): 253–72

Simon, H.A., Guetzkow, G.K. and Tyndall, G., 1954. *Centralization vs Decentralization in Organizing the Controller's Department*, New York: American Books – Stratford Press

Swieringa, R.J. and Weick, K.E., 1987. 'Management Accounting and Action', *Accounting, Organizations and Society* 12(3): 293–308

Thompson, G., 1986. *Economic Calculation and Policy Formation*, London: Routledge

1987. 'Inflation Accounting in a Theory of Calculation', *Accounting, Organizations and Society* 12(5): 523–43

Tinker, A.M., 1980. 'Towards a Political Economy of Accounting: An Empirical Illustration of the Cambridge Controversies', *Accounting, Organizations and Society* 5(1): 147–60

1984. 'Theories of the State and the State of Accounting: Economic Reductionism and Political Voluntarism in Accounting Regulation Theory', *Journal of Accounting and Public Policy* Spring: 55–74

1985. *Paper Prophets: A Social Critique of Accounting*, New York: Praeger

Tinker, A.M., Merino, B.D. and Neimark, M.D., 1982. 'The Normative Origins of Positive Theories: Ideology and Accounting Thought', *Accounting, Organizations and Society* 7(2): 167–200

Tomkins, C. and Groves, R., 1983. 'The Everyday Accountant and Researching his Reality', *Accounting, Organizations and Society* 8(4): 361–74

Tribe, K., 1978. *Land, Labour and Economic Discourse*, London: Routledge & Kegan Paul

Wardell, M. and Weisenfeld, L.W., 1991. 'Management Accounting and the Workplace in the United States and Great Britain', *Accounting, Organizations and Society* 16(7): 655–70

Waterhouse, J.H. and Tiessen, P., 1978. 'A Contingency Framework for Management Accounting Systems Research', *Accounting, Organizations and Society* 3(1): 65–76

Watts, R.L. and Zimmerman, J.L., 1986. *Positive Accounting Theory*, Englewood Cliffs, NJ: Prentice-Hall

Whyte, W.F., 1955. *Money and Motivation*, New York: Harper & Row

Wildavsky, A., 1964. *The Politics of the Budgetary Process*, Boston: Little, Brown

Willmott, H.C., 1983. 'Paradigms for Accounting Research: Critical Reflections on Tomkins and Groves' "The Everyday Accountant and Researching his Reality"', *Accounting, Organizations and Society* 8(4): 389–405

Zeff, S.A., 1978. 'The Rise of "Economic Consequences"', *The Journal of Accountancy* December: 56–63

# 2    Early double-entry bookkeeping and the rhetoric of accounting calculation

*Grahame Thompson*

## Introduction

One way of approaching accounting is to locate it within the wider framework signalled by the term 'calculation'. Accounting then becomes a form of calculation, indeed a sub-form of economic and financial calculation. This way of approaching accounting has the advantage of setting it within a wider context. With respect to early forms of accounting, one can plot the connections between accounting and a more general turn in the analytical mind associated with the emergence of a range of calculative political and economic discourses arising during and after the late Middle Ages. Accounting can then be positioned alongside such regulatory programmes as Cameralism, Oeconomy, Physiocracy and other latterday economic discourses. Accounting can be viewed as in principle on a par with these other practical regulatory configurations rather than as existing in their shadow. Accounting can be placed on an equal analytical footing with economics, instead of continually deferring to economics because of the latter's seemingly more secure intellectual domain. This is the way I have approached the analysis of accounting and economics elsewhere (Thompson, 1986, 1987, 1991, 1994), and which I pursue below in the context of the emergence of the double-entry form in the early sixteenth century.

The term 'calculation' as used here has two interrelated meanings. The first refers to those techniques of calculation akin to arithmetic manipulation. This is a relatively uncontroversial use of the term. It focuses on the detail of how economic and financial assessments of activities are carried out, and how these feed into decision-making processes. The second use of the term refers to the context in which such calculations take place. It is concerned with elucidating the conditions of existence of calculative mechanisms and their effects. Calculation in this sense can refer to political calculation or legal calculation, as well as to economic, financial and managerial forms of calculation.

This way of locating accounting as a particular form of economic calculation entails an emphasis upon the *institutional matrix* in which accounting emerged. In the context of the sixteenth century, this involves attention to the role of three crucial institutions: the Church, the pedagogic apparatuses, and the publishing house. Along with the better explored role of the commercial organizations during the period, these institutions provide the contours in which we can understand how and why accounting in its particular 'modern' form emerged. For calculation can be regarded as an effect of the practices and mechanisms of particular organizational forms and agents. Calculative practices run through, and are articulated within, institutions. They are not determined by an essential principle but are dispersed through a range of what can be ambiguous and sometimes contradictory practices. It is with a view to specifying how these practices of calculation inhere within definite institutional and organizational configurations that we address the conditions of existence of the rhetorical formulation of early double-entry bookkeeping (DEB) in this chapter.

To explore the rhetorical nature of early DEB in this manner is distinct from an endorsement of 'the model of language' that underpins much of the contemporary analysis in terms of rhetoric. The model of language, or linguistic turn as it is often referred to, has become a central methodological device in the analysis of a wide range of phenomena in the humanities and social sciences. If somewhat belatedly, a concern with the linguistic and rhetorical characteristics of discourse has also affected the progressive accounting literature (e.g. Arrington, 1987; Lavoie, 1987; Lehman and Tinker, 1987). Whilst the issue of exactly what this 'new rhetoric' involves is the subject of considerable debate (e.g. Perelman, 1979, Nelson et al., 1987; Vickers, 1988), the re-emergence of a general concern with rhetoric has been stimulated by a focus on the language model.

In stressing the institutional matrix through which were articulated the processes and mechanisms of early DEB, this chapter proposes a distinctive way of addressing the rhetorical foundations of accounting. A focus on the central role of the publishing house within this matrix is to depart from the abstract and formal approach entailed in the 'model of language'. In its place is put an investigation of the contingent and historically specific configurative mechanisms that comprise the institutional moment in the formation of discourses. Thus although all calculation involves an element of rhetorical motivation – one of the conditions of existence of calculation is the practice of its rhetorical justification – it is to the institutional aspects of such processes that we need to look, rather than to the abstract and formal properties of language.

### Why rhetoric?

Let us look briefly at the background to the recent concern with rhetoric in accounting. For rhetorical analysis has been posed as a methodological

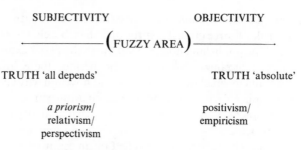

2.1  The problem of Truth

response to the classic philosophical problem of demarcating between theories in a number of disciplines. In the context of accounting, this has particular salience, as a number of authors have demonstrated (Arrington, 1987; Lavoie, 1987; Lehman and Tinker, 1987). But it needs to be posed carefully in this respect. McCloskey (1986) for instance suggests that it is *not* a Methodological response with a capital 'M'. Rather, it should be more modestly approached as part of a methodology with a small 'm'. By this McCloskey means to signal the passing of the grand philosophical claim to adjudicate between right and wrong, or between truth and falsity in intellectual discourse. A more subtle style of reasoning is called for.

One convenient way of representing these issues is with respect to figure 2.1.

This illustrates the key issues that have informed the re-emergence of interest in rhetoric and the model of language or linguistic turn. The problem of Truth[1] has traditionally been solved within philosophical discourse at either end of the spectrum in figure 2.1. Taking the right-hand pole first, here Truth can be established more or less absolutely and objectively. This is a result of the method of positivism/empiricism as usually understood. On the other hand, at the left-hand end of figure 2.1, Truth 'all depends'. Here Truth is the consequence of an overtly subjective *a priori*. It all depends upon the position from which it is judged. This illustrates the method (if it can be termed as such) of relativism/perspectivism. The analyst's theoretical *a priori* determines the Truth content of the results offered. It all depends from which perspective one begins.

It is a scepticism about the claims made at either end of the spectrum shown in figure 2.1 that has exercised many critical philosophers of late. This scepticism has highlighted the importance, and the difficulties, of conceptualizing that area falling in the middle ground between the two poles. This is sometimes referred to in the literature as a 'fuzzy' area, and it is within this grey area that much of the following discussion is located.

Any discussion of language is problematical in that there are at least two quite different ways in which language can be formulated as a category of analysis. These are consistently elided and run together in much of the literature dealing with accounting discourse (e.g. Arrington, 1987; Lavoie, 1987; Lehman and Tinker, 1987).

In the first place we have the traditional formulation of *language being a system of communication*. With this theory an already formulated message with a meaning is encoded by the speaker, forming the word, which is then transmitted to the audience in the form of a spoken message. This the audience subsequently decodes, usually on the basis of the social context of the language, or on the basis of the social characteristics of the audience. Chomsky's theory of language is a classic instance of this approach, an approach that has been of particular interest to the military. For the military the prime problem is to generate clear and unambiguous messages, which fits into the communications approach to language perfectly. It was Chomsky's brilliant achievement to relate this to a 'depth model' which looked for the foundations of language in the 'universals' of the human mind – his 'deep structures'. These deep structures are responsible for motivating meaning and encoding a message in his theory, which is then communicated by language.[2]

An alternative, and potentially more radical view of language, is to see it as a *system of signification* rather than of communication. With this approach the crucial category within language is the 'sign'. This is made up of two aspects – the signifier and the signified. Both of these exist in the realm of the concept. It is the referent that is signified by the signifier and this referent is what 'exists' outside of discourse.[3] As is well known, this Saussurian concept of language has given rise to a number of variants, perhaps the most radical of which argues that the sign constructs its own adequate signifieds. In this case it is the signifier that dominates the signified. Furthermore where this is the case, the emphasis shifts to the conditions of discourse for an understanding of the origin of meaning and sense. Under these circumstances the means of signification and their conditions of operation form the crucial sites for the construction of meaning. Thus meaning is not something already formed prior to its communication (encoded 'in advance', so to speak) for which the means of communication merely act as a transmission mechanism to an audience, which decodes the message on the basis of its 'consciousness', itself determined by that audience's social situation or circumstances. Here, by contrast, the 'play' of meaning and sense is a consequence of the play of signification, as exemplified by the system of signs that make up those very means of signification. Signs exist in the form of chains, which often 'slide' around, or under, each other. This implies that all systems of signification – one of which is given by accounting calculations – need to be 'read' for their meaning with respect to a definite pertinence rather than simply decoded. That pertinence is at least in large part given by the institutional configuration into which the system of signification is inserted.

It is this latter theory of language that has stimulated the recent interest in rhetoric as something that can specify the nature of meaning in a text almost independently of its extra discursive configuration. If rhetoric is thought to be about language as an argumentative system, where language is seen as a series of signs that constructs its own signifieds or narrative and where these signifieds directly represent the referent, then the rhetorical level is the one most adequate to the analytical procedure. In the case of accounting this would imply an almost exclusive focus upon the 'internal' dynamics of accounting rather than upon its 'external' institutional discursive configuration.

### What is rhetoric?

At first sight there might seem a simple answer to this question. For is it not just a matter of the conditions and procedures of argumentation and persuasion? Clearly this does capture something of an answer. But we need to generate a more developed response. The central feature of rhetoric for the Greeks concerned the way arguments and conversations were conducted in an attempt to persuade. Three distinct, but not separable, forms of argument have been traditionally deployed here: ethical appeals (*ethos*) involving one's own values and one's own character; emotional appeals (*pathos*) involving an appeal to the feelings of the audience; and rational appeals (*logos*) addressing the capacity to reason (which do at least abide by historically current standards of logic). The preparation of, and reflection on, these kinds of appeals is known as the invention of the argument (*inventio*). Once invented the appeals need to be organized and arranged (*dispositio*). This is then followed by the presentation of the material in an eloquent manner (*elocutio*).

This accounts for the formal arrangement of a rhetorical investigation, the object of which becomes one of uncovering these features in any text. But other problems linger. For instance, is it a 'methodological approach' or just an 'analytical technique'? Here we can signal a certain unease about exactly how to describe the kind of thing or event indicated by the term 'rhetoric': an 'investigation'?; an 'analysis'?; a 'method'?; an 'approach'?; a 'technique'? Clearly it has certain methodological pretensions of an analytical kind. These are signalled directly above. But describing it as an approach would seem to suggest something both looser and wider – a rather grander claim would seem to be being indicated.[4]

The predominant way in which rhetoric is described in the literature on economics and accounting is to treat it as an analytical method. Indeed there is one dominant way of dealing with it which is to describe it as a 'conversation' (e.g. Klamer, 1984, in the case of economics, and Arrington, 1987, in the case of accounting). Thus the investigative problem in the case of accounting would be to elaborate the forms of language in which disputes about accounting have been couched, and to elucidate the rhetorical power of these in shaping the field of comprehension, meaning and sense they engendered. Clearly a conversation is a rather gentle form of argument and we may want to draw a distinction between 'soft rhetoric' and 'hard rhetoric' on this basis. Thus the conversational soft rhetoric would be the kind of thing that goes on in the senior common rooms and seminars of American liberal arts colleges and universities, while a more robust hard rhetoric could characterize the argumentative form of public discourse. But in trying to make this distinction we can begin to see the shortcomings of the emphasis on rhetoric as such. It is towards a more critical view of the linguistic model and rhetoric analysis that I now turn.

### Problems with rhetoric and the model of language

To have a polite civilized conversation with someone, or even an argument with them, requires some stringent preconditions. In the first place, it presupposes that both parties 'speak' the same language. In the case of the social sciences this cannot always be guaranteed. Very different theoretical *a priori* can be involved in debates, demonstrating deep and often irreconcilable differences in outlook. How can these always be resolved by debate? Perhaps the best that can be said under these circumstances is to be able to recognize the difference and leave it at that.

But this then invokes the second precondition: that a certain rationality, and a commitment to it, must underlie the basis of any conversation or argument. It is not just by chance that modern German rationalist philosophers like Gadamer and particularly Habermas are invoked by, for instance, Arrington (1987) and Lavoie (1987) in their advocacy of the 'rhetoric of conversation' for accountancy. For both Gadamer and Habermas construct their theoretical systems of 'communicative rationality' on an elaborate edifice of enlightened and rationalistic behavioural foundations. To question whether this is always likely to be the case, or even *ever* likely to be the case, is not to decry rational argument or advocate an irrationality in its place. It is merely to register a scepticism, itself predicated on the actual experience of modern German history. Thus even to accept a difference and leave it at that requires a rational maturity often lacking in the actual practice of day-to-day social intercourse, let alone political debate and struggle.

Perhaps, then, the distinction between soft and hard rhetoric can be overdrawn. But in one sense we might like to try and preserve it. There is at least hope that a conversational, genuinely dialogical form of discourse could be organized, in which the mutual non-antagonistic exploration of positions is undertaken. Indeed, some have argued that this is the actual way in which all thinking is organized (Billig, 1987). Against this, however, we should recognize the 'pursuit of mastery', which can unhinge the dialogical character of discourse in its quest for a monological persuasive objective. If there is a genuine wish to convince 'the other' in any discussion, argument or conversation the dialogical moment may never quite arrive.

The problem with respect to accounting is this: can we understand its history simply in terms of the development of a communicative rationality? Whilst one does not wish to dismiss this aspect of its history the broader issue is to 'place' accounting's rationali*ties* in the context of their wider discursive configurative determinations. Only then – in the context of a conception that opens the non-rationalistic to an institutionalized rationality – will an adequate history be specifiable.

In an attempt to open this issue up in a concrete manner, the rest of this chapter concentrates upon the emergence of DEB within the rhetorically and institutionally rich environment of the late Middle Ages and early Renaissance period. This analysis invokes the names of Peter Ramus and Luca Pacioli as key figures in the period. But in so doing it also emphasizes another key element; the development of printing. Printing, and the 'printerly', is seen here as a more appropriate and alternative metaphorical investigative device to the 'model of language'. Printing displaces the ontological nature of the speaker or the writer of language into an institutionalized practice and a technology. The importance of this is drawn out later.

### The decline of rhetoric and the rise of accounting

In the 1550s, the Protestant priest Peter Ramus was heralding the final decline of the ancient rhetorical tradition. Some 50 years earlier a Franciscan priest Luca Pacioli had heralded the beginning of modern accounting. Are there connections between these two events? This is the issue explored in this section. Of course any connections here are not simply between these two figures as individual writers. Rather they are between a certain set of intellectual issues that each of them exemplified. The discussion is organized around three separate but connected points: the problem of 'belief' in the sixteenth century; the role of pedagogic reform; and the relationship between an oral, a written and a printed culture which was in a process of radical transformation at the time. Thus, as mentioned in the introductory remarks, *three* institutional practices in the construction of the discourse of accounting in this period are highlighted: the Church; the university/school; and the publishing house.

Aho (1985) has produced one of the most successful overtly rhetorical investigations of accounting with his analysis of the invention of DEB.[5] Aho (1985: 22) summarizes his argument as follows:

Instead of arguing that DEB was originally devised to serve exclusively informational or theoretical ends, this author suggests that its purpose was largely rhetorical – that is, to justify an activity about which there existed in medieval Christian Europe a considerable suspicion; namely commerce itself. In other words, we submit that DEB was neither an outgrowth of the spirit of Renaissance science nor of Thomistic logic – a position held by Weber Sombart – but of the art of rhetorical discourse.

Aho goes on to provide an exemplary rhetorical account by unpicking Pacioli's text according to the sets of threefold categorizations outlined above when discussing the formal organization of a rhetorical analysis. He suggests that DEB partly answers an ethical problem first by integrating profit-seeking into a Christian cosmos (thereby avoiding charges of the sin of avarice) and second by providing a 'just' explanation of business activity via the double-entry form which balances debits with credits, advantages with sacrifices, receipts with payments, and so on. In doing this it also served an aesthetic function of bringing bookkeeping into a realm of geometric and proportionate equivalences. These were classic rhetorical devices of the time, it is suggested.

There is much to admire and agree with in Aho's analysis. However there is a wider range of issues and problems in which it must be set if we are to account fully for the importance of DEB, of Pacioli, and of the demise of rhetoric as a legitimate intellectual tradition.

Clearly Pacioli was answering multiple questions in his texts – ethical, juridical and aesthetic. Crucial to the development of DEB was the notion of *balance*. This is recognized by Aho. But a focus on writing draws out a further dimension. For, as Hoskin and Macve (1986) suggest, DEB appeared as a consequence of a new way of textual writing, generated during the thirteenth and fourteenth centuries, mainly by clerical pedagogues. The systematic writing of accounts is seen by them in terms of a textual complexity involving first the 'doubled' character of the money sign (to be given and to be received in an exchange), and then its transformation into a 'double-sign' (a representation of a representation of value in the form of an account entry). Only after a long and hesitant development did the 'doubled-sign' and the 'double-sign' manifest themselves in the form of the double writing on paper of paper money. Furthermore, it was a formal organization of the relationship between interconnected entries of this

2.2 Painting of Pacioli completed in 1495 by Jacopo Barbari
*Source:* Taylor (1942, opposite p.196, Anderson, Roma)

double writing in books of account that created the notion of a *balanced account* late in the fifteenth century. This itself created a new measure of control over flows of goods and money.

There is, then, a kind of 'internal' history of writing within which DEB can be located, one that is strikingly illustrated by Hoskin and Macve's rich analysis. Such a focus on the practice of writing highlights the importance of addressing the institutional embeddedness of DEB, and the ways in which it expresses an emerging calculative rationality. In what follows I concentrate on and develop this explicit institutional setting of early DEB. Given that a good deal has been written about the institutional matrix of commerce and banking in which it developed, I do not elaborate this element. Instead, I begin with the impact of the Church and its increasingly uncertain status during the later part of the period.

### The Church and the rhetoric of DEB

The uncertainty of the position of the Church in the late fifteenth and sixteenth century stemmed from complex developments within theology on the one hand, and from the emergence of secular philosophical and scientific discourses on the other. The complexity of religious belief in the sixteenth century is well captured by Lucien Febvre's masterly analysis of the possibility of its antithesis – 'unbelief' – during the period (Febvre, 1982). Interestingly, in part this led to a major intellectual revival of classical studies, particularly of Greek thought which was appealed to by all sides for authority (just as it is tending to be used today in a similar period of intellectual uncertainty[6]). In addition, this growing intellectual turmoil was fostered by the invention of printing by Gutenberg in Mainz during the second half of the fifteenth century. Indeed, one of the ways the Church tried to keep a control over these events was to ban printing (e.g. by the edict of Paris in January 1535). Such attempts proved futile in the long run as discussed at greater length in a moment (see also Febvre and Martin, 1976).

Many of these themes can be seen in play in the work of Pacioli. For instance, take the famous portrait of him painted in 1495 and reproduced as figure 2.2. Pacioli, dressed in a friar's habit, is shown instructing the young Duke Guidobaldo of Urbino, a noted patron of mathematics. On a table are the symbols of mathematics – compasses, a geometrical diagram, an open copy of Euclid's *Elementa*, and (probably) a printed copy of Pacioli's own mathematical treatise (the *Summa de Arithmetica, Geometria, Proportioni et Proportionalita* – Everything about Arithmetic, Geometry and Proportion – first published in 1494, see figure 2.3). Drawn on a slate is one of the five perfect solids of Plato to which Pacioli points with his baton. His other hand indicates a place in the *Elementa*. In the upper left part of the

2.3 Title page of Pacioli's *Summa*, 1523 edition (the original 1494 edition did not have a title page) *Source:* Brown (1905, opposite p.108, Edinburgh Chartered Accountants' Library)

painting is a rather curious but resplendent crystal polyhedron (possibly an icosahedron). This hangs almost suspended in mid-air and is the true object of Pacioli's gaze.

The composition of this painting is revealing. Pacioli is a teacher as well as a priest. His mode is instructional. The crystal poly(icosa?)hedron is symbolic on a number of counts. It represents the eternal truth and clarity of mathematics. Pacioli was one of those responsible for the upsurge of mathematical thinking in the sixteenth century, a good deal of which was mystical rather than 'scientific' (Rose, 1975).[7] For Pacioli and others the Greeks symbolized this truth and clarity. But there is another level at which the mathematical impedimenta shown in the picture work, particularly the hovering poly(icosa)hedron. This relates to their religious significance. God himself had worked the world in a mathematical form. To worship God is to partake of this divine project. Hence the hovering poly(icosa)hedron can be read as symbolic of God's work (if not of God himself), and hence worthy of the reverent gaze it gets in the picture from God's disciple on Earth. (Pacioli's other major work, first published in 1509, was entitled *Divina Proportione*, see figure 2.4.)[8]

For Pacioli everything was symmetry and proportion. 'Even Rhetoric gains in elegance from proper harmony' ('Introduction to the *Summa*', Taylor 1942: 193). Pacioli's larger project was to *re-emphasize a belief in order sanctified by God*. It was not simply to justify the practice of commerce as something not antithetical to Christian doctrine (although clearly it was this in part). The project was rhetorical in so far as Pacioli was responding to a question or problem posed for religious belief more generally. But that question was posed outside of the protocols of language in a formal sense. It was posed by the nature of theological belief, and by the institutional requirement of the Church.

### DEB and the pedagogical apparatus

It was mentioned above that Pacioli was a teacher. He held a number of teaching posts in central Italian universities during his life, and was a personal tutor to many of the wealthy and famous of the time. In connection to this we can now raise a more general issue of the relevance of teaching reform to the popularization of Pacioli's books, and in particular of the 'method of Venice' – DEB – that formed a major part of the *Summa*. Here we take up another institutional theme in the construction of the discourse of DEB.

The scholasticism of the late Middle Ages remained under sharp attack during the early part of the sixteenth century in the works of Peter Ramus. Ramus was above all else interested in pedagogy. He was concerned to

**proportione**
O pera a tutti glingegni perfpi
caci e curiofi necefaria One cia
fcun ftudiofo di Philofophia:
Profpectiua Pictura Sculptu
ra: Architectura: Mufica: e
altre Mathematice: fua/
uiffima: fottile: e ad/
mirabile doctrina
confequira: e de
lectaraffi:cõva
rie queftione
de fecretiffi
ma fcien/
tia.

M. Antonio Capella er uditiff. recenfente:
A. Paganius Paganinus Characteri
bus elegantiffimis accuratifsi
me imprimebat.

2.4  Title page of Pacioli's *Divina*, first published in 1509
*Source:* Morison (1969, p.1)

reform the practices of teaching current in the universities of his day (Ong, 1974). To this end he developed a formidable battery of textbooks and other writings (not all published under his own name) which remained in circulation, and which were used for over two centuries in some cases. There were three separate but interrelated aspects to this project – Ramus' *Dialectic*, his *Rhetoric*, and his *Method*. The *Method* served to tie the *Dialectic* and the *Rhetoric* together. While all three are highly nuanced in his writings I try only to outline their main features here.

For Ramus, dialectic has two aspects: invention and judgement. 'Invention' refers to a kind of testimony or human opinion that lodges a statement. This is supplemented by 'judgement' which is cultivated by the calm mind and refers to a kind of logic. These two features, or dialectic, are organized to be capable of creating a *conviction*. They are designed to create a *confidence* in something, or a trust in it. Whilst this is seen as an effect of reason in the sense of a means of inferring a conclusion, it is not a form of reason seen as a way of getting at a *Truth* which is sure, commonsensical and thoroughly scientific in the modern meaning of these terms. Thus the logic that operates in this schema is not a 'scientific logic'. Rather, it is more a 'logic of probability' where the debate or discussion generates the likelihood, and where the probable has to be sufficient, if not to decide between alternatives at least to result in a practical decision or action. Rendered into the concern with teaching, invention underlies the art of practice, while judgement that of exercise. The resultant art of dialecting becomes defined as a doctrine of teaching or discoursing *well* – never mind its *Truth* value.

Rhetoric is linked closely to dialectic in this process, but it is also radically separated from it. Rhetoric has to do with communicating and expressing. It has to do with the voice and the audial aspects of creating a persuasive conviction. But with Ramism, in an important and novel way, the specifically and overtly rhetorical aspects of Rhetoric are denied and spirited away. Ramism 'derhetoricizes' Rhetoric, so to speak. It puts Rhetoric under the shadow of the Dialectic, so that it is subject to the ordered dialectic of invention and judgement. The Ramist drive towards curriculum simplification and orderliness hastened this process of denying the rhetorical moment to classroom practice and exercise. The textbook order, so crucial to the Ramist 'method', came to dominate its particular conception of rhetoric. Rhetoric in turn became more of a secondary ornamentation to the main intellectual business of invention and judgement.

What about the Ramist method which served to tie the other two aspects together? 'Method' can be defined quite generally as a series of ordered steps gone through to produce, with certain efficiency, a desired effect. Thus it is a routine of *efficiency* in the first instance. Ong (1974) suggests that this conception of method did not exist in the sixteenth century and this was not the Ramist method. In the sixteenth century method was seen more as a pursuit or investigation in its own right, with no necessary objective involving the generation of new and absolutely confirmed knowledge. Thus it was still set in that tradition which emphasized argument and dialogue in an open investigatory stance. In addition, method was closely associated with curriculum organization and pedagogical procedure. It did not have that judgemental character associated with the Methodology of today (see also Gilbert, 1960).

Ramus took up the issue of method very much in the tradition of its pedagogical meaning. He emphasized *orderly arrangement* above all else. Thus method came to denote the orderly arrangement of the *topics* within discourse.[9] A 'topical logic' was constructed (a form of class logic in fact) in which it was of central importance where things fell in an ordered and hierarchical series of places. In practice, Ramus was able to generate a highly sophisticated and successful textbook style of presentation which was enduring. This was at least in part because he was able to produce a clearly spatialized documentation of how a discourse works. This was his decisive advantage in the teaching situation. With this advantage went an acceptance, almost unconsciously, of the more 'theoretical' aspects that lay behind and supported the generation of his textbook style and the books he prepared on Dialectic, Rhetoric and Method. They embodied their own 'methodology' in a self-reflexive way within the analysis that was offered of the nature of discourse, one that was lodged in the teaching books themselves.

But this was not all. Ramus was able to capitalize on a number of general and some would argue momentous, social and technological developments of his time. Of particular importance was the development of writing and printing. As mentioned above, the effect of Ramus' method was to institute a formal spatialization into the representation of discourse. This was associated with a profound transformation in the way in which thinking in a general sense was beginning to be conducted. The development of *writing*, already alluded to, was partly responsible for mobilizing this transformation. Writing creates a space for a kind of silent discourse – an internal, comtemplative type of thought (Clancy, 1979; Saenger, 1982). But in addition it is above all else a 'visual' form of thought – it relies on the visualization of discourse. In this capacity it is vitally dependent on a spatialization of words, and the order of presentation of arguments. This offered the vital link to the success of Ramus' method. Two things followed. In the first place, the Ramist method met the growing implication of the development of a written culture. Secondly, its subordination of dialogue, verbal argument, disputation and so on, i.e. of rhetoric, to the dictates of dialectic reasoning also met the implication of the growing internal and contemplative mode of thinking. It silenced a robust and public form of rhetoric, reducing it to mere communication. From now on, the work of the intellect went on within the dialectic only, rather than within a system which included rhetoric and dialectic in a complex combination and where neither was given a preference. This 'prior' form of thinking the nature of thinking, where there had been no distinction between rhetoric and dialectic, was more suited to an environment in which the spoken word formed the content of discourse – where personal verbal testimony and listening constituted the typical modes in which knowledge was invented and consolidated.

### DEB and the printing house

During the period in which Ramus was working writing itself was being transformed. Indeed it was probably this development that was decisive in the consolidation of the idea of method Ramus pioneered. With the printing of textbooks, embodying both the relative ease of study via their style of presentation, and the 'method' implicit to them, these features became duplicable and endurable. What is more, printing reinforced the ordering and spatialization of the visual text. It demanded a more diagrammatic form of presentation, breaking up the text into its constituent parts with headings, paragraphs, a tight compact style of composition, and so on. The portability of such books deepened the individualized, silent character of learning and knowledge creation, particularly in the humanities (Eisenstein, 1979, and below).

This transformation brought about by the invention of printing, together with the issue of pedagogical reform, were central to the success of Pacioli and DEB. Let us turn now to look at the background conditions in which Pacioli wrote, and the manner in which he presented his own analytical programme.

It is well known that Pacioli did not 'invent' DEB. As Taylor has noted, he specifically stated that he was merely writing down the system that had been used in Venice for up to 200 years (Taylor, 1956: 180). According to Peragallo (1938: 54–5) and others, Benedetto Cotrugli actually finished a written manuscript containing a presentation of double-entry in 1458 (*Della Mercatura et del Mercante Perfetto*), some 40 years before Pacioli's *Everything about Arithmetic, Geometry and Proportion*, but it remained unpublished. A glance at any of the many books documenting the historical development of accounting in the Middle Ages and early Renaissance also demonstrates that the double-entry method was relatively widely deployed, if in an elementary form, before Pacioli wrote (e.g. Brown, 1905; Peragallo, 1938; Zerbi, 1952; Yamey, Edey and Thompson, 1963; see also Chatfield, 1974 and Sapori, 1970).

What marks out Pacioli's treatise was the fact that his was the first book on the subject, and was the first to be printed. This was its decisive advantage. It led in turn to a great many imitators. Indeed these quickly improved on the original. While they more or less copied and duplicated Pacioli's own exposition (Geijsbeek, 1914), they added worked examples and illustrated with specimen accounts. These were not contained in the *Summa*, though it did give some guidance on how to handle debit and credit ledger entries as shown in figure 2.5. An additional first advantage for Pacioli was that he published the *Summa* in the colloquial Italian, rather than in the more usual Latin. Combined with a definite touch for the colloquial language (Geijsbeek, 1914: 27), this secured Pacioli a readership that did not seem to have been tapped before.

Hugh Oldcastle's *Profitable Treatyce* and Jan Ympyn's *A Notable and Very Excellent Woorke*, both published in 1543, were the first English and Dutch treatments of DEB respectively, and were near enough exact duplications of Pacioli's *Summa*. Ympyn's book was translated into English in 1547. Oldcastle's book seems to have been lost, and the earliest existing systematic English treatment is to be found in John Mellis *A Briefe Instruction* published in 1588. This is also heavily dependent upon Pacioli and Ympyn, and it contains specimen accounts.

All of these early books and many later ones, were written in an instructional style. They were meant to act as textbooks.

The number of books on accounting published in English from the middle of the sixteenth to the beginning of the nineteenth century is shown in table 2.1. Clearly, after 1550 the number of books published expanded rapidly. But it is difficult to gain an accurate impression of who actually read these books. Chartier's analysis (1987) of the reading habits of the French in the late Middle Ages and early modern period does not once mention the existence of books on accounting held in the private libraries or household inventories of citizens, not even those of merchants. (I have not been able to find any comparable analysis of English reading habits at the time.) Thus one would expect the impact of these kinds of books *qua* printed books to have been largely confined to academic circles, at least in the first instance. Only gradually did they begin to have an added impact on those merchants not already familiar with rudimentary accounting procedures of the double-entry type.

Pacioli's own books were mainly about mathematics. The *Summa* contained five parts: arithmetic and algebra; their use in trade reckoning; bookkeeping; money and exchange; pure and especially applied geometry.

Cali che acade mettere ale recordançe del mercante.

Utte lemafferitie di casa o di bottega che tu ti truoui. Ma vogliono essere per ordine.cioe tutte le cose di ferro da perse con spatio da potere agiongnere se bi sognasse.E cosi da segnare in margine quelle che fussino perdutte o vendute o donate o guaste.Ma non si intende masseritie minute dipoco valore. E sare ri cordo di tutte le cose dottone da perse comme e detto. E simile tutte le cose distagno. E si mile tutte lecose dilengno.E cosi tutte le cose dirame.E cosi tutte le cose dariento e doro zc. Sempre con spatio di qualche carta da potere arrogere se bisognasse.e cosi dadare notitia di quello che mancasse. Tutte lemalleuerie o obbzighi o promesse che promettessi per ql che amico. e chiarire bene che e comme. Tutte lemercantie o altre cose che ti fosseno las sate i guardia o a serbo di pstaça da qlche amico.e cosi tutte lecose ch tu pstassi a altri tuoi amici. Tutti limercati conditionati cioe compre ovedite come p ereplovno cotrato cioe ch tu mi mandi con lepzossime galee che tornerano dingbliterra tanti cantara di lane dilimi stri a caso che le sieno buone e recipienti. Jo ti daro tanto del cantaro o del cento o verame te ti mandaro alincontro tanti cantara di cottoni. Tutte le case o possessioni o bottegbe o gioie che tu affitassi a tanti duc.o a tante lire lanno.E quando tu riscoterai ilfitto aloza ql lidinari sanno a mettere al libzo comme disopza ti dissi.Pzestando qualche gioia o uasella menti dariento o dozo a qualche tuo amico per otto o quidici giozni diqueste tale cose no si mettono al libzo.ma sene fa ricozdo ale ricozdançe.perche fra pochi giozni lai bariauere. E cosi per contra se a te fossi pzestato simili cose non li debbi mettere al libzo.Ma farne me mozia alericozdançe perche pzesto lai a rendere.

Comme si scriuono lire e soldi e danarte picioli e altre abzeuiature.
Lire soldi danari picioli libbze once danarpesi grani carati ducati fiozin larghi.
℔ ₷ ₰ p libbre ℥ ₰p g°. ₭ duc. fio.laf

<table>
<tr><td>

Cómeſidebbe dettare le ptrie de debitozi.
Mcccc° Lxxxxiij°.
Lodouico dipiero foreſtaí devare a di.xiiii.nouembre.
1493.₷.44.f.1: ₰.₷.porto contati in pstaça.posto caſ ſa auere.a car. 2 ₷ 44 ₷1 ₰8.
E a di.18.detto ₷.18.f.11.₰. 6.promettemo p lui a marti no dipiero foraboschi a suo piacer posto bere i qsto.a c.2.₷ 18 ₷11 ₰6.

Caſſa i mano di ſimone da leſſo bobeni de daí adi.14. nouembre 1493. ₷.62.f.13. ₰.2.da francesco dantonio caualcanti in qsto a c.2 ₷ 62 ₷13 ₰6.

Martino di piero fora bo schi de dare a di.20.nouem bre.1493.₷.18.f.11.₰.6.por to luimedesimo contati po sto caſſa a car. 2. ₷ 18 ₷11 ₰6.

Francesco dantonio caual cati de dare a di.12.di noue bre.1493.₷.20.f.4.₰.2.d.p misse anostro piacer p lodo uico dipiero foreſtaí a c.2. ₷ 20 ₷4 ₰2.

</td><td>

Come ſi debbe dittare leptite di creditori.
Mcccc° Lxxxiiij.
Lodouico dipiero fozeſtaí de hauere a di.22.nouembre 1493.₷.20.f.4.₰.2.ſono p parte di pagamento.E per lui celia promiſſi a nostro piacere fracesco datonio. caualcati posto dare a c. 2.₷ 20 ₷4 ₰2.

Caſſa in mano di ſimone daleſſo bobeni de hauere a di.14.nouembre.1493.₷.44. f.1.₰.8.alo douico di piero foreſtani in qsto. a car. 2. ₷ 44 ₷1 ₰8.
E a di.22.nouembre.1493 ₷.18.f.11.₰.6.a martino di piero foraboschi.a ca.2. ₷ 18 ₷11 ₰6.

Martino di piero fora bo schidi hauere a di.18.noue bre.1493.₷.18.f.11.₰.6.gli pmettemo a suo piacere p lodouico di piero foreſtani posto obbi bere iqsto a c.2.₷ 18 ₷11 ₰6

Francescho datonio caual canti de hauere a di.14.no uebre.1493.₷.62.f.13.₰.6. reco lui medesimo ptan po sto caſſa dare a.car.2. ₷ 62 ₷13 ₰6.

</td></tr>
</table>

2.5 Page from Pacioli's *Summa*, dealing with ledger entries
*Source:* Geijsbeek (1914, p.80)

Table 2.1. *Number of books on accounting published in English, 1543–1800*

| Years | Number of books[a] |
|---|---|
| 1543–1550 | 2 |
| 1551–1600 | 8 |
| 1601–1650 | 11 |
| 1651–1700 | 49 |
| 1701–1750 | 92 |
| 1751–1800[b] | 175 |

*Notes:*
[a] Includes different editions of the same book.
[b] Some later editions of books first published before 1800 are included here.
*Source:* Calculated from Yamey, Edey and Thompson (1963).

Printing lent itself readily to mathematical and geometrical exposition. Indeed it was indispensable to it. This was also the case with accounting. According to Eisenstein (1979), printing changed the whole way in which culture was henceforth generated and understood. To begin with it stimulated an interest in the past rather than the future. It led to a fascination with ancient wisdom, to a recovery of what had been known rather than a discovery of the new. Instead of the single-minded focus on a single book it opened up the possibility of a wide focus on a range of books. A manuscript culture kept books 'hidden' and singular because of their rarity and frailty. Printing undermined this and brought into focus a set of often conflicting interpretations contained in many manuscripts and books that could be assessed together. The diversity of manuscripts on accounting, for instance, with all their local variation, were brought together by people like Pacioli to study before a printed exposition of their general rules and orders could be undertaken.[10] Others did the same, often eventually reaching different interpretations and conclusions about these rules and orders. Pacioli's reputation as expositor of DEB spread quickly in the first half of the sixteenth century as his printed text was reworked and translated into all the major European languages.

Printing made it possible to present accounting material, together with mathematics and geometry, in a way that embodied the idea of an ordered and rule-governed uniformity. This innovation is most pertinent from the point of view of establishing why Pacioli is still recognized as the 'father' of

DEB. He paid particular attention to methodological exactness and the mastery of detail. Clearly this type of account, at least in part, met the requirements of a growing commercial culture. But the fact that it did not penetrate into all capitalist organizations for some 400 years or more should make us wary of attributing too much to this concern for exactitude and detail.[11] What was more crucial for its growing popularity was that it suited the printed form in which it became embodied. Ong (1971) and Eisenstein (1979) have argued that the Ramist method outlined above takes an itemized approach to discourse highly reminiscent of the printing process itself. Pacioli's method did much the same thing: it imposed organization on a subject by imagining it as made up of parts fixed in space.

This was particularly true of the idea of balance, so crucial to the development of DEB as noted above. Genuine double-entry did emerge in a paragraph form, but it was the tabula, bilateral form that soon dominated, greatly facilitating the summation of items and their alignment. A book could then be easily closed, with assets appearing on one side and liabilities plus owners' equity on the other. With its printed exposition, the double-entry method became the standard against which other methods were measured and found wanting. Without such a technology the full impact of the method could never have been realized, since it relied on a careful alignment and spacing of the entries, text and figures which could only be properly reproduced and widely understood in a printed form. We have already seen something of this in figure 2.5, showing the printed way debit and credit items were handled in the *Summa*. Figures 2.6 and 2.7 reinforce this. Figure 2.6 demonstrates the way Pacioli handled the categorization of the intricacies of proportions and their organization. Quantified and spatialized tableaux of this character became a *way of thinking* after the invention of printing made them durable and easily duplicable. Figure 2.7 shows the difference between a handwritten page of the *Summa* and its printed form. Again, the tidiness and spatialized nature of the latter make it much easier to read and therefore comprehend.

The pagination of a printed presentation helped further to reinforce the almost stark spatialization and non-precisability of the financial picture that DEB constructed of the enterprise. Printing helped consolidate a deliberative, diagrammatic, silent, private and calculative mode of thinking. In this way it helped 'turn' the analytical mind. It stimulated that calculative approach so typical of commercial practice.[12] It did not just 'represent' it. The very mechanism of keeping a record of account in this manner located that turn of mind in a practical manifestation. Of course this did not happen overnight, immediately after the *Summa* was first published. Accounts were still kept and presented by firms in a handwritten form until well into the present century in many cases. Rather, what printed

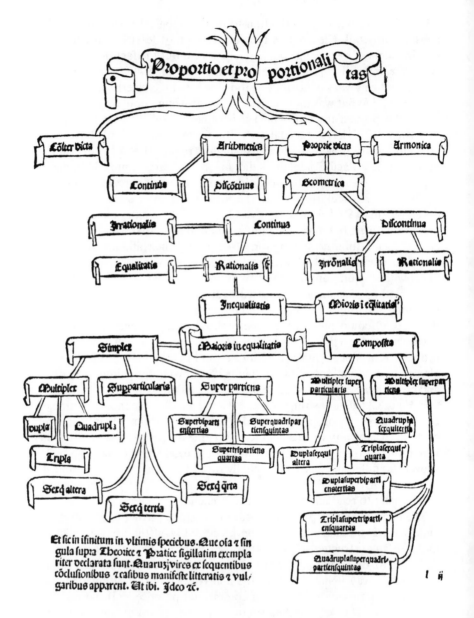

Et sic in ifinitum in vltimis fpeciebus. Que ofa z fin
gula fupra Theorice z Pratice figillatim exempla
riter declarata funt. Quarumj vires ex fequentibus
coclufionibus z cafibus manifefte litteratis z vul/
garibus apparent. Ut ibi. Ideo zc.

2.6 The organization of proportions: from the *Summa*
*Source:* Geijsbeek (1914, p.26)

« Apresso. per le ℞ sorde zoe quelle che non sono discre-
» ti uoglio metere. qui vna regola per la qual sempre
» in infinitum te aprosimarai piu cbel compagno. onde
» auoler trouare ditte ℞ sempre tien questa. via. prima
» troua la sua ℞ diritamente commo fai laltre. e quando
» tuaj trouata la prima ℞ fane proua. e uedi quanto lapassa
» ditto numero. alora. torai quello piu. zoe quella differentia
» e partirala. per lo dopin de questa prima ℞. e quello che uenira
» de dito partimento. trarale de dita prima ℞. Elo ri-
» manente sira ℞ secondo di quel tal numero. poi faraj
» la proua. anche di questa seconda ℞. e uederai quanto la so-
» perchia ditto numero. e anche quel piu che ti dara questa seconda
» ℞ partiralo per dopio de questa seconda. ℞ e quello che ne
» uen chauaralo. de ditta seconda ℞ e lo rimanente sira
» ℞ terza de dito numero. poi amo dito faraj proua euederai
» quanto la passi ditto numero. e pigliarai anche quella differentia
» e partirala sempre perlo dopio dela ℞. che te da. tal differentia
» e sempre chaua quello che neuen dela ℞ sola. Elo rima-
» nente sira laltra ℞. piu prossimana. e così va proce-
» dendo in infinito. e guarda chauar sempre riparti-
» menti dele ℞ schiette. e non dele dopiate Verbi gratia
» ℞ prima. de. 6. sie. $2\frac{1}{2}$ e questa passa. de $\frac{1}{4}$ parti
» questo. $\frac{1}{4}$ qual. e / differentia. per lo dopio della prima ℞ zoe

2.7 A page from the *Summa*: handwritten and printed; the original facsimile of Pacioli's handwriting is to be found in ms. no.3129 in the Vatican Library

*Source:* Taylor (1942, opposite p.133)

instructional textbooks on accounting like that produced by Pacioli did was to familiarize and popularize the method amongst a widening range of commercial establishments. This was done initially at the behest of experts rather than actual bookkeepers who did not prepare books on DEB in its early stages of development. Accounts could still be kept in a handwritten form, as indeed they were, with a good deal of the calculations conducted in the head, but the printed orderliness, repetition and durability 'directed' the account formulation and presentation process in a particular way.

## Conclusions

This chapter began by suggesting that accounting be regarded as an instance of a broader category of economic calculation. One of the aims has been to assess recent proposals that accounting should be investigated and adjudicated in terms of rhetoric and the 'model of language'. The argument has been that while this appeal to rhetoric is not without its interest or without positive and useful results, it is not robust enough to cope with the sharp differences of intellectual and political life. The rationality of argument can easily break down. Polite conversations can become strained. Often the construction of intellectual advance along the lines of the outcome of civilized conversation is actually an *ex post* rationalization or *reconstruction* of the event.

One of the main problems with rhetoric remains who sets the questions, or where they are set. In responding to this, the protocols of language are just not sufficient. The argument has been that we need to look to the institutional moment in the construction of the discursive for help. The discursive domain of economic and financial assessment is typified by a significatory complex of calculative practices that are highly specific and institutionally conditioned. In the case of early DEB and Luca Pacioli discussed here, such an approach involved examining three interrelated institutional mechanisms which articulated the 'birth' of the double-entry method in the fifteenth and sixteenth centuries: the Church; the educational apparatus; and the printing/publishing regime at the time. Pacioli was writing at the peak in the power and security of the Church. The manner in which he presented DEB reflected that power and security. But there is a curious way in which the more intensely an institution celebrates the certainty of its position, the more it reveals its underlying unease. The stormclouds for the Church were gathering well before the late fifteenth century, though they did not break until 20 years later when Luther began publishing his attacks on religious orthodoxy.[13] The growing 'crisis' in the institution of the Church presents one set of contours in which we must view Pacioli's particular rhetorical formation and delivery, and the manner in which he presented DEB.

But this was not the only important influence on the formation and delivery of DEB. The manner of its delivery and reception was also influenced by the pedagogical debates and reformulation of teaching practices at the time. Here I have concentrated upon the role of Ramism as an exemplary illustration of these changes, indicating what they implied for the presentation of discourses like DEB. Ramus was writing in a period when Pacioli's text was being popularized as a teaching text by Oldcastle, Ympyn, Dafforne and others, as they copied, refined and published their own versions.

This leads to the final institutional context in which the emergence of DEB needs to be considered. It has been argued that the 'printerly' character of DEB was decisive in securing its place against rival systems. It met the implications of a 'printerly culture', the characteristics of which were themselves also emerging at the time through the invention of printing and the publication of printed books. This again secured Pacioli a central place in the history of DEB as the author of the first printed exposition of the method.

When one adds these elements together, and introduces into the picture the final institutional site of commercial and banking changes that many others have analysed, a 'governable entity' (as I would prefer to term it, see n. 11) – the firm, as distinct from its owners, proprietors, managers or workers – became a possibility and was eventually established.

Finally, we can ask a key question addressed to the analysis offered by this chapter – 'Is accounting rhetorical?'. In responding to this, the answer is a qualified 'yes'. It is rhetorical in as much that accounting is arguing and persuading, like any other calculative discourse. But, of itself, this answer is not terribly useful. It has been suggested that the terms of a rhetoric are extradiscursive/linguistic. They are institutionally set. The specification of that institutional matrix, its form and consequences, remains the critical analytical problem. What is said, how it is said, and why it is said, while clearly an effect of language, need to be 'placed' in their contingent institutional context before the 'reasons' for all of this can be properly identified. Approaching accounting as one among many calculative practices conceived in this way provides a robust analytical device for the understanding of modern as well as ancient accounting procedures.

NOTES

This chapter is partly based upon Thompson (1991).
1. Truth is given a capital 'T' to denote its specifically philosophical connotations – i.e. as an absolute Truth.
2. For a general linguistic analysis that tries to develop a *rapprochement* between grammar and rhetoric along these lines, see Gray (1977).

3. This is somewhat more problematical than indicated by these remarks in that not all signs have a real referent, e.g. mythical beasts like the centaur.

4. Rhetoric is thus definitely not akin to a positivistic analysis that first generates a theory or set of hypotheses (or single hypothesis) and then proceeds to test this against a real domain of facts. Nor is it a method that tends to logically construct (or even deconstruct) the terms of an analysis, proposition or method – this would involve an attempt to subject the text to the criteria of rational consistency and logical order (in the modern sense of those terms). Rhetoric in its modern discredited sense – associated with disreputable practices of propaganda and cajole – is also ruled out, as is the idea of rhetoric as a complementary practice to the 'symptomatic reading' which uncovers the silences, absences and lacunae in a text.

5. I am grateful to Anthony Hopwood for having drawn my attention to this article by Aho.

6. See Ong (1971, 1974); Febvre (1982); Vickers (1988). There are two basic ways the Greeks can be deployed. One is to make an appeal to them for *authority*. The other is to use them to signal a *difference*. This latter is clearly the more progressive.

7. Pacioli was not a great mathematician but more a popularizer of mathematics. For instance he gets only a passing mention in Kline's monumental history (Kline, 1972: 237).

8. For the source of these none too original remarks about Pacioli see Taylor (1942). Taylor carries part translations of the *Summa* and the *Divina*, mainly their introductions. Various full translations of that part of the *Summa* dealing with accounting exist. I have used the one contained in Geijsbeek (1914). Morison (1969) provides a translation of that part of the *Divina* dealing with the aesthetic of alphabetical letters and their construction.

   There is clearly more to this painting than has been elaborated here. Does Pacioli in fact gaze at the poly(icosa)hedron or *through* it towards an invisible writing of the Truth of which the poly(icosa)hedron is the only visible sign? In addition, it is perhaps God and Plato that act as the true double framers for Pacioli's gaze. (I thank an anonymous referee for suggesting these possibilities.)

9. Topics are the 'things' or subject matter of dialetic which came to be known through the places in which they were stored in memory.

10. Perhaps Eisenstein (and others) may have exaggerated the *novelty* of reading habits initiated by the advent of printing in the fifteenth century. Saenger (1982) presents the revisionist case that silent (or quiet, at least) reading was a well established feature of scholastic and lay intellectual life in the early and high Middle Ages. Word separation in writing was introduced from the tenth century and thirteenth-century scholastic writers produced texts with elaborate cross-referencing, displaying well developed synthesizing powers (Saenger 1982: 386). Saenger's point is that the forms of tabula orderings so clearly consolidated by the advent of printing were in common usage within an earlier written culture, something confirmed by the existence of written double-entry formulations well before Pacioli's printed exposition.

11. The obstacles to the rapid universalization of DEB are interestingly discussed in Hoskin and Macve (1986). One of the ways of developing the implications of Pacioli's project would be to set it in the context of the notion of a 'governable

subject'. Thus DEB is part of that condition which creates a commercial entity separate from those who own it, manage it, or work in it. This notion is developed in Miller and O'Leary (1987), though note how my formulation treats the enterprise as an *entity* rather than a *subject*. For a discussion of the implications of this difference see Thompson (1986, ch. 7).

12. A different example of the importance of the early development of printing concerns the emergence of actuarial practice. This relied heavily upon the ordering embodied in printing and was of central importance to the twin developments of the insurance market alongside the statistical skills needed to operate it effectively. Again this embodied a calculative turn of mind in a practical manifestation.

13. Saenger (1982: 414) suggests that the silent reading of the thirteenth and fourteenth centuries may have fostered the insecurities in faith and devotion that led to support for John Calvin three to four generations later.

REFERENCES

Aho, J.A., 1985. 'Rhetoric and the Invention of Double Entry Bookkeeping', *Rhetorica* 3(1), Winter: 21–43

Arrington, C.E., 1987. 'The Rhetoric of Inquiry and accounting Research', *European Accounting Association*, 10th Congress, London, March

Billig, M., 1987. *Arguing and Thinking: A Rhetorical Approach to Social Psychology*, Cambridge: Cambridge University Press

Brown, R., 1905. *A History of Accounting and Accountants*, Edinburgh: T.C. & E.C. Jack

Chartier, R., 1987. *The Cultural Uses of Print in Early Modern France*, Princeton, NJ: Princeton University Press

Chatfield, M., 1974. *A History of Accounting Thought*, Hinsdale, IL: Dryden Press

Clancy, M.T., 1979. *From Memory to Written Record: England 1066–1307*, London: Edward Arnold

Eisenstein, E.L., 1979. *The Printing Press as an agent of Change*, vols 1 and 2, Cambridge: Cambridge University Press

Febvre, L., 1982. *The Problem of Unbelief in the Sixteenth Century*, Cambridge, MA: Harvard University Press

Febvre, L. and Martin, H-J., 1976. *The Coming of the Book: The Impact of Printing 1400–1800*, London: New Left Books

Geijsbeek, J.B., 1914. *Ancient Double-Entry Bookkeeping*, Houston, TX: Scholar Book Co

Gilbert, N.W., 1960. *Renaissance Concepts of Method*, New York: Columbia University Press

Gray, B., 1977. *The Grammatical Foundations of Rhetoric*, The Hague: Mouton

Hoskins, K.W. and Macve, R., 1986. 'Accounting and the Examination: A Genealogy of Disciplinary Power', *Accounting, Organizations and Society* 11(2): 105–36

Klamer, A., 1984. *The New Classical Macroeconomics*, Brighton: Wheatsheaf

Kline, M., 1972. *Mathematical Thought from Ancient to Modern Times*, Oxford and London: Oxford University Press

Lavoie, D., 1987. 'The Accounting of Interpretations and the Interpretation of

Accounts: The Communicative Function of the "Language of Business"', *Accounting, Organizations and Society* 12(5): 503–22

Lehman, C. and Tinker, T., 1987. 'The "Real" Cultural Significance of Accounts', *Accounting, Organizations and Society* 12(5): 503–22

McCloskey, D., 1986. *The Rhetoric of Economics*, Brighton, Wheatsheaf

Miller, P. and O'Leary, T., 1987. 'Accounting and the Construction of the Governable Person', *Accounting, Organizations and Society* 12(3): 235–65

Morison, S., 1969. *Fra Luca de Pacioli of Borgo San Sepolcro*, New York: Kraus Reprint Co

Nelson, J.S., Megill, A. and McCloskey (eds.), 1987. *The Rhetoric of the Human Sciences*, Madison: University of Wisconsin Press

Ong, W.J., 1971. *Rhetoric, Romance and Technology*, Ithaca, NY: Cornell University Press

1974. *Ramus: Method and the Decay of Dialogue*, Cambridge, MA: Harvard University Press

Peragallo, E., 1938. *Origin and Evolution of Double Entry Bookkeeping*, New York: American Institute Publishing Co

Perelman, C., 1979. *The New Rhetoric*, Notre Dame: University of Notre Dame Press

Rose, P.L., 1975. *The Italian Renaissance of Mathematics*, Geneva: Libraire Droz

Saenger, P., 1982. 'Silent Reading: Its Impact on Late Medieval Script and Society', *Viator* 13: 367–414

Sapori, A., 1970. *The Italian Merchant in the Middle Ages*, New York: Norton

Taylor, R.E., 1942. *No Royal Road: Luca Pacioli and His Times*, Chapel Hill, NC: University of North Carolina Press

1956. 'Lucia Pacioli', in A.C. Littleton and B.S. Yamey (eds.), *Studies in the History of Accounting*, Homewood, IL: Richard D. Irwin: 175–84

Thompson, G.G., 1986. *Economic Calculation and Policy Formation*, London: Routledge

1987. 'Inflation Accounting in a Theory of Calculation', *Accounting, Organizations and Society* 12(5): 523–43

1991. 'Is Accounting Rhetorical? Methodology, Lucia Pacioli and Printing', *Accounting, Organizations and Society* 16(5/6): 572–99

1994. 'Accounting for economics and the economy', forthcoming in *Accounting, Organizations and Society*

Vickers, B., 1988. *In Defence of Rhetoric*, Oxford: Clarendon Press

Yamey, B.S., Edey, H.C. and Thompson, H.W. (eds.), 1963. *Accounting in England and Scotland: 1543–1800*, London: Sweet & Maxwell

Zerbi, T., 1952. *Le Origin della Partita Doppia*, Milan: Carlo Marzorati

# 3 Writing, examining, disciplining: the genesis of accounting's modern power

*Keith Hoskin and Richard Macve*

## Introduction: towards a disciplinary history of accounting

Accounting is an ancient practice with a distinctive modern power. The invention of the paradigmatic form of modern accounting, double-entry, can be dated to the fourteenth century at the latest (de Roover, 1974; Thompson, 1991). But is was not till the nineteenth and twentieth centuries that accounting attained its modern significance with the emergence of Cost and Management Accounting, Financial Reporting, accounting as a recognizable and respectable profession, and systems of accountability.

Accounting's history therefore poses a central and uncomfortable question: why the long gap between the invention of the double-entry technique and the development of accounting's modern significance? Explanations couched purely in terms of economic utility are inadequate, for there has never been a clear link established between accounting's use and the improvement of rational economic decision-taking. Thus most famously Yamey (1964) refuted the 'Sombart thesis' showing that there was no direct connection between the rise of Renaissance capitalism and the invention of double-entry bookkeeping (DEB). And in the modern context putative links continue to prove tenuous, unstable or illusory. So the possibility looms increasingly large that a new quality of understanding is needed in order to make sense both of accounting's history and its modern power.

We propose that such an understanding can be constructed from a 'disciplinary' perspective, where the focus is on accounting the *practice*, as a form of writing and examining. For at the simplest level of its inscription, accounting is a technology that writes value, and presents in that writing a space for examination – be it of physical flows, monetary values or human performance, of past events, present states or future possibilities.

Such a perspective derives initially from the work of Michel Foucault. It proposes that accounting's history is best approached as a problem in 'power-knowledge' relations (Foucault, 1977, Gordon, 1980).[1] For accounting functions simultaneously, to an ultimately undecidable limit, as a form of both power and knowledge: it disciplines behaviourally even while it provides expert disciplinary information, and it does both by the way as a practice it turns events into writing and subjects them to examination.

However we are not thereby suggesting that accounting writes and examines in precisely the same way in all times and places. On the contrary, we follow Foucault in perceiving certain discontinuities in history, moments when power-knowledge practices change in fundamental and significant ways. In analysing accounting we discern two distinct phases in its history since the Middle Ages: a first stage beginning in the twelfth century when the development of new (though not yet modern) practices of writing and examining enabled the invention of the double-entry format; then a second phase beginning from the late eighteenth century when our familiar forms of written, graded examination were first developed, and when modern forms of 'discipline', stretching from normalizing techniques of behavioural control to the network of modern academic disciplines, first took shape.

The key to our approach therefore lies in the first place in uncovering how new forms of writing and examining first get established; and the counterintuitive heart of our analysis is that each time fundamental change begins in the apparently marginal field of education. What changes at such moments is not human learning as such – for learning is a process like language, constantly eluding capture since it can be captured only through historically specific forms which are always both more and less than the process itself – what changes is the historically specific structuring of the way in which humans learn *to* learn.[2]

That moves the focus to educational practices – the humdrum microtechnologies of everyday educational experience – and how occasionally in history such practices, though virtually unnoticed, change significantly. Our thesis here is that, when such changes take place, they restructure the way humans learn to learn, and that once that has happened those humans begin to reshape the possible patterns of power-knowledge relations. Sometimes the activity can be traced only to the educational elite in general, sometimes to specific individuals, but in either case the apparently marginal in history becomes the central focus of attention.

In one respect this extends Foucault's own insights on the genesis of the modern disciplinary world in the late eighteenth century. For as he acknowledged in his major work *Discipline and Punish* (1977), there was one key power-knowledge technology that emerged at that time, where 'the superimposition of the power relations and the knowledge relations assume ... all its visible brilliance' (1977: 185): the examination. The modern examination manifested, as Foucault saw (1977: 185), a new 'power of writing'. First, it turned students into a 'field' wherein knowledge would be diffused, as they were made to write for examination; second, it made it possible to generate for each individual examinee (and a whole population of examinees) a written 'archive' of their performance; third, these examinations, in awarding numerical marks, generated a new power of calculation, rendering individuals into a population of 'calculable persons' as each person's marks contributed to, and simultaneously marked a deviation from, a newly-establishable population 'norm' (1977: 184–7). Such a form of examination promoted both behavioural discipline and the cause of disciplinary knowledge.

But where Foucault saw just this one power-knowledge breakthrough engineered by writing and examining, a more fine-grained historical analysis shows a two-stage process. What was developed in the late eighteenth century was examination in its modern form as the *written graded examination*, developed first within elite institutions of higher education such as Cambridge, where its first form was the Mathematics Tripos (Hoskin, 1979).

However there was an earlier moment when writing and examining came together in the educational world to produce a new level of knowledge-power: in the twelfth century with the invention of the university. This was the first Western institution to impose formal examination, though at that time it took the *oral* and *ungraded* form of the disputation and recitation (Hoskin, 1979). This also, in its time, promoted a new power of examining and writing. Firstly, students confronting the apparatus of examination came to learn that real reading was silent critical reading (named first by Abelard as *inquisitio*), focused on the critical examination of texts and the search for the hidden intention presumed to lie beneath the surface of words; secondly, within this university world the first 'alphanumeric' sign systems were developed (i.e. systems using both alphabetic letters and arabic numerals), along with the visually-oriented layout of texts to promote information retrieval.

Thus we propose an extension to Foucault's analysis of power-knowledge relations, an extension which may help to gain a new purchase on the conundrum of how knowledge practices come to constitute forms of power. For, we suggest, the hyphen that both links and differentiates power and knowledge relations is an educational one, namely the educational practices through which at any given time we learn to learn.[3] In both the twelfth and the eighteenth centuries new modes of writing and examining made possible a new power-knowledge configuration, in each case with an enhanced role for the power of knowledge.

But most significantly for our interests here, one particular power-knowledge precipitate each time was the development of a new writing of accounting. In the first case it was the invention of the double-entry format. In the second it was the development of the modern forms of accounting and accountability, which then, in a process usually seen in reverse, *made possible* the emergence of our familiar modern economic discourses focused on productivity, profitability and performativity (see ch.10 in this volume).

Today virtually all humans learn to learn under a regime of writing, examining and grading, to the point where such practices appear simply given, as quasi-eternal aspects of experience. Consequently the structuring of the real is increasingly dominated by two principles that express directly the power of these practices to structure both the external world and the self within: these principles we name 'grammatocentrism' and 'calculability'.

The first of these terms denotes the way in which power and knowledge are increasingly exercised through writing. Both modern organizations and individuals are grammatocentric, i.e. centred on writing, in a world where the written takes priority in a historically new way. We operate and succeed via texts, handbooks, plans, data, models, budgets, accounts, etc.; at a meta level we construct expert (discipline based) accounts of the accounts, meta narratives, meta analyses and so on.

Meanwhile humans increasingly discover that there is no quality that cannot in principle be quantified. The mark, we suggest, was the technology that initiated the drive towards this ubiquitous calculability. First deployed in institutions like Cambridge and the French *Grandes Ecoles* in the late eighteenth century (Hoskin, 1979, 1990) it did not just put a number on performance, it put a quantifiable value on the person, providing for the first time in history an objective measure of human success and failure.[4] The mark functioned both as an account of past performance, and as a currency conveying a quantified expression of human value; when aggregated, marks became a measure of the underlying competence or 'ability' of the self, and by extension of the population of selves.

In a world where the principles of grammatocentrism and calculability are so widely disseminated, accounting has discovered a new power to be more than just a technology measuring and recording transactions and flows of goods and money – more indeed than just the double-entry form of bookkeeping. It has become one particularly privileged way of measuring and restructuring man as the 'calculable person' (Miller and O'Leary, 1987; Miller, 1992); it has also come to play a strategic role in the development of a new, grammatocentric kind of 'managing by the numbers', exemplified in the emergence of what Alfred Chandler (1977) has called the 'modern business enterprise'.

Under the disciplinary analysis this breakthrough is more than just an economic change. The modern business enterprise does not emerge as a response to some imputed economic 'need' (an invocation more magical than explanatory), for it does not appear when 'need' should demand it, during the English Industrial Revolution. Instead it emerges, as Chandler has shown, in the then-economic backwater of the USA, beginning in the 1830s and 1840s, as the first organization in history where managers manage other managers and do so via the sort of numbers found in the now-ubiquitous reports, forecasts, norms and ratios of business life.

This is a manifestation of the new double power of discipline. For the pioneers of the new business practices prove not to be businessmen as such, but graduates of the US Military Academy at West Point. Though founded in 1801, West Point was reformed in 1817 by the introduction from the French *Ecole Polytechnique* of a rigorous new educational regime based on constant writing, grading and examining; and, as we shall show, it was individual graduates of this regime who translated its disciplinary practices into the business arena, thus initiating the first managerial businesses.

The genesis of modern business therefore marks a transformation broader and deeper than just an economic change; it is one particularly dramatic sign that a new power-knowledge regime had begun to take shape, a regime which is predicated on the practices of writing, examining and grading and whose underlying principles remain today grammatocentrism and calculability.

This then is the outline of our new disciplinary approach to understanding accounting's modern power. Let us now proceed to show in more detail how such simple practices as writing and examining could have such transformative yet little-noticed historical effects.

### The Western medieval invention of DEB

For some time it has been clear that double-entry is a Western medieval invention. No such system is to be found in Graeco–Roman antiquity (de Sainte Croix, 1956; Macve, 1985), nor in Arabic culture (Udovitch, 1979). One explanation for its absence in the Graeco–Roman world, advanced by de Sainte Croix (1956: 64), is that double-entry was virtually unthinkable in the absence of an arithmetical notation like arabic numerals. For without a zero there could be no system of place value, and so columnar arrangement of numbers offered no special advantage. Thus there is no systematic use of opposed columns and little tabulation within columns, let alone any integrated journal–ledger system.[5]

Yet the presence or absence of arabic numerals alone is not a sufficient explanation for this development. Certainly arabic numerals played a significant role in the medieval Western world, as they enabled a new interrelated writing of word and number to form an 'alphanumeric' system of notation.[6] But what is now apparent is how the introduction of arabic numerals formed just one part of a more general shift in the modes both of writing and reading, a shift which predates the introduction of the new numerals and which in one key respect directly affects them: for it is only in this European context, from around 1200, that the numerals are rewritten into their familiar modern number forms where for instance zero becomes written as '0' (Lemay, 1977).

The underlying shift in reading and writing, it now seems, began by the early twelfth century, and at the apparently simplest levels: as a rewriting of writing centred on increasing the rational spatialization of texts (Rouse and Rouse, 1982), and as a shift in the culturally dominant mode of reading away from reading aloud, the culturally approved mode of reading in antiquity, to silent reading (Saenger, 1982).[7] As a result, from the twelfth century on and at first within the world of elite education, humans began to engage with both the visible technology of writing and the invisible technology of reading in systematically new ways. In particular, in the elite institutions they began to *examine*, first texts and then people, to the point where the institutions themselves began to change before 1200 into the first examining and degree-giving institutions: the universities.

It is at that point that new power-knowledge possibilities began to take shape. Over the next two centuries the new practices of reading, writing and examining came to generate a range of new forms of knowledge-based power: (1) a new social power for the elite who emerged from the examining system as the first university graduates, (2) new 'apparatuses' of power constructed out of the application of writing and examining, and (3) a new 'writerly' power discovered (through silent critical reading) as residing both within signs themselves and in their layout.

It is, we suggest, through analysing and following these changes that the ultimate development of the double-entry format can be explained. Each of these three developments in knowledge-power contributed to establishing a new significance for accounting. Taken together they emphasize how double-entry was not just a pure-knowledge technical breakthrough but a manifestation of the power accruing to the new ways of writing, reading and examining. They show how double-entry is a power-knowledge not a pure-knowledge invention.

### Accounting and the university elite

A long-standing traditional view has been that double-entry was an innovation developed by medieval merchants because of the expanding demands of trade. But such a view now seems more and more untenable, not least because it overlooks the degree to which the increased status and visibility of accounting was linked to the world of administration, a world which from the twelfth century on was increasingly dominated by the new university-educated elite.

The emergence of this elite is marked particularly by the changing definition and increasing status of the term *magister* (Southern, 1982; Baldwin, 1982). Southern points out that before 1135 the term had been restricted to a specific category, the masters in charge of a cathedral school. But it quickly developed into a term designating the status of scholars 'as professional men' (1982: 135). Baldwin takes the story a stage further, showing how, by the late twelfth century, *magistri* were becoming key figures in governmental administration: the French court having 'at least a dozen', and the English court by 1202 having over 20. And as this happened they acquired a new title as *magistri officiales*, at first a bishop's chief legal officer, but soon, as a generic term, the 'official'. Thus we see here the constitution of a historically new category, the credentialled professional. In this respect the oldest profession is that of the professors.[8]

These masters and officials were not slow to recognize accounting's administrative utility. As Michael Clanchy has pointed out, up to the mid-thirteenth century 'the great majority of clerks and accountants ... were trained at universities' (1975:685). But theirs was more than just a utilitarian response. For this university elite, rather than merchants, were also those who first developed a genuine 'arithmetical mentality'.

Alexander Murray (1978) decisively lays the old ghost that the credit for this should go to the merchant: his role is 'not that of a pioneer or even a patron of pioneers' (1978: 194). Instead, it was the pedagogues and scholars who pioneered the new mentality, for instance by producing in the 1100s the first handbooks showing how to use arabic numerals in the pen-and-paper system of algorism (Evans, 1977). And it was within the academic context that arabic numerals got one of their first regular uses, as a means of facilitating information retrieval.

As medieval university scholars produced huge new texts – annotated editions of the Bible, commentaries on the Church Fathers, texts in Canon Law, etc. – they devised a range of new techniques to enable the precise designation of textual locations. As they did so (Rouse and Rouse, 1979: 34) they 'were nearly unanimous in their rejection of roman numerals as being too clumsy ... in the course of the thirteenth century [arabic numerals] supersede roman numerals and letters ... for use in foliation; and the use ... for line-numbering before mid-century is one of the earlier instances of routine wholesale use'. Thus it now appears increasingly clear that the leading exponents and beneficiaries of the new concerns with numeracy and accounting were not at first merchants but the university graduates.[9]

### From inquisition to accounting: new apparatuses of knowledge-power

Changes in the practices of learning also generated new knowledge-power in a more intimate, less immediately obvious way, for the shift in elite culture away from reading aloud towards silent reading produced one particular new kind of critical hermeneutic approach to texts. The beginnings are small. Pedagogues such as Abelard (c. 1120 AD) began to develop this new critical reading of texts, requiring the careful compilation and comparison of apparently contradictory passages (Smalley, 1957).[10] This new reading, undertaken with a view to reconciling such contradictions, Abelard named *inquisitio*, for 'through inquiring we perceive the truth'.[11]

But such a powerful form of reading, silent, critical, appraising, was not long restricted to the examination of texts. Before 1200 a new concern, not found in antiquity, with establishing the 'intention' of an author became widespread – indeed this also 'seems to have originated in Abelard's philosophical writings' (Haring, 1982: 185). The technique was then also extended to the formal examination of students, who had to prove their own competence in the skill of critical reading by undertaking disputations in oral defence of some thesis.

Here lies the genesis of formal academic examination, with its new power-knowledge dilemma. For the student it was an ordeal, carrying the threat of ignorance exposed, but its successful negotiation led to admission into the guild of masters as a qualified expert, and a subsequent internalized commitment to examination as a specially valuable apparatus for the extraction of truth. Within a generation the new graduates had developed three such apparatuses: Confession, Purgatory and the Inquisition.

Confession, while not a new practice as such (Hoskin, 1984), shifted from being concerned with sinful acts (the surface of sin) to inquiring into the deep-seated *intentions* underlying them: this new inquisitorial reading of the self is first found in the work of a Paris scholar, Alan of Lille's *Liber Poenitentialis* published in 1202, a work which changed the whole focus and power of Confession within the Catholic rite.[12] Purgatory on the other hand is a new invention of this era, as Jacques le Goff (1981) has shown. In 1150 there was no such theological location but by 1190 the Parisian scholars, undertaking their Abelardian critical reading, had imposed a unified coherence on minor and previously unconnected passages in the Bible referring to 'purgatorial fire', the bosom of Abraham, and Limbo, and coalesced all three into a new and specific place. The invention of Purgatory (a third place found only in the Catholic rite) thrust God into the role of Great Examiner in the Sky, testing each sinner, appraising their sin, and deciding who should be admitted into the Elect.

Finally there is the judicial form of Inquisition which first took shape around 1220 (Hamilton, 1981). This was perhaps the most deadly and powerful application of the new technologies: a combination of (1) new scholarly writing techniques such as indexing, collating and cross-referencing, used to trawl through depositions and identify potential heretics, and (2) the new critical reading, or *inquisitio*, which was deployed to examine suspects in person and uncover the truth of heresy lying beneath the surface. And who were the first Inquisitors? Members of the new mendicant orders, the Franciscans and Dominicans, recruited in the first place from universities (Hamilton, 1981: ch.3).[13]

Such power-knowledge changes would be of only tangential interest if it were not the case that the same amalgam of writing and examining produces two further new apparatuses of more direct relevance to accounting: the audit and 'control', both of which are more closely related to these apparatuses and to each other than is generally recognized.

Both terms are Latin neologisms absent from ancient classical Latin. The 'audit', or hearing of accounts may, as Clanchy has suggested (1979: 215), reflect the continuing power of the old tradition that real reading was reading aloud. Thus Abbot Samson of Bury St Edmunds (c. 1185 AD) 'heard' the weekly account of his expenditure, and when the Franciscans arrived in England the superior 'heard the first annual account' (which showed such overspending that he never wanted to hear an account ever again). But that, we suggest, is only half the story. The audit as power-knowledge apparatus also embodies the power of the new critical practice of *inquisitio*. Abbot Samson, Clanchy also notes, inspected his rent register almost every day 'as though he could see therein the image of his own efficiency as in a mirror' (Clanchy, 1979: 215).

The audit in this respect constitutes a translation of the new learning practices of the academic world. Just as students had to combine the silent critical reading of texts with the oral proof of their competence in the formal event of the examination, so the audit exercised the same double power: first, a silent inquisitorial reading of the network of books, as the auditor through careful examination and cross-referencing got them to yield up their hidden truth; second a formal examination where the auditor now 'heard' what the accounts and their stewards had to say in response to stringent oral questioning.

This certainly seems to reflect the way in which power was exercised by auditors over stewards in the examination of estate accounts from the thirteenth century on (Drew, 1947; Noke, 1981). Such stewardship accounts were still quite traditional, typically recording information about receipts and payments of money and produce in a way little changed since ancient Rome. But now the final account comprised not just the transactions that actually did occur, but those which the auditors estimated *should* have occurred. In other words, in their practice the auditors were going beneath the surface of the actual figures to derive true 'expected' yields. Then upon completion of the formal oral audit, they regularly surcharged the bailiff or reeve for the calculated excess.[14] Thus, though this was far from the modern detailed surface procedures of accounting and audit, structurally the audit was enacting power-knowledge relations in a way that continues to the present.

As to 'control', this medieval neologism displays the knowledge-power directly derivable from the rewriting of writing. For it refers to a new kind of textual form, the 'counter-roll' (in Latin it is the *contra-rotulus*, in French the 'contre-rolle', with its first usage being dated around 1220 at the English court). This roll was not a simple copy duplicating original primary data (something found in all bureaucratic cultures) but a new *third* roll introduced to be both a check and a precis of primary records already kept in duplicate.[15]

The evidence tends to suggest that the term emerges from an accounting context, in the Exchequer, which had by 1200 a well established system of accounting based on the use of wooden tally-sticks as the primary record of transactions. With the tally system each transaction was recorded in duplicate by first cutting varying-sized notches across the tally, and then splitting it lengthwise into a larger part (the stock, given as a receipt) and the smaller foil (kept as the central record). For further accuracy relevant details of the transaction were written onto both parts of the tally and into the current Exchequer Roll. But by 1200 a whole system of extra checks involving the rewriting of writing had been introduced, as we know from the *Dialogue of the Exchequer* (Johnson, 1983) written by Richard Fitz Nigel, an Exchequer official. Each transaction was now entered twice in writing, once into the Treasury Roll, and once into the Chancery Roll, while officials oversaw each scribe for accuracy. But in addition, there sat at a separate bench a new official who kept a 'third Roll' which excerpted key entries from the full transcript and is described as containing 'the Laws of the Realm and the secrets of the King'.

This, we suggest, is the roll which by 1220 became known as the *contra-rotulus*. It marks a new kind of written power: an abridgement both of essential rules of procedure and of significant transactions and decisions. Already such a 'counter-roll' in a simple way encapsulates the two complementary functions of control as it is conventionally defined today: (1) to be a check on the essential accuracy of data and the honesty of functionaries and (2) to produce a condensation and clarification of data enabling a critical overview of the wider situation. And again we find the educational connection, for according to Fitz Nigel the man who introduced the 'third Roll' was a university graduate and *Magister*, one Thomas Brown, trained in Italy before coming to the English court in 1160.[16]

*From the rewriting of writing to the double-entry format*

Finally there is the textual transformation in accounts themselves, eventuating in the double-entry format. Here there is a direct parallelism between educational and supposedly economic change, for the rewriting of accounts follows and mirrors the more general rewriting of writing within the scholarly world.

If we look first at the accounting progression we find, on the basis of the evidence collated by de Roover (1974: 121ff.), that the earliest surviving medieval accounting record, from 1157, is no more than 'a few figures jotted down on three scraps of paper'. However, by 1221 a rudimentary form of visual awareness is found in a Florentine account book which has loans entered in paragraph format and space for noting repayments, each of which is separated by a punctuation mark.[17]

At this stage the arrangement is still basically chronological and simple, with the accounting text being constructed as a narrative of past events rather than a structure oriented to future information-retrieval (there is not for instance an account for each client). But by 1300 the Fini account book contains 'accounts for operating results and expenses as well as the usual personal accounts for receivables and payables'; it also cross-references each entry as both a debit and a credit. Around the same time the Farolfi ledger adopts a still more sophisticated layout. All entries have cross-references to corresponding debits and credits, and amounts are now placed in extension columns where they can be easily totalled. Finally, by 1340 in northern Italy another textual re-organization, into tabular or bilateral double-entry layout, has taken effect. De Roover finds Genoese bankers using the tabular layout in 1313 but still only in single-entry. However, by 1340 the accounts of the stewards of the Genoa commune can be seen to have developed a full double-entry format, where each debit is matched by and cross-referenced to a corresponding credit in a bilateral layout.

If we then shift back to the more general history of writing, we find that each stage of this textual transformation is anticipated within the scholarly world. Paragraphing was one of the earliest layout changes found in the early 1100s as the concern with silent meaningful reading of texts took over from the dictates of reading aloud. By the 1160s the layout of the Bible was well advanced towards complex columnar organization. Traditionally it had been laid out in a two-column format, without glosses or explanatory comments. Now scholars produced a text in one column, centre-page, flanked by two narrower columns of glosses with key words underlined and tie-marks linking gloss and text (Rouse and Rouse, 1982: 208). By 1170 a text of the Psalms is laid out with three columns of apparatus at either margin supporting one column of text, one cross-referencing to the other

Psalms, the second cross-referencing to other books in the Bible and the third containing scholarly citations complete with primitive quotation marks. As Rouse and Rouse (1982: 209) comment of these devices: 'we still use virtually all of them today, save that we have moved the marginalia to the foot of the page.'

A century later, by 1250, texts had become sophisticated information-rich grids. Such techniques as chapter and verse division, paragraphing, punctuation and marginal symbols had become commonplace features of pedagogic and scholarly texts, and in that process as noted above arabic numerals had replaced roman ones in foliation and line numbering. At the same time a whole range of new secondary texts were evolving to facilitate information retrieval, like the alphabetically ordered index, the concordance and the catalogue.

The analogues to the textual changes in accounting are manifest: a century before the development of double-entry we already find the principles of columnar layout, alphanumeric discourse, cross-referencing, indexing, and the integration of primary and secondary texts. These technologies quickly became taken for granted, part of the mental furniture of those who learned within the new visualist textual world, where by now real reading was silent reading beyond all question. Thus double-entry, as a textual format, mirrors a new quality of textuality that had already taken over the elite literate world. 'Mirroring' is indeed the apt metaphor, for the thirteenth century was the quintessential age of the book as Mirror (as expressed in the title of Vincent of Beauvais' encyclopaedic *Speculum Maius*, which was then made up of subsidiary mirrors, the *Speculum Naturale, Historicale* and *Doctrinale*). Double-entry is a particular kind of mirror book, embodying the balanced and interconnected writing of the equal and opposite signs of debit and credit – or rather, with its journals, cash books and ledgers, it was like Vincent's *Speculum* an interconnected series of such books.

Of course, once having achieved its new format accounting could develop its own distinctive power. Having grafted onto the simple form of chronological narrative the new impersonal format of the mirror book it could develop a new discursive voice; instead of just being a narrative of transactions, it could become a critical commentary *upon* them. Thus by the fifteenth century we find 'anticipations' of much later practices: for instance, as de Roover points out (1974: 123), Italian merchants:

had begun by 1400 to use accounting as a tool of management and control ... by developing the rudiments of cost accounting, by introducing reserves and other modes of adjustment such as accruals and deferred items, and by giving attention to the audit of balance sheets.

At the same time, the case of double-entry underlines the fact that new information technologies do not in themselves effortlessly transform the world. While accounting was occasionally deployed to striking economic effect (Solomons, 1968), for over four centuries forms of accounting including double-entry had in general a remarkably limited impact. Accounting in itself was certainly not a profession (bookkeepers and accounts clerks lay well below that threshold), and there is ample evidence (de Roover, 1974; Yamey, 1977) that ledgers and balances were kept sporadically even in large and successful businesses; even the East India Company used accounting practices which gave only limited attention to annual profit measurement (Yamey, 1977: 21, 26). Meanwhile annual audit, the use of the accounting data for prediction and cost control, the development of a systematic concern with the changing value of assets over time: these are all conspicuously absent from the majority of business enterprises. As late as the Industrial Revolution, the extent of accounting's use was still limited, being mainly for financial stewardship purposes, as a check on honesty, or for very rudimentary forms of cost control.

Taken overall, such premodern approaches to accounting had a temporal orientation facing more towards the past than the future. Accounting faced the past insofar as it was a record of what had happened and what workers or stewards did or did not do (and it faced the present insofar as it produced more or less timely and updated financial statements); but it seldom faced the future to be used, like now, as a means of predicting or shaping future activity or exerting a constant and watchful accountability over the future performance of workers, managers and directors. In short, accounting exercised a kind of control which aimed to conserve loss rather than maximize gain. It did not operate as part of something one might call 'management'.

All this would change, dramatically and swiftly, during the nineteenth century, particularly in the USA. Yet, as must by now be clear, the explanation for this transformation cannot easily be sought in any technical transformation in accounting itself, since double-entry had existed by this time for some five centuries. Furthermore it cannot be put down in any straightforward economistic way as accounting emerging smoothly to meet the new economic 'demand' of industrialization, for neither management nor accounting played any noticeable role in the Industrial Revolution in Britain.

As Sidney Pollard concluded in *The Genesis of Modern Management*, as late as 1830 in Britain (1) there was no specialist field of knowledge representing 'a management science or at least a management technology', and (2) there was no workforce category who could be designated a 'managerial class' (1965: 250). There were, of course, enterprises which used accounting and disciplinary techniques, often quite extensively: the Crowley Iron Works (c. 1710) for instance and, from the 1770s on, Wedgwood's pottery near Stoke-on-Trent and Boulton & Watt's manufactory in Birmingham (McKendrick, 1970: Pollard, 1965; Thompson, 1967). But even recent re-evaluations of the evidence (e.g. Fleischman and Parker, 1991) fail to discover an *integrated* management structure taking shape. Cost experiments (such as those of Wedgwood) were not utilized to coordinate production, control costs and maximize productivity on a *regular* basis. What appears to be lacking is any approach which simultaneously analysed both financial and *human* performativity, rendering the interrelated but separable values of products and persons jointly calculable. Instead, as Alfred Chandler details in *The Visible Hand* (1977), these managerial breakthroughs were first developed in the USA from the 1830s.

### The genesis of modern business: the West Point connections

The modern business enterprise is the first organization in history to consist, as Chandler puts it, of 'many distinct operating units ... managed by a hierarchy of salaried executives' (1977: 1). It is the first system where managers manage other managers and report upwards to senior executives; and where each department/division 'has its own set of books and accounts which can be audited separately from those of the large enterprise'. As Chandler emphasizes, the competitive advantage of the modern business enterprise lies in its capacity for 'administrative coordination', which has proven over the past century to engineer 'greater productivity, lower costs and higher profits than coordination by market mechanisms' (1977: 4). It is a system which has, essentially, to be run and managed 'via the numbers'.

As Chandler describes it, the beginnings of modern business are to be found in two unlikely sites. Single-unit management 'had its genesis in the United States at the Springfield Armory' (1977: 75). As a result of innovations such as detailed quality control and inventory accounting systems, Springfield played a major role in the development of the 'American System of Manufacture', the first system to succeed in achieving integrated mass production using interchangeable parts (1977: 72). Meanwhile multi-unit management was being pioneeed on the US railroads. This occurred initially on the grandiosely-named Western Railroad (which ran all the way west from Boston to Albany, New York), where a line-and-staff system of organization was introduced following an accident in 1841. This was 'the first modern, carefully defined, internal organizational structure used by an American business enterprise' (1977: 97).

Yet these two distinct developments can now be shown to be linked aspects of one transformation. The pioneers of the new business practices in both arenas had an unusual profile. As Chandler (1977: 95) concedes, they:

were a new type of businessman. It is worth emphasizing again that they were salaried employees with little or no financial interest in the companies they served. Moreover most had had specialized training.

But what the key pioneers, both at Springfield Armory and on the railroads, had in common is the *same* specialized training as cadets at the US Military Academy at West Point (indeed the first two pioneers were classmates, graduating together in the Class of 1819); and West Point in 1817 had been transformed into perhaps the most 'disciplinary' educational institution that existed at that time.

*Towards grammatocentrism and calculability: the West Point educational revolution*

In 1817 Sylvanus Thayer was appointed as West Point's fourth Superintendent, and immediately introduced from the French *Ecole Polytechnique* both its new scientific curriculum (based on texts written by the great French scientists of the day) and its disciplinary pedagogy based on the constant deployment of writing, examination and grading.[18] In addition, Thayer added a managerial dimension all his own, running the Academy like a modern CEO, issuing his orders in writing and setting up his own line-and-staff system. Under Thayer, therefore, students encountered the powers of writing, examining and grading with an unprecedented intensity.

First, the imposition of a regime of calculability was swift and comprehensive. By 1819 Thayer, expanding on the French precedent, had developed a marking system used in every subject and in every class enabling the cumulative ranking of each individual cadet. Each student performance was graded (initially on a system running from $+3$ to $-3$, later from $+3$ to 0 with quarter-point gradations); and each cadet's 'account' was kept in a Weekly Class Report summated each term and then, after factoring in the results from the twice-yearly examinations, totalled up for a final Annual Merit Roll. This ranked every cadet in the Class on a weighted cumulative total of all marks obtained, and each yearly total was then carried forward so that at the end of his four years every cadet had a specific graduating position. In addition, from 1826 Thayer added a numerical demerit system for Conduct and integrated the demerit score into each individual's account before calculating the Merit Roll positions, completing the system in 1832 when he introduced a cut-off point of 200 demerits above which expulsion was immediate and without exception. Thus was a new kind of human accountability instituted in the most rigorous form by an alphanumeric combination of numerical and linguistic judgements.

At the same time Thayer set up an intensely grammatocentric managerial regime. Even though West Point had under 300 cadets when he took over, he set up a line-and-staff system which separated the Academy into two divisions, which were then sub-divided down into companies, with strict reporting always in writing in continual relays of communication up and down each line of command. Significantly this system culminated not with Thayer himself but with his second-in-command, the Academy's Commandant.[19] Meanwhile Thayer himself operated outside these lines, setting policy, collating reports and coordinating the whole system via a central 'Staff Office', with the assistance of a personal clerk and two cadets.

Thayer thus established himself as a separate locus of authority. He became a ghostly presence, hardly ever seen by most of the cadets, knowing them principally through the individual files kept meticulously by his clerk. In their everyday lives he 'entered the picture only as a court of last resort' (Fleming, 1969: 50), and those summoned to formal interviews were disconcerted to discover how much he knew of them despite the lack of personal contact – in fact through reading off slips prepared from the files and pasted inside the pigeon holes on his desk: a kind of VDU data base before the computer. In many respects the Thayer system recalls Foucault's 'panopticism', as a system with the power to see into every aspect of individual life while the source of its vision remains invisible. But it was specifically a *grammatocentric* form of panopticism, whose *modus operandi* was constant writing, grading and examination.

The net outcome of Thayer's innovations was that disciplinary power and disciplinary knowledge could be simultaneously internalized in a new and potent way. The graduates of the Thayer system were both highly trained in the scientific disciplines (particularly maths and engineering) and in the wider uses to which writing, grading and examining could be put to engender human productivity and accountability. Having learned to learn under this unprecedented disciplinary human success system they could go out to translate its practices into the business arena.

### West Point graduates and the genesis of managerialism

Chandler has tended to play down any West Point connection, noting (1977: 95) that while two of his 'pioneers of modern management', George Whistler of the Western Railroad and George McClellan of the Illinois Central, had military experience, these two 'were the least innovative of the lot'. He concludes that the military model had only an 'indirect impact on the beginning of modern business management' and that 'there is little evidence that railroad managers copied military procedures' (1977: 95–7).

We would agree with Chandler insofar as these pioneers were not translating *military* procedures as such: but our review of the evidence suggests that what they were translating instead was Thayer's West Point procedures. Chandler's global conclusion appears at the least premature: in particular where two graduates of West Point's Class of 1819 are concerned, the above-mentioned George Whistler and his classmate Daniel Tyler.

Whistler now appears to have played a major innovatory role since the first known railroad line-and-staff system is traceable directly to his tenure as Superintendent of the Western Railroad between 1838 and 1842. Tyler at the Springfield Armory merits a similar accolade. For the development of an economically effective system of labour and cost control now appears attributable to a time-and-motion study he undertook in 1831 (50 years before Frederick W. Taylor's scientific management), a study which for the first time established norms of production and unit cost. But the point we stress is that both these initiatives, for all their surface differences, draw on the disciplinary practices of Thayer's West Point: Thayer's organizational structure in Whistler's case, and his calculative system of accountability in Tyler's.

### Accountability at the Springfield Armory

Taking the Springfield Armory case first, Chandler's view (1977: 73-4) is that single-unit managerialism was initiated under the Superintendency of Roswell Lee, which ran from 1815 to 1833. As noted by historians of technology (e.g. Deyrup, 1948; Smith, 1985), major steps towards the successful achievement of interchangeable-part manufacture were made at Springfield under Lee, including standardized go/no go gauges, division of labour, quality control, plus a meticulous 'double-entry' bookkeeping system (Chandler, 1977: 73).[20]

However the history of technology is not necessarily the history of business innovation; and there are two major problems here. First, it is now apparent that Lee's innovations did not produce *economic* breakthrough. Paul Uselding's detailed re-analysis of Springfield's production and cost figures shows that there were virtually no efficiency gains in costs or productivity over the 1815–33 period; breakthrough actually occurred only after 1841 (Uselding, 1972, 1973).[21] Second, careful re-examination of Lee's uniformity initiatives shows that they were not managerial at all (nor indeed was his accounting system a double-entry one). What has happened in the Springfield Armory case is that technological innovation has been mistakenly equated with managerialism and so the detail of what took place has not been properly assessed.

The available records on the National Armories are fortunately copious (e.g. Deyrup, 1948; Smith, 1977), which makes it possible to distinguish the differences in the technological and business histories to a high degree. And what the detailed evidence shows is that Lee, while pursuing technological improvement, ran the workforce in a traditional and premodern way, aiming at maintaining good stewardship (i.e. minimizing loss of materials through poor quality work, damage or pilfering) and promoting good conduct via such traditional tactics as rules on attendance and proper behaviour plus fines or expulsions to enforce the rules.[22] Furthermore the evidence also shows that he never attempted to exert a *managerial* form of control focused on cost minimization and productivity maximization, the twin paths to the modern goals of profitability and performativity.

In the first place Lee's accounting system made administrative coordination unlikely since it was in charge/discharge not double-entry format: Lee accordingly used it as it was most easily used, to operate separate lines of control tracking reciprocal interchanges between individuals on the stewardship principle. In one set of charge/discharge accounts flows of materials were tracked, but in physical terms only; in separate payroll accounts the record of each individual's payments were kept; meanwhile the work returns recorded actuals, ensuring simply that each worker was paid for actual pieces made (for piece-workers) or hours worked (for fixed-wage earners). Such a system set up relays of reciprocal obligation passing from individual to individual, but Lee never developed it to integrate plant-wide financial and performance data and thus coordinate performance across the whole workplace.

In the second place there was no tracking of time taken per piece manufactured or even enforcement of regular hours: the skilled workforce came in, as an 1819 armory inspection remarked, 'as many hours as they choose' (Dalliba, 1823: 543). Thus there was no way of establishing norms of performance or pay (what the average worker should achieve or earn). Instead Lee followed a very different approach, setting his wage rates 'in line with but slightly above wages at other armories' with further cost-of-living adjustments (Deyrup, 1948: 105–6). Thus over the period up to 1830 wages tended to rise while productivity remained static, as evidenced for instance by a suspicious uniformity in each barrel-welder's monthly production, which as Deyrup drily puts it (1948: 110) 'implies . . . considerable excess productive capacity'.

Under these circumstances it is not surprising that, as Chandler acknowledges, Lee failed 'to obtain more effective internal coordination and so speed up the flow of materials through his establishment' (1977: 74). His was not a system equipped with practices geared to going beneath the surface of actual performance and costs, towards establishing objective *norms* of what could be done and/or effective quantified measures of worker *accountability*.

However, those are the innovatory principles given shape by Tyler's 1831 time-and-motion study, as recorded in Tyler's own *Autobiography* (1883). In January 1831 the US Ordnance Department appointed him as the first independent Inspector of Contract Arms, and sent him to Springfield. Once there he quickly saw the slack built into Lee's regime. Tyler then goes on (1883: 21–2):

Early in the month of February I commenced my examination of the Springfield Armory, and during six months ... I kept watch in hand, timing every operation into which the manufacture of the musket was divided ... never leaving until I was satisfied ... that I had arrived at the exact time necessary for the performance of each particular task. In this way I came to know accurately what the workmen could earn daily at ten hours' service under the Government prices, and I was enabled to determine ... first what the fair price was for each division of 'piece work' and second the exact working time necessary to produce a Springfield musket.

In this inspection the power of disciplinarity finally penetrates into the workplace, as Tyler deploys the practices he had internalized at Thayer's West Point: examining, grading performance, establishing norms and rendering humans objectively accountable. It penetrates further the following year as a Board of Inspection (which includes Tyler) formally recommends a total reform of the work culture. The terminology used, as reported by Deyrup (1948: 169) is significant. For the Board's report:

divided the Armory workers into six classes according to the degree of skill and intelligence necessary for each occupation and established for each group a standard wage for a ten hour day, capable of being earned by a workman of average skill and energy ... From questioning the workforce and examining the Armory's pay-roll the board made recommendations as to appropriate piece rates and the number of pieces which should constitute a good day's work.

'Classes', 'intelligence', 'standards', 'examining': this is certainly a discourse of normalization (cf. Miller and O'Leary, ch. 4 in this volume); but at the same time it is one which imports into the business world the terminology of *educational* disciplinarity.

There remains, of course, the historical problem pointed out by Uselding. Why, if this system was such a breakthrough, did cost and productivity efficiencies not occur until 1842? The reason, as Tyler's 'Autobiography' makes clear (1883: 21–2), was that the Springfield workforce quickly recognized what was at stake and organized what in the short term proved a successful strategy of resistance. They wrote to the Secretary of War and even made a direct appeal to President Andrew Jackson, to such effect that the Board's recommendations were overruled. So the old piece-rates and work practices remained in place. In 1834 Tyler resigned his commission, recognizing that he was not now going to achieve rapid promotion.

However with the inauguration of President William Harrison in 1841 a reformist agenda was introduced, a new military Superintendent was appointed and a three-man 'civilian' Board of Enquiry was appointed to review the work practices at Springfield. Significantly the board included both the ex-West Point Professor of Mathematics and Tyler himself. Its recommendations, adopted in January 1842, were directly drawn from the 1832 Board. Fixed hours of work were introduced, a time-log was kept of the hours actually worked by piece-rate workers and the piece-rates were set according to the 1832 tariff, thus succeeding in 'reducing the wages to the point previously recommended' (Tyler, 1883: 22).

The productivity and cost outcomes were dramatic, as is highlighted in the figures for the barrel-welding shop. This was one of the most highly-skilled tasks, and one where there was no technological change in production methods over the whole period from 1820 to 1859; yet even so, from 1842 the average number of barrels welded per man went up from a figure never above 2500 before 1840 to around 4000 by 1843, while piece-rates dropped from an average of c. 27 cents up to 1841 to 13 cents by 1844 (Deyrup, 1948: appendix D, tables 5 and 6).

Here, then and not in Lee's earlier uniformity initiatives, lies the previously-hidden genesis of modern single-unit management. What took place at Springfield was a power-knowledge revolution which, by introducing the writing and examining practices which could *integrate* the surveillance and control of time, activity and cost, made the modern concerns with productivity, performativity and profitability articulable.

### Line-and-staff structure on the Western Railroad

Meanwhile, over the same period but in a different surface way, the Thayer system was penetrating railroad business culture as Tyler's classmate George Whistler developed the first known line-and-staff system. Again, though, the chronology has been not quite clear and the provenance of the system has failed to command much attention.

According to Chandler (cf. Salsbury, 1967: 185), the system was introduced following a head-on collision in November 1841 on the single-track line the Western had just opened through western Massachusetts. As a result in only six weeks Whistler set up a management system with clear lines of authority, structured round a central staff office plus three operating divisions. Transportation and Machinery divisions had their separate heads while he personally had direct line responsibility for the Roads division in addition to running the central Staff Office. Within each line information flowed up and down through three regional managers who in turn had local managers below them. In Chandler's words, Whistler succeeded in 'fixing definite responsibilities for each phase of the company's business, drawing solid lines of authority and communication for the railroad's administration, maintenance and operation' (1977: 97).

However, though Whistler's success is not in doubt, the details of the story require reconsideration. First re-examination of the archives shows that Whistler introduced the system not in 1841 but two years earlier when the railroad first opened. For the initial *Regulations* he drew up in 1839 already had the three divisions, plus the detailed division of responsibilities between each line, and the central Staff Office. So he does not invent the system following the 1841 crash, instead he just streamlined it then, to eradicate confusion and overelaboration in the command chain. But that chronological change then raises in acute form the issue of how this organizational system, without apparent business precedent, came so easily to Whistler's hand.

Chandler's own preferred solution was that it was a response to technological innovation such as the telegraph (1977: 95), which made a new kind of long-distance administrative coordination feasible; but this now becomes questionable since Samuel Morse only developed the telegraph in 1842–3. On the other hand, there is to date no evidence of any prior analogous system in use in any business context.[23] And Whistler's career before joining the Western also offers an unlikely source of inspiration.[24]

However it turns out that he had, while a cadet at West Point, a particularly close acquaintance with Thayer's grammatocentric line-and-staff administrative system. By an intriguing coincidence, when in 1817 Thayer was choosing two cadets to form his initial Staff Office, he chose Whistler as his Cadet Staff Sergeant. Thus it was not just on the Western Railroad that Whistler was a pioneer: he had helped Thayer set up the line-and-staff system in the first place.

Hence as at the medieval moment, it becomes apparent that there are direct but overlooked links between the educational and economic worlds. The time-and-motion study and the line-and-staff system have the same genealogy, leading back to Thayer's West Point system. Therefore where Chandler sees two separate lines of innovation in single-unit and multi-unit organizations, we would see two aspects of one disciplinary transformation. What was established under the guise of 'administrative coordination' was a new power of writing, examination and grading.

### 'Management by the numbers': accounting on the Pennsylvania Railroad

The Springfield Armory and the Western Railroad constitute only a first step towards the establishment of the modern business enterprise, and so of the principles of grammatocentrism and calculability at the heart of economic discourse. The more visible and decisive step comes in the 1850s on the Pennsylvania Railroad. We return once more to Chandler's history.

Following the earliest innovations there were, he argues, in the 1850s two further significant structural developments (1965: 37–40):

> One was the building of a separate Traffic Department to administer the getting and processing of freight and passengers. The other was the creation of a central office manned by general executives ... [who] concentrated less on day-to-day operation and more on long-term problems of cost determination, competitive rate setting and strategic expansion. In both these developments the Pennsylvania made the largest contribution.

The Pennsylvania Railroad was begun in 1847, under inauspicious circumstances.[25] Yet by 1870 it had by effective management and strategic development become the dominant railroad in the USA. Indeed Chandler goes so far as to say (1965: 22):

> So effective was their work that the Pennsylvania not only became the largest business enterprise in the nation (if not the world) but also was just as famous for being one of the most efficiently administered.

Not coincidentally, it is here that accounting began to move from marginality to centrality in business practice.

The team that ran the Pennsylvania Railroad in those early years included some truly significant individuals: J. Edgar Thomson, its first Chief Engineer; Thomas A. Scott, hired as a Station Agent in 1850, the Railroad's Vice-President by 1858 and by 1862 appointed to be Assistant Secretary of War in charge of railroads on the Union side in the Civil War; and Scott's protege, Andrew Carnegie, hired in 1853 at the age of 17, who rose to Divisional Superintendent before striking out into an even more spectacular career in iron and steel. In any understanding of the rise to global dominance of modern accounting-based economic power these men must play a key role: particularly Carnegie, since his success was built upon importing the Pennsylvania Railroad management system into the manufacturing sector.[26]

Carnegie's success simply serves to underline the significance of the innovations introduced on the Pennsylvania. And there the person who must take centre stage is Thomson's No. 2, Herman Haupt. For it is Haupt who introduced the first genuinely 'divisionalized' organizational structure (formally published in the 1857 *Organization Manual*) and who also set up the Traffic Department (Ward, 1971).

The chronology is as follows. Haupt's earlier career had been as a surveyor, bridge designer and principal of an Academy: initially hired by Thomson as a surveyor in 1847, he was quickly promoted because of his outstanding and speedy surveying work and in early 1849 was appointed

Superintendent of the Railroad, reporting directly to Thomson. Immediately, at Thomson's request, he went round the leading railroads and got details on their organizational and personnel practices, and by the end of March had prepared a best-practice organizational plan, largely based on the Baltimore & Ohio system. But where the latter created one department for Working of the Road and one for Collection and Disbursement of Revenue, Haupt divided responsibility among four departments, Transportation, Maintenance of Way, Motive Power and Maintenance of Cars, all reporting to himself as Superintendent. At the same time he created a General Transportation Office concerned solely with 'regulating all the other offices on the line and in securing accuracy and uniformity in their accounts' (Ward, 1971: 78).

Here we see the application of the grammatocentric approach, establishing a system which depends upon constant writing and guarantees an expanding role for writing, as it is able to bring more and more functions into the ambit of administrative coordination *within* the organization. At the same time Haupt imposed a new regime of calculability drawing particularly on accounting data. From 1851 he was including summary but detailed operational data in the *Annual Report*, data which was derived from the accurate and timely information which poured in on a daily basis to the central Traffic Office (Ward, 1971: 82–3). As a result Haupt was soon effectively managing by the numbers.

Among his accounting based decisions Ward notes the following. In 1850 he costed the toll sheet issued by the directors and suspended it because it did not cover full costs. In 1851, having identified on the basis of the accounting returns an opportunity to expand westward passenger traffic he initiated a strategy of getting immigrant traffic from New York to Pittsburgh to travel via the Pennsylvania, even though he had to strike deals with so many other railroads and canal companies that he retained only $1.55 out of a $5.25 through ticket (Ward, 1971: 82–3). And in strategic costing vein, while Thomson tended to favour a fixed 'high toll on a relatively low volume of freight', Haupt, having studied the freight volume, 'analysed the fixed and variable costs ... and determined that the rates could be drastically lowered' (Ward, 1971: 81). He also introduced discounts for large shippers, for those who shipped in full carload lots and for those who offered return-journey business.

Haupt's initiatives appear to mark the watershed in the emergence of managerialism, for here we see, combined with the earlier calculative technologies promoting accountability and productivity, the accounting technologies to promote systematic cost control and profitability. By 1857 the company was keeping '144 basic sets of accounting records' (Chandler, 1977: 110), an information load so great that a separate Accounting Office was hived off. With Carnegie then exporting the Haupt management system into manufacturing, and with other railroads having to follow the system in order to compete and survive, the rules of US business discourse were soon definitively changed. Businesses began to be reconstructed in the image of the proactive, future-oriented organization, managed by the numbers and thoroughly grammatocentric.

But why should Haupt be the man to produce this integrated system for managing by the numbers? It turns out that, like Daniel Tyler and George Whistler, he is one more product of West Point. However he is from the next generation, graduating in the Class of 1835 by which time the full Thayer system had been developed, including the sanction of expulsion for those over 200 demerits.

Intriguingly that system, by Haupt's own admission, marked a major turning point in his life. He entered West Point in 1831 aged only 13, and spent his first two years in card-playing and novel-reading and collecting his share of demerits caring, as he says, 'but little how nearly I approached the limit if it was not exceeded: a very unwise course'.[27] But at the end of his Sophomore year in June 1833 he ended up on precisely 200 demerits, and believed he was about to be expelled. As humiliation loomed he underwent a conversion experience and resolved, in his own words, to 'turn over a new leaf, renounce cards and novels and apply myself to study'. From that moment on he became a total devotee of the disciplinary way of life, beginning with his own self-discipline. Indeed, the private academy he ran in Gettysburg before joining the Pennsylvania was itself run on the Thayer principles, right down to the demerit system for conduct.

Thus once more we find the educational connection. And in this case the special significance of the Pennsylvania Railroad, both in itself and as borne out by the subsequent success of Carnegie, is that it brings to fruition the kind of accounting based managerial system that can survive any one individual. Haupt in fact severed his links with the Pennsylvania in 1856. But he had already put together a system, based now on grammatocentric structure, a general commitment to calculability and a specific commitment to the constant use of accounting, which no longer needed him in person.

### Conclusion: knowledge-power and the power-knowledge conundrum

At the close of his analysis of the pioneer organizations, Alfred Chandler reflects on the overkill of the new divisionalized structures of the US railroads, with their meticulous accounting and their detailed disciplinary procedures (1977: 120); from the economic standpoint:

the innovation made . . . in organization, accounting and control went beyond mere necessity. The railroads could have operated well enough with only rudimentary organizational structures, without the line and staff distinction, without an internal auditing staff.

The same of course applies to Thayer's original disciplinary system. In every case there is more than a purely economic–rational discourse, for there is more at stake than just an economically optimal outcome. What we are confronting instead is a new kind of power-knowledge regime which made possible the new power of economics, not the other way round.

That is why we see the emergence of modern accounting not as the 'practical' response of men faced with new entrepreneurial challenges, sensibly devising ways to capture the data needed for rational economic decisions – for in that sense no 'practical' man would have invented modern accounting practice, the outputs of which are not at all what is obviously needed for such purposes (e.g. Macve, 1985). Instead, we see modern accounting emerging as a powerful new way of 'writing the world' which like the modern examination embodies the power relations and knowledge relations of a disciplinary (and self-disciplinary) culture.

The power-knowledge apparatuses of accounting have continued to expand: to Management Accounting has been added Financial Reporting, and the intensifying spread of systems of accountability. Now accounting increasingly penetrates into the public governmental world as well as the private sector, for as John Meyer has pointed out (1986: 354) 'contrary to much earlier speculation, real bureaucratization ... has made such a weak advance'. Weber's high bureaucracies are giving way to accounting-led organizations which both give more space for calculative individual initiative and locate the power over individuals in more dynamic flexible control systems which ultimately empower them to discipline their selves in a constant play of accountability and responsibility.

Meanwhile at the social level, accounting, like fields from medicine to plumbing (Bledstein, 1976), has taken advantage of the new written graded examination system to effect the classic shift into modern professionalization. Before the end of the nineteenth century, the first professional bodies were established, all, like the Institute of Chartered Accountants in England and Wales (Jones, 1981), quickly setting up qualification systems based on taking written, graded examinations.[28] And at the 'writerly' level accounting, like other emergent academic fields, has discovered how to rewrite itself into ever more sophisticated disciplinary forms, with its scholars adopting the standard *parvenu* tactic of drawing on high-status neighbouring fields like economics, statistics and mathematics for legitimacy: an understandable tactic, though one destined to lead to constant theoretical puzzlement and disappointment insofar as it leads such scholars to believe that accounting is thereby rendered into a field of pure-knowledge rather than power-knowledge relations.

However that is a minor and local problem. The larger picture is that accounting – as a form of social power, as an apparatus of knowledge-power, as an academic field, and as a technology embedded within the self – has established itself as a practice seemingly indispensable, something we can neither avoid nor simply transcend. Instead, with both accounting and examination, we find ourselves bound up in a continual process of trying to reduce their inadequacies and arbitrary effects, yet always, in so doing, extending their power and scope.

NOTES

1. Foucault's argument was not simply that 'knowledge is power' in the old Baconian sense; rather that 'power and knowledge directly imply one another: that there is no power relation without the correlative constitution of a field of knowledge, nor any knowledge that does not presuppose and constitute at the same time power relations' (Foucault, 1977: 27). The question Foucault left pending is precisely *how* power and knowledge come to imply one another, for clearly not all knowledge is powerful nor all forms of power knowledge based.
2. For the first sustained formulation of the idea of 'learning to learn', or 'deutero-learning' see Gregory Bateson's *Steps to an Ecology of Mind* (1973). There Bateson advanced the possibility 'that "learning to learn" is a synonym for the acquisition of that class of abstract habits of thought ... which we call "free will", instrumental thinking, dominance, passivity, etc.' (1973: 140).
3. Indeed it is possible to discern a hidden educational connection within Foucault's own work (Hoskin, 1990). For a key Foucauldian term such as 'discipline' is itself in its etymology an educational term. The Latin *disciplina* is a collapsed form of *disci-pulina*, which means getting learning (the disci- part) into the child (puer/puella). Thus from its genesis discipline was an educational term intertwining both knowledge and power relations.
4. Earlier grading systems such as ordinal ranking (used by the Jesuit schools to stimulate rivalry from the sixteenth century) lacked this dimension: ranks compare, enable the emulation of the best, but do not in themselves confer an independent numerical value on each individual performance or construct performance norms.
5. Of course this would not necessarily explain double-entry's absence in the Arabic world. On the other hand, expecting to find double-entry there just because the culture used arabic numerals would be to reduce the question to purely one of notation.
6. Mathematically this is of transformative significance as increasingly forms of mathematical discourse are constructed by interweaving number and letter forms: by the seventeenth century mathematicians have developed the $x,y$ notation for algebra, logarithms, the differential calculus. This, be it noted, happens only when arabic numerals encounter the Western alphabet sign system, arabic script being not alphabetic but a syllabary lacking vowels (Havelock, 1975).
7. Saenger suggests that this shift is the end result of an initially simple rewriting of texts which had begun centuries earlier with the adoption of word division (not generally used in ancient texts), probably as an aid to word recognition as Latin

became less and less familiar to the Celtic priest-scholars of the so-called Dark Ages. By the twelfth century, the use of word division had promoted a greater visualist recognition of writing as a medium in its own right, rather than just a supplement to speech. As scholars began to learn that silent reading was real reading, they began to inhabit a more silent 'writerly' world. They began to use visualist metaphors to denote reading (no longer referring to texts being 'heard'), and also described composition as something written personally rather than dictated to a scribe (Saenger, 1982: 386–9).

8. It is no coincidence that the four 'old' professions, the Law, the Church, Medicine and Teaching correspond to the four medieval university faculties, Law, Theology, Medicine and the Liberal Arts (Hoskin, 1986). Their university base defined them until the nineteenth century as the sole fields that could claim to possess all the attributes conventionally taken to define a profession: (1) monopoly in competence within the domain of specialization, (2) autonomy concerning the right to control entry to the field of expertise and (3) a body of esoteric knowledge access to which is obtained through qualification via formal examination.

9. This is underlined by the growth in thirteenth-century universities, alongside the liberal arts, of a training in notarial and accounting skills under the title of the *ars dictaminis*. Clanchy (1979) observes that a law and business school may have existed in Oxford from the reign of King John (1199–1216) and there were (Richardson, 1941) a number of flourishing such schools in the fourteenth century.

10. As Smalley points out, this was in part possible because of the rewriting of authoritative texts into topically organized collections of differing pronouncements which visually 'showed up' contradictions: Abelard's own *Sic et Non* was precisely such a collection.

11. In a crucial passage in the prologue to the *Sic et Non* Abelard sets up the new three-stage progression from doubting to inquisition to truth; in the Latin it reads 'dubitando enim ad inquisitionem venimus; inquirendo veritatem percipimus' (Smalley, 1957: 96).

12. Its new power is then legally reinforced by the written requirement published by the Fourth Lateran Council of 1215, also dominated by graduates, that confession should be regular and serious.

13. Ironically it is these men who invented the prison-reformatory whose invention Foucault in *Discipline and Punish* located in the eighteenth century. Unrepentant heretics were burned, but there were far more who in the face of the uncompromising apparatus of the Inquisition recanted. Such people were still contaminated by their prior apostasy, and so by 1250 the prison-reformatory was developed to house these 'penitents' (Hamilton, 1981: ch. 5), who were condemned to be segregated from society until such time as they were purified of their sin.

14. As Drew (1947) points out, the surcharges might be two or three times the official's annual salary, therefore phenomenal slack must have been recognized as part of the 'truth' in the 'actual' figures.

15. It appears that it was invented at the English court, since they alone in Europe kept central records on rolls rather than in books.

16. There may be a special accounting connection here since within the Exchequer

the foil was also known as the counter-tally or *contratalea*, and the Keeper of the foils was already by 1155 known as the *contrataleator*; perhaps it is on this analogy that the new roll became known as the *contrarotulus*, and its keeper as the King's 'controller' or *contrarotulator*, both of which terms are found in the first usages cited from 1220. For citations see Latham (1981), under *contrarotulus*.

17. However where a large number of transactions attached to a loan, space often ran out and 'the bookkeeper was forced to crowd in additional entries as best he could' (de Roover, 1974: 122).

18. This system had been introduced into the *Ecole Polytechnique* by Gaspard Monge in the 1790s. The development of examination based laboratory training there has its analogue in the contemporaneous development of new written graded examinations at Cambridge in the mathematics Tripos (Hoskin, 1990).

19. The system penetrated right down to the minutiae of individual activity. Any cadet wishing to object to or deviate from prescribed routine had to do so in writing up the appropriate line of command. Permits for visits or leaves had to be made in writing giving details of time, place and persons involved. Even excuses for delinquencies had to be in the prescribed written form and handed in to the Commandant within one hour of the publication of the 'crime'.

20. Smith, the leading historian of the US Ordnance system, similarly notes that Lee pursued 'the grand object of uniformity' including a system of quarterly returns 'based on standard double-entry bookkeeping' (1985: 57).

21. From 1842 'there is a dramatic growth in the efficiency of both factors, with labour efficiency growth outstripping that of capital efficiency' (Uselding, 1972: esp. 303–4). By way of contrast, under Lee's superintendency there was only 'a leveling out in the fluctuations of output per worker and cost per musket' (Uselding, 1973: 79).

22. Lee is very much in the English disciplinary tradition of Wedgwood and Boulton & Watt. But then, as Jonathan Prude points out, the English approach was quite widespread in rural Massachusetts, where it had been introduced in the textile factories. 'Advanced' discipline would entail a clock-regulated workday backed up by a 'system of room overseers, fines, blacklists and occasional beatings' (Prude, 1983: 37). This was still very much a regime ruled by Foucault's 'punishment on the body' rather than the disciplining of the person.

23. There is an argument (O'Connell, 1985) that the US Engineering Corps had by the early 1830s an effective management structure. Insofar as it did it may suggest a further West Point influence. However our reading of the system suggests that it was a bureaucratically comprehensive rule system with no effective lines of accountability built in.

24. Working backwards, he had been, while on secondment from the US Army, a railroad surveyor and a designer of (not very successful) locomotives, and before that a junior officer in the US Survey and Assistant Professor of Drawing at West Point.

25. Until the mid-1850s it began not in Philadelphia, but 50 miles west, while its Western division was separated in the Alleghenies from the Eastern division by the Allegheny Portrage Railroad.

26. A point underlined by Chandler: Carnegie introduced from the Pennsylvania the voucher system of accounting, so that each department 'listed the amount and cost of materials and labor used on each order as it passed through the sub-unit ... These cost sheets were Carnegie's primary instrument of control ... The minutest details of cost of materials and labor in every department appeared from day to day and week to week in the accounts. The men felt and often remarked that the eyes of the company were always on them through the books' (Chandler, 1977: 267–8).

27. The information comes from Haupt's own 'Memoirs of Herman Haupt up to the age of Twenty-One, When he married', written in 1889. Our thanks to Professor Jim Ward of the University of Tennessee for providing us with a copy of this manuscript.

28. In every case (Hoskin, 1986) modern professions simultaneously define their special body of knowledge and construct the means of specialist entry and accreditation by first establishing a written graded examining system. This applies also to the old professions (see n. 8 above). Medicine, for instance, well before it developed its *scientific* basis, modernized in this way around 1800.

REFERENCES

Baldwin, J., 1982. 'Masters at Paris from 1179 to 1215: A Social Perspective', in R. Benson and G. Constable (eds.), *Renaissance and Renewal in the Twelfth Century*, Oxford: Clarendon: 138–72

Bateson, G., 1973. *Steps To an Ecology of Mind*, London: Paladin

Bledstein, B., 1976. *The Culture of Professionalism*, New York: Basic Books

Chandler, A., Jr., 1965. 'The Railroads: Pioneers of Modern Corporate Management', *Business History Review* 39: 16–40

1977. *The Visible Hand: The Managerial Revolution in American Business*, Cambridge, MA: Harvard University Press

Clanchy, M., 1975. 'Moderni in Education and Government in England', *Speculum* 49: 671–88

1979. *From Memory to Written Record: England 1066–1307*, London: Arnold

Dalliba, J., 1823. 'Armory at Springfield', *American State Papers: Military Affairs* 5(246): 538–53

de Roover, R., 1974. *Business, Banking and Economic Thought*, Chicago: University of Chicago Press

de Sainte Croix, G., 1956. 'Greek and Roman Accounting', in A. Littleton and B. Yamey (eds.), *Studies in the History of Accounting*, London: Sweet & Maxwell: 14–74

Deyrup, F., 1948. *Arms Makers of the Connecticut Valley: A Regional Study of the Economic Development of the Small Arms Industry, 1798–1870*, Smith College Studies in History 33, Northampton, MA: Smith College

Drew, J., 1947. 'Manorial Accounts of St Swithun's Priory, Winchester', *English Historical Review* 62: 20–41

Evans, G., 1977. 'From Abacus to Algorism: Theory and Practice in Medieval Arithmetic', *British Journal for the History of Science* 10: 114–31

Fleischman, R. and Parker, L., 1991. 'British Entrepreneurs and Pre-Industrial Revolution Evidence of Cost Management', *Accounting Review* 66(2): 361–75

96    *Keith Hoskin and Richard Macve*

Fleming, T., 1969. *West Point*, New York: Morrow
Foucault, M., 1977. *Discipline and Punish*, London: Allen Lane
Gordon, C., 1980. *Power/Knowledge: Selected Interviews of Michel Foucault, 1972–77*, Brighton: Harvester
Hamilton, B., 1981. *The Medieval Inquisition*, London: Arnold
Haring, N., 1982. 'Commentary and Hermeneutics', in R. Benson and G. Constable (eds.), *Renaissance and Renewal in the Twelfth Century*, Oxford: Clarendon: 173–200
Havelock, E., 1975. *Origins of Western Literacy*, Toronto: Ontario Institute for Studies in Education
Hoskin, K., 1979. 'The Examination, Disciplinary Power and Rational Schooling', *History of Education* 7: 135–46
   1984. 'Confession: A Review', *Theory and Society* 13(5): 736–42
   1986. 'The Professional in Educational History', in J. Wilkes (ed.), *The Professional Teacher*, London: History of Education Society: 19–28
   1990. 'Foucault Under Examination: The Crypto-Educationalist Unmasked', in S. Ball (ed.), *Foucault and Education*, London: Routledge: 29–53
Hoskin, K. and Macve, R., 1986. 'Accounting and the Examination: A Genealogy of Disciplinary Power', *Accounting, Organizations and Society* 11(2): 105–36
   1988. 'The Genesis of Accountability: The West Point Connection', *Accounting, Organizations and Society* 13(1): 37–73
Johnson, C. (ed.), 1983. *Richard Fitz Nigel's Dialogue de Scaccario*, Oxford: Clarendon
Jones, E., 1981. *Accountancy and the British Economy*, London: Batsford
Latham, R., 1981. *Dictionary of Medieval Latin From British Sources*, London: Oxford University Press
le Goff, J., 1981. *La Naissance du Purgatoire*, Paris: Gallimard
Lemay, R., 1977. 'The Hispanic Origin of our Present Numeral Forms', *Viator* 8: 435–62
McKendrick, N., 1970. 'Josiah Wedgwood and Cost Accounting in the Industrial Revolution', *Economic History Review*, New Series 23: 45–67
Macve, R., 1985. 'Some Glosses on "Greek and Roman Accounting"', *History of Political Thought* VI(1/2): 233–64
Meyer, J., 1986. 'Social Environments and Organizational Accounting', *Accounting, Organizations and Society* 11(4/5): 345–56
Miller, P., 1992. 'Accounting and Objectivity: The Invention of Calculating Selves and Calculable Spaces', *Annals of Scholarship* 9(1/2): 61–86
Miller, P. and O'Leary, T., 1987. 'Accounting and the Construction of the Governable Person', *Accounting, Organizations and Society* 12(3): 235–65
Murray, A., 1978. *Reason and Society in the Middle Ages*, Oxford: Clarendon
Noke, C., 1981. 'Accounting for Bailiffship in Thirteenth-Century England', *Accounting and Business Research* 11: 137–51
O'Connell, C., 1985. 'The Corps of Engineers and the Rise of Modern Management, 1827–1856', in M. Roe Smith (ed.), *Military Enterprise and Technological Change*, Cambridge, MA: MIT Press: 87–116
Pollard, S., 1965. *The Genesis of Modern Management*, London: Arnold
Prude, J., 1983. *The Coming of Industrial Order*, Cambridge: Cambridge University Press

Richardson, H., 1941. 'Business Training in Medieval Oxford', *American Historical Review* 47: 259–80

Rouse, R. and Rouse, M., 1979. *Preachers, Florilegia and Sermons*, Toronto: Pontifical Institute of Medieval Studies

1982. '*Statim Invenire*: Schools, Preachers and New Attitudes to the Page', in R. Benson and G. Constable (eds.), *Renaissance and Renewal in the Twelfth Century*, Oxford: Clarendon: 201–28

Saenger, P., 1982. 'Silent Reading: Its Impact on Late Medieval Script and Society', *Viator* 13: 367–414

Salsbury, S., 1967. *The State, the Investor and the Railroad: Boston & Albany, 1825–1867*, Cambridge, MA: Harvard University Press

Smalley, B., 1957. '*Prima Clavis Sapientiae*: Augustine and Abelard', in D. Gordon (ed.), *Fritz Saxl: A Volume of Memorial Essays*, London: Nelson: 93–100

Smith, M. Roe, 1977. *Harpers Ferry Armory and the New Technology: The Challenge of Change*, Ithaca: Cornell University Press

1985. 'Army Ordnance and the "American System" of Manufacturing, 1815–1861', in M. Roe Smith (ed.), *Military Enterprise and Technological Change*, Cambridge, MA: MIT Press: 39–86

Solomons, D., 1968. 'The Historical Development of Costing', in D. Solomons (ed.), *Studies in Cost Analysis*, 2nd edn, London: Sweet & Maxwell

Southern, R., 1982. 'The Schools of Paris and the School of Chartres', in R. Benson and G. Constable (eds.), *Renaissance and Renewal in the Twelfth Century*, Oxford: Clarendon: 113–37

Thompson, E., 1967. 'Time, Work-Discipline and Industrial Capitalism', *Past and Present* 38: 56–97

Thompson, G., 1991. 'Is Accounting Rhetorical? Methodology, Luca Pacioli and Printing', *Accounting, Organizations and Society* 16(5/6): 572–99

Tyler, D., 1883. 'His Autobiography', in *Daniel Tyler: A Memorial Volume*, New Haven: privately printed

Udovitch, A., 1979. 'Bankers Without Banks: The Islamic World', in R. Lopez (ed.), *The Dawn of Modern Banking*, New Haven: Yale University Press

Uselding, P., 1972. 'Technical Progress at the Springfield Armory, 1820–1859', *Explorations in Economic History* 9: 291–316

1973. 'An Early Chapter in the Evolution of American Industrial Management', in P. Cain and P. Uselding (eds.), *Business Enterprise and Economic Change: Essays in Honor of Harold F. Williamson*, Ohio: Kent State University Press: 63–84

Ward, J., 1971. 'Herman Haupt and the Development of the Pennsylvania Railroad', *Pennsylvania Magazine of History* 95: 73–91

Western Railroad, 1840. *Regulations for the Government of the Transportation Department*, Springfield, MA: Merriam, Wood

Yamey, B., 1964. 'Accounting and the Rise of Capitalism: Further Notes on a Theme by Sombart', *Journal of Accounting Research* II: 117–36

1977. 'Some Topics in the History of Financial Accounting in England, 1500–1900', in W. Baxter and S. Davidson (eds.), *Studies in Accounting*, London: ICAEW: 11–34

# 4  Governing the calculable person

*Peter Miller and Ted O'Leary*

Between 1900 and 1930, theories of standard costing and budgeting became a central part of the accounting literature. This profoundly transformed cost accounting, and massively expanded its domain. Henceforth, cost accounting was to be concerned with the future as well as the past. Cost accounting was no longer to be limited to ascertaining only the actual costs of production or activities (Nicholson, 1913; Church, 1917; Epstein, 1978). Standard costing and budgeting made it possible for accounting routinely to address questions of waste and efficiency in the employment of resources, whether human, financial or material. Standard costing enabled the calculation of variances at the level of the profit of the total firm, at the level of material or labour use in production, or at the level of every accountable person within the firm.

Existing histories of accounting note the importance of standard costing. For Sowell (1973), standard costing entailed the development of a set of techniques and a theoretical rationale for the 'scientific' predetermination of the costs of raw material, labour and overhead, as well as for the analysis of the variance of such costs from the actual or historical costs. Solomons (1968) identifies similar themes across a range of writers, in particular Harrington Emerson (1919) and Charter Harrison (1930). But such histories tend to limit themselves to either a detailed and careful chronology of ideas and techniques (Sowell, 1973), or to a narrative of progress in which standard costing becomes a key stage in the development of accounting to ever-increasing levels of sophistication (Solomons, 1968). The 'weaknesses' of the early outlines of standard costing, such as those provided by Emerson, are highlighted. And the history of accounting becomes the unfolding of a socially useful complex of techniques, whose underlying logic is one of progress.

Our concern with the transformation brought about by standard costing is different. We locate it on the plane of the government of economic life, understood as an ensemble of culturally and historically specific ways of representing and acting upon individuals and activities within the 'economic' realm (Miller and Rose, 1990). The government of economic life in advanced Western nations, we argue, should be understood in a dual sense as an ensemble of *rationalities* and *technologies*.

By 'rationalities', we mean the changing vocabularies or discursive fields through which collective meaning is given to the ideals that set out the objects and objectives of government (Gordon, 1991; Rose and Miller, 1992). The government of economic life, we argue, consists in a multiplicity of programmes which seek to administer the actions of individuals in conformity with wider political norms. Concerns with efficiency, with industrial accidents, with labour turnover and absenteeism, with the rise of the large corporation, with international competitiveness and much else besides are articulated at the level of the enterprise in ways that are congruent with wider cultural ideals (Miller and O'Leary, 1989, 1994).

By 'technologies', we mean all those calculations, techniques, apparatuses, documents and numerous other devices for acting upon individuals, entities and activities in conformity with a particular set of ideals. For it is by means of technologies that rationalities of government are made operable within the enterprise. Understood in this dual sense, as an ensemble of rationalities and technologies, the government of economic life consists of attempts by authorities to act on the conduct of others, to shape their beliefs and behaviour in directions deemed desirable. The enterprise is the principal site for the government of economic life. Here, the political ideals of a democratic society come to be linked up to more local concerns. Attempts to govern individuals so as to improve productivity, reduce costs, or enhance competitiveness may seem natural and self-evident responses to the problems faced by firms. But, we argue, they should be understood as historically contingent devices, constitutive elements of particular modes of governing economic life.

Standard costing can be viewed in these terms as a technology of government, for it made possible a new form of government of persons within the firm. Standard costing and budgeting provided a new way of thinking and intervening that promised to render visible the inefficiencies of the individual within the enterprise. It supplemented the traditional concerns of accounting with the fidelity or honesty of the person. Cost accounting was now to embrace individuals, and to make them accountable by reference to prescribed standards of performance. Efficiency was to be an individual as well as a collective phenomenon. In making the activities of individuals visible and governable in this manner, standard costing helped foster the calculated management of life (Miller, 1992). Standard costing thereby helped bring about a significant shift in the mode of exercise of power in advanced industrial societies.

Standard costing was not an isolated phenomenon. Within the firm, it was closely allied to that vast project of standardization and normalization that has been called 'scientific management'. Standard costing and budgeting emerged in a reciprocal relationship with scientific management. And the complex formed by these twin technologies of government was itself linked to developments beyond the firm. For at the same time that standard costing and scientific management were seeking to standardize and normalize economic life within the firm, a number of other initiatives were seeking a related normalization of social life. In Britain and the US there was a discourse of 'national efficiency', which deployed the notion of efficiency in different sites and in relation to a range of concerns including government, industry and social organization. And a number of other dreams and schemes sought, in different locales, to promote the notion of a nationally administered social order. These included the ideal of government through expertise articulated by the pragmatists in the US, the Fabian socialists in the UK, and others, as well as practices such as psychological testing and intelligence testing. These diverse strategies and practices were only loosely related to each other. Yet they helped to support and articulate the ideal of a rationally administered social order in which efficiency would be made visible at an individual as well as a collective level.

Let us turn first to analyse the manner in which standard costing set out a conception of efficiency as something that could be made visible and calculable at the level of the individual within the enterprise.

## Making inefficiency visible and calculable

The proliferation of practices of standard costing between 1900 and 1930 can be charted clearly. Take this classic statement by Garcke and Fells (1911: 3–5), concerning the role of systematic cost accounts and their relevance for managerial action:

it is only by means of systematic records that leakage, waste, and fraud can be prevented, and that employers can know the cost of any article of their manufacture, and be able to determine accurately and scientifically, not merely approximately and by hap-hazard, the actual profit they make or loss they sustain, not only on the aggregate transactions during a given period, but also upon each individual transaction.

In a similar manner, Dickinson (1918, cited in Garcke and Fells, 1911: 7–8) states the principal objects of a modern cost system. They should comprise:

(1) Ascertaining the cost of the same product at different periods in the same mill, or at the same period in different mills, and so to remedy inequalities in cost by reducing all to the results shown by the best.
(2) The provision of an accurate, running book of inventories on hand, so facilitating reduction in stocks and capital invested to the lowest state consistent with efficiency.

(3) The preparation of statistical information as to costs of parts, quantity, and variety of output, relative efficiency of different classes of labour, and relative costs of labour and material, between different mills and periods.

(4) The preparation of periodical statements of profit and loss in a condensed form, readily giving directors all material information as to the results of the business.

These statements are admirable in their rigour. But in limiting themselves to *actual* costs, they provide no place for a conception of standard or predetermined costs, and hence no means of quantifying the variance of actual from standard.

By 1930, and on both sides of the Atlantic, things had changed. There was a new language of cost accounting, and a new set of devices for the keeping of cost accounts. The key terms of this new language of cost accounting were 'the standard cost', the 'variance analysis', the 'budget' and 'budgetary control'.

The inadequacies of the past were vehemently proclaimed, as in this statement by Charter Harrison (1930: 8):

The most serious defect of the job-order cost plan was that it failed, most utterly and dismally to achieve what should be the primary purpose of any cost system, namely, to bring promptly to the attention of the management the existence of preventable inefficiencies so that steps could be taken to eliminate these at the earliest possible moment.

And the promise of the novel technique of standard costing was equally vigorously declared (Harrison, 1930: 12):

one of the primary advantages of standard costs . . . is that the clerical work involved in the operating of a properly designed standard cost system is very much less than that required to operate any complete job-order cost plan. That this is so is evident when it is considered that with standard costs we are dealing with the principle of exceptions, that is to say with variations from the standards.

But more than a simple technical innovation was at stake. With standard costing and the analysis of variances it was now possible to attach norms and standards of behaviour to every individual within the firm. Efficiency could be individualized and rendered visible. Exponents of this novel technology did not hesitate to point out its advantages in this respect (Harrison, 1930: 27–8):

We have increased the efficiency of the average man because we have applied the principles of scientific management to his work – instead of letting him proceed haphazardly we have set before him carefully determined standards of accomplishment rendered possible by standardization of conditions, and have given him scientific training supplemented by an efficiency reward. We have combined mechanical sciences and psychology, with the result that today every man, woman and child in this country is reaping the harvest.

With this step, cost accounting was transformed. With this novel technique came a transformation in the possibilities of governing the individual person within the productive machine. No doubt the initial formulations of standard costing lacked the precision they gained later. Indeed, it was not always clear whether a standard was considered to be an ideal or an attainable target; nor was the possibility of actually locating the source of waste entirely clear (Solomons, 1968: 41). And no doubt the deployment of standard costing within firms was not always immediate, and was influenced by local concerns and issues. But, when analysed in terms of the government of economic life, it is not the truth value of standard costing, or the extent to which it delivered efficiency gains to individual managers that is of concern. Rather, what is of interest is the transformation that standard costing made possible in the government of individual conduct within the enterprise. Henceforth, departures from standards and norms could be made visible and calculable at the level of each individual within the firm. Thus did standard costing help transform the government of economic life.

### Detecting hidden wastes

Standard costing owed much to that movement which, originating in the US, came to be given the label 'scientific management'. As Solomons (1968) has remarked, F.W. Taylor's paper of 1903 on 'Shop Management' contains many of the essential elements of what would later become standard costing. Accounting historians have drawn attention to another leading proponent of scientific management ideas, Harrington Emerson (Sowell, 1973; Epstein, 1978). Not only did Emerson's work on efficiency explicitly envisage something akin to a standard costing (Emerson, 1919), but he appears to have exercised a strong influence on Charter Harrison's elaboration of a fully integrated standard costing and budgeting system in 1930 (Sowell, 1973).

Scientific management, as set out in the introductory pages of F.W. Taylor's celebrated *Principles of Scientific Management* (1913), sought to advance national efficiency through attacking the vast wastes which had secreted themselves within the daily actions of every individual. For Taylor, the core issue was that wastes of human resources are hidden, in contrast with the ready visibility of wastes of natural resources (1913: 5–6):

We can see our forests vanishing, our water-powers going to waste, our soil being carried by floods into the sea ... We can see and feel the waste of material things. Awkward, inefficient, or ill-directed movements of men, however, leave nothing visible or tangible behind them. Their appreciation calls for an act of memory, an effort of the imagination. And for this reason, even though our daily loss from this source is greater than from our waste of material things, the one has stirred us deeply, while the other has moved us but little.

Scientific management sought to address this invisibility and intangibility of the wastes arising from the actions of individuals. A 'scientific' knowledge of the exact extent of such wastes would be the first step. The second step would be the systematic elimination of such wastes. Taylor was joined in his crusade by others such as the Gilbreths. Long-established practices in trades such as bricklaying were to be dissected and analysed in terms of the wastes that inhered in all the minute components that such an activity was composed of (Drury, 1915). Taylor himself pointed to the need for a 'science' of mundane tasks such as shovelling and pig-iron handling.

Inefficiency was seen by scientific management to be intrinsic to lay knowledges and practices. Whether these took the form of trades, crafts, or traditional practices, the activities of individuals in such fields were to be scrutinized for their possible wastefulness. Scientific management sought to appropriate the life of the individual at work, to act upon it in order to optimize the efficiency of each individual action. No matter how minute or apparently trivial the activity, according to scientific management much could be gained by an attentiveness to each and every movement of the individual.

Scientific management articulated the principle that 'expert' interventions were needed if individuals were to give their best in their work, whether it was on the shop floor, in the office, or in a multitude of other locales. Such interventions were not only necessary in the interests of efficiency and the elimination of waste. They were legitimate also, for managers might now direct and control the actions of individuals on the assured basis of science and expertise.

Scientific management reflected the almost messianic role for the engineering profession envisaged by some of its leaders in the US (Emerson, 1919: 5):

To attain the high efficiency of the atomic energy of the fish, the high mechanical efficiency of the bird, the high lighting efficiency of the firefly, is not an ethical or financial or social problem, but an engineering problem; and to the engineering profession, rather than to any other, must we look for salvation from our distinctly human ills, so grievously and pathetically great.

The efficiency of the individual was considered to be something that could be acted upon and improved, rather than something fixed. Success and greatness were seen to be the result of organization and training, rather than accidents of birth. 'In the future', according to Taylor (1913: 6–7):

it will be appreciated that our leaders must be trained right as well as born right, and that no great man can (with the old system of personal management) hope to compete with a number of ordinary men who have been properly organized so as efficiently to cooperate.

All social institutions might be conquered by this new scientific principle. Whilst Taylor's proposals originated in the factory:

It is hoped, however, that it will be clear ... that the same principles can be applied with equal force to all social activities: to the management of our homes; the management of our farms; the management of the business of our tradesmen, large and small; of our churches, our philanthropic institutions, our universities, and our governmental departments (Taylor, 1913: 8).

But more might be achieved if efficiency norms could be given monetary form. Indeed, from an early date scientific management writers had recognized the potential of an efficiency measure grounded in costs saved and profits earned. As early as 1886, for example, H.R. Towne, then president of the American Society of Mechanical Engineers and a mentor of Taylor's, had wanted to construe the engineer as an economist (Towne, 1886). For Towne, an engineer's contribution to the goal of efficiency should be judged principally in terms of economics. Efficiencies were deemed true only if they could ultimately be represented as costs saved.

Such sentiments were echoed later by Harrington Emerson (1919), who argued that engineers and accountants needed to collaborate in the task of detecting and analysing inefficiencies. And the figure of G. Charter Harrison, whose claims to title spanned the professional bodies of industrial engineering, chartered accountancy and cost accountancy, and whose writings provided the first full articulation of standard costing (Solomons, 1968), helped to cement this temporary alliance.

The engineering concept of scientific management was thus made visible and calculable in financial terms. The earlier concern of cost accounting with the registration of the movements of workers and materials as they 'attached' themselves to production (Epstein, 1978) was augmented. Efficiency and inefficiency were individualized. The worker was represented as almost certainly inefficient, needing to be enmeshed within the routinely applicable calculative apparatus of standard costing. Taylorism insisted that each worker be singled out, to be rewarded or punished on the basis of his or her individual performance (Taylor, 1913; Haber, 1964). When one ceases to deal with men in large gangs or groups, said Taylor (1913: 69–70):

and proceeds to study each workman as an individual, if the workman fails to do his task, some competent teacher should be sent to show him exactly how his work can best be done, to guide, help, and encourage him, and, at the same time, to study his possibilities as a workman.

But over whom was this individualizing gaze to be exercised? It is clear that the leaders of the scientific management movement envisaged that their principles could embrace everyone. No task or person was considered too lowly, or too important, to escape. Both physical and mental work were deemed legitimate and appropriate objects of attention. Despite that aspiration, scientific management remained trapped at the level of relatively mundane physical tasks (Drury, 1915). Its principal technology for intervening, the time-and-motion study, was hardly equipped for anything more.

An escape route was provided by standard costing and budgeting, allowing the normalizing aspirations of scientific management to move away from the factory floor. Standard costing and budgeting made it possible for a particular mode of government of economic life to move upward through the corporate hierarchy. At least in principle, an individualizing mode of government could now embrace everyone within the firm. As Harrison stated (1930: 27–8), explicitly linking standard costing and scientific management, and setting out a much broader agenda that embraced the executive:

We have increased the efficiency of the average man because we have applied the principles of scientific management to his work . . .

Our accounting methods today are the best evidence of our failure to apply scientific management principles to the development of our executives. For the five-dollars-a-day man our accounting records clearly set up the objective and the accomplishment in comparison therewith. But when we come to our records for executives what do we find? . . . Of accomplishment, it is true that our profit and loss account tells the story of the ultimate result, but of executive objectives shown in relation to the accomplishment, our records are silent.

Standard costing had already enmeshed the shop floor worker within a calculus of efficiency. According to Harrison (1930: 27–8), it should now move on, by means of the budget or profit plan, to do the same for executives:

No man can realize his fullest possibilities, whether he be a five-dollar-a-day trucker in the factory or a five-thousand-dollar-a-year executive, unless he has before him at all times (1) a carefully determined objective, (2) records showing the relationship between accomplishment and this objective, and (3) if he has failed to realize the objective, information as to the causes of such failure. Standard costs furnish the factory superintendent with this information as regard factory costs, and standard profit or budget systems give the executive this information as regards profits.

The engineers (e.g. Emerson, 1919) had envisaged that standard costing would be no more than an appendage to their principles of scientific management. It would be a convenient way of giving calculable form to the core data that the engineer would supply. But accounting's facility for expressing in monetary form the standardizing ambitions of the engineers effected a surprising metamorphosis. The normalizing aspirations of scientific management could be extended to a much larger group. The firm itself could be defined as a particular type of space, one in which efficiency and rationality might be made the operative principles.

From Taylor onward, the government of economic life within the enterprise has been extended and modified. An army of experts of the soul has continued the attempt to govern the lives of individuals in their depths and details (Rose, 1990). The alliance between standard costing and scientific management has been supplemented by industrial psychology. Monitoring and observation might have begun with the worker on the factory floor. But the dream of those experts of the soul is that eventually every employee would be reached. Actions and outputs might be the starting point, but eventually even motivations would be opened up to this individualizing form of inspection. As Hugo Munsterberg was to state (1913: 3):

Our aim is to sketch the outlines of a new science which is to intermediate between the modern laboratory psychology and the problems of economics: the psychological experiment is systematically to be placed at the service of commerce and industry.

Just as Taylorism had sought to manage the bodily movements of the worker, industrial psychology sought to know and to manage the psyche of the individual in the enterprise. Relative to the 'helpless psychological dilettantism' (Munsterberg, 1913: 56) of those who had endeavoured at earlier times to motivate the worker, industrial psychology attempted to establish for itself a privileged position based on its claims to expertise and its promise to provide a practical contribution to the goals of civilization. Along with standard costing and scientific management, industrial psychology sought to place itself above the fray, to set itself apart from sectional interests. It appealed to efficiency and the ends of organizations as goals beyond the reach of politics. In the words of Munsterberg (1913: 20): 'psychotechnics does not stand in the service of a party, but exclusively in the service of civilisation'. The factory was to be the laboratory of this new expertise, and its object would be individual differences. The stated contribution of the industrial psychologist was to recommend a person–task fit congruent with individual wellbeing and the exigencies of efficiency (Myers, 1920).

Not surprisingly, these promises proved difficult to keep. Moreover, this early psychology of individual differences was superseded by a more complex psychology that focused on the group and the interactions of those who composed it (Miller, 1986). But accounting inherited much of these early ambitions to govern the actions of the individual in accordance with the overall aim of enhancing the productivity of the enterprise. To any project of enmeshing the individual within norms of efficiency, an expert psychological selection process, as well as psychological intervention in interpreting task performance variables, would be declared essential. The issues of executive decision-making (Miller and O'Leary, 1989) and the budgeting process (Argyris, 1952) were central to this problematizing of individual performance. Through these mechanisms, an individualizing mode of governing economic life moved firmly up the corporate hierarchy.

### The efficient nation and the efficient individual

It is the adaptability of the word 'efficiency' that gives it much of its persuasive power. The term efficiency can operate in different sites and be applied to diverse activities and objectives. It can be deployed within the firm as a way of giving meaning and significance to the aspirations of standard costing and scientific management. It can be applied with equal force to a collectivity such as the nation. And it can serve as a relay between distinct and otherwise unrelated entities, helping to link up local sites with each other, and with wider entities such as the nation.

The forming of a reciprocal relationship between the firm and the nation was central to the success of standard costing and scientific management. The notion of efficiency helped establish such a reciprocal relationship. For although concerns with the collective efficiency of the nation were expressed in ways that differed from those applied to the enterprise, relays were established between these two sites. Efficiency was problematized and made quantifiable by multiple devices and interventions. Statistical deviations from a norm were central to the individualization of difference, both at the level of the firm and of the nation. A visibility was attached to individuals, in relation to disparate issues such as productivity, intelligence and health, and their contribution to collective efficiency made knowable. A plethora of techniques of socio-political management made possible observation of, and intervention in, the minutiae of the everyday lives of individuals. Efficiency was made operable at an individual and a collective level in diverse sites.

The notion of efficiency provided an organizing theme for diverse debates and arguments in the early years of this century, such that one can speak of a discourse of national efficiency. The forming of this discourse of national efficiency was important for the rise of so many practices that sought to establish a congruence between interventions in locales such as the firm and the school, and macro level concerns with the wellbeing of whole populations. The notion of efficiency emerged as a 'convenient label' under which could be grouped a range of assumptions, beliefs and demands concerning government, industry and social organization (Searle, 1970;

Hays, 1959; Haber, 1964). The notion of efficiency was used in different ways by different commentators. There were of course divergences of opinion on matters of social and industrial policy. And the way in which the notion of efficiency was used in the United Kingdom was different from the way in which it was articulated in the United States. But with due recognition of these variations in mode of deployment it remains the case that the notion of efficiency gave common meaning and significance to the concerns and ambitions of disparate actors and agencies.

In Britain, a discourse of national efficiency was elaborated not only in the writings of Taylorism, but in journalistic writings, the arguments of politicians, as well as in medical and para-medical writings. The question of national efficiency was seen to be at heart a matter of social organization. Germany and Japan were held up as models or exemplars of a form of social organization which promoted efficiency through the incorporation of science in the art of politics. Britain was held to be wanting in relation to such models of national efficiency.

The need for a fundamental reappraisal of the nation's political and moral values was proclaimed in extreme form by the British writer Arnold White (1901), in his demagogic book *Efficiency and Empire*. Most of this material had appeared in newspaper articles the previous year. In these writings, White depicted a country stumbling through successive disasters and scandals, such as those of the Boer War. Inefficiency was identified as the central problem, and was considered by White to derive from physical and moral deterioration. The middle classes had, he argued, become largely 'a class of pleasure-seekers', whilst the working classes 'artificially restrict their labour' (White, 1901: 310). Meanwhile, drink exercised its despotism over all social groups. The result was a softening of the fibre of the ruled and the rulers alike. Beyond certain institutions, such as the Army, the Navy and the Police, the population was seen to consist mainly in 'hospital out-patients, enfeebled with bad air, sedentary lives, drink, and disease' (White, 1901: 107–8). In short, the nation was rapidly degenerating, and the State was doing virtually nothing to prevent this. Something had to be done, according to White, for the efficiency of the nation depended on the efficiency of the individuals who comprised it.

White was only one of many journalists and commentators to suggest the need for new political ideals, ones that would give expression to a programmatic concern with 'national efficiency'. But if these concerns were expressed at the level of the nation as a whole, it was in 'private' locales such as the firm, the school, and the home that the efficiency of the individual became an object of concern, and came to be regarded as something that sapped the strength of the nation. Such locales became key sites within which the quest for profit or health was to be linked to the quest for national efficiency. For the quest for profit within the enterprise was seen to depend on much the same capacities as the ability of the nation to fight a war.

Experts of varying kinds, including cost accountants, industrial psychologists, medics and others, were called upon to objectify and act upon the individual in such locales to remedy matters and to foster national efficiency. The 'private' domains of the enterprise and the family became the repository of various hopes and aspirations of a more 'efficient' nation. The arguments and appeals of politicians reinforced such ambitions. Whilst an astute politician such as Rosebery shied away from White's journalistic excesses, he admitted to being in 'substantial agreement' with White's opinions (Searle, 1970: 54).

Efficiency was also a key term in relation to the articulation of a role for expertise within the machinery of government. The purpose of the State was to promote the 'good life' of its citizens, and to develop the moral nature of the individual (Dyson, 1980: 192). To achieve this, the application of scientific knowledge and training was held to be necessary. For some, this meant leaving key decisions in the hands of experts, whilst for others it meant transforming politics and public administration into sciences. The latter found its institutional form in the founding of the London School of Economics and Political Science by the Webbs at the end of the nineteenth century. The principle at work here was that 'social reconstructions require as much specialized training and sustained study as the building of bridges and railways, the interpretation of the law, or technical improvements in machinery and mechanical processes' (quoted in Searle, 1970: 85).

The appeal to expertise as a way of enacting a wider concern with social efficiency was a theme that cut across party politics. Expertise, or so it was hoped, would reconcile interventions in diverse locales with macro level aspirations. Rosebery, the leader of the 'Liberal Imperialists' called for government by 'scientific methods'. Asquith, for his part, suggested that social reform should be carried out 'not as a moral question ... but as a question of social and imperial efficiency (quoted in Collini, 1979: 83–4). Underlying these varying shades of opinion was the common theme that expertise might help reconcile a recognition of the vital economic and political implications of formally private activities, with the concern to refrain from extending the domain and powers of the State (Rose and Miller, 1992). Experts could thus enter into an alliance with politicians and other authorities, translating concerns with inefficiency and the strength of the nation into the vocabulary of cost accounting, scientific management and industrial psychology.

In the US, the notion of efficiency was equally central in political argument, even if it differed in terms of the issues to which it was applied and the exact content that it was given. The progressive era, as one author has expressed it, 'is almost made to order for the study of Americans in love with efficiency' (Haber, 1964: ix; Hays, 1959). The 'efficiency craze' of the progressive era consisted in 'an outpouring of ideas and emotions in which a gospel of efficiency was preached without embarrassment to businessmen, workers, doctors, housewives and teachers' (Haber, 1964: ix). Efficiency referred here to a personal attribute, to a mechanical principle equivalent to the output–input ratio of a machine, to a commercial efficiency in the form of profit, and to efficiency conceived as a relationship between persons. It is this last sense that is most significant for the 'politics of efficiency'. For in this case efficiency meant social efficiency, which in turn meant social organization.

The 'politics of efficiency' accorded a central position to the links between democracy and expertise. Scientific wisdom and expertise were to be used to advance the cause of 'good government', whether at the site of the municipality or the factory. 'Democracy' was to mean government for the people based on the *facts*, a partnership between the expert and the citizen which was essential to good government (Haber, 1964: 110). Efficient government was to be achieved by means of government experts acting in the interests of citizens. Since citizens could no longer realistically achieve the level of expertise required:

Citizens of larger cities must frankly recognize the need for professional service in behalf of citizen interests . . . Even efficient private citizens cannot deal helpfully with expert governmental questions. Efficient citizens will evidence their efficiency by supporting constructive efforts for governmental betterment (cited in Haber, 1964: 112).

The language of efficiency suffused federal bodies such as the Presidential Commission on Economy and Efficiency, which was replaced by a Bureau of Efficiency when the Wilson administration took office (Haber, 1964: 113–14). And the language of efficiency appeared also at state level, many states soon setting up their own efficiency commissions. Wisconsin began in 1911, and by 1917 at least 16 states had formed such commissions. These bodies focused principally on consolidating state agencies, improving cost accounting techniques, and granting more power to the governor (Haber, 1964: 115).

The language of efficiency was reinforced by the notion of a rationally administered and managed social order. In the USA, pragmatism articulated such a conception. Pragmatism envisaged the creation of a space within which human rationality would actively shape and reform social organization. In the UK, the New Liberalism (Freeden, 1978) played a similar role. Figures such as Hobhouse set out a conception of an active role for the human mind in the overall process of evolution. Social science would, or so it was argued, contribute to the better control and directing of human progress. Just as natural science could serve human needs, so too could social science be harnessed and adapted to the purposeful achievement of ends.

These conceptions of a rationally administered social order allowed social reform to be conceived in a manner analogous to the reform of the enterprise. Both required the elimination of inefficiencies. If the efficiency of individuals was to be enhanced, this would be achieved through a reconstruction of their interactions so as to minimize collective wastes. Reform would take as its central object the links between individual behaviour and the collective goals of society. Social science expertise could thus enter into a dual alliance with the individual and with the State, assisting both in the purposeful improvement of the social order. Industrial psychology and intelligence testing could play a role in such interventions just as readily as could accounting. For by individualizing efficiency, each of these practices would make operable the macro level concern with efficiency and a rationally administered social order.

The notion of efficiency thus gave meaning and significance for interventions in a diverse range of locales. The way in which it was deployed, and the domains to which it was applied, varied between the USA and the UK. But it is this mobility and flexibility of the term that allowed it to be invoked in such a multiplicity of locales. And it fitted the domains to which it was applied because, at least in part, those domains were to be remade in accordance with the aims and aspirations of 'efficiency'. The difficulty of providing a clear definition of the term was not a limitation but a strength. For it provided an opening into which experts such as accountants, engineers, industrial psychologists and many others could insert themselves. Such experts would seek to make operable at a local level the wider concerns with national efficiency.

### Conclusion

The argument of this chapter is that we need to understand the transformation brought about by the invention of standard costing as part of a shift in modes of government of economic life. Standard costing has been located as a key component within an ensemble of practices that sought to make the actions of individuals visible and calculable in relation to norms and standards. The 'success' of standard costing and budgeting was its ability to give financial form to attempts to govern the actions of individuals. The ensemble of practices addressed here has been analysed at the level of the firm, in particular through the interrelations of standard costing and scientific management. It has also been analysed at the related level of the nation, in the discourse of national efficiency, and in the attempts by diverse bodies of expertise to normalize and govern populations of individuals.

The transformation brought about by standard costing was profound. It enabled the individual within the firm to be surrounded by calculative norms and standards. Between the worker and the boss was interposed a calculative apparatus that claimed neutrality and objectivity. Imperatives of efficiency could henceforth be traced back to this calculative apparatus, rather than to the will of the boss. This expertise of efficiency sought to remove itself from the disputed and conflictual terrain of politics, and sought to set itself above the fray. Discipline was to be founded on a knowledge of the facts deemed true, and on deviations from a norm.

This attempt to govern economic life within the firm can be viewed as part of that ensemble of discourses and practices that Michel Foucault has done so much to analyse, an ensemble that 'exerts a positive influence on life, that endeavours to administer, optimize, and multiply it, subjecting it to precise controls and comprehensive regulations' (Foucault, 1981: 137). Of course, to speak of the positive and productive nature of modes of government in this way is not to endorse such mechanisms, as one commentator seems to think (Moore, 1991: 773). Rather, it is a matter of examining the capacity of certain practices to generate effects, to produce outcomes, to make operable certain programmes of government. It is a question of seeking to analyse a particular mode of exercise of power, one that acts upon the actions of others who are faced with a field of possibilities. For, as Foucault has remarked, 'Power is exercised only over free subjects, and only insofar as they are free' (Foucault, 1982: 221). Power presupposes rather than annuls the capacities of agents (Gordon, 1991: 5). Power in advanced liberal societies is a matter of 'making up' (Hacking, 1986) citizens endowed with various capacities, and capable of bearing a kind of regulated freedom. The general principle here is well expressed by Rexford Tugwell, government advisor, economics professor, and staunch advocate of the applications of scientific management to the wider society (1933: 17):

Is it possible that, instead of appealing to sets of emotions of an immediate and piecemeal sort, the problem of motivation might be resolved by fixing in each individual mind a rationale of ends to be tried for, and of the means available? For if this cannot be done, it seems very little use to hope that group action will ever become coherent and cooperative in a larger, a genuinely social sense.

To identify such mechanisms of government is not to presuppose that a liberal society is 'fundamentally imprisoned' (Moore, 1991: 773). There may be linkages between carceral institutions and other sites of government such as factories, but this does not make them equivalent (Deleuze, 1986). Nor do such mechanisms produce totally obedient individuals. A liberal society is neither a myth, nor a society in which government does not take place. To grasp the diverse ways in which power is exercised in advanced liberal democracies, we need to abandon the political vocabulary structured by oppositions between coercion and consent, sovereignty and autonomy, public and private, and the like (Rose and Miller, 1992). We need to examine the shifting alliances between the various authorities that seek to govern a multitude of aspects of economic, social and personal life. In particular, we need to examine how the 'private' enterprise becomes a vital locale for the government of the economic life of the nation, how bosses, managers and workers become the loci and relays of changing sets of political objectives.

Doubtless, the devices and tactics addressed in this chapter are related to the development of capitalism (Miller, 1986). For the accumulation of capital is paralleled by the accumulation of persons. The adjustment of the conduct of individuals to the productive apparatus has been a continuing concern for capitalist industry. But technologies and rationalities of government have an irreducibility which needs to be analysed, and without subjecting such analysis to the injunction to discover always, underneath practices of government, the play of capital accumulation (Neimark, 1990: 109). As François Ewald has remarked, we need to examine liberalism 'not just as an economic form but as the functioning principle of power in capitalist societies' (cited in Gordon, 1991: 27). Modes of government have their own regularities and chronology, and it is these that we have sought to attend to here.

We have sketched only briefly the different dimensions of the transformation in the government of economic life brought about by standard costing and budgeting. We have not traced the subsequent transformations in the calculative technologies of accounting, and their links with changing modes of government. There is no doubt much to be gained by undertaking a comparable analysis of the ways in which accounting is modified through the incorporation of a 'behavioural' dimension. Equally significant would be to study the redefinition of cost accounting as management accounting following the Second World War, at least in part by the deployment of the notion of the decision-maker. And the shift in the roles of cost accounting as advanced manufacturing systems are increasingly widely installed is an issue of profound contemporary significance for the government of economic life (Miller and O'Leary, 1994). The analysis provided here of standard costing and budgeting simply identifies some of the practices and principles set in place in the early decades of this century. The roles of accounting within changing modes of government of economic life is something whose significance is only just beginning to be appreciated.

NOTE

This is a condensed and revised version of Miller and O'Leary (1987).

REFERENCES

Argyris, C., 1952. *The Impact of Budgets on People*, New York: Controllership Foundation
Church, A.H., 1917. *Manufacturing Costs and Accounts*. New York: McGraw-Hill
Collini, S., 1979. *Liberalism and Sociology*, Cambridge: Cambridge University Press
Deleuze, G., 1986. 'Un Nouveau Cartographe', in G. Deleuze, *Michel Foucault*, Paris: Editions de Minuit
Dickinson, A.L., 1918. *Accounting Practice and Procedure*. New York: Ronald Press
Drury, H.B., 1915. *Scientific Management*, New York: Columbia University Press
Dyson, K., 1980. *The State Tradition in Western Europe*, Oxford: Martin Robertson
Emerson, H., 1919. *Efficiency as a Basis for Operation and Wages*, New York: Engineering Magazine Co
Epstein, M.J., 1978. *The Effect of Scientific Management on the Development of the Standard Cost System*, New York: Arno
Foucault, M., 1981. *The History of Sexuality*, vol. 1, Harmondsworth: Penguin
    1982. 'The Subject and Power', afterword to H.L. Dreyfus and P. Rabinow, *Michel Foucault: Beyond Structuralism and Hermeneutics*, Brighton: Harvester
Freeden, M., 1978. *The New Liberalism*, Oxford: Oxford University Press
Garcke, E. and Fells, J.M., 1911. *Factory Accounts*, 6th edn, London: Crosby Lockwood
Gordon, C., 1991. 'Governmental Rationality: An Introduction', in G. Burchell, C. Gordon and P. Miller (eds.), *The Foucault Effect: Studies in Governmentality*, Hemel Hempstead: Harvester Wheatsheaf
Haber, S., 1964. *Efficiency and Uplift: Scientific Management in the Progressive Era, 1890–1920*, Chicago: University of Chicago Press
Hacking, I., 1986. 'Making up People', in T.C. Heller, M. Sosna and D.E. Wellbery (eds.), *Reconstructing Individualism: Autonomy, Individuality, and the Self in Western Thought*, Stanford, CA: Stanford University Press
Harrison, G.C., 1930. *Standard Costing*, New York: Ronald Press
Hays, S.P., 1959. *Conservation and the Gospel of Efficiency*, Cambridge, MA: Harvard University Press
Miller, P., 1986. 'Psychotherapy of Work and Unemployment', in P. Miller and N. Rose (eds.), *The Power of Psychiatry*, Cambridge: Polity Press
    1992. 'Accounting and Objectivity: The Invention of Calculating Selves and Calculable Spaces', *Annals of Scholarship* 9(1/2): 61–86
Miller, P. and O'Leary, T., 1987. 'Accounting and the Construction of the Governable Person', *Accounting, Organizations and Society* 12(3): 235–65
    1989. 'Hierarchies and American Ideals, 1900–1940', *Academy of Management Review* 14(2): 250–65
    1994. 'Accounting, "Economic Citizenship" and the Spatial Reordering of Manufacture', *Accounting, Organizations and Society* 19(1): 15–43
Miller, P. and Rose, N., 1990. 'Governing Economic Life', *Economy and Society* 19(1): 1–31
Moore, D.C., 1991. 'Accounting on Trial: The Critical Legal Studies Movement and its Lessons for Radical Accounting', *Accounting, Organizations and Society* 16(8): 763–91
Munsterberg, H., 1913. *Psychology and Industrial Efficiency*, London: Constable

Myers, C.S., 1920. *Mind and Work*, London: University of London Press

Neimark, M., 1990. 'The King is Dead. Long Live the King', *Critical Perspectives on Accounting* 1: 103–14

Nicholson, J.L., 1913. *Cost Accounting*, New York: Ronald Press

Rose, N., 1990. *Governing the Soul: The Shaping of the Private Self*, London: Routledge

Rose, N. and Miller, P., 1992. 'Political Power Beyond the State: Problematics of Government', *British Journal of Sociology* 43(2): 173–205

Searle, G.R., 1970. *The Quest for National Efficiency*, Oxford: Blackwell

Solomons, D., 1968. 'The Historical Development of Costing', in D. Solomons (ed.), *Studies in Cost Analysis*, 2nd edn, London: Sweet & Maxwell

Sowell, E.M., 1973. *The Evolution of the Theories and Techniques of Standard Costs*, Alabama: University of Alabama Press

Taylor, F.W., 1913. *The Principles of Scientific Management*, New York: Harper & Bros

Towne, H.R., 1886. 'The Engineer as Economist', *Proceedings of the American Society of Mechanical Engineers*

Tugwell, R., 1933. *The Industrial Discipline and the Governmental Arts*, New York: Columbia University Press

White, A., 1901. *Efficiency and Empire*, London: Methuen

# 5    Accountancy and the First World War

*Anne Loft*

A.J.P. Taylor writes that 'the House of Commons did not realise what it was doing' when, in early 1916, it added a clause to the Defence of the Realm Act (DORA) concerning the price which the war ministries would pay manufacturers for war supplies which it purchased from them. That price was to be the cost of making the items in question, plus an allowance for profit. This allowance for profit was to be based on the profit usually earned by the factory or workshop before the War (Taylor, 1970: 66; Lloyd, 1924: 58–60). This legislation represented a decisive move away from the principle beloved of the majority of MPs, that of letting the market set the price. It was an almost complete reversal of the policy put forward earlier in the War by the President of the Board of Trade, who had told the House of Commons that: '[n]o government action could overcome economic laws, and any interference with those laws must end in disaster' (quoted in Taylor, 1970: 41).

Cost-plus pricing is, in theory, a relatively simple concept; but, as was soon to be discovered, its implementation is not. For a start, accurate and up-to-date records of materials and time spent on jobs were a basic requirement; waste and faulty goods also needed to be carefully recorded. Then there were the more technical issues: most factories produce more than one type of product, they had to decide how to allocate joint costs as well as factory and office overheads to the different items produced. To operationalize this principle required manufacturers to have comprehensive and accurate cost accounting systems, but at the time the legislation was passed many had only very elementary systems in operation. It also required the government to have the means to check the figures which manufacturers provided, but few in the civil service had that ability. It is hardly surprising in the circumstances that in the ensuing months of the War cost accounting became a topic of great interest both to manufacturers and to those organizing the rapidly expanding war ministries. By 1919, the Deputy Minister of Munitions could report to the House of Commons that, from being something which manufacturers were suspicious of, cost accounting had now 'become an integral part of the method of most up-to-date industrial firms' (113 HC. Deb. 5s, col. 485).

This chapter deals with the way in which accountancy and war intersected, via cost accounting. The War had profound effects on the practice of accountancy and on its practitioners. In turn, accountancy also affected the War, for it came to play a role in the 'battle' on the home front for controlling production and managing the economy.

The First World War marked a fundamental change in the relationship between the citizen and the State, and between the manufacturer and the State. The lives of individuals were to be shaped by orders from above concerning everything from their freedom of movement to their conditions of work (Taylor, 1970: 25–6). Manufacturers became the subject of intensive government scrutiny, and a plethora of regulations. For many of them what they made, whom they employed, what they paid for their raw materials, and the prices they received for the finished goods were controlled. They were subject to much higher levels of taxation, and taxation took new forms such as Excess Profits Duty and Munitions Levy. State control penetrated the enterprise to an unprecedented degree, and accounting was one of the techniques which enabled this. Although the controls were not always successfully implemented in their own terms (profiteering and inefficiency remained rife), they fundamentally transformed the terms of the relations between State and industry.

There were other consequences. Accountants gained a social status and a degree of acceptance which had been absent before the War. This derived from the prominence which their war work brought them, not only with regard to cost accountancy, but also with regard to the other financial consequences[1] of the massive conversion of the economy to war production. The work carried out by cost accountants grew in status as its importance in enterprises grew. After the War, imitating the now very successful chartered accountants, an attempt was made to professionalize the occupation. These enhancements in social status and in the aspirations of practitioners were not without impact on accounting itself. In Britain, the relatively high status of accountants and accountancy can be linked to its widespread use as a tool of management.

### Cost accounting and accountants prior to the First World War

Prior to the First World War, professional accountants, with a few notable exceptions, were not interested in cost accounting. It was not part of their repertoire, and nor was it desired by them. To appreciate this negative view of cost accounting in the UK prior to the First World War, let us begin by tracing briefly the development of the accountancy profession, and then looking at the basic details of the history of cost accounting up to the War.[2]

In the mid-nineteenth century a profession of accountancy began to develop in Britain: first in Scotland in mid-century, and later in England with the formation in 1880 of the Institute of Chartered Accountants in England and Wales (ICAEW). As they began to restrict entry by introducing compulsory examinations and gradually making a period of clerkship compulsory, then in 1885 an association (the Society of Accountants and Auditors) was formed for those who had been excluded, its members becoming known as incorporated accountants.[3] Originally, most of the work of chartered accountants was concerned with bankruptcy. But as legislation was introduced to protect shareholders, the preparation of financial statements, and the audit of them, gradually became more important to them, and to the incorporated accountants.

By the eve of the First World War a number of new associations for accountants, catering for those excluded from the others, had come into existence. Attempts to create a statutory register of accounting practitioners (as had been done for, amongst others, the medical profession) floundered. It was still unclear who, and what, was 'an accountant', and in what ways an accountant differed from a bookkeeper. The self-identity of the profession, and the acceptance of their identity by others, was only weakly developed.

For manufacturers, the Great Depression of 1873–96 had brought increased competition and price-cutting. Associated with this had been a growing interest in what it cost to make things. By the end of the nineteenth century, Britain seemed to be leading the world in terms of the technical development of costing systems. Nevertheless, it was only in exceptional circumstances that a costing system was to be found in industry (Solomons, 1952: 17). It was not until the early decades of the twentieth century, and in the US, that the theory and practice of cost accounting grew in association with the efficiency and scientific management movements (cf. Miller and O'Leary, ch. 4 in this volume). In the UK, the combination of traditional family firms and strong unions did little to encourage interest in cost accounting systems in practice. To establish a comprehensive system required a standardization and organization of production which was found only exceptionally. Discussions of costing systems in engineering journals such as *Engineering* and *Mechanical World* (for it was here that costing was discussed) suggested that while some manufacturers were advanced in this respect, others had no systematic system. To find out what it cost to make something required, in many cases, combining factory records of production, and records from the accounts office (which were kept independently).

Prior to the First World War, costing systems were the province of engineers, estimators and cost clerks. Professional accountants (of which more below) typically regarded cost accounting as something rather beneath their dignity. This is well illustrated by the response of the ICAEW to a chartered accountant who, on his return from several years in the US, put up a plate describing himself as 'Chartered Accountant and Efficiency Engineer'. He was accused of using a term which was 'discreditable to a Chartered Accountant' (*The Accountant*, 28 June 1919: 552).

### 1914–15: the beginning of the War, and the failure of competitive tendering

When the War started in 1914, it was not expected that it would last very long. Indeed, when Kitchener stated that he believed that the war would last three years and require a million men, the Foreign Secretary, Edward Grey, commented that it was 'unlikely, if not incredible' (Stevenson, 1984: 49). It is hardly surprising that the Army contracts department of the War Office did not consider it necessary to change their normal procedures for obtaining supplies, which, until then, had been based on competitive tendering.[4]

However, the scale of supplies ordered by the War Office to equip and feed the large numbers who volunteered in the early months of the war was so great that shortages of all types of finished goods and raw materials developed. The result, not surprisingly, was rapid price rises and profiteering by unscrupulous traders. Firms tendering for government contracts set prices high because raw materials were continually rising in price. Despite problems, the Liberal Government was reluctant to interfere. Having spent their lives arguing for free trade, the prime minister, Herbert Asquith, his foreign secretary, Herbert Gray, and other members of the Cabinet, resisted the idea that industry would have to be centrally organized for large-scale war production (Lloyd, 1924; Pigou, 1947; Taylor, 1970).

By March 1915, profiteering had reached a level which even staunch supporters of free trade could not tolerate. The government invoked an old regulation allowing the requisition of items at 'a fair market price in the opinion of the purchasing officer' to prevent profiteers making 100 per cent profit on the sale of sandbags to the government (Lloyd, 1924). It could hardly be said that the existing system of purchasing was working well, the shortages of munitions for the troops was becoming a sensitive issue, especially the shortages of shells (Taylor, 1970). The trade unionists accused employers of taking 'malicious advantage of the war' to 'reap huge profits' (*The Times*, 20 March 1915). At a Labour conference the suggestion that all profits in excess of 10 per cent should go to the State was met with hearty approval (*The Times*, 20 March 1915). The government was obliged to pay attention to the opinions of trade unionists, for they were a powerful force at this time, and their cooperation was needed if 'dilution' (the use of unskilled and semi-skilled workers to do work traditionally reserved for skilled craftsmen) was to be introduced. Dilution was essential if war production was to be increased, for large numbers of skilled workers had left to fight. Trade unionists were concerned that dilution would lead to employers making even greater profits at their expense. In the so-called 'Treasury Agreement', trade union leaders accepted dilution and the lifting of restrictive practices. But in doing so they imposed a number of conditions, one of which being that some limitations would be placed on profits (Stevenson, 1984).

The issue of the control of profiteering became the subject of debate in the national press. In an article in *The Times* (23 March 1915) it was suggested that the problem of the unrest caused by profits could be solved by all government contract work being priced at prime cost plus a standardized profit based on the type of work, the cost figures to be checked through an audit by supervisors. However, in the 'City Notes' of the same edition the complications of limiting profits were commented upon, and it was remarked that if a Government Department was to decide what unreasonable profits were it would 'have a great deal of difficult accounting to do' (*The Times*, 23 March 1915).

### The Ministry of Munitions and cost accounting

A culmination of these and other problems, such as the shortage of munitions, led to the collapse of the Liberal Government (Taylor, 1970: 55–6). In May 1915 a coalition government was formed. Lloyd George took command of the new Ministry of Munitions, which had taken over the duty of supplying munitions to the army from the War Office. A major survey of the machinery, capacity, and working practices of British industry was initiated, questionnaires being sent to 65,000 manufacturing workshops (Adams, 1978). Control over the munitions industry was extended through the Munitions of War Act of July 1915, which incorporated the conditions of the Treasury Agreement. Factories regarded as essential to the manufacture of munitions were designated 'controlled establishments' and wages, conditions and the organization of work came under the control of the State. There was even an attempt to limit profits to prewar levels through the so-called 'munitions levy'. The Ministry initiated the construction of a number of national factories to meet the demand for shells (Pigou, 1947; Stevenson, 1984; *The Accountant*, 30 June 1917). The cost of producing armaments was an issue of great concern, but remained a problem, the Undersecretary at the Ministry of Munitions writing in his diary on 12 August 1915 that: 'For some time I have been getting very anxious about the Financial Arrangements; about the nature of some of the contracts and so on. The astounding thing is that nobody seems to be able to tell us what things cost to make' (Addison, 1934: 116).

In order to deal with the problem of 'what things cost to make', Samuel Lever, a chartered accountant who had spent much of his working life in the US, was brought home to London from New York in late 1915 to be Assistant Financial Secretary to the Ministry of Munitions. He was to be in charge of: 'arrangements for cost accounting, for the control of the cost of new munitions factories, for revising our present tenders and so forth' (Addison, 1934: 119).

Pigou writes that by late 1915 overall control was still only at an 'elementary stage'. Instead of competitive tendering and individual contracting, there were now collective agreements in operation between the government and business associations. However, this only led to different problems. For instance, the government wanted to reduce the price of certain items supplied by members of the Brass-Makers' Association to the government ordnance factories, but the Association resisted because the armament firms, which they also supplied, were willing to pay the higher price. Each control which was introduced seemed to lead inexorably to further controls. For example, as a consequence of metal prices being fixed at the end of 1915, supplies of metal had to be allocated between competing users by means of a priority system (Pigou, 1947: 112–13).

There seemed to be no way of establishing a 'fair market price' for many of the items required for fighting the war, because there was no open market for items such as shells. For many other items, the demand of the army was so great that the market was distorted: in June 1917, it was estimated that the War Office had, in the almost three years of war up to that date, purchased 35 million knives, forks and spoons, and 400 million pounds of bacon (*The Times*, 29 June 1917). Thus it was that in early 1916 a new clause was introduced into the Defence of the Realm Act. This specified that in determining the price 'regard need not be had to the market price, but shall be had to the cost of production of the output so requisitioned, and to the rate of profit usually earned in respect to the output of such factory or workshop before the war' (quoted in Lloyd, 1924: 58–60). The power to examine manufacturers' books was given through a general clause which gave the government the right to verify particulars 'in such a manner as they may direct' (Lloyd, 1924: 58–60).

Costing was becoming important, and a Board of Trade investigation was set up to investigate costing in the engineering trades. When it finally reported in 1918, one of the things it emphasized was the enormous variation in the state of costing systems: whilst 'all efficient firms' had proper systems of costing, in others the systems were based on 'conventional rates of wages' from several years previously; worse still, 'certain large works' had 'no systems of costing at all', and it could be 'assumed that most small works have a costing system more or less reduced to rule of thumb' (Cd 9073, 1918: 11).

In general, three basic ways of ascertaining costs were used by the Ministry of Munitions: first, technical costing, in which engineering experts analysed the process of production and calculated what it ought to cost; secondly, accountancy costing, which relied on examination of the contractor's books in order to find out what things actually cost to make; thirdly, by comparison with the costs of items made in National Factories if the same items were being produced, a method particularly used where shells were being produced (Ministry of Munitions, n.d., vol. 3, pt. 2, ch. 1: 10–11). Contracts were usually either fixed price (negotiated beforehand), or based on actual costs plus an allowance for profit. Some were entered into on the rather unsatisfactory basis that the price would be settled later (Ministry of Munitions, n.d., vol. 3, pt. 2, ch. 1: 16–35; ch. 2: 59).

The success of these controls in reducing profiteering was much debated, both during and after the War. Not surprisingly there were problems, and some of these are outlined in the history of the Ministry (Ministry of Munitions, n.d.). However, there were also achievements: in October 1916 Samuel Lever explained to Parliament how the Ministry of Munitions had compelled the big armament firms to reduce their prices for shells:

The Ministry consulted accountants and engineers, and having arrived at what they considered the actual cost, set to cut the price of shell bodies. The big armament firms said the work could not be done for the prices named by the Ministry. The firms were then asked to produce their costs, and, as the Ministry had the power under the Munitions Act to see the firms' books, they immediately brought the prices down. The price of shell bodies had now been cut between 25 and 30 per cent (quoted in *The Times*, 11 October 1916: 5).

The indirect insinuation that the firms had been profiteering led the chairman of Cammell Laird & Co. (Ltd) to protest; but Lever was backed up by Addison, and in the debate most Members of Parliament supported them (the debates were reported verbatim in *The Times*, 25 October 1916). In *The Accountant*, it was suggested that the problem for the firms was that they had 'no adequate Cost Accounts' and 'no effective control over costs'. They had to reduce their prices because they had no accurate cost figures to justify them, not because they were making large profits at the expense of the country. Thus 'the real triumph of Mr. Lever consisted in his being able to show them, by means of a proper accounting system, how economies could be effected and production cost reduced' (*The Times*, 24 February 1917: 186).

The Ministry of Munitions employed special teams of cost investigators to check the costs of suppliers.[5] It was estimated that in 1917 alone there were about 2500 technical estimates made, and about 1000 accountancy investigations carried out by the Ministry of Munitions. These were led on the accounting side by qualified accountants (chartered or incorporated), and on the technical side by engineers (Ministry of Munitions, n.d., vol. 3, pt. 2, ch. 2: 58). In the official history of the Ministry of Munitions, it was noted that there was 'great difficulty' in 'finding competent persons'; this is supported by the comment of one manufacturer after the War that the government 'sent us men from heaven knows where to investigate the cost'. However, he went on to remark that 'of course as time went on they got more experience. They were bound to get it going [from] one place to another' (*The Cost Accountant*, March 1922: 186).

The Ministry of Munitions' own records were a disastrous mess, according to Marriner (1980). The prioritizing of production above all else meant that making records of transactions took second place. After the enormous scale of the problems was revealed in 1917, intensive efforts were made to rectify the situation. Contractors were asked for statements of all materials, components and loans made to them since 1915, and a specially set up unit, called the 'breakdown gang' tried to reconcile their records with those of the Ministry. Unfortunately, as Gilbert Garnsey (a prominent chartered accountant employed by the Ministry) noted, many contractors' books 'were in as bad a state as ours' (Marriner, 1980: 138).

The issue of profiteering kept raising its ugly head. A select committee set up to investigate the financial methods of the Ministry of Munitions reported in March 1918 that munitions firms were making large profits. In the sample they examined, the companies were making nearly twice what they were before the War, even after deduction of the munitions levy (*The Times*, 12 March 1918). One of the reasons why companies could make large profits was that for many items the level of acceptable costs had to be set at the level of the least efficient producer; and there were many which were inefficient. Small factory owners were encouraged to switch to producing war supplies by the huge scale of the contracts on offer, even when they did not possess the most appropriate machinery and skills for efficient production. This enabled others who were producing more efficiently to make large profits legally. However, many merely cheated. As Hobsbawm (1969: 275) writes, this was 'a paradise for profiteers'. It was simply impossible to establish strict enough controls to prevent exploitation. Many stories were told, one of a managing director who refused to set up a systematic cost accounting system. On investigation, it was revealed that he was charging all of his overheads to each of the contracts he was working on for five different government departments (reported in *The Accountant*, 19 June 1920: 723).

However, industry, especially the engineering sector, changed radically during the war under the pressure of the introduction of unskilled labour and the requirements of mass production. The number of specialized works concentrating upon a single product increased; and in the engineering sector, instead of items being produced to order, many began to be standardized and made for stock; a development already established in America (Cole, 1917; Pollard, 1962; Littler, 1982; Hannah, 1983). As a result of these developments, the organization of work within many of the larger factories became more rationalized. These basic changes made it easier to instal costing systems; for accurate and comprehensive cost accounting systems rely on accurate and comprehensive records of production, records which are much easier to keep where this rationalization has occurred. Together with government demands for information about costs, these factors encouraged the establishment of cost accounting systems[6] and the growth and spread of expertise in the area.

Knowledge about cost accounting, and expertise in using the techniques, spread in various ways. However, technical books and journals were probably important given that there were few courses in cost accounting at universities, and colleges of commerce taught only the basic principles.[7] Technical magazines such as the British edition of the American magazine *System*, contained articles on costing. However, the systems described tended to be rather elementary, many being based on pre-printed cards which could be purchased from salesmen.

One important source of information was seemingly E.T. Elbourne's book *Factory Administration and Accounts*, of which some 10,000 copies were sold during the war, principally among the executive staffs of the government contracting firms (Urwick and Brech, 1940, vol. 1: 149). First published in 1914, this book synthesized administrative methods with the planning of production and control of stock. It was very detailed and lent itself to being used as a guide to manufacturers. At its re-issue in 1918 the *Ministry of Munitions Journal* commented that it must already be known to many of the readers. The book emphasized the importance of accurate cost accounting, and laid out a system of accounts which could be used. The staff chart illustrated clearly the place of the 'Works Accountant and Estimator', a figure whose importance Elbourne drew attention to (Elbourne, 1914: 30–1).

Another means by which techniques of costing spread was through the Ministry of Munitions' inspectors, and through their work with cost accounting. In the case of the production of shells, government experts developed a sophisticated system of cost accounting for the National Shell Factories based on 'special costing forms'.[8] Apparently many private shell manufacturers took up the offer to use the forms, and this enabled the production of more accurate cost records (Ministry of Munitions, n.d., vol. 3, pt. 2, ch. 1: 12–13).

Although the new cost accounting systems were not always successfully implemented in their own terms (there remained profiteering and inefficiency), their establishment had several important consequences. First, cost accounting was brought to the attention of manufacturers, and many either installed a system or improved their existing one. Secondly, it marked a fundamental alteration in the possibilities that there were for State and industry to relate to each other. The State surveyed, controlled and inspected industry: what it cost to make things was to be visible not just to the manufacturer, but also to the State for regulatory purposes.

### Chartered accountants and costing

This 'coming into the light' of cost accounting (as one contemporary writer described it) had important consequences for the clerks and accountants who established and operated the new systems. Prior to the War, few professional accountants in the UK were interested in cost accounting. Their work was concerned initially with the financial aspects of bankruptcy (and, in Scotland, other legal and trustee work), and later came to focus mainly on the preparation and audit of financial accounts. Imitating the working practices of the more established professions, in particular law, they worked in professional offices and took on articled clerks whose parents paid a premium for the privilege. They considered themselves far superior to those accountants who worked in commerce and industry, and who were involved with such techniques as cost accounting. However, during the War many of these chartered and incorporated accountants became involved with cost accounting.

As accounting became a means by which government could exert control over industry, the employment of chartered and incorporated accountants by government departments rose. In early 1916, when conscription was introduced, the work of professional accountants was declared to be of national importance.[9] Married accountants of over 31, and single accountants of over 41, were excused military service as they were engaged in a certified occupation. At this point around a third of them had already left to fight as volunteers (*The Accountant*, 22 January 1916). Public criticism meant that they were excluded from the second list of certified occupations issued in 1916,[10] but government pressure brought them exemption again in 1917, although the conditions for obtaining it were more onerous (Garrett, 1961).

By July 1918 there were about 340 chartered and incorporated accountants in the finance, contracts, accounts and audit departments of the Ministry of Munitions (*The Incorporated Accountants' Journal*, July 1918: 187). Many of these would have been concerned with aspects of cost accounting. M. Webster Jenkinson, Controller of Factory Audit and Costs, commented that 'quite 200 of the men on his staff at the Ministry had learned a good deal about costs' (*The Accountant*, 18 January 1919: 46).[11] Others were employed on similar activities at the War Office and the Admiralty. In national and other government factories, accountants were apparently to be found 'acting not only in their usual capacity, but as managers, commercial superintendents, cost accountants, and stores accountants' (*The Accountant*, 5 January 1918: 1). Even those who remained in the profession became involved with costing, for example prominent firms of chartered accountants were selected by the Ministry of Food to be District Supervising Accountants and investigate the books of any manufacturer or trader on the instruction of the Ministry (Lloyd, 1924: 318). Others came into contact with costing through having to deal with their clients' problems with government contracts and the new, and higher, forms of taxation, namely the munitions levy and excess profits duty.

With this elevation of the significance of cost accounting went an elevation of its status. It began to be seen as essential knowledge for the accountant. It began to appear in examination questions of the ICAEW. Whilst immediately prior to the War a few questions had appeared in the examinations on this subject, they were very general. In the Intermediate Examination of 1911 the question was asked: 'What are cost accounts? State shortly how they are prepared and give an example' (ICAEW Archives). However, from the May 1918 examination the proportion of questions which involved a knowledge of cost accounting increased dramatically, as did the level of knowledge of the subject required to answer them. In the auditing paper, questions appeared on the auditing of costs (ICAEW Archives).

When the inadequacy of the Ministry of Munitions' accounting systems came to light, a select committee on national expenditure recommended that the War Office should order the release of qualified accountants from the Army for National Service in the Ministry (reported in *The Times*, 12 March 1918: 3). This appears not to have been implemented in practice (*The Incorporated Accountants' Journal*, July 1918: 188). The Deputy Chairman of the Appeal Tribunal of the House of Commons, G. Bettesworth-Piggott, wrote to the *Daily Telegraph* criticizing the long period of articled clerkship required to qualify, asking why, if gunners and airmen could be trained in a few months, accountants could not? But his critique appears not to have had any effect.

After the War, eminent accountants were knighted for their war effort. These included M. Webster Jenkinson, Gilbert Garnsey and Samuel Lever, who had served in key positions at the Ministry of Munitions (*The Accountant*, 10 May 1919: 396). This was the first time that accountants had obtained such honours, and clearly illustrates the rise in social standing and social acceptance that the War had brought them. Prior to the War, the question of whether or not accountancy was really a profession had been a matter of debate. During the War, members of the chartered and incorporated bodies of accountants achieved formally the legal status of being defined as members of a profession. This occurred when legislation enacted to introduce excess profits duty allowed for the exemption of members of professions; an exemption which led to the necessity for clarifying precisely which occupations were professions (*The Times*, 19 May 1916). In the first census after the War, accountants were included for the first time in the list of 'professional' rather than 'commercial' occupations (Census, 1921).

Given their general lack of enthusiasm for cost accounting before the War, it is ironic that the work of accountants with costing in the War played such an important part in their move towards the professional status they so desired. After the War there was a major crisis in the ICAEW. The 'old guard', who wanted to return to the way things were before the War, were faced by a group of reformists who wanted change in the internal organization of the Institute. The reformist group sought more democracy, positive action to educate more accountants in costing and efficiency matters, as well as a reduction of the obstacles to those joining the profession which took the form of the payment of premiums and the necessity of serving long articles. M. Webster Jenkinson and Gilbert Garnsey were prominent activists in this matter, and Jenkinson declared at a meeting that 'they say an army fights on its stomach; in the coming commercial struggle the British manufacturer has got to fight on his internal records' (Annual General Meeting of the ICAEW, reported in *The Accountant*, 10 May 1919). Ultimately, the reformists were fobbed off with promises of reform which came to very little. An attempt the same year to create an association of chartered and incorporated accountants with an interest in cost accounting, to be called 'The Costing Association', failed due to opposition from the two professional bodies (for more details, see Loft, 1986, Loft, 1988, ch. 5). During the interwar period, growing numbers of chartered and incorporated accountants left the profession to work in industry.[12] Regarded by the leaders of the profession as second-class members, it was not until 1945 that an accountant employed in industry was permitted to sit on the governing board of the ICAEW (Locke, 1984: 123).

### Cost clerks and cost accountancy

The importance given to cost accounting during the War had implications beyond its effects on qualified accountants. It also affected the large numbers of clerks and assistants who were involved with the processing and analysis of the figures involved.[13] Many clerks had volunteered in the early days of the War. Indeed, the 'Pals' movement was actually instigated at a crowded meeting in Liverpool on 28 August 1914, at which Lord Derby invited the clerks of the city to form their own battalion with the guarantee that those who 'joined together should serve together' (Stevenson, 1984: 50). The government soon recognized that a shortage of clerks was developing, and a government investigation was set up to look into the matter. This reported in 1915 that the number of men of military age in clerical and commercial employment was over 300,000, of which perhaps half would be available for military service (Cd 8110, 1915: 3). The report suggested that women would have to be employed, but that it should be made clear to them that the work was temporary and only for the duration of the war. Special training courses were to be set up for them of between one and three months' duration. Among the subjects covered were the 'calculation of cost of goods, trade discount and simple interest' and 'the elementary principles of double-entry book-keeping' (Cd 8110, 1915: 8–9).

The War brought change to the nature of the work which women were involved in. Previously employed largely as typists, they began, of necessity, to move into and take over jobs which previously had been the almost exclusive province of men (Walby, 1986; Zimmeck, 1988). Whilst before the War the women employed in the offices of chartered accountants were almost exclusively typists, during the War they worked as audit clerks, previously the unchallenged province of men (Kirkham and Loft, 1993). In factories they moved into jobs as cost clerks where the lower levels of clerical work came to be seen as women's work. Indeed, a manufacturer complained about a clerk who resigned his job to take a better paid one completing pay and timesheets at Woolwich Arsenal, writing that such work was 'surely women's work' (*The Times*, 22 September 1915: 9).

One of the by-products of these developments was that the newly recruited substitutes, whether women or men, learnt about accounting. At the Ministry of Munitions it was reported that whilst chartered and incorporated accountants had been recruited to direct accountancy work, the 'clerical work had necessarily to be done by those of less experience; the accountant clerks and the book-keepers of peace-time are in the trenches, but their substitutes are training on, and are becoming more efficient every day' (reported in *The Incorporated Accountants' Journal*, July 1918: 187).[14]

Immediately after the War, and building on the new visibility of cost accounting, a professional accountancy association, the Institute of Cost and Works Accountants (ICWA), was formed on 8 March 1919. The founders stated that the principal aim of the Institute was to 'provide for the business community the professional cost accountant who can be considered quite as worthy of the confidences of the business community as the legal profession and Chartered Accountants are at present' (*The Cost*

*Accountant*, December 1922: 217). They emphasized that the Institute was for cost accountants, and not for cost clerks, writing that 'as an Audit Clerk is presumably in a preliminary stage to a professional accountant, so also a Cost Clerk is in the same relation to a Cost or Works Accountant' (quoted in Loft, 1990: 103). These were strange comparisons. For the large majority of cost accountants were employees whose allegiances were to their employers, not to 'the business community'. Only small numbers (around 5 per cent) were independent cost consultants (Loft 1990: 103). As an employee, a cost accountant could scarcely take on an articled clerk in the same way that chartered accoutants took on audit clerks.

The fledgling ICWA was assisted by the support of a number of the country's leading industrialists, although this support may have been given for motives other than ones intrinsic to the advance of the costing profession. Indeed it is possible that this support was linked to a desire to see office staff become aspiring members of professions, rather than have them join clerical unions which were in their heyday.[15] Lord Leverhulme, their first President, had experienced great trouble with unionized office staff at Port Sunlight; and Herbert Austin warned them of its dangers (Loft 1990: 103). Despite their assistance, the ICWA failed to obtain a royal charter. One of the opponents was the ICAEW, who lodged a petition with the Privy Council arguing that the ICWA should not be given a charter because 'such persons are not engaged in professional work, but are employed in the service of traders' (*The Accountant*, 5 May 1923: 683).

This attempt at professionalization was linked with the increasingly bureaucratic nature of the office hierarchy. The job of the ordinary clerk declined in status over this period,[16] the rapid feminization of the lower levels of clerkdom probably helping to accelerate trends already in exis-tence. But contrary to what happened in most other occupations, where women were dismissed after the War, many women remained in clerical work (Zimmeck, 1988; Walby, 1986). The nature of office life had changed, secretarial and routine clerking work had become work for women, or to be more exact, work for young women in the period between leaving school and getting married. Comparing the 1911 and 1921 censuses, the number of male clerks was little changed, but the number of female clerks more than tripled, increasing from 18 per cent of all clerks employed to 43 per cent (Kirkham and Loft, 1993). In order to advance in the office hierarchy, paper qualifications were important for young men who aspired to jobs such as company secretary and cost accountant. As university was out of the question for the majority, and since those who went were unlikely to aspire to be a cost accountant, the way forward (for boys – girls had few chances) was to enter the accountancy office of an industrial firm as a trainee, and to take classes at evening school in their spare time.[17] Cost accounting slowly became a career possibility for boys from the lower middle class who, a generation before, would have aimed only at being a clerk.

Thus the War had an impact not only on the practice of cost accounting, but also on its organization. The status acquired by chartered and incorporated accountants, combined with the new visibility of cost accountancy, were factors leading to the setting up of a professional association for cost accountants. Although it had relatively few members in the interwar period (less than 1000), it provided a centre of expertise in the area, a centre for the creation and spreading of cost accounting knowledge by means of local meetings, national conferences and the Institute's professional journal. The War was instrumental in defining what a cost accountant was, and what the cost accountant's role in the factory was.

## Accounting, reconstruction and national efficiency

There was a general expectation that the end of the War would bring a new industrial and social order, and during the War ambitious plans were made by the State towards a vision of reconstruction. These plans went far beyond the reconversion of industry to peacetime production. They embodied a vision of a new Britain in which Capital and Labour would work in harmony towards the creation of a newly efficient British State (Johnson, 1968). By the close of the War these ideas had achieved a general acceptance. They even found favour in the pages of the orthodox economic journal *The Statist*, and it was possible to find autocratic industrialists arguing in favour of such reforms as 'democratic management' (Mowat, 1955: 21; Child, 1969: 47). This apparent *volte-face* was not unrelated to the political and social problems which loomed at the close of the War. The spectre of the Russian Revolution, the growing trade union membership, and events such as a police strike in London in mid-1918, struck fear into the heart of the Establishment (Mowat, 1955; Hyman, 1975). The vision of reconstruction was being forged in a combination of fear and hope: fear of revolution, hope that the successes of the War could be repeated on the industrial front in peacetime.

Reconstruction was to involve a new approach to management. In an official publication entitled 'Scientific Business Management', the Ministry of Reconstruction opened with the words '[t]he prosperity of an industry and every man concerned in it is intimately bound up with the efficiency of management' (Urwick and Brech, 1949, vol. 2: 101–2). The Industrial Reconstruction Council held six meetings on this subject, of which two were directly concerned with cost accounting. Under the title 'Costing in

Relation to Scientific Management', J.H. Boyd, Director of 'Costs and Efficiency Methods' at the Central Stores Department of the Ministry of Munitions, spoke of the importance of scientific management in curing industrial unrest, and illustrated how cost systems could contribute, describing them as 'the foundation on which scientific management must be built. They enter very largely into the whole structure, and finally supply the roof' (Boyd, 1919: 40). The other lecture which dealt with cost accounting was given by M. Webster Jenkinson. He discussed the importance of costing systems to the efficient use of labour, and the importance of making efficiency data available to workers, commenting that 'costs form a full scale contour map of a business ... all interested in the direction of the business must therefore, study the map in order that they pick their way along the difficult path of industrial management (Webster Jenkinson, 1919: 185).

The appearance of cost accounting as an element in this vision of the future of Britain was shared by some of the intellectual elements of the Left, the most prominent being Guild Socialist G.D.H. Cole, and Sidney Webb of the Fabian Society. Webb was author of the official programme of the Labour party, 'Labour and the New Social Order', adopted in 1918. In his vision of the future, management was to depend on the reports of 'disinterested experts'. He gave the cost expert as a specific example of this role, writing '[t]hink, for instance, what it would mean to a particular factory to receive a report from an efficient outside costing expert, and to find out exactly what each component and every process was costing' (1920: 14). Thus despite the different social ends sought by the Establishment and by the Left, the means which they expected to use had elements in common, including this explicit belief in the value of technical experts such as cost accountants.

In the year following the end of the War the country went through an unprecedented period of political and economic turbulence. But by the end of 1919 the 'cutting edge of revolution and of reconstruction alike had been blunted' (Mowat, 1955: 35). The vision of reconstruction was quickly forgotten in the economic depression of the early 1920s; and the discussion of the potential of cost accounting to solve the problems of the nation disappeared from the public arena.


### Conclusion

before the First World War costing was hardly ever thought of, it was a very rum old subject and hardly anybody bothered with it ... by the time the war ended they were all cost conscious, they'd had all this trouble during the war finding out what the costs were.[18]

At the beginning of the War Churchill had said that there would be 'business as usual'. At the end of the War he talked of the 'extraordinary improvisation without parallel in any country in the world which took place in our industrial system' (Ministry of Munitions, n.d., vol. 3, pt. 1, ch. 1: 11).

During the War, the relationship between the State and its citizens 'altered profoundly' (Middlemas 1979: 14). The mass of people became, for the first time, citizens whose lives were shaped by orders from above. Their food was limited and its quality changed by government order, their freedom of movement restricted and their conditions of work prescribed (Taylor, 1970: 25–6). There was also a fundamental change in the relationship between the State and industry. Prior to the War, there was little regulation, apart from that concerning working hours and conditions. During the War, the concept developed that the nation had a productive capacity which should be used in the most efficient way possible. In the name of this aspiration to efficiency, huge amounts of information were collected and analyzed with the aim of realizing the potential of the nation.

But the principle of free trade was deeply embedded in British society. Cost accounting came into the light as an unintended consequence of the compromise made between free trade and a command economy. As profiteering had become an important political issue, what things cost to make had emerged as a seemingly fair criterion on which to base the government's payment for war supplies. Costing apparently enabled the government to align the practices of manufacturers with the objectives of controlling war production *without* directly taking over control in individual plants. The concept appeared that this internal visibility in the enterprise could be 'pulled out' and exposed to the governmental gaze.

Accounting thus became, indirectly, a tool of regulatory intervention, a tool which helped to sustain the uneasy compromise between the principles of the free market and total government control. Accountancy contributed to the processes of governance as an 'indirect' mechanism for aligning economic conduct with socio-political objectives (Miller and Rose, 1990). In this case, the attempted alignment was between the practices of individual manufacturers, and the overall objectives of controlling war production.

The intersection between accountancy and war altered not only the practice of accountancy, but had an impact on the organization and status of accountancy work. As Hopwood writes: 'for better or for worse, it has been the accountant who has been concerned with making the abstract concept [of cost] into a concrete instrument of governance in organisations and society at large' (1990: 9). As a consequence of their involvement in government contracting, the war ministries, and other war work, the accounting profession, in the form of chartered and incorporated accountants, was brought 'prominently forward', as Ernest Cooper, a senior chartered accountant wrote (1921: 554). For the first time, professional accountants were officially recognized as a profession and appeared on the honours lists. This elevation in the status of accountancy is significant, for it foreshadows accountancy's rise to prominence in the management of British industry. Moreover, it has doubtless contributed to the financial, rather than production orientation of British management (Armstrong, 1987).

In industry, the cost accountant became more visible. An indirect consequence of this was the creation of a professional body for cost accountants, one that aimed to be like chartered accountants. In a European context, this was exceptional. In other countries the connection between engineering and costing was stronger than that between accounting and costing.

Cost accounting played a part in the vision of reconstruction which developed in the latter years of the War. It was envisaged that, released from the straightjacket of war production, manufacturers and workers would be able to strive together to recreate Britain as an efficient manufacturing nation. One of the members of the corps of experts who were to provide the efficiency data was the costing expert, providing the 'lantern which throws the limelight' on 'obstacles to production efficiency' (Webster Jenkinson, 1919: 186). Within the enterprise accounting was to provide a 'truth' about production which would enable its efficient management; and the sum of efficient enterprises would be an efficient nation. Such was the Utopian vision of accountancy that emerged during the First World War, and that, in different forms, has animated other attempts to foster efficiency in the twentieth century.

A number of different intersections between accounting and war have been discussed in this chapter. What is illustrated above all else is that accounting is more than a purely technical matter outside the realm of the social, for the techniques and practice of accountancy are fundamentally bound up with social and organizational change. By examining accounting in a society under enormous stress, namely Britain in the First World War, it is possible to reveal some of these linkages and to indicate the multiple origins of accounting.[19] In particular, the social status and aspirations of its practitioners have been shown to be intrinsically linked to the practice of accountancy within organizations. The development of accounting cannot be separated from the fortunes of the occupational groups who carry out its work, and who 'market' its techniques.

NOTES

1. For example the expansion in scope and amount of taxation.
2. This section is based on Loft (1988: ch. 3).
3. In 1908 it changed its name to the Society of Incorporated Accountants and Auditors (SIAA).
4. However, some 'special relationships' had been entered into with producers of specialized armaments, for which there was no general market (Trebilcock, 1966: 365–7).
5. The DORA regulations concerning pricing also applied to the purchases of the Admiralty (who dealt with their own munitions purchases, as well as those of ships and other naval accessories), and the War Office which supplied the army with everything other than munitions. These also had their teams of cost investigators.
6. These developments apply mainly to larger factories, in smaller ones (which were often family-run) organization still tended to be a matter of 'rule of thumb', likewise costing.
7. It is notable that during the war lectures in cost accounting were introduced into the curriculum at the London School of Economics (LSE), one of the foremost institutions for the study of commerce (Dev, 1980: 4). However one student complained that these lectures, given by Professor Dicksee, were intended for students working for a university degree, and were 'purely theoretical'; he wanted to know where he could obtain 'practical instruction' for it seemed that 'neither factory costing or scientific management are taught anywhere in London' (*The Accountant*, 19 May 1917: 482).
8. A sophisticated system of costing was developed for the National Shell Factories 'which should yield for each process of shell manufacture a statement of the output, its cost in material, wages and establishment charges, and the extent to which each of these items was affected by faulty workmanship' (Ministry of Munitions, n.d., vol. 3, pt. 2, ch. 1: 12–13).
9. This refers only to men of course, women could not practise as chartered or incorporated accountants because they were barred from both the ICAEW and the SIAA (and the Scottish associations) until the end of the war (see Kirkham and Loft, 1993).
10. It is unlikely that the general public understood the necessity for accountants. I noted a reference to 'Accountant Cuthberts' (Siday, 1919), 'Cuthbert' being a slang word for a government employee or officer shirking military service (Partridge, 1937).
11. It is unlikely that they knew much about cost accounting when they began the job; Miles Taylor, a chartered accountant who had learned about such matters in the US, asked 'how many men at the Admiralty, War Office, Ministry of Munitions – or the Coal Controllers! knew the first thing about it?' (reported in *The Accountant*, 5 April 1919: 277).
12. This process was to have important effects on British industry, for many of them ultimately obtained positions of authority such as that of finance director (see Armstrong, 1987).
13. This, it must be recalled, was an era when most records were kept and processed by hand. Machinery to process such records was in its infancy, although was

quickly being taken up by larger firms (the 'Office Machinery Association' presided over by Professor Dicksee of the London School of Economics was vigorously encouraging its use by manufacturers).

14. For instance, at the Admiralty Costs Investigations Department 69 qualified accountants were assisted by 78 assistant accountants, 47 clerical staff and 103 recorders (117, HC. Deb 5s, Cols. 937–8).

15. In general union activity and membership reached a peak in the immediate postwar period; and apart from the year of the General Strike, 1921 marked the highest number ever of days lost due to stoppages (Pelling, 1976).

16. In 1911 clerks were placed in the highest social class (Class 1) (although at this time evidence suggests that their status was declining rapidly); by 1921 they had fallen to Class 2 and by 1931 to Class 3 (there were 5 classes in all) (Hakim, 1980: 566).

17. Some insight into life for cost accountants and clerks at this period is given in interviews with some of the (then) young men who became members of the ICWA in the 1920s (published in Loft, 1990).

18. Ernest Laidler FCWA, talking about his experiences as a trainee cost accountant in the 1920s with Armstrong Whitworth & Co. (Ironfounders) Ltd (quote from interview with author in 1984; see Loft, 1990: 131–5).

19. It is interesting to compare the intersection of accounting and war in Britain with that in Germany, where the government did not attempt to use cost accounting to regulate industry as in Britain; however accounting and accountants were brought to the public's attention through scandals over profiteering (Gallhofer and Haslam, 1991).

REFERENCES

Adams, R.J.Q., 1978. *Arms and the Wizard: Lloyd George and the Ministry of Munitions 1915–1916*, London: Cassell

Addison, C., 1934. *Four and a Half Years: A Personal Diary from June 1914 to January 1919*, London: Hutchinson

Armstrong, P., 1987. 'The Rise of Accounting Controls in British Capitalist Enterprises', *Accounting, Organizations and Society* 12(5): 415–36

Boyd, J.H., 1919. 'Costing in Relation to Scientific Management', address to the Industrial Reconstruction Council, 1919, reproduced in *The Accountant*, 12 July: 33–40

Child, J., 1969. *British Management Thought*, Hemel Hempstead: George Allen & Unwin

Cole, G.D.H., 1917. 'Scientific Management', in G.D.H. Cole (ed.), *Some Problems of Urban and Rural Industry*, Oxford: Ruskin College

Cooper, E., 1921. '57 Years in an Accountants Office', *The Accountant*, 22 October: 553–63

Dev, S., 1980. 'Accounting and the LSE tradition', London: London School of Economics

Elbourne, E.T., 1914. *Factory Administration and Accounts*, London: Longmans

Gallhofer, S. and Haslam, J., 1991. 'The Aura of Accounting in the Context of a Crisis: Germany and the First World War', *Accounting, Organizations and Society* 16(5/6): 487–520

Garrett, A.A., 1961. *History of the Society of Incorporated Accountants 1885–1957*, Oxford: Oxford University Press

Hakim, C., 1980. 'Census Reports as Documentary Evidence: The Census Commentaries 1801–1851', *Sociological Review* 28(3): 551–80

Hannah, L., 1983. *The Rise of the Corporate Economy*, 2nd edn, London: Methuen

Hobsbawm, E.J., 1969. *Industry and Empire*, Harmondsworth: Pelican

Hopwood, A.G., 1990. 'Accounting and Organisation Change', *Accounting, Auditing & Accountability Journal* 3(1): 7–17

Hyman, R., 1975. 'Foreword', in R. Hyman, *The Frontier of Control*, London: Pluto Press: vii–xli

Johnson, P.B., 1968. *Land Fit for Heroes: The Planning of British Reconstruction 1916–1919*, Chicago, University of Chicago Press

Kirkham, L.M. and Loft, A., 1993. 'Gender and the Construction of the Professional Accountant', *Accounting, Organizations and Society* 18(6): 507–58

Littler, C.R., 1982. *The Development of the Labour Process in Capitalist Societies*, London: Heinemann

Lloyd, E.M.H., 1924. *Experiments in State Control at the War Office and the Ministry of Food*, Oxford, Clarendon Press

Locke, R., 1984. *The End of Practical Man*, Greenwich, CT: Jai Press

Loft, A., 1986. 'Towards a Critical Understanding of Accounting: The Case of Cost Accounting in the UK, 1914–1925', *Accounting, Organizations and Society* 11(2): 137–69

  1988. *Understanding Accounting in its Social and Historical Context: The Case of Cost Accounting in Britain 1914–1925*, New York: Garland

  1990. *Coming into the Light: A Study of the Development of a Professional Association for Cost Accountants in Britain in the Wake of the First World War*, London: CIMA

Marriner, S., 1980. 'The Ministry of Munitions 1915–1919 and the Government Accounting Procedures', *Accounting and Business Research* 10(37A): 130–42

Middlemas, K., 1979. *Politics in Industrial Society. The Experience of the British System since 1911*, London: André Deutsch

Miller, P. and O'Leary, T., 1987. 'Accounting and the Construction of the Governable Person', *Accounting, Organizations and Society* 12(3): 235–65

Miller, P. and Rose, N., 1990. 'Governing Economic Life', *Economy and Society* 9(1): 1–31

Ministry of Munitions, n.d. unpublished official history, 8 vols., British Library reference BS28/12

Mowat, C.L., 1955. *Britain Between the Wars, 1918–1940*, London: Methuen

Partridge, E., 1937. *Dictionary of Slang and Unconventional Language*, Henley: George Routledge

Pelling, H., 1976. *A History of British Trade Unionism*, 3rd edn, Harmondsworth: Penguin

Pigou, A.C., 1947. *Aspects of British Economic History, 1918–1925*, London: Macmillan

Pollard, S., 1962. *The Genesis of Modern Management*, Harmondsworth: Penguin

Siday, G.A., 1919. *Profiteering: In Relation to Cost Accounting. A 20th Century Hoax*, London: E.J. Larby

Solomons, D., 1952. 'The Historical Development of Costing', in D. Solomons (ed.), *Studies in Cost Analysis*, 2nd edn, 1968, London: Sweet & Maxwell: 1–52

Stevenson, J., 1984. *British Society 1914–45*, London: Allen Lane

Taylor, A.J.P., 1970. *English History 1914–1945*, Harmondsworth: Pelican

Trebilcock, R.C., 1966. 'A "Special Relationship" – Government, Rearmament, and the Cordite Firms', *Economic History Review* 19(2): 364–79

Urwick, L. and Brech, E.F.L., 1949. *The Making of Scientific Management*, 2 vols., London: Management Publications Trust, 1940

Walby, S., 1986. *Patriarchy at Work: Patriarchal and Capitalist Relations in Employment*, Cambridge: Polity Press

Webb, S., 1920. *The Root Cause of Labour Unrest: An Address to Employers and Managers*, Fabian Tract 196, London, Fabian Society

Webster Jenkinson, M., 1919. 'The Worker's Interest in Costing (A Factor of Industrial Reconstruction)', address to the Industrial Reconstruction Council; reproduced in *The Accountant*, 8 March: 185–95

Zimmeck, M., 1988. '"Get Out and Get Under": The Impact of Demobilisation on the Civil Service, 1919–32', in G. Andersen (ed.), *The White-blouse Revolution: Female Office Workers since 1870*, Manchester: Manchester University Press

# 6 Accounting and labour: integrations and disintegrations

*Philip Bougen*

Accounting has been viewed as being essentially constructive. Central to this role is its capacity to integrate organizational activities, processes and resources. By establishing plans, measurements and controls, an organizational world is constructed of technical coherencies and integrations. One target for these calculations is labour. By making labour aware of organizational goals and standards, and then by coupling technical surveillance with appropriate inducements, accounting seeks to make labour more physically productive. These technical integrations generate tangible consequences for labour. They specify what is physically required of labour, and assist in the determination of appropriate financial rewards. Although accounting produces other more complex phenomena, as a cautionary observation, labour can associate accounting methods with physical exertion, compensation levels, work procedures and job security.

Other constructive aspects of accounting also have been explored. The basis of this perspective was that this collection of seemingly innocuous techniques possessed enabling and facilitative properties which exceeded the objective of mere technical integrations. Again, the theme was one of constructive accounting integrations, with labour again a target for their application and with enhanced labour productivity still an objective. However, the integrations now were more than mere technical solutions to technical requirements. Instead, it was accounting's integrations with other managerial control methods which were considered significant. More specifically, attention was directed towards accounting's contribution to the establishment of various managerial 'regimes of truth' (Foucault, 1980). Regimes of truth can be considered as amalgamations of assorted rules, measurements, discourses and philosophies employed by management to render labour more responsible to the application of technical integrations and controls. One means of achieving this objective is by management convincing labour of the scientific foundations and necessities (Hopwood, 1987) of these integrations and controls. By contributing to the production of partial and partisan realities and facts (Burchell *et al.*, 1980; Loft, 1986; Meyer, 1986; Ogden and Bougen, 1985), accounting can be tactically mobilized by management to legitimize their prerogatives. Accounting was now viewed as being more subtly implicated in the conduct of organizational power relationships, helping to maintain the relative subordinated position of labour within organizations (Miller and O'Leary, 1987).

If accounting has been viewed as being essentially constructive, accounting has also conceptualized labour as being essentially destructive. The underlying thesis of this perspective was that the productive capacities of accounting integrations could be jeopardized by the destructive predispositions of labour. As regards accounting's technical integrations, it has been argued for some time (Caplan, 1966) that accounting control methods were based upon a set of assumptions which adopted a narrow and pessimistic view of the contribution of labour to organizational functioning. Labour was considered to be lazy, ignorant and wasteful, only entering into the scope of accounting concerns when their reactions to technical accounting procedures threatened to jeopardize the successful managerial accomplishment of organizational goals. As such, these reactions were carefully labelled as the behavioural consequences of necessary technical imperatives and managerial actions. Consequently, they could be attributed to either imperfectly designed and explained accounting techniques, or to pathological labour behaviour. From either perspective they remained a technical issue. This analysis was clearly underpinned by the belief that labour should not be allowed to disrupt the assumed smooth flow of the injection, operation and progression of technical accounting integrations.

As regards labour's interaction with managerial regimes of truth, much less has been explicitly stated. Managerial regimes of truth are often premised upon silences and exclusions, with the productive capabilities of such regimes being linked to their capacity to demonstrate that certain organizational arrangements are beyond contention. By presenting itself as merely a technical apparatus (Hopwood, 1985), accounting contributes to this perception. The claims of accounting to provide technical integrations between organizational goals, performance, and measurements creates an organizational reality based upon supposed technical coherencies. It also helps to ensure that organizational events are framed and evaluated solely upon technical criteria. This adoption of a profile of technical substance, coherence and purpose offers accounting the capacity to erect barriers around itself, effectively silencing labour voices. Little is heard of labour experiences and judgements of accounting systems. The exploration and accumulation of local labour experiences with the consequences of accounting systems rarely enter the research agenda. Consequently, labour voices are left unheard, and stories are left untold about the connections between accounting numbers and physical exertion, compensation levels, work procedures and job security. The knowledges and evaluations that labour has of these relationships are thus marginalized and prevented from disrupting the assumed smooth flow, and self-evident desirability, of accounting's constructive capacities.

This chapter will critically examine some of the issues relating to this constructive–destructive classification. More particularly, it considers how, and with what effects, accounting can become implicated with destructive and disintegrative organizational processes. This requires that the constructive contributions and capacities of labour be considered. The constructive aspects of labour can be examined from two perspectives. At one level, labour makes physical contributions to output, profitability and company survival. As with the physical effects of accounting systems upon labour, these should not be underestimated. Equally significant, however, is the existence of labour's own regimes of truths: the productive capacities of their own knowledges, discourses and philosophies. Labour can accumulate and assemble its own experiences and perceptions of the interactions between accounting and various organizational activities. The accumulation and assembling of its own experiences and perceptions of organizational life can produce a critical awareness of its position within workplace power arrangements and relationships. Such an exercise offers labour the opportunity to compare and contrast its own regimes of truth with those of management, particularly as regards the relative integrity and status of the knowledges underpinning them. These comparisons can be of assistance to labour by enhancing its understanding of the mechanisms and processes by which its relative position within workplace power arrangements is formulated and maintained. This suggests that if one was to examine the distinct though overlapping arenas in which accounting and labour interact within organizations, opportunities should exist to observe and evaluate the parallel processes of simultaneous productive and destructive relationships.

Historical case study evidence – based on the profit sharing scheme at the Renold Company – will be used in the analysis to explore these issues. Three related themes are emphasized.

First, the case study illustrates some of the obvious deficiencies in our knowledge of accounting and labour. It examines how and why accounting became integrated with some of the substantive and tangible issues important to labour. It shows how labour experienced the effects of accounting methods and calculations on wage levels, bonus payments, increased managerial surveillance and control, changes in work practices and redundancies. Accounting produced real physical consequences for labour at its operational points of impact. It also contributed to the production of increased labour effort and output. This allowed the organization to survive and ultimately to report record profitability. Labour was also productive in this relationship. It was the physical efforts and sacrifices of labour which allowed the achievement of these organizational goals. This theme, therefore, is one of *constructive integrations*.

Secondly, one can see the Renold case as an analysis of management–labour relationships. Once again, accounting is involved in this process, but now in a more complex and contingent manner. Its association with various discourses, rules, philosophies and imperatives informs these processes of industrial interaction. The case study illustrates one company's experiences over a substantial period of time in the evolution and operation of a particular managerial regime of truth. Labour was its intended target, with accounting calculations and procedures being placed as pivotal components of its intended application. Accounting became entangled in a web of heterogeneous elements: the practices and rules of scientific management; a managerial philosophy of paternalism; the dictates of financial markets; managerial discourses of business science; notions of common sense; joint consultation dialogues; and a scheme of profit sharing. The issues at stake here are the more problematic, although equally important, ones of power, legitimacy and trust. Accounting, and its association with this regime of truth, can be shown to have both constructive and destructive capacities. It assisted in the production of managerial power and legitimacy. It also contributed to their destruction.

Labour also had access to its own regimes of truth. Again, a heterogeneous assembly of elements was involved. There was labour's own first-hand knowledge of factory activities and changes in work methods. Labour adopted at certain times discourses of conciliation, and at other times revolutionary concepts of ideologies and class, exploitation and deception. Trade union institutions operated simultaneously with managerially inspired joint consultation committees. Accounting was implicated in all of these arenas. Accounting numbers and descriptions contributed to an enhanced labour confidence in the legitimacy of its own regimes of truth. It was also the destructive properties of accounting numbers which motivated management to limit the opportunities for labour to voice their opinions and experiences. The theme here is one of *constructive and destructive integrations and disintegrations*.

Thirdly, the Renold case illustrates some of the limits and boundaries as regards the constructive and destructive characteristics of accounting. It considers some of the dividing lines between what accounting is able to do, and what it cannot do; its legitimacies and illegitimacies; and its continuities and discontinuities. In particular it examines *clashes* of truths, of knowledges and of experiences, and their effect upon relationships. The case study material, by dealing with a substantial period of time, captures some of the dynamics and consequences of the clashes between the managerial and labour regimes of truth. One can assess the limits and boundaries, and the contexts and antecedents of managerial and labour evaluations of their respective regimes of truth. This notion of the dynamics of accounting and labour being both constructive and destructive, and existing in an integrative and disintegrative relationship constitutes the third theme. This theme is one of *fragility*.

The detail and dynamics of these three aspects of accounting's constructive–destructive capacities will now be considered.

### The Renold profit sharing scheme

In 1921, the Hans Renold company of Manchester, UK, introduced a profit sharing scheme which operated for a 10-year period. The scheme was conceived and designed as a vehicle for the interweaving and anticipated resolution of a number of urgent managerial issues. The company's competitive position had deteriorated with declines in market share and reductions in selling prices. In 1919 it had made a net loss of £3000 on the year's trading (Tripp, 1956: 119), the first such occurrence in its history. Furthermore, in the post First World War period the disruptive effects of the War had also to be addressed. During the War, 99 per cent of all output was on munitions contracts. The company was confronted therefore by the need to introduce new products, technologies and work practices into the factory (Tripp, 1956: 104). The War had also seen other developments within the factory with increases in the number of new employees and deteriorating 'mutual confidence' between management and labour (Renold, 1950: 17). This had led in 1917 to the trade unionization of the factory, which was consistent with national trends of an increase in socialist organization and in trade union growth and militancy (Hinton, 1973). A means of avoiding 'a general break down of works morale' (Renold, 1950: 18) was required. The profit sharing scheme and its various associations and connections had a strategic function to produce managerial solutions to these problems. By its interactions with various direct control methods, the scheme was designed to render labour more physically productive. The scheme was also a pivotal component of a more elaborate managerial regime of truth, intended to justify and explain both this and other anticipated constructive integrations.

Although the War and the instabilities of its aftermath triggered the need for urgent action, the roots of the profit sharing scheme had no single point of origin. The scheme blended scientific management, accounting, employee education and managerial paternalism in a pragmatic and idiosyncratic manner. There was no continuity of intent, such that the scheme was the outcome of a singular and inevitable series of events. However, key antecedents can nonetheless be identified. An organizational infrastructure and culture existed which influenced the decision to introduce the scheme, helped to shape its content, and impacted upon its progressions and regressions. The scheme can be viewed, therefore, as the focal point of a particular managerial regime of truth, one consisting of a complex ensemble of managerial methods of controlling labour, each having its own history and trajectory within the company.

### An emerging regime of truth

The company was founded in 1879 by Hans Renold, a Swiss engineer. He was first and foremost a trained and highly competent mechanical engineer to whom quality and efficient workmanship were critical. Hans Renold was a disciple of the principles of scientific management and, along with his son C.G. Renold, created 'a generation ahead of its time ... a truly outstanding illustration of British scientific management in practice' (Urwick and Brech, 1946: 169). Standardized information flows, organization charts and merit rating had all been established prior to the War, contributing to remarkable improvements in the profitability and financial strength of the company from 1903 to 1919 (Tripp, 1956).

The productive contributions of labour within the factory to these achievements were also considerable. Work methods had been substantially changed; unskilled labour had replaced skilled; and a payments by results scheme had been implemented (Ministry of Munitions, 1922, vol.4, pt.1: 33–4; Bougen, 1988). Operating in parallel to the principles of scientific management was a comprehensive cost accounting system. The company had commenced 'with one machine man and his boy, and a bookkeeper' (Tripp, 1956: 125), significant in that when confronted by a whole number of start-up problems the keeping of accounting records was considered of prime importance. In 1900 a 'scheme of costing' was introduced which 'would be considered modern even today' (Renold, 1950: 13), and by 1914 a cost manager had been employed (Tripp, 1956: 162). This early commitment to cost accounting was untypical of much of British manufacturing industry which introduced cost accounting later, as a direct consequence of government intervention during the First World War (Armstrong, 1987; Loft, 1986). In the Renold Company, the integrations of accounting with other technical control methods centred on the physical productivity of labour within the factory.

A further productive element also existed within the factory. Although less direct and tangible as a method of control, the managerial style and the cultural climate Hans and C.G. Renold sought to create were also significant. At one level, this consisted of a series of benevolent paternalistic gestures by management towards labour. These ranged from canteen facilities, health services, and a pleasant physical work environment to a shorter working week and higher than district average wage rates. Management viewed these as contributing to labour loyalty, trust and low labour turnover (Bougen, 1988: 14). However, these measures were components of a much wider-ranging and complex managerial philosophy and tactic of control. In a number of contexts C.G. Renold (1917, 1921, 1927, 1928, 1929a, 1929b, 1950) explored the intellectual and practical rationale of constructing a comprehensive theory for the management of labour. A critical theme was that the productive elements of labour could be enhanced by paying attention to what was viewed as its destructive tendencies. A number of interlocking elements constituted the philosophical and ideological basis for what was an emerging managerial regime of truth. However, its components were not radical departures from previous managerial concerns, but instead tapped into the technical and cultural infrastructure evident in the company's past.

C.G. Renold believed that the acceptance by labour of the managerial prerogative to determine workshop relationships could not be taken for granted, since 'the work of very many men, probably of most is given more or less unwillingly' (Renold, 1921: 210). In particular, it was in the workshop where the employee 'meets and resents the *arbitrary* exercise of authority' (Renold, 1921: 209) that such problems were most manifest. It was there that 'the workers are irritated beyond measure by the inefficiency and blundering in *organization and management* which they detect on every side' (Renold, 1917: 161–2, emphasis is added in all cases).

C.G. Renold's concern with labour unease about the basis of managerial prerogatives led him to consider some 'devolution of management' (Renold, 1929a: 10). This he envisaged as the introduction into workplace relations of various joint consultative bodies whereby the physical meeting of management and labour would offer management the opportunity to construct and to explain the new basis for authority which concerned him. 'It is indeed, a positive duty on the part of every employer . . . to seize every opportunity to discuss management and business problems with his workpeople . . . greater knowledge, on the part of the workers, of the actual problems of industry is the best hope of the future' (Renold, 1921: 211).

This 'greater knowledge' would consist of management 'Tell[ing] them what it is all about, what the problem is, and how you are seeking to tackle it' (Renold, 1927: 24). More critically, C.G. Renold recognized the possibility of coupling profit sharing (with its financial inducement to labour to participate in discussions) with the education of labour (1921: 233):

A generous scheme of profit-sharing would be of great help in this connection. One of the difficulties of giving the kind of information necessary under this head is that the worker so often does not really believe that efficiency in industry is his affair ... A profit-sharing scheme, therefore, which made successful administration a direct and living issue to workers no less than to management and shareholders, would make the giving of full information about the progress of a business much easier. Under such a scheme full accounts of the manufacturing activities of the business could quite well be laid before a committee of workers ... Under such circumstances, business and management problems could be discussed with the very greatest freedom.

Not only would profit sharing, therefore, make employee education a more relevant exercise for labour, but it would also facilitate the disclosure of accounting information. The notion of employee education, whilst being presented as a neutral and mutually beneficial process, carried with it an assumption that not only would management be the educators but that the curriculum would be based on managerial priorities and perspectives. It was also to be underpinned by the technical methods of scientific management and accounting as the basis for the managerial control of labour. There would, therefore, be the resort to management by 'facts' (Renold, 1929a: 764–9):

Scientific management finds perhaps its culminating expression in the work of the Financial Controller, or in the Cost Accounting Section of the Finance Department ... They aim at laying down beforehand what is expected, based on a study of all the relative facts.

More critically (1929a: 767), this was perceived as being compatible with themes of industrial democracy:

It may be pointed out that there is nothing incompatible between scientific management and the development of schemes of 'Industrial Democracy' ... Indeed the more management can be based on ascertained facts and follow predetermined procedures the more possible it is to take the workers into consultation.

C.G. Renold had, therefore, created a basis for managerial prerogative, one that could be integrated with his existing interest in joint consultation and profit sharing. The disciplines of scientific management and cost accounting were to provide the intellectual and operational foundation for this endeavour.

There existed now both the philosophical basis and the vehicle for the introduction of the Renold regime of truth. Its intended target was labour, and its goal was to make labour more productive. It was anticipated that this would be achieved by both the direct application of formal controls, and by the legitimation of these methods via the interconnected process of labour education and the financial inducements of a profit sharing scheme.

Underlying these individual policies was a theme of anticipated constructive integrations, and of a managerial regime of truth in which at least some of these connections would be made visible to labour and subjected to discussion. The anticipated inclusion of labour within the consultative process was envisaged by management to possess constructive potentialities. The inclusions, however, were tactical in nature, since the agenda underpinning them was a product of managerial design. The possibility of potentially destructive consequences from the process was clearly not anticipated by management. More particularly, management had not anticipated that labour would bring with them an agenda and a philosophy based upon their own personal experiences and knowledges, and that these would provide a basis for evaluating management's projected constructive integrations. In other words, labour regimes of truth existed in parallel to, and often in conflict with, those of management.

### Operationalizing the managerial regime of truth

A profit sharing committee comprising management and employee representatives was established in June 1920 to explore, for a six-month period, the basis for the scheme's introduction. The scheme commenced in January 1921 and operated until the end of the decade. Although profit sharing does not require a formal management–labour body to monitor its performance, the committee was to continue in existence throughout the life of the scheme. It was explicitly designed by management as an arena for the articulation and reinforcement of their particular regime of truth. The formally recorded minutes of these monthly committee meetings provide important insights into the dynamics and clashes of truths, knowledges and experiences.

Profit sharing conceptualizes the organization as an amalgamation of shared values and priorities, and envisages that any disagreements between organizational interests can be accommodated and ultimately absorbed by the search for financial gain and by the division of any such gains. The Renold scheme explicitly adopted this focus, with the labour representatives being asked to view the organization as a coalition of capital, staff and labour (Committee Minutes – henceforth CM – July 1920). This was more than a statement of ideological intent, since it was also to constitute the operational mechanics for the determination of distributable financial rewards under the scheme. Thus it integrated the scheme's technical calculations with the underlying managerial philosophy. C.G. Renold argued that such a scheme could only operate by deciding: 'What were the main interests concerned in industry ... the general nature of the services rendered by each ... and the payment of those services' (CM, 19 July 1920).

Table 6.1. *Organizational relationships and profit sharing*

| Outgoings | Income |
|---|---|
| *Raw materials* | Sales |
| *Wages & salaries* | × |
| *Other expenses* | Selling prices |
| Minimum payment for the use of capital | |
| *Wages of capital* | |
| *Total expenses* | *Total income* |
| Surplus to be divided between | |
|   (I) Capital | |
|   (II) Staff | |
|   (III) Labour | |

Since such questions strike at the very roots of organizational relationships, many conceptualizations of the issues were available. C.G. Renold's answer was to present the scheme illustrated in table 6.1.

The choice of an accounting income statement, raising problems as it does of the selection, definition and measurement of items to be included, might not appear the most obvious framework for analysis. However, it had the effect of injecting accounting issues into the arena from the start. C.G. Renold proceeded to explain the scheme's format (CM, 19 July 1920):

the income of the business depended on the quantity of goods sold multiplied by the price. Price, therefore, was an essential factor. That was the first point to be noted in the scheme.

The selling price of the product, which parenthetically one might observe was beyond the control of labour, was therefore central to the scheme. There had also been introduced a somewhat unusual item, termed the 'Wages of Capital' which had been categorized alongside more conventional factory expenses. As regards the 'Wages of Capital' (CM, 19 July 1920):

Which had been included as an expense was really nothing more than a sufficient return to attract enough Capital ... if a business were to continue ... it must be able to pay the 'Wages of Capital' just as it must be able to pay the Wages of Labour. That is to say, the 'Wages of Capital' were in the nature of an expense, not a surplus.

The 'wages of capital', therefore, were to be viewed, and indeed were to be accounted for, as analogous to the wages paid to labour, being expenses of

Table 6.2. *The calculation of a profit sharing surplus (CM, 19 July 1920)*

| Outgoings | Income |
|---|---|
| 1. Manufacturing:<br>   Raw materials<br>   Wages & salaries<br>   Other expenses | Works output<br>×<br>Standard works cost |
| *Surplus*<br>2. Other expenses | Works output<br>×<br>Standard admin. cost |
| *Surplus*<br>3. Wages of capital | Works output<br>×<br>Capital allowance |
| 4. Selling:<br>   Wages & salaries<br>   Other expenses | Sales<br>×<br>Standard selling cost |
| *Surplus*<br>Total expenses | Total income =<br>Sales<br>×<br>Selling price |
| *Total surplus* | |

the period rather than appropriations of profit, reinforcing the assumed equivalency between labour and capital. C.G. Renold then clarified how the distributable profit sharing surplus was to be computed: 'some way had to be found of measuring the activities of *each section* of the organization by itself, namely, a price for its work of service . . ., that is to say, the "selling price" must be divided up into parts attributable to the various sections of the business or groups of expenses, thus giving a *standard cost* of each' (CM, 19 July 1920).

The tabulation used to describe the key relationships is illustrated in table 6.2. Once again, accounting classifications were given a high profile in the scheme's underlying structures, with table 6.2 making it clear that there was to be a coupling of accounting controls and profit sharing. This disaggregation of the company into 'sections', and the introduction of standard costs, ensured that the operational mechanics of the scheme were intertwined with the planning and appraisal of sub-unit performance.

The committee was also informed that the scheme's foundations were *'not guesswork but founded on facts and figures'* (CM, 4 August 1920), whereby actual costs could be compared against standard and where 'If the former were less than the latter a surplus would be manifest, a definite proportion of which would be divided' (CM, 4 August 1920).

The calculative procedures of the scheme were reinforced by additional administrative rules. Whilst the committee had no executive powers, 'it would be given freedom of discussion and criticism of anything appertaining to the success of the business' (CM, 14 October 1920), since (CM, 15 November 1920):

the Directors must safeguard the position that they could go to the public for money ... which would not be the case if the Directors had devolved their powers of control to a committee of employees.

Resort to the imperatives of the financial markets as a basis for policy was compounded by the argument that the 'wages of capital' could be justified by *'financial experts* [who] held the view which could be well substantiated that it was practically impossible to get people to lend their money at a fixed rate' (CM, 19 July 1920). By this stage, therefore, the contribution of the scheme to the establishment of a managerial regime of truth was becoming entangled with a discourse conveying more general meanings and priorities for management–labour relationships. Themes of 'facts and figures', 'going to the public for money'; and 'financial experts' had already been introduced. Furthermore, when C.G. Renold addressed a mass meeting of employees to explain the scheme, they were told that they were to receive: 'a first hand knowledge of business problems ... a conviction that you are getting a square deal ... [and] increased earnings when there is a surplus'.

Labour was expected to be physically productive within this scenario (CM, 18 December 1920), since:

unfortunately ... this scheme is being launched just at a time when trade is bad and likely to get worse ... [but] ... what the workers can do is, by reducing costs, enable us to reduce our prices to such a level that the employment in the works may be kept up to the present level.

The strands of the regime of truth were now becoming more complex and contingent. Coalitions of interests, financial bonuses, and cost control systems had now become intertwined with other anticipated productive themes. Employee education, business problems, external market constraints, price reductions, and the safeguarding of employment had all been introduced as relevant issues within the profit sharing scheme. However, this seemingly heterogeneous mixture of elements had strategic managerial purposes. The profit sharing scheme was intended to serve as a vehicle for assorted anticipated productive integrations. Labour was to be the target for both increased technical control and the targeted recipient of an educational process designed to legitimate these controls and other managerially-determined organizational relationships. As a key component of the profit sharing scheme, accounting was to be injected as an anticipated constructive element in both processes.

However, if management had brought to the committee their own anticipated agenda and regime of truth, so too had labour. The nature and evolution of this labour regime of truth, and its subsequent clashes with managerial priorities, became more evident as the scheme progressed. However, from the very outset labour brought with them an amalgamation of concerns, discourses and knowledges. One of the roots of the scheme lay in the trade unionization of the workforce and the more general expression of national radical labour sentiments. There existed a perceived managerial need to dilute some of the associated local pressures. Throughout the existence of the profit sharing committee there operated a parallel trade union based arena for management–labour meetings. Some of the labour representatives attended both forums (Bougen, 1988). Management clearly saw their relationship with the trade union as being a matter of negotiation, whilst the profit sharing committee was intended to be consultative in nature. As C.G. Renold (1950: iii) argued, 'Negotiations implies that there are *divergent* interests to be reconciled. Consultation implies a basis of *common* interest in ... enterprise'. This existence of dual mechanisms created an immediate tension. It offered the potentially productive prospect of financial rewards by participation in the scheme, but with a recognition that this should not dilute or even destroy the integrity of their bargaining position with management in other arenas.

This theme of the productive and destructive capacities of the scheme for labour is of significance for what was subsequently to transpire. In initial meetings of the profit sharing committee, the labour representatives assailed management with a whole series of wide-ranging questions and observations (CM, 19 July 1920, 20 September 1920: Bougen, 1988: 89–90):

What was the Capital which was to be entitled to the minimum return spoken of? ...
Establishment charges were too high relative to producing wages ...
Why should Capital have any share of the surplus at all? ...
Would past profits have been sufficient to pay a bonus? ...
What happens if the selling price falls? ...
Why allow the shareholders the chance to share in excess profits?

These statements clearly indicate that labour brought to the arena their past experiences as well as their current concerns with organizational relationships: some antecedents of their own regime of truth. However, the scheme offered labour more than the opportunity for its mere articulation. It also offered the constructive and destructive possibilities of laying it alongside the managerial regime of truth. C.G. Renold had designed the committee as an explicit forum for the making visible of what he saw as a series of singular, continuous and legitimate facts, knowledges and truths. Labour had brought with them their own regime of truth. Evaluations and judgements of truth or falsehood, legitimacy or illegitimacy, continuity or discontinuity, whilst impossible within a contextual vacuum, now became possible. As the scheme and the committee meetings unfolded and developed, the accumulation of past arguments, of what was claimed to govern a position or a statement, and of associated personal and local knowledges and experiences, created the environment for subsequent clashes of truths and the exposure of their relative validities.

### Some physical consequences of the scheme

With its clear emphasis on cost reductions, coupled with associated changes in work methods and technology, the mechanics of the scheme generated numerous tangible consequences. Over the period 1913–28, output per employee increased by 'nearly two and a half times' (Renold, 1928). Furthermore, when directly questioned by labour in one of the meetings as to the scheme's contribution towards this, a management representative commented that '*he had no doubt whatsoever* that it had considerable effect' (CM, 4 October 1921). One labour representative directly linked the scheme with the increased application of formal controls and organizational change (CM, 3 November 1924):

From the production point of view it had been an unqualified success, . . . it gave the management the opportunity of studying operations and setting schedules.

The scheme contributed to the introduction of increased accounting controls within the factory. In 1929, by which time the profit sharing scheme had been operating for nine years, C.G. Renold gave a detailed description of the company's accounting control system, defining it as 'one which has been under development *for the past ten years*' (Renold, 1929b: 1). The system contained many similarities to the data requirements and accounts of the profit sharing scheme. Cost classifications, account headings, the basis of responsibility allocation, time period of feedback, and the process of budgetary review were identical for both. The scheme also contributed to the improved financial performance of the company. The company went from making a loss at the scheme's inception, to the earning of record profits when it was terminated. The company also survived a severe national economic recession, characterized by massive declines in industrial production, real income and employment (Aldcroft, 1970).

Critical to this survival were the reduced selling prices of the company's products financed by the increased output and cost efficiencies contributed by labour (Bougen, 1988). The relationship between increased efficiency and the amount and method of rewarding labour for its productive contributions, were issues of recurring significance. The scheme generated some profit sharing bonuses for labour, particularly in the very early and in the latter stages of its existence. However, throughout the life of the scheme, these payments were considered by labour as too infrequent and too insufficient a reward for their efforts (CM, 3 November 1924) in that:

while they had undoubtedly cooperated as far as production was concerned, they had received next to nothing in the financial benefits derived from that production.

Indeed, at one stage the scheme was described by labour within the committee as approaching '*exploitation or rate-cutting*' (CM, 16 January 1925). Labour's persistent concern with the shortage of bonus payments was no doubt compounded by the fact that in 1926 the mechanics of the scheme were unilaterally changed by management. A new scheme was introduced during a period of more prosperous trading conditions, when substantial bonus payments to labour would have been likely under the terms of the old scheme. The new scheme based any bonus payments to labour not on corporate profits but on the amounts of dividends paid to shareholders, thus explicitly introducing an element of managerial discretion. It also provided for preferential bonus payments to monthly salaried staff. The labour response to these two changes was to note (CM, 8 February 1926) that:

the view of the average worker would be that the Directors desired to change the scheme because at last the workers looked like getting something worth having

and (CM, 23 September 1926):

right from the inception of the Profit sharing scheme there had been talk of one thing above all others, namely 'cooperation' – the team spirit, identity of interest, etc., the principle of which was now being challenged by putting one section in a privileged position. What were the manual workers likely to think of a scheme which gave special benefits to their superintendents . . . It looked like a bribe to the superintendents, etc., to press for work which could not be obtained by ordinary means.

The theme of the raw exercise of a differential power advantage by management and its destructive impact upon labour's perceptions of the integrity of notions of 'cooperation' will be discussed later. At this stage, one can merely note that in the eyes of labour the scheme did not produce sufficient financial rewards, and that it had been changed to ensure that this remained the case.

Labour experienced other effects of the scheme, and these too must be evaluated alongside the contributions labour made to the financial improvement of the company. There were wage reductions in 1921, as district engineering rates were revised downwards, with further reductions of between 8 per cent and 25 per cent in 1922. Labour employment was also cut back by 25 per cent in 1922, with 272 workers being 'paid-off' (Bougen, 1988: 136). Furthermore, some employees linked this with the scheme, although one labour representative dissented, arguing that 'the scheme has helped to retain workers in employment over a longer period rather than the reverse, as some are inclined to think' (CM, 6 March 1922). Nevertheless, it is clear that at least some employees had made this direct association between the scheme and cutbacks in labour.

Whilst it is impossible to evaluate fully the scheme's physical consequences in isolation of events and effects in other associated arenas, one can highlight some issues of relevance for subsequent analysis. The scheme assisted in the survival of the company and ultimately in the reporting of record profits (Bougen, 1989: 228). It was productive in that a combination of cost accounting and other formal physical controls linked to its operations were introduced which contributed towards greater labour productivity. It also produced some additional remuneration for labour in terms of profit sharing bonuses. The fact that these were paid whilst reductions in the standard wages of labour were being negotiated is illustrative of the more significant problem of attempting to attach some singular and total rationale to the physical events. As already indicated some employees believed that the scheme had contributed to employment, others believed the contrary. This issue had arisen in March 1922 and persistently recurred. So, for example, by September 1923 a labour representative was arguing that by promoting 'maximum activity' the scheme had *increased* employment since during the recession '*we are . . . one of the few firms who are active at the present time*' (CM, 17 September 1923). However, the number of employees was reduced by 25 per cent. Similarly, the Committee meetings clearly illustrated that labour never believed that they had received sufficient financial rewards for their contributions, yet as C.G. Renold commented (CM, 15 September 1924):

We are still paying wages considerably in excess of district rates. This excess – something like £10,000 per annum – is really a sort of anticipated profit sharing distribution.

Examining the contribution of accounting to these physical consequences requires similar caution. From a managerial perspective, accounting controls and calculations as introduced by the profit sharing scheme's mechanics clearly generated some of the anticipated constructive results. Accounting integrations contributed to the enhancement of labour productivity and efficiency, and thereby assisted in the improvement of corporate performance. At a fundamental level, accounting numbers were used by management to tighten their control over labour actions within the factory. Not surprisingly, therefore, labour made the connection between the scheme, its accounting based calculations, and the 'press[ing] for work which could not be obtained by ordinary means'. Once again, a set of physical consequences of accounting integrations. Furthermore, the concern of labour with the financial payments from the scheme, which were also dependent upon accounting calculations, again indicates a direct link between accounting and its tangible impact upon labour. Clearly, therefore, labour could forge a strong network of relationships between accounting procedures, managerial controls, physical exertion and financial rewards as established within the terms of the scheme. More insight into these issues will be obtained by examining further dimensions of the scheme's consequences in other arenas.

### Facts, science and education

An explicit component of the managerial regime of truth was to educate labour in the factual and scientific basis of managerial decision-making: to convince labour that changes within the factory and their impact upon labour were not the product of discretionary managerial choice but were instead necessary, legitimate and *explainable*. Certainly, C.G. Renold seemed genuinely to believe that this was the case. He was, therefore, sufficiently confident to make visible to labour some of the components of his regime of truth. A committee was established as the forum for these discussions. From the very outset accounting and scientific management principles had been placed via the scheme's computational mechanics as key props of his educative endeavour. Subsequently, vast amounts of data were presented by management to labour. Layer after layer of accounting costs, selling prices, standard allowances, and profit figures were disclosed (Bougen, 1988). Furthermore, the entire factory was subjected to the scrutinization of activities by the stop-watch, and to the 'scientific' restructuring of work methods. C.G. Renold encouraged labour to study the data, to ask questions and to consider problems from a managerial perspective. So, for example, when labour raised the issue about machinery lying idle, C.G. Renold 'promised that *chapter and verse* in justification ... should be looked up and presented (CM, 17 February 1921) noting that: 'this was a good example of the kind of criticism which the Directors desired to get'. C.G. Renold was not to be disappointed in this regard as labour provided instance upon instance of factory issues they wished explained. Labour questioned management on a whole range of topics, 'expensive schemes were experimented with ... departments were overstaffed with non-producers ... unnecessary expenditure [was] incurred in splitting up and moving departments' (CM, 11 April 1921). Labour increasingly employed their own local knowledges, experiences and observations of workshop activities as a basis for their questions. They sought explanations for the scrapping of 2½ million parts of raw materials and their impact upon bonus payments (CM, 23 April 1923) and for why 'we are working overtime and running a night shift' yet 'there was no profit to distribute' (CM, 17 September 1923). If management was to be conducted on the basis of facts, labour sought access to the relevant facts.

Equally significant was the labour scrutinization of the scheme's accounts and other accounting numbers. C.G. Renold had mobilized accounting as a key element of his regime of truth. Within the factory he saw accounting's successes. The integration of accounting techniques with a package of other formal controls dramatically increased efficiency and output. However, the potential of accounting to legitimize managerial prerogatives and to act as an educative vehicle for the propagation of managerial solutions proved more problematic. An interlocking multiplicity of accounts was created, enabling management to integrate the new control system with corporate performance and hence with profit sharing bonuses. This complex and sophisticated accounting system offered management the opportunity to couple and decouple tactically the relationships between the accounts in their dealings with labour. They could emphasize the integration of corporate and profit sharing performance as an explanation of company losses and the lack of bonuses. At other times, the absence of bonus payments could be detached from corporate performance and explained by constraints determined by the control system. However, although C.G. Renold sought the labour evaluation of accounting numbers upon his own criteria, he could not compel labour to detach their own abilities, knowledges and experiences from the evaluation. In other words, labour retained access to its own regimes of truth.

So, for example, when the accounts failed to correspond to labour's own perception of factory events, this fuelled controversy. For instance, when the result for the Camshaft Department showed a deficit, a labour representative commented (CM, 23 April 1923):

that he and the Superintendent of the department were extremely surprised at the result because so far as they could judge everything was going swimmingly.

At the next meeting (CM, 16 May 1923) management conceded that:

The only question asked in the meeting was in regard to the Camshaft Chain figures on the trading statement, in which it appeared there were some errors.

Similarly, ambiguities in what constituted accounting principles or 'good' accounting practice also generated discontent. Labour acquired a sufficient grasp of various accounting methods and their impact upon the scheme to interrogate management on their interpretation of a whole array of calculative procedures. The accuracy of provisions for falling stock values (CM, March 1921), and the significance and impact of either the immediate write-off or the amortization of 'exceptional' costs (CM, 23 April 1923) were unearthed by labour. As labour recognized that management had the discretion to select accounting methods, they found accounting numbers a potent source of ammunition (Burchell *et al.*, 1980) to embarrass management as regards the 'scientific' bases of these choices. So stock valuations meant that 'the question of profit or loss depended altogether upon the Director's decision' (CM, 14 August 1922), and that the managerial choice of transfer prices offered management the discretion as to where profits would be recognized (CM, 8 September 1923), with a corresponding impact upon bonus payments.

However, such labour challenges constituted more than mere irritations for management. C.G. Renold in particular not only saw his quest for the legitimization of the factual basis for management evaporate, but also saw labour increasingly obtain the 'upper hand' in discussions. This was vividly illustrated when he sought to respond to a labour challenge as to why external contractors rather than existing employees were being used on certain work. His initial answers contained arguments of *'probably* lower cost ... and ... *it is hoped* that greater efficiency will result' (CM, 24 March 1924). Labour responded (CM, 22 April 1924) that:

they were in a position to see what was going on and it was their belief that much of the work that was done by outside concerns could not possibly be done as well nor as cheaply as by the inside staff. No proof had been supplied that this is not so.

C.G. Renold's subsequent explanations 'that it had not been possible to get *the particulars of cost comparisons* ... so it is not possible to obtain *the true cost*' (CM, 19 May 1924) triggered off a series of discussions over a six-month period about the wider issues of managerial abilities and powers. Initially, C.G. Renold exercised unilateral power in that *'it was therefore proposed to suspend the question sine die'* and with the plea for assistance in *'warding off questions or investigations'* (CM, 5 January 1925). More significant, however, was a subsequent statement (CM, 26 January 1925) in which he spoke of:

strain ... and also how far the policy decided upon could be explained and justified to the Committee. He said there were a great many things the Board would be able to accept and act on with less explicit evidence than was considered necessary to go to the Committee. The Directors were able to act, to a certain extent, on general impressions which was quite a sound basis of action among persons who were in close touch with things and with one another, but these impressions could not be expected to satisfy a Committee like the Profit Sharing Committee.

The circulation of power within the Committee was such that C.G. Renold in this speech admitted that managers often had to act upon '*general impressions*' and upon local knowledges rather than on systematic calculations. Ultimately, so successful were labour's own knowledges and perceptions as a basis for challenge that in the latter years of the scheme's existence C.G. Renold relegated and ultimately excluded accounting calculations from the Committee's agenda (Bougen, 1988). This action seemed to deprive labour not so much of a credible calculative base with which to understand managerial policies and to monitor performance, but of a source of ammunition to expose the fragilities of managerial decision-making.

C.G. Renold's attempt to educate labour as regards the systematic rigour of managerial decision-making was both short-lived and unsuccessful. He failed to convince labour that a factual and scientific body of knowledge governed his statements and actions. The disintegrative properties of accounting numbers in this context were such that management was compelled to resort to the unilateral exercise of power to exclude the issue from the committee's agenda. This was seen as necessary to prevent the further erosion of their already shaky status as 'experts' in the eyes of labour. Moreover, the committee's activities incrementally adopted a profile and momentum of their own based upon past statements, postures and discussions. As such, it is critical to recognize that for both labour and management it became increasingly irrelevant whether any accounting system could accurately measure performance in the Camshaft Department for so short a period as one month. It became equally irrelevant whether accounting principles would ever be able to provide a coherent and consistent solution to the issue of the timing of expense recognition for exceptional costs. It also seemed to matter little that C.G. Renold's elevation of local knowledges and managerial intuition as a basis for decision-making perhaps accurately reflected the constrained and urgent necessities of many managerial decisions. It was not an issue of whether these realities and statements were either true or false, legitimate or illegitimate *per se*, but that in the context of C.G. Renold's regime of truth they contravened the stated aspiration and criterion to make visible and to explain to labour the bases of managerial actions. They also contravened the very rationale of the committee, its existence, and its many discussions. From this perspective, the discourses and events appeared to labour as false and as illegitimate, particularly when the raw exercise of power was used by C.G. Renold to impose a new and discontinuous reality upon the committee's agenda, and thereby upon labour.

Within this process, the roles of accounting were significant. From a managerial perspective, the regime of truth was intended to act as an educative and legitimizing force that would facilitate the introduction and operation of the new control system and attendant changes in work method. Accounting, and its integrations with the assorted themes of scientific management, joint consultation and profit sharing was strategically placed by management as a part of his endeavour. Certainly, accounting was constructive in that it constituted an essential ingredient for the operationalization of the scheme, providing as it did its measurement criterion. This also had the productive effect of allowing management to subject the factory to the stop-watch and to restructuring, on the pretence that it was essential for the calculation of profit sharing bonuses. However, within this arena these were the limits to its productive contributions. Even with its own calculative domain, accounting numbers failed to convince labour that they were being subjected to management by fact and by science. Instead, management was forced to concede that judgements and assumptions were inherently involved in accounting calculations. Equally significant, however, was labour's insistence that accounting numbers failed to correspond to their own observations and knowledges of factory events. From a labour perspective, therefore, accounting numbers produced for them the tangible evidence with which to confront management as regards the questionable rationale of many of the physical changes they were being subjected to within the factory. As the scheme progressed, these challenges also gave labour the increased confidence to question more directly the wider aspects of managerial decision-making, again from the perspective of their own local knowledges. This development and evolution of a labour regime of truth and its clashes with managerial objectives and priorities provided the basis for labour to discredit components of the managerial regime of truth. Not only was managerial decision-making shown to lack a scientific rationale, but the basis also now existed for labour to expose the fragile nature of other managerial statements.

### Communities and coalitions of interest

It should be apparent by now that C.G. Renold's aspirations to employ the scheme and its various integrations as a means of promoting the company as a 'community of interest' proved problematic.

As indicated earlier, labour brought to the committee their own regime of truth. From the very outset they expressed a commitment to ensuring that their financial rewards from the scheme should be appropriate for their efforts. In the first year of its operation they were concerned that they 'considered it unsatisfactory that . . . extra efforts on the part of the workers should only result in safeguarding the wages of capital' and 'that the scheme was working wholly in the direction of stabilizing capital' (CM, 4 March

1921). Such a discourse was clearly premised upon some fundamental discontent with the underlying financial relationship between capital and labour as determined within the scheme. In addition, labour also expressed a more cynical view of the motives and power of management since: 'what guarantee the workers would have that ... the management would not modify the scheme to suit some new conditions' (CM, 4 March 1921).

This is exactly what transpired. However, at the same time labour did seem willing to give the scheme a fair hearing. At the first Annual General Meeting of the scheme, before the assembled workforce, a labour representative argued 'we must take the long view, men with common sense do not expect bonuses at present'. This meeting ended with the scheme 'being carried unanimously, with *acclamation*' (CM, 6 March 1922). There were also other instances when labour seemed to exhibit some genuine interest in the cooperative aspects of the venture (CM, 17 September 1922):

What we ought to aim at is greater security and the consolidation of what we have already gained ... and that is what the Company and, he believed, the Directors had in mind.

Such sentiments evaporated as the scheme progressed. Activities in other arenas of the scheme's operations certainly contributed towards this. Wages were cut; work methods altered; and the labour force was reduced. Labour was more productive but few bonuses were paid, with the scheme then being unilaterally altered by management. Similarly, the alleged scientific basis of management prerogatives had crumbled under labour scrutiny, with management again unilaterally enforcing their decision to cease the disclosure of information to labour. These events, not unexpectedly, generated a labour cynicism towards any notion of 'communities'.

However, other issues increasingly came to the fore. The company's history and C.G. Renold's personal predispositions had, at least at one level, consistently exhibited some commitment to the theme of cooperation. Assorted paternalistic managerial measures in the workplace, and early company experiments with consultative groups of employees had been used. There was, therefore, a residue of past cooperative associations and gestures. As the scheme and events unfolded, however, there were to be significant shifts in both managerial and labour attitudes. Although articulated within the context of the performance of the scheme, these issues were underpinned by wider concerns and priorities.

One component of the labour regime of truth was the connections labour established between the relative position of labour within the factory and more general social and economic relationships (CM, 17 September 1923):

All the workers were aware of the instability of the worker's lot. A good many have had bitter experience of it ... In the ordinary course of events a worker might spend 10, 15, 20 or even 30 years in the service of a firm without it bringing him any security whatsoever or immunity from abrupt dismissal either through industrial depreciation or some perhaps quite trivial reason. This is entirely wrong. The workers' domestic atmosphere should be much easier and reach further into the future. This is impossible under present conditions.

It was, therefore, not only the personal experiences and knowledges of factory activities which informed labour's perceptions of the scheme and its relationships with management, but also its accumulated knowledge of conditions outside the factory, *'the workers' domestic atmosphere'*. Labour attempts to grapple with the differential powers and privileges of industrial relationships increasingly began to dominate their dealings with management. For example when, under the reformulated terms of the scheme, monthly staff were to be entitled to a larger share of the profit sharing bonus, this initiated radical labour criticisms both of the economics and of the social relationships implied by the change. Labour demanded a *'claim to share in [the] ownership of reserves'* of the Company (CM, 27 May 1929) and:

that a pro rata distribution of the fund is the only equitable basis and would have it apply from the highest paid to the lowest paid worker, that is to say, including Directors and Managers, etc., at one end and juniors at the other, as all contribute in some measure to the profitability.

The employment of more radical categories of economic calculation and more caustic rhetoric coincided with C.G. Renold's recognition that the scheme's attempts to generate a community of interests were incrementally being eroded. In 1927, C.G. Renold asked the committee 'whether the meeting had tended to strengthen the feeling of community of interest by arousing enthusiasm'. A response that 'one member stated that in his opinion not one in twenty was interested beyond what he got out of the scheme' (CM, 18 October 1927) must have been viewed as disappointing. By 1929, in justifying changes to the scheme, C.G. Renold argued that the Board of Directors needed to be free 'from the study of Profit Sharing and allied problems' (CM, 27 May 1929). By this stage the scheme's 'community' basis had disintegrated to such an extent that profit sharing was now viewed as an *'allied problem'* for management. Indicative of this was the subterfuge surrounding the scheme's termination. In May 1927 it was minuted for the committee that the rules of the scheme were to be modified so that any restructuring of the Company would automatically necessitate the scheme's abandonment. No mention of any likely future restructuring was made. However, C.G. Renold had been involved in merger discussions for many years, with the idea having been raised as early as 1919 and with discussions taking place intermittently over the next 10 years (Tripp, 1956: 131–5). Certainly, by 1927, when the change in the scheme's rules was initiated, a merger seems to have been decided upon. C.G. Renold was at least aware, therefore, when introducing the rule change that in the future it would have considerable impact upon the scheme and upon labour. However, no such explicit reference was made by management at either the meeting in question or at subsequent meetings to the likelihood of a future merger. Notions of cooperation, discussion and visibilities had been replaced by prerogative, subterfuge and secrecy.

One can best understand the contribution accounting made to this state of affairs in the context of the antecedents of the scheme's introduction and their relationship to the historical development of a corporate infrastructure. Two recurring themes dominated the company's history prior to the introduction of the scheme. First, there existed a significant technical or calculative core as regards factory activities. Concern with workmanship and output, the introduction of planning and control methods, and the early employment of a bookkeeper in the company all illustrate the importance attached to the managerial quest for the quantitative integration and improvement of the physical productivity of labour within the factory. At the same time, however, there also existed a managerial interest in the development of a cultural infrastructure within the factory. Assorted paternalistic gestures aimed at improving the physical condition of labour, such as canteen and health facilities, operated in parallel with wider-ranging attempts to produce labour loyalty and confidence. Early experiments with workshop committees and joint consultative arrangements are examples of this managerial interest. Clearly, both influences were essentially concerned with making labour more productive inside the factory. However, the profit sharing scheme was intended by management as a more ambitious exercise in their dealings with labour. Although the central aim remained the improvement of corporate performance by increasing labour productivity, the linkages between the various strands of this endeavour were now to be made more explicit and open, and were anticipated therefore to be even more productive. The scheme, with its quite explicit blending of tighter controls, management by facts, and notions of community of interest offered labour a financial inducement to cooperate with management in the discussion of these issues. The profit sharing committee was established for this very purpose. Unlike, therefore, the dominant theme in many other managerial regimes of truth, a tactical purpose of the scheme was the notion of partial inclusions rather than complete exclusions.

The making visible of connections and integrations, and the inclusion of labour voices, was clearly premised upon C.G. Renold's personal confidence in the legitimacy and persuasiveness of his own regime of truth to overcome any initial labour suspicions of the scheme. Therefore, when secrecy, subterfuge and, more significantly, the exercise of raw power were deemed necessary to silence labour voices, more was at stake than the inability of accounting numbers to convince labour of the primacy of managerial versions of events over their own personal knowledges and observations.

Management had aspired to rid their methods and tactics of control over labour of any perceived partisan qualities by resort to fact, science and knowledge. The profit sharing scheme, its committee, the disclosure of information, and the whole process of making visible components of their regime of truth illustrate the managerial objectives in this arena. In other words, it was anticipated that the factory would be perceived as a community and as an agreed coalition of interests. The making visible of relationships constituted as it were *the contract* both formal, in the case of profit sharing bonuses, and informal as regards resort to discussion and intellectual argument, between management and labour. It was the managerial overstepping of this contractual limit which perhaps had the greatest impact upon the progression of the scheme. Management unilaterally exercised raw power and changed the terms of the scheme disadvantageously for labour. They withheld accounting information from labour and secretly planned for the strategic termination of the scheme. Within the context, antecedents, and dynamics of the management–labour relationship these all seemed to labour illustrations of repression. Management could not claim that the cost figures were true, to labour they came to be viewed as false. Management could not argue that legitimate changes in the rules of the scheme were required to satisfy external financial agents, to labour they now appeared illegitimate. Neither could management argue that their decision-making needed to pay attention to local knowledges; to labour that case now seemed inadmissible.

Labour had seen the circulation of power. It had entered a managerially predetermined arena for the articulation and operation of a particularly elaborate managerial regime of truth. But labour had stripped bare the inconsistencies between managerial discourse and managerial action, and had seen re-emerge intact the unilateral imposition of managerial power and prerogatives. It is hardly surprising that notions of communities and coalitions had also disappeared.

### Some concluding observations

The chapter commenced by observing that accounting has typically been viewed as essentially constructive. One way in which it achieves this is by its capacity to integrate at a technical level various organizational activities and resources. As an important element in organizational operations, labour is an obvious target for this process. It was argued that accounting has also been viewed as having other constructive and productive capacities. These relate to accounting's contribution to other more indirect methods of controlling labour. These were referred to as managerial regimes of truth, which seek to promote to labour a managerial perspective that assorted organizational purposes, methods, and imperatives are necessary, factual and therefore beyond contention. One consequence of this is the effective silencing of labour voices and the relegation of labour experiences and knowledges to the margins of interest and validity. Again, there is a central theme of management seeking constructive accounting integrations. It was argued that both of these constructive roles for accounting were premised upon the perceived necessity of reducing or eliminating the potentially destructive predispositions of labour. Whether by the stricter physical control of labour, or by the more subtle method of exclusion and silencing, the aim was to prevent labour from jeopardizing the smooth flow of accounting's constructive capabilities.

From one perspective, the Renold case study material illustrates how accounting controls were employed within the factory to enhance labour productivity, and how such controls did in fact succeed in achieving greater physical output at lower cost. At the same time, a detailed regime of truth was established by management with the anticipated objectives of justifying both the necessity and the factual foundations of these work changes. However, the regime of truth had another more ambitious objective. This was to locate these changes within a wider managerial objective of educating and convincing labour of the overall legitimacy of managerial prerogatives and associated organizational structures and industrial relationships. To achieve this end a complicated, and in many ways a sophisticated series of interlocking methods was used by management. A profit sharing scheme was created which sought to integrate a heterogeneous set of philosophical and calculative priorities. Profit sharing bonuses were to be intertwined with accounting and scientific management calculations, with themes of consultative dialogue, with employee education, and with the alleged scientific bases of managerial decision-making. One can make a reasonable case that the regime of truth introduced into the Renold Company would have appeared to possess a reasonable opportunity for a smooth implementation and operation. It was based upon elements in which historically the company had considerable strengths and past experiences. The company was a pioneer in the application of accounting and scientific management practices, with C.G. Renold himself an acknowledged expert and writer on industrial relationships. Perhaps more significant, however, was a labour willingness at the commencement of the scheme to give the exercise a fair and reasonable hearing. It is worth recalling that the First General Meeting of the profit sharing scheme concluded with 'acclamation' from the assembled workforce. A combination of financial inducements and promises of forging a new partnership between management and labour seemed powerful reasons for labour to participate in the scheme.

Accounting integrations were clearly constructive in that company output and profitability were increased. It should be noted that this was achieved with the full cooperation of labour. This fact was claimed by labour, and subsequently confirmed by management. The Renold material indicates that accounting's obsession with the destructive capacities of labour is misplaced. However, limits existed to the productive capabilities of accounting. The case study reveals both some of the destructive consequences of accounting integrations, and the fragility of its constructive capabilities.

It is important to recognize that the Renold regime of truth was to be based upon planned inclusions, transparencies and discussions. Although these bases were all strategically determined by management and were anticipated to be under their control, nevertheless the theme was one of making linkages between various organizational processes and structures more explicit. It was also one of tactically allowing labour experiences, knowledges and voices to be heard.

It was these aspects of the scheme which led to its downfall. They also led to the disintegration of the managerial regime of truth and to the emergence of accounting's destructive properties. At one level, C.G. Renold was compelled to attempt to convince labour of the technical integrity of the scheme: that changes in work methods, tighter controls and greater efficiency did not calculatively justify the paying of bonuses. Increasingly, however, he was also compelled to wrestle with the philosophical integrity of the scheme and the inconsistencies which were becoming more apparent. Despite the rhetoric of coalitions, of communities of interest and of the scientific bases of organizational relationships, management was forced to resort to raw power to determine appropriate outcomes and to silence labour.

As it became increasingly apparent to labour that the scheme was not living up to their expectations in terms of cash bonus payments, other aspects of the scheme and of its overall integrity entered into the arena. As labour scrutinized the technical accounts of the scheme, seeking out meanings and explanations, they observed the difficulties C.G. Renold had experienced in attempting to explain away arbitrary accounting allocations and judgements. As management became increasingly embarrassed both by their failure to justify scientifically their decisions and then by their resort to traditional prerogatives, the scheme's accounts took on increased

significance for both parties. Management sought to relegate the significance of accounting for the scheme's operation. From a managerial
perspective, accounting numbers were simply offering labour the opportunity to embark upon destructive forays into managerial prerogatives. For
labour, however, accounting constituted ammunition, producing means to
penetrate the rationale of the scheme and managerial motives. As accounting became destructive for management, it became constructive for labour.
However, the constructive capacities of accounting for labour were to
exceed its role as an irritation or as a means of embarrassing managerial
arguments and positions.

What commenced for labour as a relatively passive exercise, for the most
part reacting and responding to managerial initiatives and claims, progressively became more significant. Labour had clearly brought to the Committee its own regimes of truth. Initially, labour merely presented its
opening partisan postures, speculating on the scheme and its potential
impact upon labour. Management, with its own agenda and its own
associated regimes of truth, undertook the same exercise. The adoption and
expression of partisan positions was understandable. From such a perspective, the existence of two distinct though interdependent regimes of truth
being analysed and reformulated during the course of the Committee's
discussions became particularly informative. As labour began to appreciate
that their probing of the scheme's accounts resulted in a managerial
inability to explain their technical integrity, they launched a wider-ranging
set of challenges to managerial interpretations of events. As the fragility of
many managerial positions and statements was exposed, labour gained
increasing confidence in the validity of its own regimes of truth. The notions
of science, facts, and coalitions with their managerially promoted connotations of neutrality creaked and ultimately crumbled under labour
scrutiny. Consequently, labour gained an even greater degree of confidence
in its own regimes of truth, since it was its local knowledges of factory
events and its own observations of the increasing inconsistencies and
discontinuities between the rhetoric and realities of managerial motives
which underpinned their challenges. These clashes of truth reveal much
about the potentialities and limitations of accounting as a constructive and
destructive force, and about the limits and boundaries of its operations.

Management had established the starting rules, and predetermined the
anticipated parameters of the profit sharing scheme, both in terms of its
calculative properties and the intended agenda of discussions. However, the
unfolding of events and relationships was neither predictable nor fully
under their control. As the scheme progressed, both the credibility of the
technical calculations of the scheme, and the fragility of many managerial
positions, caused the relationships between management and labour to

shift. The dynamics of the processes in this transformation were implicated in many ways with accounting.

The partisan nature of the managerial regime of truth was exposed as labour considered that the physical consequences of the scheme, for example bonus payments, redundancies and changes in work method, were working solely to the advantage of management. Under such circumstances, the fragility of managerial concepts of coalitions, cooperation, education and science could not be buttressed by accounting calculations. Labour's initial hesitancy to treat its own observations as illegitimate developed into a more tangible confidence in its own regimes of truth. Management's inability to erode this conviction either by its actions or by its arguments resulted in labour increasingly coupling the logic of various factory activities with the profit sharing experience. As it did so, the partial and partisan characteristics of accounting descriptions and measurements became apparent to labour. The realities management sought to convey to labour by various accounting methods became increasingly at odds with labour's own personal knowledges. At this stage, the fragility of accounting's capacities as either a constructive or destructive element was highlighted. Accounting continued to contribute to greater labour productivity, but it did so as a restrictive integrative control technique, buttressed by the exercise of raw managerial power. Its other anticipated productive contributions evaporated as the fragility of the managerial positions and postures it sought to support were exposed by labour. As the inconsistencies and discontinuities between managerial claims for the scheme, and its local and tangible effects upon labour unfolded, accounting contributed to the further disintegration of industrial relationships both within the scheme and inside the factory.

NOTE

1. This chapter draws on material documented in Bougen (1988, 1989) and the study should be viewed as being complementary to this previous work.

REFERENCES

Aldcroft, D.H., 1970. *The Inter-War Economy: Britain, 1919–39*, London: Batsford
Armstrong, P., 1987. 'The Rise of Accounting Controls in British Capitalist Enterprises', *Accounting, Organizations and Society* 12(5): 415–36
Bougen, P.D., 1988. *Accounting and Industrial Relations: Some Historical Evidence on Their Interaction*, New York: Garland
     1989. 'The Emergence, Roles and Consequences of an Accounting Industrial Relations Interaction', *Accounting, Organizations and Society* 14(3): 203–34
Burchell, S., Clubb, C., Hopwood, A.G., Hughes, J. and Nahapiet, J., 1980. 'The Roles of Accounting in Organizations and Society', *Accounting, Organizations and Society* 5(1): 5–28

Caplan, E.H., 1966. 'Behavioural Assumptions of Management Accounting', *Accounting Review* 41(3): 496–509

Foucault, M., 1980. *Power/Knowledge*, Brighton: Harvester

Hinton, J., 1973. *The First Shop Stewards' Movement*, London: Allen & Unwin

Hopwood, A.G., 1985. 'Accounting and the Domain of the Public: Some Observations on Current Developments', *The Price Waterhouse Public Lecture on Accounting*, University of Leeds

1987. 'The Archaeology of Accounting Systems', *Accounting, Organizations and Society* 12(3): 207–34

Loft, A., 1986. 'Towards a Critical Understanding of Accounting: The Case of Cost Accounting in the UK, 1914–25', *Accounting, Organizations and Society* 11(2): 137–69

Meyer, J.W., 1986. 'Social Environments and Organizational Accounting', *Accounting, Organizations and Society* 11(4/5): 345–56

Miller, P. and O'Leary, T., 1987. 'Accounting and the Construction of the Governable Person', *Accounting, Organizations and Society* 12(3): 235–65

Ministry of Munitions, 1921–22. *History of the Ministry of Munitions*, 4 vols., London: War Office

Ogden, S. and Bougen, P.D., 1985. 'A Radical Perspective on the Disclosure of Accounting Information to Trade Unions', *Accounting, Organizations and Society* 10(2): 211–24

Renold, C.G., 1917. 'Workshop Committees', in A.W. Kirkaldy (ed.), *Industry and Finance: War Expedients and Reconstruction*, London: Pitman

1921. 'Workshop Committees', in A.W. Kirkaldy (ed.), *British Labour: Replacement and Conciliation 1914–21*, London: Pitman

1927. 'Relations in the Workshop', *Manchester Guardian* 30 November

1928. 'The Nature and Present Position of Skill in Industry', *The Economic Journal* 38, December: 593–604

1929a. 'Scientific Management', in J. Lee (ed.), *Pitman's Dictionary of Industrial Administration, Volume II*, London: Pitman

1929b. 'Budgetary Control in the Organization of Hans Renold Ltd', papers presented to the International Management Institute, Geneva, Switzerland

1950. *Joint Consultation Over 30 Years*, London: George Allen & Unwin

Tripp, B.H., 1956. *Renold Chains: A History of the Company and the Rise of the Precision Chain Industry*, London: George Allen & Unwin

Urwick, L.F. and Brech, E.F.L., 1945–8. *The Making of Scientific Management*, 3 vols., London: Management Publications Trust, 1946

# 7 The politics of economic measurement: the rise of the 'productivity problem' in the 1940s

## Jim Tomlinson

In the late 1940s, the concept of productivity rose to a wholly new prominence in discourse about the economy in the UK. This discursive shift signalled a twofold movement in attempts to measure and account for economic activity. On the one hand, at the macroeconomic level, the rise of a concern with productivity can be seen as linked to the rise of measurement of the national economy as part of the growth of national economic management. On the other hand, a concern with productivity was linked to a rapid escalation in attempts to regulate the enterprise in the name of increased output and efficiency.

This second, microeconomic, aspect can be further broken down into two components. First it may be characterized as an attempt to get enterprises to 'account' for themselves in a new way, by attempting to impose new criteria of action and new responsibilities upon them. More specifically, part of this process of governmental attempts to change enterprise practices was an attempt to change their accounting regimes, to get them to measure productivity as part of everyday management activity.

In this context, the purpose of this chapter is threefold. First, to describe and discuss the neglected issue of the conditions of existence of this rise of 'productivity' as a concept deployed in national economic accounting and management. Secondly, to locate the new governmental concern with enterprise productivity in the context of changing relations between government and enterprises more generally. Thirdly, to describe and assess the attempts to change accounting practices in the name of enhanced productivity.

### The concept of productivity

Productivity was not, of course a new *word* in the late 1940s. As Leyland (1952: 381) notes 'Before the war the word productivity was largely confined to academic discussion. Today it is common currency'. And in that prewar period even the amount of academic discussion was limited, and seems in particular to have led to very little applied work.

For public policy, concern with productivity has historically arisen in three contexts.

First, from a focus of unemployment, and the argument that real wage growth was outstripping productivity increases and so reducing the demand for labour. This issue was, for example, discussed by the Economic Advisory Council to the government in the early 1930s, but seems to have led neither to much empirical work on productivity, nor to any clear conclusions (Keynes 1973, ch. 3, 1981: 405–7; Howson and Winch, 1977: 59–60). This same issue informed some of the wartime discussions of productivity, but again without leading very far (PRO, 1944).[1]

Secondly, productivity has come into focus when output has been supply constrained, and when the level of output has been a pressing concern of government. The obvious example of this is in wartime. The First World War, by calling on British industry as a key war resource, focused attention on that industry's efficiency, especially on such issues as costing (Loft, ch. 5 in this volume). This concern was then extended into the peace (Kirby and Rose, 1991). In the context of the 1919–20 boom and the consequent supply constraints, this government interest led, for example, to the establishment of a Committee on Increased Production, which conducted an enquiry into levels of output per person per hour in comparison with 1913. Little came of this in the face of the slump from the middle of 1920. But its work reflected in a broad sense the same concerns as were to make productivity so important after the Second World War – a desire to increase total output in a fully employed economy, and a belief that other countries, notably the US, were doing better in regard to output per head (PRO, 1920).

Thirdly, concerns arising from the perception of a supply constrained economy have led to international comparisons which in turn slide into a concern with international competitiveness. This change of emphasis is apparent in the interwar period in the work of the Balfour *Committee on Industrial and Commercial Efficiency*, whose remit was very much to investigate Britain's competitiveness (Balfour Committee, 1927–9). However, it did not take the discussion of productivity beyond generalities.

In the 1930s the real wage–productivity link was not pursued with any enthusiasm. And with mass unemployment, the concerns arising from a supply constrained economy were unsurprisingly absent. In sum, before 1939 concern with productivity was episodic, underdeveloped and ill-focused.

From 1939, the wartime context of output constrained by the supply of resources fundamentally altered the immediate concerns of economic policy. Whilst on the macroeconomic side it led to 'Keynesian' national income planning and a complex and comprehensive web of controls, on the 'supply side' government took on a revolutionary role in attempting to raise output at both industry and enterprise level. Most obviously, Ministries like those of Supply and Aircraft Production intervened in existing firms or created new firms in support of what, in retrospect (but not at the time) could be called a massive government-driven productivity drive.

At the accession of the Labour Government in 1945 its prime economic policy concern was unemployment, and its principal fear was that an immediate postwar boom would be quickly followed by slump, as had been the case following the First World War (Tomlinson, 1987a). But this concern quickly shifted to a linked focus on the balance of payments and the expansion of output (Cairncross, 1985; Tomlinson, 1990, ch. 8). In the short run, the balance of payments problem was not the competitiveness of British goods, but their availability. For much of their term in office the Attlee government was trying to get greater output from a fully employed economy in order to supply export markets, increase investment and last (and very much least) expand domestic consumption. This led logically to a concern with productivity, i.e. getting more output from more or less given resources.

In the case of national economic management, in the sense of 'Keynesian' manipulation of aggregate demand, one of the preconditions was the existence of national income accounts, which would provide government with some measure of the national economy against which to assess its interventions. Whilst private efforts had been made to provide such data before 1939,[2] it was only in wartime that such measurement was under-taken by government in order to design appropriate fiscal policy (Sayers, 1956, ch. 2; Stone, 1951; Keynes, 1978, ch. 2).

Similarly, one precondition for a coherent productivity drive was data on productivity. However, such data was strikingly absent at the end of the War. It might be thought that the national income accounts would have provided a basis for at least good estimates of production. But in fact most national income calculations at this time were calculated from the income not the output side (e.g. Stone, 1977; Clark, 1932). Basically this was because production data were available on a systematic basis only from the Census of Production which was not only infrequent (1907, 1924, 1929, 1935) but more importantly covered only about 50 percent of national income, excluding services, distribution and government entirely. National income estimates had been built up from Census of Production data, by, for example, Flux (1913, 1924, 1929, 1933). But these estimates were rudimen-tary, and usually production data were used only to check figures derived from income data (e.g., Clark, 1932). By 1945 the situation was improved by the introduction of an index of production, although the basis for this was problematic before the first full postwar Census in 1948.

Hence, at the beginning of the production campaign in early 1946, Ministers were lamenting that 'As the campaign is concerned so largely with increasing productivity, the Committee is particularly concerned over the lack of facts or statistics bearing upon productivity' (PRO, 1946a). The main response was the appointment of L. Rostas as the first civil servant in the Board of Trade concerned with compiling productivity figures.[3] His first Report was produced in early 1947 (PRO, 1947a). It stressed the difficulties in finding the raw data for such calculations, including, for example, the lack of a common industrial definition in the production and employment figures. But, much more important, was the fact that Rostas chose to attempt to get round these difficulties by using one highly specific measure of productivity, that of physical output per person. In doing so he inaugurated a long debate about what significance, if any, could be attached to the productivity numbers which informed so much of the policy discussion of the late 1940s.

In principle, measuring productivity is simple – it is a matter of comparing (changes in) total inputs into a production process with (changes in) total output. This is what in modern jargon is called total factor productivity. In practice, such calculations are much less simple. Above all, they require some measure of capital input which, even if it is agreed what this means conceptually, is always difficult to calculate. In addition, such calculations require some measure of output across sectors. For marketed goods this looks quite simple, using market prices. But these prices may, of course, be distorted by all the factors that stop market prices reflecting 'true' values – oligopoly and monopoly, cartels, dumping, etc.

In the 1940s, these problems of conceptualization and measurement were added to by the simple absence of data – for example on the capital stock (Lomax, 1956). Indeed, the first serious attempt to measure capital productivity in the UK does not seem to have been made until 1960 (Reddaway and Smith, 1960). Moreover, in the 1940s prices were widely controlled and/or subsidized, so that market values were an especially poor guide to 'true' values at this time. To try and circumvent some of these problems by focusing upon labour productivity had an especial appeal as the relevant measure in the 1940s. As Rostas was to argue in defence of his emphasis on this approach, labour productivity was central because 'given the quantity and quality of available resources, it is largely the productivity of labour which determines the standard of living' and 'its importance is however enhanced in periods like ours when there is full employment'. Also, he argued, labour was the almost universal element in production and thirdly 'the more practical reason for choosing labour productivity as our subject is that labour as an input factor is a measurable quantity while such a factor as capital is not easily measurable' (Rostas, 1955: 33–4).

This pragmatic approach was far from illogical. It fitted with the 1940s' emphasis on manpower as the constraining factor in the economy and the difficulties in rapidly increasing capital investment. But it had a number of significant weaknesses. First of all, labour productivity is not a measure of efficiency, as economists never tire of pointing out (e.g. Farrell, 1957: 253; Reddaway and Smith, 1960: 17). Hence its implications are far from clear – in particular, as Jewkes (1946) emphasized, the common Anglo–American comparisons of productivity, in which Britain fared badly, were not a good measure of the competitiveness of British products against those from the US.[4] More particularly, labour productivity figures capture the effects of a whole range of determinants; as Rostas emphasized, they by no means simply reflect the 'contribution' of labour to output (PRO, 1947a; Rostas, 1952: 23). But the counterpart to this is that labour productivity 'does not give us any information on the factors determining these productivity levels' (Rostas, 1955: 34). But labour productivity not only fails to pinpoint the causes of productivity differences, it threatens to give a wholly illegitimate emphasis to labour effort in determining such differences. This latter danger was apparent in the 1940s, and the government was keen to reject such a conclusion (PRO, 1946b, 1947a). Nevertheless, this conclusion *was* widely drawn, and it bedevilled the productivity debate in the 1940s and into the 1950s, to the extent that productivity became widely used as synonymous with intensity of labour effort (Andrews and Brunner, 1950: 199; more generally, Nichols, 1987).

The strategic origins of the 1940s' policy concern with productivity can thus be seen to have emerged out of the desire to expand supply in the face of unprecedented balance of payments problems in a fully employed economy. (There was also a tactical concern to respond to US criticisms of British economic performance at a time of extensive borrowing from the US.) But once this initial concern moved beyond generalities it acquired a focus which was by no means implicit in it, especially a focus on labour productivity. This focus on labour productivity served to shape subsequent policy discussion. We may contrast this with the development of national income accounting. 'National income' is a concept equally as problematic as productivity, but at least in the UK the initial development of National Income Accounts was clearly subordinate to a policy objective – matching aggregate supply and demand to minimize inflation. The situation is quite different with productivity, in that here a particular form of measurement became embedded in the policy apparatus at an early stage, before the policy had moved much beyond governmental rhetoric. A distinctive relationship between forms of economic calculation and economic policy can thus be detected in the case of productivity.

### Policy instruments

A coherent policy on productivity clearly requires much beyond a means of measurement. At best it requires a coherent doctrine of the determinants of productivity and a portfolio of policy instruments to affect those determinants. All policy programmes will no doubt fall short of such an ideal, but such an ideal provides a starting point for understanding the shortcomings of the Attlee government's policies on productivity.

First, we may note that only a minority strand in the Labour Party traditionally saw it as a party of industrial modernization. It was mainly a party of welfare and economic stability, grounded in a strongly adversarial view of economic activity. Intellectually it was grounded, broadly, on a combination of trade union voluntarism and Fabian centralization (e.g. Durbin, 1985). This found little room for the analysis of that crucial institution of industrial modernization, the capitalist enterprise, which was largely viewed as a site for struggle over wages and/or a source of (illegitimate) economic and political power (Tomlinson, 1982; Hotten, 1988). Correlatively, there was little interest in, or knowledge of, industrial management.

If accurate for the pre-1939 period, these broad generalizations would have to be qualified by 1945. Many of the leading Labour Ministers of 1945–51 served through the War as ministers concerned with economic issues, and this gave them an unprecedented insight into the activities (and failings) of British industry. Men like Dalton and Cripps (both Chancellors of the Exchequer under Attlee) in particular were, by 1945, keenly interested in reforming British industry and management, drawing particularly on the extensive wartime Board of Trade enquiries into British industrial efficiency (Middlemas, 1986: 53–7; Barnett, 1986, pt. III). Nevertheless, the switch in concern under the 1945 government from unemployment to production and productivity could not draw on a clear doctrine relating those problems to questions of industrial organization and management.

In 1945 Labour's policy for industry was dominated by nationalization, and that approach to industry did tend to crowd out attention from the 80 percent of industry that remained in private hands (Mercer, 1991b). Beyond monopoly policy Labour had little to say in 1945 on the private sector (Mercer, 1989, 1991a, 1992). Hence policies in this area tended to be *ad hoc*, combining some of the possibilities suggested by the Board of Trade and other Ministries during the War with responses to the immediate circumstances of the late 1940s.

It is possible to list a whole range of policy initiatives under the broad heading of Labour's attempts to raise productivity (for surveys, see Tomlinson, 1991a, 1992). These would include attempts to raise the quality of management (funding the foundation of the British Institute of Management (BIM)); attempts to offer State management consultancy (the Production Efficiency Service of the Board of Trade); attempts to get operations research applied in industry (the Special Research Unit of the Board of

Trade); attempts to increase industrial research and development (by expansion of the Department of Scientific and Industrial Research and encouragement of Industrial Research Associations or IRAs). Better known perhaps is the establishment of Development Councils (DCs) (Planning, 1951; Henderson, 1952; Mercer, 1991b), and the establishment of the Anglo–American Council on Productivity (AACP) (Carew, 1987, ch. 9; Tomlinson, 1991c). Finally, there is the largely unexplored encouragement of Joint Production Councils, in turn linked to a whole range of initiatives to improve 'human relations' in British industry (a point returned to below).

All these instruments can be looked at in the context of Labour's productivity drive. But, with the exception of the AACP, their concerns were not wholly or simply assimilable to that concern. This is partly explicable by the fact that the most important of them (DCs, the AACP, the BIM, the IRAs) were not agencies of government but bodies which operated to a greater or lesser degree autonomously of government. Indeed, the government was usually keen to maintain precisely such an arm's-length relationship with the private sector, getting them to take responsibility for achieving increased production and productivity. Only towards the end of the Labour Government was it being clearly argued that such an arm's-length relationship had failed and more direct involvement of government at enterprise level was required (PRO, 1950a, 1950b).

This arm's-length strategy had a number of implications. First, it was embedded in, and was to depend upon, a tripartist approach to policy-making where unions, employers and government would get together in a number of forums to discuss policy issues. Thus there was the National Production Advisory Council for Industry, and Regional Boards for Industry below it; the National Joint Advisory Council for wage issues; the Economic Planning Board (from 1947), and a range of other such organs. But these were all consultative in character, and the government looked to unions and, more usually, employers to *execute* decisions. This approach was explicitly made by Cripps in relation to the productivity campaign. He told the two sides of industry that the primary responsibility for increasing productivity must lie with them, not with government (PRO, 1948b).

Secondly, these consultative mechanisms mainly operated via representative bodies of employment – at the apex, the Federation of British Industry (FBI) and the British Employers' Confederation, but below this a whole range of Trade Associations. Trade Associations in particular were not just bodies to represent employers, but also acted as crucial agencies for *operating* government policies – most notably the myriad controls which Labour operated over the allocation of raw materials, intermediate and consumer goods (Rogow, 1954; Rogow and Shore, 1955; Mercer, 1989). Government accepted this role for the Associations in the absence of any other available mechanism, the Associations embracing it as a way of keeping many decisions in their hands and out of those of the government. Hence Trade Associations played a pivotal role in controlling private industry, and gave them great leverage over the policy-making process.

Given both the government's strong commitment to consultative and cooperative relations with private industry, and the embedding of employers' associations in the policy-executing institutions, little was possible where employers judged it politic to resist government initiatives. The Development Council initiative came to very little in the face of FBI-orchestrated opposition; the FBI role on the AACP was minimalist; and employer opposition prevented any possibility of Joint Production Committees being made compulsory (trade unions, by contrast, certainly at the leadership level, were extraordinarily compliant with the productivity drive, see Tomlinson, 1991b).

This does not mean that employers campaigned against the productivity drive – such a move would hardly have been politic in the late 1940s. But they were largely able to channel and resist the government's initiatives, especially insofar as they threatened managerial autonomy. The reasons for such opposition were partly political – a desire to resist what was widely seen as the excessive ambitions of a meddling government. But, in addition, it needs to be noted that for all the talk (and actuality) of economic crisis in these years, these were good years for most employers – profit levels rose sharply, giving little incentive for employers to change their practices (e.g. PRO, 1948a). In the absence of German and Japanese competition, the sellers' market guaranteed even the most backward employer easy money (Barna, 1949).

The limited and often negative response of the private sector raises a general question about the status of the government's 'productivity drive': if it were possible for certain actors to divert, stall or block such a policy, to what extent can we still refer to such an initiative as more than an empty wish? At its simplest level, this phrase is appropriate because of the scale of government activity in this area, activity in the sense of speeches made, committees established, policy mechanisms examined. But in another sense 'drive' is misleading if it suggests a tightly-knit set of policies with a clear programme of action attached. The concern with productivity, as already suggested, led to and drew upon a range of initiatives with no central origin point, strategic orientation or straightforward points of contact with enterprise. Further, the government was ideologically committed (and, arguably, politically constrained) to act mainly *indirectly* to change enterprise behaviour. Even in the newly nationalized industries there was a rapid realization of the incapacity of government to act directly on enterprise behaviour (PRO, 1949e).

For the macroeconomic reasons already noted, there were compelling economic reasons why a rhetoric of the 'productivity drive' should be constructed out of these diverse elements. But just as most physical controls over the economy were effectively 'sub-contracted' to Trade Associations and the like, so the productivity drive was mainly pursued through other bodies, semi-autonomous agencies, the AACP or, probably more importantly, fully autonomous institutions like Trade Associations and the FBI. Part of the problem of the drive was that it relied largely for its success on a degree of cooperation from the private sector. To the extent that this cooperation was unforthcoming, the elements of that 'drive' were immensely difficult to assemble, and maintain, as a coherent and purposive entity.

Towards the end of the Labour Government's first period in office some stocktaking on the relationship with private industry was undertaken, notably by the President of the Board of Trade, Harold Wilson. Part of this was an attempt to change the law relating to Development Councils, of which only four were established by the government, a disappointing result given their central role in the Government's policies for the private sector. Wilson proposed that the legislation on DCs be amended to give government a much bigger say in the industry's affairs, by acting as a channel for the execution of government decisions, rather than as purely advisory bodies. In pursuit of this, Wilson called for rights for the DCs to inspect the books of firms deemed inefficient (PRO, 1950a).

More broadly, Wilson addressed the whole issue of the relation between the government and the private sector, asserting that in this area 'we have almost a vacuum in socialist thought' (PRO, 1950b, para. 2). He argued for new forms of governmental intervention in private companies, especially in relation to the primary objectives of raising productivity, given that 'The forces of competition, particularly in conditions of full or near-full employment seem to be singularly ineffective despite the text-books' (PRO, 1950b, para. 4). He stressed throughout that the key corporate decisions are made at board level where the government has little impact, and argued for government Directors on company boards alongside a range of other policy options such as nationalized firms (rather than sectors) to compete with private firms.

Nothing came of these proposals in the face of Labour's loss of office in 1951. But they do register the conception of a clear policy failure by Labour in this area, and one where the productivity objective was central. We have already suggested some of the reasons for this failure in Labour's long-held ideological and political positions *vis-à-vis* the private sector, as well as the constraints faced by the government in the face of a powerful and recalcitrant private sector.

At a lower level of generality it may be asked what doctrines about the enterprise and its reform were in play in the late 1940s, and how far they acted to inhibit or advance the productivity drive. This is especially pertinent because some commentators have seen that drive as a significant bridgehead for attempts to import 'scientific management' into the UK, especially via the AACP (Carew, 1987, ch. 9).

## Standardization, costing and budgeting

'Scientific management' is a vague concept, and there is little agreement on what might be included under that heading. Here the focus will be on two industrial practices which are generally accepted to be part and parcel of the notion. First, is standardization of output, a way of seeking to facilitate the realization of scale economies; and, secondly, standard costing and budgeting, a mechanism for attempting to manage production processes through close scrutiny of deviations from attainable norms (Miller and O'Leary, ch. 4 in this volume).

Certainly standardization of output was taken seriously by various government bodies in the late 1940s. This seems to have been pressed especially by the Ministry of Supply during the War period, and was also pushed by other bodies such as the Engineering Advisory Council (PRO, 1948c, 1949a, 1950a). There was an official committee on standardization in engineering, the Lemon Committee, which reported in favour of more standardization in this area in 1949 (HMSO, 1949).

However, much of the initial impetus to this concern came from large-scale public purchasing of munitions during wartime. When this declined postwar, employers increasingly seem to have emphasized the diversity of their markets, and therefore the dangers of overstandardization of output, especially in the case of final as opposed to intermediate goods (PRO, 1949b; Andrews and Brunner, 1950).[5] In addition, there was the seemingly key issue of how far government was to have a role in standardization. Respondents to the Andrews and Brunner survey (1950: 207-8) recognized the benefits gained in textiles and engineering from wartime compulsory simplification and standardization, but the general employers' posture was to resist any such central role for the government. For example the FBI tried to use the establishment of a specialist committee on standardization under the AACP to squash the Ministry of Supply committee on that issue (PRO, 1949c: AACP meeting, November 1948). Employers were also resistant to a semi-official body like the British Standards Institution (BSI) (as opposed to industry by itself) having any role in initiating standards, or government any role in enforcing them (PRO, 1949a). The Lemon Committee seems to have largely followed this view, and lent over backwards to avoid any suggestions that the BSI should play a more positive role (PRO, 1949b).[6]

The overall picture on standardization is that many employers recognized its potential benefits, but retained a belief that it could easily go too far in British conditions. The government itself pressed the issue quite hard. The Special Research Unit of the Board of Trade, for example, was largely concerned with the links between standardization and productivity (PRO, 1946c, 1947b, 1947c). But industry was insistent it proceed at its own slow pace.

The deficiencies of British cost accounting, and the absence, in particular, of systems of standard costing and budgeting, were a common feature of reformist approaches to British industry in this period. For example, almost all the Working Parties set up to look at (mainly consumer) industries under Labour reported unfavourably on the position in this regard (PRO, 1948e). For example, the Working Party Report on Cotton (1946: 132) remarked that 'it is broadly true to say that the industry as a whole lacks adequate knowledge of its cost structure'. The deficiencies of British industry in this regard were especially emphasized by the reports of the AACP. Many of the reports on individual industries stressed the link between American management efficiency and costing systems, a link summed up in typically hyperbolic fashion by Hutton's review of the AACP, where he argues 'management is measurement' and where the key characteristic of American management is that 'all measurements are part of the planning, costing or reaching of targets and because only those measures are made which have relevance to these operations' (Hutton, 1953: 49). The AACP also sent a specialist team to the US to report on management accounting, which produced the argument that the key to American efficiency was American costing and budgeting procedures, and recommended that British management 'in considering the future and preparing plans, should make the fullest use of budgeting and forecasting, based on accounting and costing data' (AACP, 1950: 14–16).

There is little evidence that all this spate of recommendations had much effect on British industry. The impressionistic evidence suggests that 'the thought in many entrepreneurs' minds that cost accounting was just another new-fangled administrative overhead could not easily be dislodged' (Stacey, 1954: 202; Parker, 1969: 1–11; Armstrong, 1987). The reasons for this very limited advance of standard costing cannot be ascertained easily. But plainly, along with the very limited movement on standardization, it was linked to the slow progress of 'scientific management' as a whole in Britain. However, before this broad point is addressed, something needs to be said on the attempts in the 1940s to instal direct accounting for productivity in British enterprises.

Whilst the early discussions of productivity focused on intercountry differences, it was soon recognized that, if the productivity campaign was to move from rhetoric to action, some more precise pinpointing of the issue was required. Hence Rostas was keen to move quickly towards detailed studies of productivity in different industries – though he faced resistance on this from the FBI (PRO, 1948d: Meeting 3 November 1948). But even such detailed measurement would not make productivity central to management's daily agenda – for that productivity needed to be part of everyday management accounting. Such a course was actively promoted by the BIM, which in 1949 published two booklets on the subjects *Indices of Productivity* and *Measurement of the Effectiveness of the Productive Unit* (see also PRO, 1949d).

In the first of these documents, L.P.C. Tippett, a well known expert on the cotton industry, commended the use of labour productivity measures as a stimulus to management. However, the discussion of his paper at the BIM conferences showed widespread lack of enthusiasm for the idea, many arguing that profitability was the key aim of firms, and that productivity measures focused too much on the production as opposed to the selling side of businesses.

In the second of these booklets, Sir E. Smith and Dr R. Beeching attempted to construct a sophisticated system of productivity accounting, again based on labour productivity. They took on board the problem of capital's contribution to productivity by trying to measure this contribution in terms of indirect labour units. This elaborate effort (similar to Marxist attempts to construct a general labour theory of value by dated labour inputs) also received a less than enthusiastic response, both because of the complexity of the system and the focus on production as the only element in efficiency.

In later years others were to attempt a similar task of incorporating productivity measurement directly into management practices (e.g. Davis, 1955). But as a review of Davis' book in the *Productivity Measurement Review* (1956a) pointed out:

Many of the advantages of productivity measurement as such could be derived from a simpler, if less elegant method; on the other hand the many managers, especially in large firms, who would like to be provided with a set of simple indications of the effectiveness of their business operations might be better advised to look for such indications in other directions.

An earlier article in the same journal (1956b) had questioned the whole idea of extending productivity measurement from the national economy to the individual firm:

In a government policy designed to increase standards of living, that is, to increase National Product per capita, it is obviously desirable that the basic element, average output per man-hour, should be as high as possible. From the point of view of the individual firm, the desirable target may be quite different. There is no particular reason why the firm should try to reach the highest possible output per man-hour. The classical function of the entrepreneur or of management is to find the most profitable combination of output factors, and it is possible – and even likely – that with labour being relatively cheap in Europe, it will not be to the advantage of a European firm to reach the high ouput per man-hour which may be a condition of survival for an American firm.

A survey of British businessmen in the late 1940s pointed out that some kind of productivity measures could be constructed from the most elementary forms of cost accounting, and this was what businessmen usually meant when they replied positively to questions about productivity accounting. There was no sense that such figures formed part of the day-to-day management process (Andrews and Brunner, 1950: 199–200).

The idea that direct measurement of productivity was an important element in raising productivity seems to have been taken seriously by the accounting bodies. For example, the Institute of Cost and Works Accountants (ICWA) set up a Joint Committee with the Institute of Production Engineers (IPE) in the belief that 'It is the measurement of productivity at the factory level that has been considered by the Joint Committee, for it is by using these ratios that industrial efficiency can be improved' (ICWA/IPE 1951: 6). '[T]hese ratios' referred to the range of productivity measures linking outputs to inputs. Like most discussions at this time the report assumed that labour productivity would be the normal measure of productivity, whilst recognizing the partial nature of that measure (ICWA/IPE 1951: 5–6).

These attempts at making productivity measurement a key part of the managerial task at plant level do not seem to have got very far. Lack of permeation to practising managers has already been noted. But in addition the Report of the AACP team on *Management Accounting* (1950: 6) made clear that in the US, that Mecca of high productivity, 'industry makes little attempt to measure productivity, preferring to rely on unit costs'.

Indeed, it would seem that the AACP report was notable for bringing out how the Americans did not have new techniques of measurement to offer, but rather differed from Britain in the intensity and speed of deployment of cost information, and its use as a vital management tool (AACP, 1950; *Accountant*, 1951). So productivity measurement often came back to questions of accurate costing, and standard costing techniques. In this context, output per man would be just one ratio amongst several (PRO, 1951).

But the measurement of labour productivity was not just one more 'technical' costing device. It is clear from the contemporary literature that the one element in the attempts to reform the calculative practices of enterprises which did make progress was that of the set of practices usually generically entitled work study. For example, the ICWA/IPE (1951: 17) report pointed to the desirability of standard costing techniques being based on 'the use of work evaluation methods based on time-study methods or some other forms of scientific estimate of process-time for a product'. Time-study was usually embraced with less enthusiasm by government bodies, but the Board of Trade was an enthusiastic proponent of motion-study, propagating this through an exhibition in 1945, and through the work of the Board's Production Efficiency Service (PRO, 1948f).

It is probably right to say that the main effect on the management technologies of British industry of the attempt at 'Americanization' after the Second World War was the spread of work-study. This increased usage of work-study was suggested by the Ministry of Labour's discussion of Wage Incentive Schemes (1951: 15) which noted the postwar growth of this method both as part of the growth of payments-by-results system, but also with the aim of improving production methods (see also Carew, 1987: ch. 9).

Work-study seems the one element of American mass production which quickly became fairly widely diffused through British industry. Plainly a word of warning is needed on this topic – we have little direct evidence on management practices at this time, and much of what we think we know is derived from documents or data at least one remove from the firm – from government reports, the work of managerial ideologues, etc. That said, it seems difficult to argue that scientific management, characterized as a general doctrine based on emphasis on mass production, deskilling of labour, standard cost and homogeneous production had made much headway by this period (e.g. the Working Party Report on Cotton, 1946: 185–6; more generally Elbaum and Lazonick, 1987). Certainly, it was not the main ideology informing the Labour Government's attempts to change British management practices, despite the governmental interest in standardization and standard costing noted above.

If it is possible to characterize the general approach of the Attlee Government it would be as one dominated by the ideology of 'Human Relations'. At the centre of the Human Relations prescription is the idea that 'management had to adopt a participative procedure which on the one hand allowed workers to feel some emotional involvement in the activities of the enterprise, while on the other retaining initiative and final authority firmly in managerial hands' (Child, 1969: 116). This aptly summarizes much of what many labour leaders seem to have believed in this period. Perhaps it is most obvious in the campaign to revive Joint Production

Committees (JPCs) as part of the production and productivity campaign (Tomlinson, 1987b). As far as the main proponents of JPCs were concerned, their primary purpose was not 'industrial democracy' but consultation, aiming to get the worker involved in the enterprise, but without challenging managerial prerogatives (Chalmers *et al.* 1949; Ministry of Labour, 1949, 1952, 1953).

This posture did not simply reflect the undoubted employer hostility to the perceived radical possibilities of JPCs, but linked to key themes of Labour's overall ideology. As already noted, Labour was committed to a cooperative consensual view of management of the economy in general. But, in addition, Cripps and others seem to have been strongly influenced directly by the human relations school of management ideologies (PRO, 1947d). In particular, this meant a concern with 'industrial psychology'. As Urwick wrote in 1944 'Industrial relations are primarily a matter of psychology. They must be an integral part of all management, not a segregated function. And the key to them is effective leadership at all levels' (cited in Child, 1969: 116; see also Albu, 1952).

In the 1920s and 1930s 'industrial psychology' had focused largely on personal dysfunction and its impact on work, but the human relations approach emphasized the need for the workplace to provide positive mental health (Miller and Rose, 1988, 1990: 18–23). This was the kind of work looked to as informing reform in the factory by the 'Human Factors' (sic) panel of the Committee on Industrial Productivity established in 1947 (PRO, 1947e).[7]

Of course, at a higher level of generality 'scientific management' and 'human relations' can both be seen as part of a broad tendency in the twentieth century to render the individual in production open to scrutiny and discipline in the name of increased output and efficiency. In this context human relations, like standard costing, is part of a 'vast project of standardisation and normalisation of the lives of individuals' (Miller and O'Leary, 1987: 238). But, in the shorter perspective of this chapter, the fact that human relations predominated over scientific management in the 1940s is of some significance.

This predominance of human relations has two aspects. It seems clear that it was a predominance that extended beyond managerial ideologies to both practising management and government.

As regards practising management, the pre-eminence of human relations doctrine can be imperfectly but reasonably inferred by the spread of joint consultation. This was the institutional representation of human relations *par excellence*. For example, George Schuster, both a practising manager and a managerial ideologue, made clear the links when he advocated joint consultation as the prime means 'to make each industrial unit a harmonious live co-operating community, spontaneously working together for a common purpose which is understood and accepted by all its members' (Schuster, 1952: 68). A similar linkage between human relations ideology and the practice of joint consultation is widely evident (e.g. Industrial Welfare Society, 1948, National Institute of Industrial Psychology, 1952; Scott, 1952; Lynton, 1949).

The extent of joint consultation is difficult to gauge exactly, but there seems little doubt it spread quickly in the late 1940s, following encouragement by the Ministry of Labour transmitted through many employers/ trade union joint agreements (summarized in Ministry of Labour, 1949: 118–9). Survey material suggests that in 1949 up to 73 percent of all firms in a range of major industrial sectors had joint consultation 'in practice', though the figure was biased upwards both by the differential response to the survey and the weighting towards engineering, where the practice was most widespread (Robson Brown and Howell-Everson, 1950).

### Conclusions

The pre-eminence of human relations doctrine in the 1945–51 Labour Government is in some ways curious, given the typically anti-union bias of this approach (Child, 1969: 135–6). But, on the other hand, its symmetry with other aspects of Labour's policies can be seen. These include: focus on *labour* productivity as the key economic problem (however fortuitously that may have arisen), a focus on the enterprise as a place where workers need to feel involved in order to give of their best, and a focus on industrial relations as essentially about psychology. Given the overarching macro political commitment to cooperation and consensus, these different elements fit quite readily together. So although the tensions and contradictions should not be ignored, the productivity drive can be seen as having a certain coherence as a strategy, albeit one that is highly contingent. Such coherence as existed, it should be emphasized, sprang not from an overarching grand design, but from the interplay of certain intellectual and political conditions which joined briefly in the highly specific circumstances of the 1940s. It did not survive into the seemingly 'easier' economic times of the 1950s.

Equally, it is important not to exaggerate the coherence of the productivity drive even in its 'heyday' in the late 1940s. As has been suggested above, elements of the reform of management practices, especially in the area of management accounting, were 'in play' at this time, without fitting easily into the rhetoric of human relations. Nevertheless, and especially because of a wide interest in standardization, costing methods were an important issue in the late 1940s. Although usually anxious not to be seen telling industry what to do, the government did exert some pressure for changes in this field, via such bodies as the Ministry of Supply. This concern with costing also gained some purchase from the general concern with productivity, and the issue of measurement involved in that elusive concept.

But the final conclusion of this chapter must be that the rise of the 'productivity problem' did not provide the occasion for a successful governmental attempt radically to reform management practices in general, or management accounting in particular. For all its undoubted serious concern with reforming enterprise practices, the government did not find a route into the enterprise that such a reform programme would have required.

NOTES

I am grateful to the editors of this volume for the very helpful comments on earlier drafts of this chapter.

1. During the Second World War there was also discussion of productivity trends in order to predict postwar National Income (e.g. Balogh, Appendix: 344–401 in Beveridge, 1944).
2. Studenski (1949) is the standard work on the history of National Income Accounting.
3. Rostas had already published pioneer work on productivity (1943) and (1945), and published two books on the subject in 1948 (1948a, 1948b), though none of them dealt with the postwar, but this was dealt with in his 1952 article. In 1947 his approach to productivity was strongly criticized by the President of the Royal Statistical Society (Snow, 1947) but Rostas responded vigorously. After his death in 1954, Rostas' work was credited with 'setting in motion the forces which led to the so-called "European Productivity drive"' (*Productivity Measurement Review*, 1958: 5).
4. There was a parallel debate on the relation between productivity and income per head (e.g. Arndt, 1947; Barna, 1946).
5. American commentators tended to view this idea as one more British excuse for low productivity (e.g. PRO, 1949c).
6. This position was complicated by the Treasury's cheeseparing view that the BSI should not receive government money but be reliant on industry support (PRO, 1949b).
7. The Human Factors panel took a fairly eclectic view of industrial psychology, drawing not only on the Tavistock Institute (founded in 1947) but on the older National Institute of Industrial Psychology, and also the work of Brown and Jacques at Glacier Metals, with its emphasis on strong constitutional mechanisms and explicit union recognition in the workplace.

REFERENCES

AACP, 1950. *Management Accounting*, London: AACP

*Accountant*, 1951. 'American Management Methods', *The Accountant* 10 January 1951: 141–2

Albu, A., 1952. 'The Organisation of Industry', in R.H.S. Crossman (ed.), *New Fabian Essays*, London: Fabian Society

Andrews, P.W.S. and Brunner, E., 1950. 'Productivity and the Business Man', *Oxford Economic Papers* 2(2), June: 197–225

Armstrong, P. 1987. 'The Rise of Accounting Controls in British Capitalist Enterprises', *Accounting, Organisations and Society*, 12(5): 415–36

Arndt, H.W., 1947. 'Productivity in Manufacturing and Real Income Per Head in Great Britain and the USA', *Oxford Economic Papers* 8 November: 65–80

Balfour Committee, 1927–9. *Reports on Industrial and Commercial Efficiency*, London: HMSO

Barna, T., 1946. 'Notes on the Productivity of Labour: Its Concept and Measurement', *Bulletin of the Oxford Institute of Statistics* 8(7), July: 205–16

    1949. 'Those "Frightfully High" Profits', *Bulletin of the Oxford Institute of Statistics* 11(7), July: 213–26

Barnett, C., 1986. *The Audit of War*, London: Macmillan

Beveridge, W.H., 1944. *Full Employment in a Free Society*, London: Allen & Unwin

Cairncross, A., 1985. *Years of Recovery: British Economic Policy 1945–51*, London: Methuen

Carew, A., 1987. *Labour Under the Marshall Plan*, Manchester: Manchester University Press

Chalmers, J.M., Mikardo I. and Cole, G.D.H, 1949. *Consultation or Joint Management?*, Fabian Tract 277, London: Fabian Society

Child, J., 1969. *British Management Thought: A Critical Analysis*, London: Allen & Unwin

Clark, C., 1932. *The National Income 1924–31*, London: Macmillan

Davis, H.S., 1955. *Productivity Accounting*, Pennsylvania: Pennsylvania University Press

Durbin, E., 1985. *New Jerusalems: The Labour Party and the Economics of Democratic Socialism*, London: Routledge & Kegan Paul

Elbaum, B. and Lazonick, W., 1987. *The Decline of the British Economy*, Oxford: Oxford University Press

Farrell, M.J., 1957. 'The Measurement of Productive Efficiency', *Journal of the Royal Statistical Society* 120(3): 253–78

Flux, A.W., 1913. 'Gleanings from the Census of Production Report', *Journal of the Royal Statistical Society* 76(6): 557–81

    1924. 'The Census of Production', *Journal of the Royal Statistical Society* 87(3): 351–75

    1929. 'The National Income', *Journal of the Royal Statistical Society* 92(1): 1–25

    1933. 'Industrial Productivity in Great Britain and the USA', *Quarterly Journal of Economics* 48(1): 1–38

HMSO, 1946. *Report of the Committee on Standardisation in the Engineering Industry*, London: HMSO

Henderson, P.D., 1952. 'Development Councils: An Industrial Experiment', in G.D.N. Worswick and P.H. Ady (eds.), *The British Economy 1945–50*, Oxford: Oxford University Press

Hotten, K., 1988. 'The Labour Party and the Enterprise', unpublished PhD. Dissertation, London University

Howson, S. and Winch, D., 1977. *The Economic Advisory Council*, Cambridge:

Cambridge University Press

Hutton, G., 1953. *We Too Can Prosper*, London: Chapman & Hall

Industrial Welfare Society (IWS), 1948. *Joint Consultation: A Symposium*, London: IWS

Institute of Cost and Work Accountants and Institute of Production Engineers (ICWA/IPE), 1951. *Measurement of Productivity – Applications and Limitations*, London: ICWA/IPE

Jewkes, J., 1946. 'Is British Industry Inefficient?', *Manchester School* 14(1): 1–16

Keynes, J.M., 1973. *The General Theory and After, Part 1: Preparation, Collected Writings, Volume 13*, Cambridge: Cambridge University Press

1978. *Activities 1939–1945: Internal War Finance, Collected Writings, Volume 22*, Cambridge: Cambridge University Press

1981. *Activities 1929–1931, Collected Writings, Volume 20*, Cambridge: Cambridge University Press

Kirby, M.W. and Rose, M., 1991. 'Productivity and Competitive Failure', in G. Jones and M.W. Kirby (eds.), *Competitiveness and the State in Twentieth Century Britain*, Manchester: Manchester University Press

Leyland, N.H., 1952. 'Productivity', in G.D.N. Worswick and P.H. Ady, *The British Ecomomy 1945–50*, Oxford: Oxford University Press

Lomax, K.S., 1956. 'UK Global Productivity Measurement', in OEEC European Productivity Association, *Productivity Measurement, Vol. III, Global Measurements of Productivity for International Comparisons at Branch and Industry Level*, Paris: OEEC

Lynton, R.P., 1949. *Incentives and Management in British Industry*, London: Routledge & Kegan Paul

Mercer, H., 1989. 'The Evolution of British Government Policy on Competition in Private Industry, 1940–56', unpublished PhD. Dissertation, London University

1991a. 'The Monopolies and Restrictive Practices Commission from 1949–56: A Study in Regulatory Failure', in G. Jones and M. Kirby (eds.), *Competitiveness and the State in Twentieth Century Britain*, Manchester: Manchester University Press

1991b. 'The Labour Government and the Private Sector', in N. Tiratsoo (ed.), *The Attlee Years*, London: Pinter

1992. 'Competition Policy', in H. Mercer, N. Rollings and J. Tomlinson (eds.), *The 1945 Labour Government and Private Industry*, Edinburgh: Edinburgh University Press

Middlemas, K., 1986. *Power, Competition and the State: Volume 1, Britain in Search of Balance 1940–61*, London: Macmillan

Miller, P. and O'Leary, 1987. 'Accounting and the Construction of the Governable Person', *Accounting, Organisation and Society* 12(3): 235–65

Miller, P. and Rose, 1988. 'The Tavistock Programme: The Government of Subjectivity and Social Life', *Sociology* 22(2): 171–92

1990. 'Governing Economic Life', *Economy and Society* 19(1): 1–31

Ministry of Labour, 1949. *Industrial Relations Handbook: Supplement No. 3 Joint Consultation in Industry*, London: HMSO

1951. Industrial Relations Handbook: Supplement No. 4 Wage Incentive

Schemes, London: HMSO
1952. *The Worker in Industry*, London: HMSO
1953. *Human Relations in Industry*, London: HMSO
National Institute of Industrial Psychology, 1952. *Joint Consultation in British Industry*, London: Staples
Nichols, T., 1987. *The British Worker Question*, London: Routledge & Kegan Paul
Parker, R.H., 1969. *Management Accounting: An Historical Approach*, London: Macmillan
Planning 1951: 'Development Councils', *Planning Vol.* 17, 326, March 17: 209–32
PRO, 1920. LAB 3/1 Committee on Increased Production, London: PRO
    1944. CAB 139/67 Central Statistical Office: Output Per Head
    1946a. CAB 134/188 Official Steering Committee on Economic Development, Memos, London: PRO
    1946b. CAB 134/189 Official Steering Committee on Economic Development, Memos, London: PRO
    1946c. BT 64/2316 Special Research Unit: Standardisation and Productivity, London: PRO
    1947a. CAB 134/190 Official Steering Committee on Economic Development, Meetings and Memos, London: PRO
    1947b. BT 64/2314 Special Research Unit: Standardisation and Productivity, London: PRO
    1947c. BT 64/2315 Special Research Unit: Standardisation and Productivity, London: PRO
    1947d. CAB 124/1093 Committee on Industrial Productivity, Minutes and Memos, London: PRO
    1947e. CAB 132/31–35 Committee on Industrial Productivity: Human Factors Panel, London: PRO
    1948a. CAB 134/210 Economic Planning Board, Minutes, London: PRO
    1948b. BT 195/19 Committee on Industrial Productivity: Productivity Drive, London: PRO
    1948c. CAB 134/639 Production Committee Memoranda, London: PRO
    1948d. CAB 134/591 Productivity (Official) Committee, Minutes and Memos, London: PRO
    1948e. BT 64/2313 Special Research Unit, Productivity, London: PRO
    1948f. BT 64/ 2324 Board of Trade: Production Efficiency Service, London: PRO
    1949a. SUP 14/141 Engineering Advisory Council: Standardisation in Engineering, London: PRO
    1949b. BT 105/1 AACP Standardisation and Simplification, London: PRO
    1949c. BT 195/66 AACP First Report and Subsequent Activities, London: PRO
    1949d. CAB 132/29 Committee on Industrial Productivity, Meetings and Memos, London: PRO
    1949e. T229/339 Control of Investment: Socialised Industries, London: PRO
    1950a. BT 64/2471 Amendments to the Industrial Organisation and Development Act, London: PRO
    1950b. PREM 8/1183 The State and Private Industry by H. Wilson, London: PRO
    1951. BT 64/712 AACP and the Creation of the British Productivity Council,

London: PRO

1952. SUPP 14/138 Economic Advisory Council, Minutes 1947–52, London: PRO

*Productivity Measurement Review*, 1956a. 'Review of Davis [1955]', 7, November: 37

1956b. 'Introduction', Special Number, June: 3

1958. 'Ten Years of Productivity Measurement', 14, August

Reddaway, W.B. and Smith, A.B., 1960. 'Progress in British Manufacturing Industries in the Period 1948–54', *Economic Journal* 70(1): 17–31

Robson Brown, W. and Howell-Everson, N.A., 1950. *Industrial Democracy at Work: A Factual Survey*, London: Pitman

Rogow, A., 1954. 'Relations Between the Labour Government and Industry', *Journal of Politics* 16(1): 3–23

Rogow, A. and Shore, P., 1955. *The Labour Government and British Industry 1945–1951*, Oxford: Blackwell

Rostas, L. 1943. 'Industrial Production, Productivity and Distribution in Britain, Germany and the USA', *Economic Journal* 53(1): 39–54

1945. 'Productivity of Labour in the Cotton Industry', *Economic Journal* 55(3): 192–205

1948a. *Productivity, Prices and Distribution in Selected British Industries*, Cambridge: Cambridge University Press

1948b. *Comparative Productivity in British and American Industry*, Cambridge: Cambridge University Press

1952. 'Changes in the Productivity of British Industry 1945–51', *Economic Journal* 62(1): 15–24

1955. 'Alternative Productivity Concepts', in OEEC, European Productivity Agency, *Productivity Measurement, Volume 1, Concepts*, Paris: OEEC

Sayers, R.S., 1956. *British Financial Policy 1939–1945*, London: HMSO

Schuster, G., 1952. 'Self Government in Industry', in Ministry of Labour, *The Worker in Industry*, London: HMSO

Scott, W.H., 1952. *Industrial Leadership and Joint Consultation*, Liverpool: Liverpool University Press

Snow, E.C. 1947. 'The Statistical Basis of Export Targets', *Journal of the Royal Statistical Society* 110(3): 169–86

Stacey, N.A.H., 1954. *English Accountancy: A Study in Society and Economic History 1800–1954*, London: Gee

Stone, R., 1951. 'The Use and Development of National Income and Expenditure Estimates', in D.N. Chester (ed.), *Lessons of the British War Economy*, Cambridge: Cambridge University Press

1977. *Inland Revenue Report on National Income 1929*, Cambridge: Department of Applied Economics

Studenski, P., 1958. *The Income of Nations*, New York: New York University Press

Tomlinson, J., 1982. *The Unequal Struggle?: British Socialism and the Capitalist Enterprise*, London: Macmillan

1987a. *Employment Policy: The Crucial Years 1939–1955*, Oxford: Oxford University Press

1987b. 'The 1945 Labour Government and Industrial Democracy', Brunel University, *Discussion Paper* 8702

1990. *Public Policy and the Economy Since 1990*, Oxford: Oxford University Press

1991a. 'A Missed Opportunity? Labour and the Productivity Problem 1945–51', in G. Jones and M. Kirby (eds.), *Competitiveness and the State in Twentieth Century Britain*, Manchester: Manchester University Press

1991b. 'Trade Unions and the Labour Government 1945–51', in N. Tiratsoo (ed.), *The Attlee Years*, London: Pinter

1991c. 'The Failure of the Anglo–American Council on Productivity', *Business History* 32(1): 82–92

1992. 'Productivity Policy', in H. Mercer, N. Rollings and J. Tomlinson (eds.), *The 1945 Labour Government and Private Industry*, Edinburgh: Edinburgh University Press

Urwick, L. 1944. 'Industrial Relations: Retrospect and Prospect', *British Management Review* 5(2): 56–67

Working Party Report on Cotton, 1946. Board of Trade, London, HMSO

Corporate control in large British companies: the intersection of management accounting and industrial relations in postwar Britain

*Peter Armstrong*

### Introduction

From the mid-1970s onwards, the academic partitioning of industrial relations and management accountancy has become increasingly inappropriate as a way of understanding corporate control. Accounts of post-1980s' industrial relations, however, continue to parade the traditional *dramatis personae* of industrial relations: management, trade unionism and State intervention (e.g. Batstone, 1984; MacInnes, 1987; Hyman, 1989). What is ignored in these scenarios is that industrial relations in large British companies now takes place on a terrain defined by budgetary planning and financial performance monitoring. On the accounting side, studies of trends in British management accounting practice have been equally insular. In effect, the issue has been couched in terms of progress, or the lack of it, on the tacit assumption that improved information systems would unproblematically improve the quality of management decisions (e.g. Jones, 1980; Coates *et al.*, 1983). In reality, the value of information depends on the ability of management to act on it, and this may well be subject to industrial relations constraints. For these reasons, neither industrial relations practice nor management accounting can be adequately understood in isolation from each other.

The aim of this chapter is to outline the management accounting–industrial relations interaction as it has developed in post-Second World War Great Britain. The territory is not entirely untrodden. Burchell, Clubb and Hopwood (1985) have demonstrated that the 1970s' vogue for value-added payment systems sprang from a conjunction of industrial relations corporatism and debates on accounting standards. Wardell and Weisenfeld's (1991) comparison of the development of management accounting in Great Britain and the USA has further advanced our understanding of these issues. More tangential to the present theme, a large body of literature, inspired by the Employment Protection Act 1975, has examined the disclosure of financial information by companies for collective bargaining purposes (Foley and Maunders, 1977; Cooper and Essex, 1977; Dickens, 1980; Craft, 1981; Purdy, 1981; Jenkins, 1982; Maunders and Foley, 1984; Ogden and Bougen, 1985; Owen and Lloyd, 1985; Amernic, 1985). At issue here, however, are financial reports rather than management accounting information. The context, moreover, has been that of formal bargaining rather than the day-to-day managerial conduct of industrial relations.

The strategy of this chaper is first to outline the developments in company structure and accounting control systems which form the context of postwar British industrial relations. The conventional 'industrial relations' view of developments is then considered in relation to this context, with the object of demonstrating the increased influence of accounting control systems on the managerial conduct of industrial relations from the mid-1970s onwards. The chapter concludes with a portrait of the budget-driven, line management-dominated approach to substantive industrial relations which has emerged in many large British companies, a system in which the personnel/industrial relations function appears to control only outline policies and procedures, and is otherwise relegated to a *post hoc* advisory role on the human consequences of line management action.

### Changes in company structure and control in postwar Britain

From the perspective of the 1990s, it is easy to forget that the British economy has not always been dominated by giant multi-establishment firms, controlled through dense flows of management accounting information. This scene is of relatively recent origin. Though there were large multi-plant undertakings in Britain even before the turn of the century (Payne, 1967), and although one or two of these (such as ICI) had adopted approximations to the multi-divisional form as early as 1930 (Hannah, 1976), even in the 1950s most British companies were still relatively small and organized on functional lines (Channon, 1973: 238). Management control systems were correspondingly undeveloped. A few pioneering companies, such as Austin (Church, 1979), had installed American-style management accounting systems during the 1930s, but these remained atypical. Even by the 1940s, the Industry Working Parties set up by the postwar Labour Government were highly critical of the primitive financial and cost accounting methods then used by the majority of British firms. According to Stacey (1954: 202), most British entrepreneurs of the period viewed cost accounting as 'just another newfangled administrative overhead'.

From the 1950s onwards, however, changes began to occur in both company structure and in forms of control. Between 1950 and 1970 the rate of merger and acquisition was such that industrial concentration in Great Britain rose from one of the lowest in the Western world at the beginning of the period, to one of the highest at its end (Prais, 1976). Since then, the process has continued. Organizational forms evolved with similar rapidity. By 1960, the holding company had replaced the single-function organization as the most common form amongst the top 100 companies. By 1970, the multi-divisional had become dominant (Channon, 1973: 238; Steer and Cable, 1978).

This, in turn, had implications for the development of accounting control systems. Though both holding companies and multi-divisionals involve the control of functional subsidiaries through flows of financial information, there are differences of both degree and of kind. As its name implies, the holding company basically controls operating subsidiaries through majority shareholdings. The core information flow is that of financial reporting. In the multi-divisional, by contrast, control procedures deriving from a cost accounting tradition (Chandler, 1977) permit far more detailed control than is possible through financial reports. In terms of information flow, the difference is that between a quarterly financial statement and a weekly, or even daily, battery of financial performance indicators reaching deep into the details of divisional operation. Within the multi-divisional firm, the attention of senior management is directed to any section which performs even temporarily below forecast. The reporting practices of the British GEC company during the 1970s are illustrative of this change in the nature and intensity of financial information (Williams *et al.*, 1983: 166).

In practice multi-divisionalization involved a rather more gradual extension of accounting controls than is implied in the foregoing sketch. Goold and Campbell (1987) have identified patterns of strategy formation in divisionalized companies wherein much of the initiative still lies with divisional executives. Conversely, Channon (1973), and Hill and Pickering (1986) note that there are multi-plant companies in which headquarters management continues to involve itself in operational matters. These pockets of resistance to the multi-divisional concept, however, appear to be temporary. Hill and Pickering (1986) and Marginson (1986) both report cases in which such obstructions of the characteristic multi-divisional control process have triggered off a second wave of devolution in which the power of divisional management has been reduced, so increasing the exposure of operating subsidiaries to headquarters monitoring and control. When these findings are set alongside anecdotal evidence that the more successful British conglomerates are now operating with very small headquarters staffs (Goldsmith and Clutterbuck, 1984), the implication is that these are concentrating almost exclusively on 'management by the numbers'. Consequently, one would expect the reliance of large British companies on accounting controls to go on increasing some time after the formal transition to the multi-divisional form.

Survey evidence on accounting information systems – such as it is – tends to bear out this picture, though comparisons over time are hampered by differences in sampling and methods. According to Parker (1969: 11), it was rare, in the Britain of 1960, to find a standard costing system in use. Yet a British Institute of Management (BIM) survey published in 1966, indicated that fully 70 per cent of the 100 member companies surveyed were then using standard costs. Whilst this *may* be a tribute to the forward-looking attitude of BIM member companies, it is difficult not to be sceptical. In a 1960s' study of industrial relations in 60 companies, Turner *et al.* (1977) found that fewer than one-half of them were able to separate labour from the other costs of production. By contrast, a recent survey of Britain's 100 largest companies (Marginson *et al.*, 1986, 1988) has shown that, in nearly all of the companies, headquarters management monitored raw labour costs and the unit labour costs of production against budgetary targets.

Over the same period, there were parallel developments in the reporting of aggregate operating unit performance. In 1975, a BIM survey of the Finance Directors of 223 companies (Melrose-Woodman, 1975) showed that roughly one-third of the companies were reporting quarterly financial information to senior management, with another fifth reporting monthly. Only one-fifth of the companies, however, were specifically including labour costs or the costs of production at that time. This concentration on the overall financial results of subsidiaries, rather than the detail of costs, is consistent with the reporting practices of the holding company.

During the late 1970s and early 1980s, this picture began to change. Pike's (1982) survey of capital budgeting practices in 150 major British companies revealed that, during the period 1975–80, there was a noticeable increase in the use of accounting data to decide on major investment projects, to monitor their progress, and to decide on whether to continue them. A 1980 survey of 550 companies carried out by the (then) Institute of Cost and Management Accountants (Jones, 1980), reported that over 95 per cent were preparing financial plans. Of these, about 90 per cent were reporting actual results to be compared against target at least monthly. A 1983 survey of reporting practices in 14 multi-divisionals revealed that, by then, multiple financial measures of the performance of divisions and operating subsidiaries were in general use (Coates *et al.*, 1983).

The broad picture which emerges from these studies is one of a massive expansion during the late 1970s and 1980s in the density of the management accounting information used to control operating subsidiaries within large companies, and a corresponding enhancement of the ability of head-quarters management to monitor labour costs and performance.

### The labour control problem of the 1960s: the view from industrial relations

One of the core promises of management accountancy is that of enhancing managerial control of labour costs. For this reason, the development of management accounting practice in Britain after the Second World War needs to be understood against the background of the changing labour cost problem, as this posed itself to employers and policy-makers. At least until the early 1980s, this issue was debated within an industrial relations rather than an accounting discourse. So, accordingly, were the 'solutions'.

Inherited from the prewar era was an 'official' system of industrial relations in which the typical small, functionally organized British company bargained with trade unions through the agency of an employers' association, and at national level. These negotiations set framework wage rates, normal working hours, holiday entitlements and overtime premiums. In their very nature, negotiations at this aggregated level could not concern themselves with workplace-specific issues such as manning levels or labour utilization. In any case, such matters were supposed to lie within managerial prerogative (the right of unilateral management decision), according to the national agreements inherited from the prewar era of massive unemployment and trade union weakness.

In the postwar context of relatively full employment, the reality was different. The traditional system of national bargaining, supported originally by employers as a means of 'taking wages out of competition', continued postwar in certain highly fragmented industries, such as electrical contracting. In these industries, national agreements determined actual pay (Clegg, 1976: 225). In other key industries – notably engineering – national agreements in the postwar era determined only non-pay conditions. In these cases, actual wage rates were increasingly negotiated at workplace level on the basis of the 'floor' set by national agreements.

The roots of this post-Second World War resurgence of establishment level bargaining lay principally in economic conditions. From the end of the Second World War until the late 1960s, unemployment in the UK remained below half a million. Firms in relatively prosperous areas, such as the industrial Midlands, experienced acute labour shortages. At the same time, a seller's market for British manufactures prioritized continuity of production over the containment of wage costs. On this basis there arose locally powerful shop steward organizations able to exert substantial control over working methods, despite the 'official' procedure agreements which reserved these issues for managerial prerogative. Shop stewards were also able to use the traditional preference of British management for piece-rate payment systems as a vehicle for extracting a variety of local pay increases over and above those nationally negotiated. On the issue of working methods, for example, agreements were negotiated at local level which guaranteed that no change would be introduced without *prior* agreement on new piece-rates (the 'status quo' clause, in trade union parlance). As for pay, a variety of local increases (for example, in the form of bonuses and guaranteed overtime) could be negotiated by tactically astute shop steward committees alive to the potential of subtle and not-so-subtle withdrawals of cooperation. At the aggregate level, the result was a growing gap between 'officially' negotiated wage rates and actual take-home pay. The term 'wage-drift' entered the policy-makers' lexicon.

On top of this negotiated wage-drift, Brown's important studies (1972, 1973) demonstrated that the operation of the status quo clause was adding a component of non-negotiated drift. Because of the short-run priority of meeting delivery dates over the containment of wage costs, senior line managers were tending to resolve disputes over the introduction of new methods by overruling any stand on the associated rates of pay which might be taken by the managers on the spot. The result was a selective 'slackening' of the piece-rates or time allowances for the operations in dispute. Such precedents could then be used by shop stewards' committees to argue for a general slackening of other rates in the name of 'custom and practice' – often using nugatory or entirely fictitious method changes as the occasion for negotiation. To the disgust of traditionally-minded work-study engineers, the result in some workplaces was that their time-studies became merely the first move in a negotiation between management and shop stewards. In other cases, actual job-timings were multiplied by progressively increasing 'allowances'. Nationally negotiated piece-rates would then be applied to these inflated timings, thus reconciling national agreements with levels of pay acceptable to the local workforce (Brown, 1973, ch.6).

At least in the engineering and motor vehicle industries, this was the general picture of shopfloor industrial relations during the late 1960s. At that time, cost accountants were comparatively few in number and also relatively junior in British managerial hierarchies. Thus there were probably few 'on-the-ground' advocates of standard cost systems as a solution to the problem of labour costs. Even if this had not been so, it is pertinent to ask what case could have been made for standard costing. Its supposed virtues depend on an expectation that the costs determined by work-study and current wage rates should normally be achievable. Clearly this was not then the case in British manufacturing companies. As Yetton (1976) has noted, the effect of fragmented piece-work bargaining on standard costing systems is effectively to corrupt and undermine them.

## The Donovan reforms and their industrial relations consequences

For the reasons outlined above, the 1960s' problem of wage costs and labour productivity was posed exclusively within an industrial relations frame of reference. Accordingly, it was a reform of Britain's fragmented bargaining system, rather than a development of the management accounting framework which was suggested as the solution. In the view of Fox (1966) and Flanders (1970), two prominent industrial relations pluralists of the day, the topical problems of unofficial strikes, restrictive practices and wage-drift were symptoms of a deeper 'disorder' which stemmed ultimately from the 'unofficial' system of *ad hoc* shopfloor bargaining. Believing that attempts to revive the tradition of national bargaining would be irrelevant to the issues raised at this level, and that a confrontation with shopfloor trade unionism was impractical, the pluralist proposal was to roll up the existing systems of bargaining in a new formalized bargaining structure at plant or company level. This was seen primarily as a management responsibility.

A key obstacle was the mind-set inculcated by the 'official' system of national bargaining. With industrial relations seen as a matter for the employers' associations rather than individual firms, it was difficult to convince managers that industrial relations reform was their business. For this reason, the major policy thrust came not from the employers themselves, but from a Labour Government concerned with the macroeconomic consequences of the British 'industrial relations problem'. A Royal Commission on Trade Unions and Employers' Associations (the Donovan Commission) was set up in 1965 and reported in 1968.

The Commission's proposals closely followed the pluralist prescription. The bargaining power which lay behind the disorder of the informal system was to be aggregated at a new level which would be simultaneously accessible to management action and relevant to the issues on which there was bargaining pressure from shop stewards – that of the plant or company. A condition of this reform of bargaining structure was a reform of payment systems in which the locally-determined piece-rates, which had served as the lever of grassroots' shop steward power, would be replaced by rational company-wide payment systems. *Ad hoc* bargaining was to be replaced by a recognition of the role of shop stewards within formalized procedures. Since the primary responsibility for restructuring industrial relations on this new pattern was to fall upon management, a corollary was that industrial relations would become a central element of company policy. In this task, managements were to be aided by the advice and encouragement of a standing Commission on Industrial Relations. Meanwhile, the 'outmoded' system of national bargaining was to be left to wither on the vine.

The impact of the Donovan proposals was uneven, and probably had less to do with the exhortations of the Commission than with a peripheral apparatus of legislative encouragement which came into being shortly after the Commission's report. Examples were the unfair dismissal legislation (1971) which encouraged employers to involve trade unions in disciplinary procedures and the Trade Union and Labour Relations Act 1974 which defined the rights of trade union representatives and members to time off for industrial relations activities.

In retrospect, the uneven response of employers to these initiatives is scarcely surprising. Influenced by the research experience of those academics who submitted evidence, the Commission had tended to equate the problems of British industrial relations as a whole with the situation in Midlands manufacturing. Other sectors responded according to their own traditions and experience. In the service sector, a tradition of anti-unionism, both of the 'hard' confrontational and 'soft' paternalist varieties persisted. Sectors in which small firms predominated (such as textiles) continued to bargain through the supposedly outmoded national system (Marsh, 1982; Marginson et al., 1988). To the extent that generalization is possible, the predominant response to the Donovan reforms was piecemeal and ad hoc. Some of the proposals were adopted as and when these appeared expedient. At other times and on other issues managements reverted to confrontational assertions of managerial prerogative (Purcell and Sisson, 1983).

However, a minority of Britain's larger companies restructured their bargaining arrangements along the lines recommended by Donovan (roughly speaking, the 'sophisticated moderns' described by Purcell and Sisson, 1983). An increasing number of Personnel/Industrial Relations managers were appointed at board level (compare the surveys of Brown, 1981; Daniel and Millward, 1983; Millward and Stevens, 1986 in this respect), whilst companies such as Massey-Fergusson produced formal company level industrial relations policies, which were promoted by the intellectual wing of the personnel profession as a blueprint for the future (Cuthbert and Hawkins, 1973; see also Salamon, 1987, for a contemporary industrial relations text which still pursues this line). By way of response, shop steward committees became increasingly bureaucratic and centralized in order to articulate local bargaining issues through the new plant or company level machinery (Batstone et al., 1977; Terry, 1983: 80).

In the meantime, economic and social conditions were changing rapidly. During the 1970s and 1980s, British manufacturers faced increasing competition, to which the main (sometimes the sole) managerial response appeared to be a determination to contain and reduce labour costs (e.g. Edwardes, 1983). Unemployment continued its steady rise to the 1986 peak of 3.2 million (probably over 4 million had the method of counting remained stable), thus exposing workplace trade union representatives to the experience of 'negotiating' successive waves of redundancy against the background of threatened plant closures. In short, the economic basis of the 'revolt from below' had largely disappeared, and with it the pragmatic case for the Donovan reforms. So too had any State support for the moral case for involving employees in decision-making through collective bargaining. Far from continuing to encourage a pluralist accommodation between management and trade unions, the Conservative Government of the 1980s passed four Employment Acts, each of which progressively circumscribed the ability of trade unions to organize collective action.

There are two versions of the fate of the Donovan reforms during this era of recession and repression. The popular view, fed by such spectacular demonstrations of managerial muscle as Michael Edwardes' dismissal of the British Leyland Convenor of Shop stewards for circulating a pamphlet opposing the company's corporate plan, is that they have been swept aside in a new era of 'macho management'. According to this scenario, shop stewards have been increasingly by-passed by direct management 'communications' which set out the price of avoiding yet another round of plant closures and redundancies.

To most British industrial relations academics, this popular view is a myth. Recent large-scale surveys (Batstone, 1984; Daniel and Millward, 1983; Millward and Stevens, 1986; Marginson, 1988; Brown, 1988) indicate that the institutional structure of industrial relations has remained largely intact. The Donovan apparatus of procedure agreements is not only still in operation, but appears to be extending (Millward and Stevens, 1986: 173). Managements continue to meet and bargain with shop stewards, though the coverage of collective bargaining and the range of issues may have narrowed somewhat. Meanwhile personnel practitioners remain confident – at least whilst filling in survey questionnaires – that the function is, if anything, gaining in importance (Torrington, Mackay and Hall, 1985). In fact these views may not be as irreconcilable as at first appears, since the first concerns a change in the *content* of industrial relations negotiation, whereas the second emphasizes a continuity in the *procedures and personnel* involved.

From an industrial relations viewpoint, the conclusion appears to be that the idea of a company industrial relations policy, operated through procedure agreements and staffed by professional personnel/industrial relations managers, has been adopted in a 'progressive' minority of Britain's large companies, whilst more have adopted parts of this approach on an *ad hoc* basis. In the formal sense, these bargaining reforms have largely survived the 1980s' recession, though the content of the agreements reached through them may well have changed.

The core argument of this chapter, however, is that this 'industrial relations' view of developments in the managerial control of the labour force is partial at best. Post-1980s' developments in British industrial relations need to be considered in the context of wider changes in the overall structure and control of large British companies. This forms the topic of the next section.

## The intersection of management accounting and industrial relations in the post-Donovan era

The 1960s' 'revolt from below' which inspired the Donovan Report occurred within functionally organized establishments. Typically, these were either autonomous or reported only outline financial results within a holding company framework. In both cases, relatively primitive accounting information systems allowed shopfloor bargaining to remain uncoupled from senior management policy.

The Donovan reforms were implemented, on the other hand, during a period of rapid change in company organization and management accounting systems. Operating units were being reorganized as subsidiaries of multi-divisional companies, the developing management accounting framework was increasing the ability of headquarters managements to monitor wage costs and labour productivity, and the scope for managerial action on this information was beginning to expand as unemployment began its climb towards the peak levels of the mid-1980s.

Some of these changes, of course, were noted within the discourse of industrial relations. Much of the post-1980s' research, for example, has been concerned with the impact of recession on collective bargaining (e.g. Batstone, 1984). The effects of changes in company structure have also been recognized, though these have been seen as posing problems for the implementation of company industrial relations policy in multi-plant concerns (Commission on Industrial Relations, 1974), rather than as implying changes in the overall system of managerial control. But the increasing tendency of British companies to articulate and monitor policy through the management accounting framework has generally escaped attention in industrial relations circles. An unfortunate result is that there is little evidence on the industrial relations consequences of management accounting systems, as these were being introduced during the 1960s and early 1970s. Such evidence as exists, however, indicates that, so far as labour costs were concerned, it was a control technique whose time had not yet arrived.

The theoretical potential for control was illustrated in Brown's studies of non-negotiated local wage-drift (1972, 1973). In 10 case study factories, it was demonstrated that wage-drift of this type was related to an absence of control over *ad hoc* pay decisions made by supervisors and first-line managers. Significantly, the only one of the factories which had a recognizable standard cost system was also the one with the lowest non-negotiated wage-drift (Brown, 1973: 164). However, there is evidence from the period which indicates that attempts to control wage-drift through accounting systems were likely to run into trouble. Whilst Brown's own study provided no data on the incidence of disputes, a review of the evidence by Purcell and Earl (1977) concluded that the 'first-order feedback' from wage cost monitoring systems was tending to provoke disputes by introducing local rigidities into the management negotiating position. During the mid-1970s, this was not a problem peculiar to accounting systems. Other evidence indicates that constraints of any kind on local bargaining flexibility were likely to have the same result. A survey of 60 manufacturing companies by Turner *et al.* (1977) indicated that the reform of industrial relations procedures was *also* associated with an increased incidence of stoppages, whilst Daniel's (1976) survey showed that there was an increased incidence of disputes wherever local managements were unable to reach settlement without higher authority. If British industry was not ready for the control of wage costs through budgets and standard costing, this was because it was not ready for the top-down control of wages at all.

During the late 1970s and 1980s, there are indications that this situation changed. Much of the evidence for the increased salience of accounting in connecting corporate policy with the management conduct of industrial relations is contained in Warwick surveys of factory managers (Edwards, 1987) and of industrial relations practices in large companies (Marginson *et al.* 1986, 1988). The picture is far from straightforward and there are considerable variations between companies. Nevertheless, some tentative conclusions are possible.

In certain respects, the company industrial relations policy is alive and well. There is substantial headquarters or divisional control of operating subsidiaries on policy and procedural basics such as union recognition, union membership agreements, membership of employers' associations and the handling of industrial tribunal cases. In addition, a 'framework' of substantive employment conditions is negotiated or otherwise determined at headquarters level. This includes the length of the working week, sick pay, holiday entitlements and redundancy terms (Marginson *et al.*, 1986: tables 7.1–7.4). On the issue of pay, about half of all large multi-plant companies have job evaluation schemes which cover manual employees in most establishments, a proportion which rises to 60 per cent in the case of non-manual employees (Marginson and Sisson, 1988: 97).

The staffing basis of the company industrial relations policy is also intact. There has been no decline in the numerical strength or degree of centralization of personnel departments (Marginson *et al.*, 1986: table 3.4; Millward and Stevens, 1986: 31), although the direction of establishment level personnel management from headquarters is not always in the hands of a specialist personnel department (Purcell, 1988). Nor has there been a reversal of the trend towards the professionalization of industrial relations management.[1] Notwithstanding anecdotally based alarms concerning the future of personnel management (e.g. Purcell, 1985) and the 'death of the old industrial relations game' (Tyson and Fell, 1986), most practitioners believe there has been no diminution in the importance of the personnel function (Batstone, 1984; Millward and Stevens, 1986: 39; Mackay and Torrington, 1987).

However, against this background of central control by the personnel/industrial relations function of basic policy and outline substantive conditions, the 1980s' trend in unionized companies has been towards devolved bargaining (Brown, 1988: 41).[2] The Warwick survey indicates that there is considerable management autonomy at establishment level on such issues as local payments, overtime, shift-working, and the introduction of new technologies (Marginson *et al.*, 1986; tables 5.3, 6.1, 7.10) as well as discipline, short-time working and redundancies (Edwards, 1987: 96). Despite the prevalence of company-wide job evaluation schemes, as noted above, the degree of local autonomy on pay is such that the establishment remains the most important level of bargaining on this issue (Brown, 1981; Daniel and Millward, 1983; Edwards and Marginson, 1988). The implication is that the autonomy of local managers is focused upon working methods, manning arrangements and wages – in other words, upon the immediate work–wage bargain. Local managers are also empowered to deal with disputes, where these are confined to their own establishments (as is generally the case), provided that wider issues of principle are not involved (Marginson *et al.*, 1986: 15).

At the establishment level, the industrial relations initiative now lies as much with line managers as with personnel specialists (Edwards, 1987: 94). A survey of establishment managing directors (Millward and Stevens, 1986: 43–6) indicates that they thought that their departmental line managers had more influence than local personnel managers on all industrial relations issues except the conduct of disputes not involving their own departments. They also believed that the influence of departmental line managers was increasing, whilst that of personnel departments remained static (see also Mackay and Torrington, 1987: 163; Storey, 1987).

Further insight into the division of establishment level industrial relations responsibilities between personnel and line managers in the 1980s can be gained from Daniel's (1986) survey. The involvement of personnel managers in organizational changes not involving new technology was confined to the stages after the decision to proceed had been made (Daniel, 1986: 72, 109). When new technology was involved, they tended to be excluded altogether.

The fact that line managers now take many of the key decisions on local industrial relations does not mean that the personnel function is without influence. They may well be consulted. What it does mean, however, is that the context of local decision-making on industrial relations is now that of local line management in general. Increasingly, this is one of detailed financial target-setting and performance monitoring (Kinnie, 1985). The implication is that the bargaining autonomy of establishment level line managers is strictly circumscribed by, and monitored through, the budgetary process. At more detailed levels, their performance is also monitored against targets for manpower budgets and the unit labour costs of production (Marginson, 1986, 1988), as well as profitability and such non-financial indicators as quality standards and production schedules (Edwards, 1987: 106).

There is also ample evidence that the material interests of establishment line managers are now linked to accounting indicators of performance. In the case of companies which are organized as profit centres, the lowest level of profit centre is normally the operating establishment (Marginson *et al.*, 1986, 1988), and roughly 40 per cent of the managers of these are paid some form of performance-linked bonus (Coates *et al.*, 1983). For factory managers in general, on the other hand, Edwards' data (1987: 50) indicate that variable elements in pay are more usually linked to the profitability of companies as a whole. When account is also taken of the likely informal effect of establishment performance on managerial careers (see, for example, Goold and Campbell, 1987), there can be little doubt that the career interests of establishment level line managers are materially linked to those aspects of their conduct of industrial relations which are visible through accounting reports.

Alongside this budget-driven dominance of local industrial relations issues by line management, local personnel managers continue to act as the representatives of such headquarters policy as exists. Millward and Stevens (1986: 31, 33) found that they reported to divisional or headquarters personnel managers, rather than to local line managers, and that there was frequent consultation between the different levels of personnel management on a range of industrial relations issues.

What seems to have developed is a *dual* linkage between the management of industrial relations at establishment level and corporate policy. The input of local personnel management connects to outline company industrial relations policy through contacts with personnel managers at divisional or headquarters level. The input of local line managers, on the other hand, connects to corporate policy primarily through accounting indicators of performance. Since line managers are evaluated against budgetary targets derived from a planning process which largely excludes industrial relations considerations (Brown, 1981: 41; Hill and Pickering, 1986), the *aspects* of corporate policy to which the input of local line management connects are those of manufacturing and capital investment. As the initiative on substantive issues – including productivity increases – now lies with local line management, it is likely that this second linkage between corporate policy and local industrial relations is increasing in importance relative to the first. Meanwhile corporate industrial relations policy, as articulated by local personnel management, may be reduced to smoothing out the human consequences of line management action.

### Establishment level collective bargaining within the new management accounting framework

Depending on trade union bargaining pressure, the intersection of management accounting and industrial relations may assume different forms. Where trade unions are strong enough to make positive demands, preplanned budgets may reduce the ability of local managements to reach an accommodation. Where union organization is weak, on the other hand, a line manager with an eye on the financial performance indicators may attempt to impose a pay settlement or a change in working practices which will reduce unit labour costs.

#### *Establishment bargaining under budgetary constraint*

During the 1980s and 1990s, the policy trend in large companies has been towards a devolution of collective bargaining, accompanied by a reliance on budgetary constraint as a means of retaining headquarters control. Thus Brown (1988) reported a fairly rapid trend during the early 1980s towards devolved bargaining in unionized companies. Over half the companies in that survey reported that they planned for the approaching wage round several months in advance, and about a quarter of them integrated this into the overall financial planning process.

Two case studies illustrate how collective bargaining within the budgetary regime is developing. In two companies studied by Purcell and Gray (1986), the task of face-to-face bargaining with trade unions was wholly devolved to divisional personnel departments. However, it was the task of headquarters personnel management to ensure that the divisional office contained any settlement within the budgetary framework decided at head office. By these means, it was intended that the trade unions should continue to dissipate their energies in 'bargaining' at the devolved level, without challenging the budgetary process.

In a study of the introduction of devolved bargaining at Coates Viyella, Leopold and Jackson (1990: 190) also found that, at subsidiary level

> management teams ... operated under a general financial constraint. Subsidiary companies had to prepare forward budgets containing provisions for increased labour costs for approval by the Divisional Boards before negotiation commenced. Although there was a degree of flexibility in these provisions, exceeding the budget on labour costs to a significant extent would be a very difficult step for a managing director to take.

Unfortunately Leopold and Jackson do not make it clear whether the 'flexibility' to which they refer is a genuine leeway for negotiation, or merely the normal allowance for volume variations in flexible budgets.

### Accounting performance indicators and local management initiative

When trade unions are weakened – which, with many exceptions, was the broad situation in the UK during the early and mid-1980s – the achievement of budgetary targets for labour costs may be relatively unproblematic. Accounting performance indicators may then encourage a proactive approach to establishment level industrial relations.

Consistent with this hypothesis, an analysis of 1980s' industrial relations surveys by Metcalf (1989) reveals that roughly 60 per cent of managements obtained at least one productivity concession during the manufacturing recession of the early 1980s. That this was the result of unilateral management initiative is indicated by the fact that industrial action was twice as prevalent where productivity concessions were obtained as compared to settlements where they were not. Recalling the evidence reviewed earlier that managerial policy on the work–wage bargain tends now to be made at establishment level and by line, rather than personnel managers, the indication is of unilateral initiatives by relatively junior line managers, not corporate management. This interpretation is also consistent with Metcalf's finding that productivity concessions were not obtained through formal company level flexibility deals, but through existing negotiating machinery. Metcalf's data indicate that this pattern of managerial action on 'restrictive' labour practices was sufficiently widespread to become visible at the macro level, in the unusually high growth of labour productivity during the early 1980s.

The connection between budgetary pressure and local management initiative which may lie behind these overall trends is illustrated in a case study reported by Edwards and Scullion (1982). Following a scrutiny by headquarters management of production levels and labour inputs, the managers of a small subsidiary unilaterally announced a reduction of overtime. This was in violation of an informal local agreement with shop stewards that production plans and manning levels would allow for about 8 hours of overtime per worker per week. This initiative led to a dispute.

There are indications that the 1980s' trend towards devolved bargaining may have been driven in part by a desire on the part of corporate managements to expose establishment level industrial relations to the pressures of budgetary control. In Leopold and Jackson's (1990) study of Coates Viyella, the devolution of bargaining was explicitly aimed at securing local concessions on labour utilization and flexibility in return for the annual pay round. Aiming, as they put it, to institute the bargaining of 'Something for something in place of something for nothing' the Coates Viyella management withdrew from national bargaining through the Knitwear Industries Federation and began bargaining at 16 subsidiary profit centres.

This substitution of budgetary pressure on line management for industrial relations policy also appears to be occurring in the public sector. Pendleton's (1991) study of 1980s' trends in British Rail revealed that reductions in the government grant had been transmitted to area managers as a tightening of budgetary controls. At the same time, senior management, impatient with the 'time-wasting' involved in local procedures, began to regard rigid adherence to these procedures as undesirable. At the local level, the result was a reduction in the time off given to union representatives for trade union activity, and a tendency for area managers to break local agreements in their pursuit of reduced costs.

As these case studies show, instead of acting as a constraint on local negotiations, by the late 1980s the budgetary framework was being used to stimulate a 'market mentality' amongst establishment managers, whereby they competed for investment capital with their own careers at stake (Kinnie, 1987). In the view of Purcell and Ahlstrand (1989) the consequence for industrial relations is an opportunist fixation on short-term accounting returns to the neglect of long-term human resource strategies, not to mention the cost in disputes indicated by Metcalf's (1989) data.

On the whole, the framework of budgetary control and accounting reports which inspires these local initiatives is formulated without reference to industrial relations considerations (Brown, 1981: 28; Hill and Pickering, 1986). Perhaps in recognition of this state of affairs, recent prescriptive writings on personnel/human resource management show signs of an abandonment of the claims of industrial relations as corporate policy and an acceptance of a diminished role as the executive arm of the budgetary process (see Armstrong, 1988 for a review of this tendency). In this respect, the corporate industrial relations policy may be in decline. For the time being, however, it appears that the industrial relations initiatives of establishment level managers still occur against the background of a centrally-determined procedural outline.

## Conclusions

In Britain's large multi-plant companies there are indications that, during the 1980s, the management accounting framework has played an increasing role in linking corporate policy and establishment level industrial relations. This linkage now has a dual character. On the one hand, the corporate industrial relations policies which were partly a legacy of the 1968 Royal Commission, continue to exist, in the sense that certain framework procedural and substantive issues are decided at headquarters level. Moreover, the local conduct of industrial relations is additionally influenced by contacts between corporate and establishment level personnel managers. On the other hand, the main substance of the immediate work–wage bargain is increasingly influenced by line management at the operating subsidiary level. Corporate control of this second input into local industrial relations is primarily exerted through budgetary control systems which derive from manufacturing and capital investment strategy, rather than from industrial relations policy.

Even during the manufacturing recession of the 1980s, the constraints and pressures of budgetary controls and financial indicators of performance have been associated with an increased incidence of disputes. There are indications that these have occurred because the accounting framework encourages local managers to push for flexibilities which, in practice, are used less to reorganize the production process along rational lines than to impose increased workloads (Elger, 1989). To the extent that this is the case, in the event of an economic upturn, the prognosis for the incidence of disputes under the emergent dual control system is not good.

NOTES

The author gratefully acknowledges the helpful comments made by Anthony Ferner, Keith Sisson and Peter Miller on earlier versions of this chapter.
1. For an indication of the professionalization of personnel/industrial relations management, compare Brown (1981), Daniel and Millward (1983) and Millward and Stevens (1986) on the proportion of industrial relations managers who are professionally qualified.
2. According to Purcell and Sisson (1983), the major exceptions to this trend towards devolved work–wage bargaining have occurred in companies such as British Leyland where production processes create interdependencies between plants which have prevented the adoption of sink or swim policies towards 'militant' sections of the workforce. There, the attractions of the specific

industrial relations strategies of isolating union negotiators from these work-places and neutralizing them within mass company-wide votes had, until the early 1980s, encouraged the centralization of bargaining. Even in the BL case the then managing director, Sir Michael Edwardes (1983: 89) expressed a preference for devolved bargaining – but only if this could be linked to cost or profit centres.

REFERENCES

Amernic, J.H., 1985. 'The Role of Accounting in Collective Bargaining', *Accounting Organizations and Society* 10(2): 227–53
Armstrong, P., 1988. 'The Personnel Profession in the Age of Management Accountancy', *Personnel Review* 17(1): 25–31
Batstone, E., 1984. *Working Order*, Oxford: Blackwell
Batstone, E., Boraston, E. and Frenkel, S., 1977. *Shop Stewards in Action: the Organization of Workplace Industrial Conflict and Accommodation*, Oxford: Blackwell
Bougen, P., 1989. 'The Emergence, Roles and Consequences of an Accounting–Industrial Relations Interaction', *Accounting, Organizations and Society* 14(3): 203–34.
British Institute of Management (BIM), 1966. *Budgetary Control in the Small/ Medium Size Company*, Information Summary 126, London: BIM
Brown, W.A., 1972. 'A Consideration of Custom and Practice', *British Journal of Industrial Relations* 10: 42–61
    1973. *Piecework Bargaining*, London: Heinemann
    1988. *The Structure and Processes of Pay Determination in the Private Sector: 1979–1986*, London: CBI
Brown, W. (ed.), 1981. *The Changing Contours of British Industrial Relations*, Oxford: Blackwell
Burchell, S., Clubb, C. and Hopwood, A., 1985. 'Accounting in its Social Context: Towards a History of Value-Added in the United Kingdom', *Accounting, Organizations and Society* 10(4): 381–413
Chandler, A.D. Jr., 1977. *The Visible Hand: the Managerial Revolution in American Business*, Cambridge MA: Harvard University Press
Channon, D.F., 1973. *The Strategy and Structure of British Enterprise*, London: Macmillan
Church, R., 1979. *Herbert Austin*, London: Europa
Clegg, H.A., 1976. *The System of Industrial Relations in Great Britain*, 3rd edn, Oxford: Blackwell
Coates, J.B., Smith, J.E. and Stacey, R.J., 1983. 'Results of a Preliminary Survey into the Structure of Divisionalised Companies, Divisionalised Performance Appraisal and the Associated Role of Management Accountancy', *Paper* 7 in D. Cooper, R. Scapens and J. Arnold (eds.), *Management Accounting Research and Practice*, London: ICMA: 265–82
Commission on Industrial Relations, 1974. *Industrial Relations in Multi-Plant Undertakings*, London: HMSO
Cooper, D. and Essex, S., 1977. 'Accounting Information and Employee Decision-Making', *Accounting, Organizations and Society* 2(3): 201–17
Craft, J.A., 1981. 'Information Disclosure and the Role of the Accountant in Collective Bargaining', *Accounting, Organizations and Society* 6(1): 97–107

Cuthbert, N.H. and Hawkins, K.H., 1973. *Company Industrial Relations Policies*, Harlow: Longman

Daniel, W.W., 1976. *Wage Determination in Industry*, London: PEP

1986. *Workplace Industrial Relations and Technical Change*, London: PSI

Daniel, W.W. and Millward, N., 1983. *Workplace Industrial Relations in Britain*, London: Heinemann

Dickens, L., 1980. 'What are companies disclosing for the 1980s?', *Personnel Management* 12(4): 28–30, 48

Edwardes, Sir M., 1983. *Back from the Brink*, London: Collins

Edwards, P.K., 1987. *Managing the Factory: a Survey of General Managers*, Oxford: Blackwell

Edwards, P.K. and Marginson, P., 1988. 'Trade Unions, Pay Bargaining and Industrial Action', ch. 5 in P. Marginson, P.K. Edwards, R. Martin, J. Purcell and K. Sisson, *Beyond the Workplace: Managing Industrial Relations in Large Establishments*, Oxford: Blackwell: 123–64

Edwards, P.K. and Scullion, H., 1982. *The Social Organization of Industrial Conflict: Control and Resistance in the Workplace*, Oxford: Blackwell

Elger, A., 1989. 'Change and Continuity in the Labour Process: Technical Innovation and Work Reorganisation in the 1980s', paper presented at the 'Work, Employment and Society' Conference, *A Decade of Change*, University of Durham, 14–15 September

Flanders, A., 1970. *Management and Unions*, London: Faber

Foley, B.J. and Maunders, K.T., 1977. *Accounting Information Disclosure and Collective Bargaining*, London: Macmillan

Fox, A., 1966. *Industrial Sociology and Industrial Relations*, Research Paper 3, Royal Commission on Trade Unions and Employers' Associations, London: HMSO

Goldsmith, W. and Clutterbuck, R., 1984. *The Winning Streak*, London: Weidenfeld & Nicolson

Goold, M. and Campbell, A., 1987. *Strategies and Styles: the Role of the Centre in Managing Diversified Corporations*, Oxford: Blackwell

Hannah, L., 1976. *The Rise of the Corporate Economy*, 2nd edn. 1983, London: Methuen

Hill, C.W.L. and Pickering, J.F., 1986. 'Divisionalisation, Decentralisation and Performance of Large United Kingdom Companies', *Journal of Management Studies* 23(1): 26–50

Hyman, R., 1989. *The Political Economy of Industrial Relations: Theory and Practice in a Cold Climate*, London: Macmillan

Jenkins, D., 1982. 'Disclosure of Information, Stratification and Collective Agreements', *Industrial Relations Journal.* 13(3): 57–62

Jones, C.J., 1980. *Financial Planning and Control: a Survey of Practice by UK Companies*, Occasional Paper, London: ICMA

Jones, E., 1981. *Accountancy and the British Economy: the Evolution of Ernst and Whinney*, London: Batsford

Kinnie N., 1985. 'Changing Managerial Strategies in Industrial Relations', *Industrial Relations Journal* 16(4): 17–24

1987. 'Bargaining Within the Enterprise: Centralised or Decentralised?', *Journal of Management Studies* 24(5): 463–77

Leopold, J. and Jackson, M., 1990. 'Decentralisation of Collective Bargaining: a Case Study', *Industrial Relations Journal* 21(3): 185–93

MacInnes, J., 1987. *Thatcherism at Work*, Buckingham: Open University Press

Mackay, L. and Torrington, D., 1987. *The Changing Nature of Personnel Management*, London: IPM

Marginson, P., 1986. 'Organisational Innovation and the Management of Labour', *Business History Conference*, London School of Economics

1988. 'Centralised Control or Establishment Autonomy?', ch. 7 in P. Marginson, P.K. Edwards, R. Martin, J. Purcell and K Sisson, *Beyond the Workplace: Managing Industrial Relations in Large Establishments*, Oxford: Blackwell: 183–226

Marginson, P. and Sisson, K., 1988. 'The Management of Employees', ch. 4 in P. Marginson, P.K. Edwards, R. Martin, J. Purcell and K. Sisson, *Beyond the Workplace: Managing Industrial Relations in Large Establishments*, Oxford: Blackwell: 80–122

Marginson, P., Edwards, P.K. Purcell, J. and Sisson, K., 1986. *The Workplace Industrial Relations Company Level Survey*, Report for the Economic and Social Research Council, Industrial Relations Research Unit, Coventry: University of Warwick

Marginson, P., Edwards, P.K., Martin, R., Purcell, J. and Sisson, K., 1988. *Beyond the Workplace: Managing Industrial Relations in Large Establishments*, Oxford: Blackwell

Marsh, A., 1982. *Employee Relations Policy and Decision-Making*, Aldershot: Gower

Maunders, K.T. and Foley, B.J., 1984. 'Information Disclosure and the Role of the Accountant in Collective Bargaining – Some Comments', *Accounting, Organizations and Society* 9(1): 99–106

Melrose-Woodman, J.E., 1975. *Reporting Financial Information*, London: BIM

Metcalf, D., 1989. 'Water Notes Dry Up: The Impact of the Donovan Reform Proposals and Thatcherism at Work on Labour Productivity in British Manufacturing Industry', *British Journal of Industrial Relations* 27(1): 1–32

Millward, N. and Stevens, M., 1986. *British Workplace Industrial Relations 1980–1984*, Aldershot: Gower

Ogden, S. and Bougen, P., 1985. 'A Radical Perspective on the Disclosure of Accounting Information to Trade Unions', *Accounting, Organizations and Society* 10(2): 211–44

Owen, D.L. and Lloyd, A.J., 1985. 'The Use of Financial Information by Trade Union Negotiators in Plant Level Collective Bargaining', *Accounting, Organizations and Society* 10(3): 329–50

Parker, R.H., 1969. *Management Accounting, an Historical Perspective*, London: Macmillan

Payne, P.L., 1967. 'The Emergence of the Large-Scale Company in Great Britain, 1870–1914', *Economic History Review* 20: 519–42

Pendleton, A., 1991. 'Workplace Industrial Relations in British Rail: Change and Continuity in the 1980s', *Industrial Relations Journal* 22(3): 209–21

Pike, R.H., 1982. *Capital Budgeting in the 1980s, Occasional Paper*, London: ICMA

Prais, S.J., 1976. *The Evolution of Giant Firms in Britain*, Cambridge: Cambridge University Press

Purcell, J., 1985. 'Is anybody Listening to the Corporate Personnel Department?', *Personnel Management*, September: 28–31

    1988. 'The Structure and Function of Personnel Management', ch. 3 in P. Marginson, P.K. Edwards, R. Martin, J. Purcell and K. Sisson, *Beyond the Workplace: Managing Industrial Relations in Large Establishments*, Oxford: Blackwell: 51–79

Purcell, J. and Ahlstrand, B., 1989. 'Corporate Strategy and the Management of Employee Relations in the Multi-divisional Company', *British Journal of Industrial Relations* 27(3): 396–417

Purcell, J. and Earl. M.J., 1977. 'Control System and Industrial Relations', *Industrial Relations Journal* 8(2): 41–54

Purcell, J. and Gray, A., 1986. 'Corporate Personnel Departments and the Management of Industrial Relations: Two Case Studies in Ambiguity, *Journal of Management Studies* 23(2): 205–23

Purcell, J. and Sisson, K., 1983. 'Strategies and Practice in the Management of Industrial Relations, ch. 4 in G.S. Bain (ed.), *Industrial Relations in Britain*, Oxford: Blackwell: 95–120

Purdy, D., 1981. 'The Provision of Financial Information to Employees: A Study of the Reporting Practices of Some Large Public Companies in the UK', *Accounting, Organizations and Society* 6(4): 327–38

Royal Commission on Trade Unions and Employers' Associations, 1968. Cmnd 3623, London, HMSO

Salamon, M., 1987. *Industrial Relations: Theory and Practice*, London: Prentice-Hall

Stacey, N.A.H., 1954. *English Accountancy: a Study in Social and Economic History. 1800–1954*, London: Gee

Steer, J. and Cable, J., 1978. 'Internal Organisation and Profit: an Empirical Analysis of Large UK Companies', *Journal of Industrial Economics* 27: 13–30

Storey, J., 1987. *Developments in the Management of Human Resources: An Interim report, Warwick Paper in Industrial Relations* 17, Coventry: University of Warwick

Terry, M., 1983. 'Shop Steward Development and Managerial Strategies', ch. 3 in G.S. Bain (ed.), *Industrial Relations in Britain*, Oxford: Blackwell: 67–91

Torrington, D., Mackay, I. and Hall, L., 1985. 'The Changing Nature of Personnel Management', *Employee Relations* 7(5): 10–16

Turner, H.A., Roberts, G. and Roberts, D., 1977. *Management Characteristics and Labour Conflict*, Cambridge: Cambridge University Press

Tyson, S. and Fell, A., 1986. *Evaluating the Personnel Function*, London: Hutchinson

Wardell, M. and Weisenfeld, L.W., 1991. 'Management Accounting and the Workplace in the United States and Great Britain', *Accounting, Organizations and Society* 16(7): 655–70

Williams, K., Williams, D. and Thomas, D., 1983. *Why are the British Bad at Manufacturing?*, London: Routledge

Yetton, P.W., 1976. 'The Interaction Between a Standard Time Incentive Payment System and a Simple Accounting Information System', *Accounting, Organizations and Society* 1(1): 81–90.

# 9 Value-added accounting and national economic policy

*Anthony Hopwood, Stuart Burchell and Colin Clubb*

There was a 'sudden upsurge of interest in value added' (Cameron, 1977b) in the UK during the late 1970s. The general contours of this event are fairly uncontroversial. The concept 'value-added' was a way of indicating the value created by the activities of an enterprise in a number of different sites. These sites included private companies, newspapers, government bodies, trade unions, employers' associations, and professional accountancy bodies. The concept also encompassed a variety of different practices, including financial reporting, payment systems, profit sharing schemes, economic analyses, as well as information disclosure to employees and trade unions. Prior to the late 1970s, the concept of value-added had been largely absent from these diverse sites and practices. Where it had been present, it had been an object of very limited sectional interest.

The widespread discussion of value-added within the ranks of professional accountants commenced with its appearance in *The Corporate Report*, a discussion paper prepared by a working party drawn from the accountancy bodies, and published by the Accounting Standards Steering Committee (ASSC) in August 1975. At least for accountants, this was the official debut of value-added.

*The Corporate Report* recommended, amongst other things, a 'statement of value added, showing how the benefits of the efforts of an enterprise are shared between employees, providers of capital, the state and reinvestment' (ASSC, 1975: 48). Subsequently, a first draft of a consultative document entitled 'Aims and scope of company reports', prepared by the Department of Trade, was issued on 9 June 1976 for comment. This paper, which reads very much as a commentary on *The Corporate Report*, states:

our preliminary view is that the subjects identified in *The Corporate Report* which should be given highest priority for further consideration as candidates for new statutory disclosure requirements are:
(a) Added Value;
(b) Employee Report;
(c) Future Prospects;
(d) Corporate Objectives (*The Accountant*, 1 July 1976: 13).

When the Government's Green Paper on *The Future of Company Reports* finally appeared in July 1977, one of the legislative proposals contained in it was for a statement of value-added (Department of Trade, 1977b: 7–8).

This policy debate in the realm of accounting regulation was paralleled by an increasing number of companies using value-added statements in their annual reports and for reporting to employees. 14 companies (out of 300) in the Institute of Chartered Accountants in England and Wales' *Survey of Published Accounts* included value-added statements in their *Annual Reports* for the year 1975–6 (ICAEW, 1978). This figure grew to 67 for 1977–78, 84 for 1978–79 and 90 for 1979–80 before declining to 88 in 1980–81, 77 for 1981–82 and 64 for 1982–83 (ICAEW, 1980; Skerratt and Tonkin, 1982; Tonkin and Skerratt, 1983). Other surveys indicate that more than one-fifth of the largest UK companies produced value-added statements in the late 1970s (Gray and Maunders, 1980).

The exact incidence of the use of added value in employee reports is unclear, although several commentators mentioned its popularity in this context (e.g. Fanning, 1978). It is also of interest to note its use by several winners of the *Accountancy Age* competition for the best employee report, its advocacy for the purposes of explaining company performance to employees by the Engineering Employers' Federation (EEF, 1977), and its mention by the Trades Union Congress as a possible performance indicator in the context of a discussion of information disclosure to employees (TUC, 1974).

The advocacy by the Engineering Employers' Federation of value-added was a development of its position as presented in an earlier document, *Business Performance and Industrial Relations: Added Value as an Instrument of Management Discipline*, published by the Federation in 1972. As the title suggests, added value appears in this document as part of a discussion concerned with its use 'as a practical tool of management' rather than simply as a form of presentation of financial information in company and employee reports. The particular area of decision-making in which it was envisaged this 'practical tool' could be brought into play was the one concerned with the utilization of and payment for labour (EEF, 1972:5):

The Federation therefore aims to encourage the use of added value as a discipline, so that all managers, with or without experience of accounting practices will appreciate the financial environment within which decisions affecting manpower are taken.

In the later 1977 EEF pamphlet, the discussion of the applications of value-added is taken further. Examination of its uses shifts from simply describing how it may serve as a guide to management when formulating wages policy, to describing how it may be linked more directly to earnings when serving as the basis of a value-added incentive payment scheme

(VAIPS). Moreover, around this time VAIPs themselves became the focus of widespread interest. It has been estimated that 200–300 companies were operating, or were about to implement, added value schemes in 1978 (Woodmansay, 1978).

In addition to the above uses of value-added as a vehicle for information disclosure and as a basis for determining rewards at the level of the enterprise, the category also appeared on several occasions in the context of policy discussions concerned with the performance of British industry (Jones, 1976, 1978; New, 1978). In addition, it was canvassed as a means for reforming company-wide profit sharing schemes (Cameron, 1977a) and appeared in stockbroker reports (Vickers da Costa, 1979) as a means of facilitating financial performance analysis.

### Value-added and the social

If the basic contours of the value-added event appear clear enough, on closer inspection the picture becomes more complex. To begin with, just what is value-added? Rutherford (1977:216) responded to this question by advancing a definition drawn from Ruggles and Ruggles (1965: 50):

The value added by a firm; i.e. the value created by the activities of the firm and its employees, can be measured by the difference between the market value of the goods that have been turned-out by the firm and the cost of those goods and materials purchased from other producers. This measure will exclude the contribution made by other producers to the total value of this firm's production, so that it is essentially equal to the market value created by this firm. The value added measure assesses the net contribution made by each firm to the total value of production: by adding up all these contributions, therefore it is possible to arrive at a total for the whole economy.

However, as Rutherford went on to point out, this definition did not provide a detailed prescription for the *calculation* of valued-added. Indeed, as he and other writers pointed out (Rutherford, 1978; Vickers da Costa, 1979; Morley, 1978), that calculative practice was very diverse. The treatment of depreciation varied (McLeay, 1983). A great deal of discretion existed as to the treatment of taxation, and so on. Furthermore, this calculative diversity was compounded by the fact that value-added statements were presented in a number of different formats (tables, graphs, pie charts, pictures, etc.) which in turn bore a variety of different names ('value-added', 'wealth created', 'where the money goes', etc.) (see Fanning, 1978). There were clearly very many different 'value-addeds'.

In addition, whilst value-added was a means of financial calculation, it was also a form of representation. Thus an incentive payment system might have specified value-added as a clearly defined financial category, the magnitude of which determined, according to certain well defined calculative procedures, a component of labour income (see Bentley Associates, 1975; Smith, 1978). But that financial category was also associated with a particular system of *representation*, albeit one that was thoroughly intertwined with the calculations made. The system of representation was itself composed of two strands. On the one hand, value-added, it was argued, represented wealth; to be precise it represented the wealth created in the accounting entity concerned. Furthermore, so the argument went, this representational property provided a basis for the improved calculation of certain important indices of enterprise performance, namely efficiency and productivity (e.g. Ball, 1968). On the other hand, it also was claimed that value-added has the property of revealing (or representing) something about the social character of production, something which is occluded by traditional profit and loss accounting. Value-added reveals that the wealth created in production is the consequence of the combined efforts of a number of agents who together form a cooperating team: 'Value Added measures the wealth creation which has been built up by the cooperative efforts of shareholders, lenders, workers and the Government' (Morley, 1978: 3). It followed, therefore, that value-added 'puts profit into proper perspective *vis-à-vis* the whole enterprise as a collective effort by capital, management and employees' (ASSC, 1975: 49). Together, these representational properties of value-added were presumed to make it a means for both the more rational control of production, and for the achievement of a more harmonious and cooperative productive endeavour.

In seeking to represent the company as a cooperating team, value-added played a positive role in attempts to create this cooperative harmony. This is a point that was made very clearly some time before value-added became such a widespread object of interest (Pakenham-Walsh, 1964: 268):

The growth we are interested in is a growth of the national product, growth of the national product is achieved by making changes which lead to increased production by business undertakings. This will not be realised until production is seen by managers to be the central purpose of business and until the accounting profession re-orients its practices to this view. The profit and loss orientation of accounts, and notably of published accounts, is inimical to the improvement of industrial relations without which the growth in production desired will be attenuated.

Although the antagonism between capital and labour has declined in recent years, the basic division of interest between maximising profits and providing maximum rewards for labour will continue to afflict industrial relations, unless we cease to see profits as the objective.

This representation of the roles of value-added was not universally held. As Stolliday and Attwood (1978) pointed out, there was no reason why the use of value-added should not have served as a spur to workers in their attempts to eliminate totally the claims of others in its distribution. The concept of value-added could serve to reveal different 'truths' about production to that of production as teamwork. Moreover, the concept of value-added could be seen as a way of 'misleading the workers', an attempt to gloss 'over the problem of profits' (see Hird, 1980; *Labour Research*, 1978). In this case, value-added served as a device for misrepresenting reality. It presented a picture of a unity of interests in the financial performance of a given business organization, whereas in fact there existed a basic conflict of interests. Value-added, it seems, was a distinctly equivocal social indicator.

There is a further problem concerning the roles of value-added: the calculative diversity of the concept enables it to subvert the very properties it is held to represent:

published statements of value added have, to date, been characterised by ambiguous terminology and by the treatment of items in ways inconsistent with the model of value added, and inconsistent within and between individual statements. The impression received by lay users of SVAs must be one of confusion – together possibly, with a conviction that value added, like profit can be made to mean whatever the accountant wishes it to mean (Rutherford, 1978: 52).

The advantages offered by the Value Added Statement are, however, currently jeopardised by great diversity of practice (Morley, 1978: 141).

Most of those [value-added statements] available seem to be designed to show, often by a 'sales-cake' diagram, how much of the value-added goes to the employees themselves, how much the Government absorbs and how little the shareholder receives (Vickers da Costa, 1979).

Rather than shedding or reducing conflict, value-added statements appear to be equally conducive to confusion, doubt and suspicion. This state of affairs problematizes not only the social rationality of value-added but also its technical rationality. Clearly there may be as many productivities and efficiencies as there are added values. The value-added event as it took form during the 1970s was thus not a sudden and massive outbreak of a single, unambiguous concept of value-added. Instead, the widespread discussion and use of value-added brought together under a single heading a multiplicity of differentiated 'value-addeds'. It is, we argue, this ambiguity of value-added that was central to its emergence and functioning. This ambiguity enabled it to serve as the focus of a widely differentiated field of political interest. It could appeal to groups at both ends of the political spectrum (Morley 1978: 5–6).

It is precisely this highly differentiated social space within which the value-added event took place that is our object of investigation. In what follows we have attempted to discover some of its preconditions – the factors that made possible the value-added event. This work of description and analysis has been carried out by delineating three arenas, or complexes of issues, institutions, bodies of knowledge, practices and actions within which the value-added event emerged.

### Three arenas

Each of the three arenas discussed below marks out a particular field of operations: the explication of standards for corporate financial reporting; the management of the national economy; and the functioning of the system of industrial relations. Within each arena there is charted the shifting patterns of relations between the various agencies functioning in these fields, e.g. the government, trade unions, the accounting profession, and the changes in their modes of operation and objects of concern, e.g. productivity, strikes, accounting standards.

The developments in each arena, the forming of 'problems' and 'solutions', are treated as if they had a trajectory largely independent of other arenas. No doubt this is an oversimplification. Clearly, macroeconomic management concerns with payment systems had implications for industrial relations. Conversely, the interest in industrial relations reform was linked to a concern with its effects on national economic performance. Similarly, developments in accounting standardization were related to both macroeconomic issues (in particular inflation), and the management of industrial relations (in a time of a perceived growth in the power of the trade union movement). However, the approach adopted is to analyse each arena initially as an autonomous entity, and only then in terms of its interdependencies with the other arenas. This has the advantage that linkages between one arena and another, for instance the links between issues of economic performance and those relating to the status of employees and trade unions, can be empirically investigated, rather than presuming an *a priori* necessity for such linkages to exist.

### *Accounting standards*

As already observed, value-added was characterized by considerable calculative diversity. In a survey of published value-added statements produced in the 1970s, it was concluded that 'It is difficult to capture systematically the degree of diversity present in the construction of statements of Value Added' (Rutherford, 1980). Moreover, such a heterogeneity of practice was seen as problematic for the roles, rationales and purposes that value-added was seen and mobilized to serve. Rather than promoting efficient, harmonious, productive activity, the motley collection of 'value-addeds' was seen as subverting the very roles allocated to them. Amongst other things, the calculative diversity opened management to the charge of manipulation and bias (*The Accountant*, 1978: 373).

One consequence of this perception of the problematic effects of diversity was a call for standardization (Fanning, 1978; Vickers da Costa, 1979). The relevant agency in this respect was the Accounting Standards Committee (ASC). As a result of these and other pressures, four of the accountancy bodies represented on the Accounting Standards Committee commissioned research studies of value-added. The reports issued by both the Institute of Chartered Accountants in England and Wales (Renshall *et al.*, 1979) and the Institute of Chartered Accountants of Scotland (Morley, 1978) concluded in favour of value-added reporting but added the caveat that 'Standardisation of practice is a necessary precondition to any formal requirement' (Renshall *et al.*, 1979: 38), so as 'to bring comparability to Value Added Statements and so safeguard the confidence of readers in the Statement' (Morley, 1978: 141). The study prepared for the Institute of Cost and Management Accountants was notably less enthusiastic and presented value-added as just one more addition to the kitbag of management tools which may be usefully employed in connection with employee payment systems and public relations (Cox, 1979). The issue of standardization was not raised in the report. The Association of Certified Accountants' study investigated the information needs of potential users of value-added statements and reviewed existing corporate practice in the area before discussing measurement and disclosure policy (Gray and Maunders, 1980). Two approaches to the measurement of value-added were identified, and although it was stated that 'conceptually it would seem desirable that a consistent approach be adopted one way or the other' (Gray and Maunders, 1980: 28), it was also argued that value-added reporting should be 'placed outside the restrictions established by convention' in order to facilitate its 'imaginative development' according to the decision requirements of its potential users (Gray and Maunders, 1980: 37).

The arrangements for the setting of accounting standards in the UK that served as the institutional site for these deliberations were established at the end of the 1960s in the aftermath of the considerable controversy and debate surrounding a series of company collapses and takeover battles (Zeff, 1972). However, the standards-setting programme very quickly ran into trouble, not least in relation to its stated aim of narrowing the areas of difference and variety in accounting practice (ICAEW, 1969). This was most dramatically exemplified in the case of the inflation accounting debate (Whittington, 1983).

Although initiated to maintain professional control over accounting standardization, the inflation accounting proposals of the then Accounting

Standards Steering Committee quickly engendered such a breadth and intensity of debate that the Conservative Government of the time established a committee of inquiry in the area – the Sandilands Committee (1975). In itself, the establishment of this committee was perceived by the profession as a threat to the traditional division of responsibility between the professional bodies and the government. The issue hinged on responsibility for the content and form of presentation, as well as the measurement principles, employed in corporate reports. The sense of professional crisis was further intensified by the fact that the committee was anticipated to report in a not uncritical manner during a new Labour administration whose opposition Green Paper, *The Community and the Company* (Labour Party, 1974), had also threatened the existing framework of professional self-regulation with its proposals for the setting up of a powerful Companies Commission for regulating companies and financial institutions.

In anticipation of the report of the Sandilands Committee, the Accounting Standards Steering Committee established a committee to re-examine 'the scope and aims of published financial reports in the light of modern needs and conditions' (ASSC, 1975). Until then, these wider issues had been ignored by the standard-setters. The committee's findings were published as *The Corporate Report*. In appraising current reporting practices, *The Corporate Report* evinces some concern for what it considers to be an over-emphasis on profit and goes on to argue (ASSC, 1975: 49) that:

> The simplest and most immediate way of putting profit into proper perspective *vis-à-vis* the whole enterprise as a collective effort by capital, management and employees is by the presentation of a statement of value added (that is, sales income less materials and services purchased). Value added is the wealth the reporting entity has been able to create by its own and its employees' efforts. This statement would show how value added has been used to pay those contributing to its creation. It usefully elaborates on the profit and loss account and in time may come to be regarded as a preferable way of describing performance.

In this way, value-added entered the discourse of accounting policy-making.

Value-added was seen as a performance criterion that put employees on a par with other interests in the enterprise. Moreover, this claim for an equality of status was reinforced by the stakeholder model adopted in *The Corporate Report*. Where before there only existed the shareholder (Sharp, 1971), a number of stakeholders were now recognized, each of which was deemed to have 'a reasonable right to information concerning the reporting entity' (ASSC, 1975: 17). The employee group constituted one such stakeholder. The report made the point that 'it is likely that employees will more suitably obtain the information they need by means of special purpose reports at plant or site level' (ASSC, 1975: 22). However, it went on to argue that corporate reports could be used as a check on the reliability of these special-purpose documents and could be useful to employees in evaluating managerial efficiency, estimating the future prospects of the entity and of individual establishments within a group.

However, the merits of value-added as an alternative or complementary performance indicator were not advanced in a vacuum. They were also advanced in relation to the concerns of macroeconomic management in the second half of the 1970s. There were two issues here: the debates, legislation and practical initiatives concerning incomes policy; and the issue of information disclosure to employees and trades unions. Although value-added was new to the accounting policy-making arena, it was already an issue in relation to macroeconomic management.

### Macroeconomic management

Income policies have been linked to the use of the value-added category by a number of writers (Beddoe, 1978; Cameron, 1978; IDS, 1977; Low, 1977). In every case the connection has been made via a discussion of value-added incentive payment schemes (VAIPSs). VAIPSs are group bonus schemes which are usually operated on a plant basis, thus covering both blue- and white-collar employees. The bonus pool available for distribution to employees is related to the value-added of the plant. This pool may, for example, be determined by a certain agreed percentage of any increase in the value-added per pound of payroll costs, over some agreed base figure for this ratio.

VAIPSs came very much to the fore during the period of the 1974–9 Labour Government. With the inception of Stage III of that Government's pay policy in August 1977, a 10 percent limit on wage settlements was imposed. But, and of crucial importance for VAIPSs, there was provision for agreements above this level where self-financing productivity deals had been implemented. VAIPSs had been introduced into the UK during the 1950s, and were already functioning in a number of firms (strongly supported by a number of management consultants). Since such schemes were, almost by definition, self-financing, they were well placed under Stage III to become more widely adopted.

But whilst the 'national economy' had been an object of government policy and deliberation since the Second World War (see Tomlinson, ch. 7 in this volume), what was lacking was a means by which government might act upon certain key economic variables. An incomes policy was one such means. However, incomes policies have usually been introduced only reluctantly by governments, and *in extremis*, in an attempt to resolve one of the central presumed dilemmas of modern demand management, namely to reconcile the objectives of price stability and full employment using only the instruments of fiscal and monetary policy. It was in relation to this concern that productivity growth became an important criterion for judging wage increases.

Productivity was so emphasized during the incomes policies of 1961 and 1962. The theme re-emerged during the life of the National Board for Prices and Incomes (NBPI) established by the Labour Government in 1965 and wound up on 31 March 1971. The NBPI was assigned the task of examining 'particular cases in order to advise whether or not the behaviour of prices, salaries or other money incomes was in the national interest' (see Fels, 1972: ch. 3). 'The national interest' was first specified in the White Paper, *Prices and Incomes Policy*, of April 1965 and was subsequently elaborated and modified in a series of White Papers until 1970. Initially, it required that there should be an incomes 'norm', i.e. a maximum percentage by which the wages and salaries of individuals should increase. In addition, certain exceptional circumstances in which increases above the norm were considered justifiable were also defined. Amongst these there was one which allowed for above-norm increases in pay where employees had made a direct contribution towards an increase in productivity. For certain periods during the life of the NBPI there was imposed a zero norm and the exceptional criteria became the only permissible grounds for obtaining an increase in pay. It was under this regime that productivity agreements became very popular. The NBPI's third report on productivity agreements showed that 25 per cent of all workers had been involved in productivity agreements, mainly in 1968 and 1969 (NBPI, 1968).

Subsequent investigation of these productivity deals led certain commentators to conclude that many of them were bogus, i.e. 'the productivity increase was mostly that which would have happened in any case; so that what many so called "productivity bargains" really did was to use this to justify an exceptional wage increase' (Turner, 1970: 203).

The experience, plus the *ad hoc* and piecemeal character of many productivity deals (which tended to be self-perpetuating), were the cause of concern on the part of both government and the Confederation of British Industry (CBI) (Elliott, 1978). Of perhaps even greater concern was the absence of a mechanism for linking increases in hourly rates paid to increases in productivity achieved. These concerns came to a head in discussions over the arrangements to be brought into effect with the expiry of Stage II of the 1974–9 Labour Government's incomes policy. At that time the government was keen to build a productivity element into the provisions for Stage III.

In this context, VAIPSs could be presented as model schemes. They were comprehensive in character, and maintained a continuous link between performance and reward. VAIPSs involved the use of a measurement technology that offered a solution to many of the problems that had created difficulties for the NBPI in its attempts to audit the productivity deals of the late 1960s.

However, it is important to note that the force of the claims made on behalf of VAIPSs did not rest on these features alone. In discussions of VAIPSs it is rare to find their merits presented solely in terms of their scope, self-financing character, or measurement technology. In a number of different ways, the point was nearly always made that the effective functioning of these schemes presupposes a number of changes in the intraorganizational relations of the enterprise concerned. Further, it was often made clear that these changes were considered to be of positive value in their own right. The relevant organizational changes were usually discussed in terms of 'information disclosure' and 'participation'. As one leading management consultant in this area put it (Binder, Hamlyn and Fry & Co., 1978: 18)

the contribution of Added Value requires:
(a) an open management style that will 'open the books' and welcome the increased questioning that will ensue;
(b) a preference for a more participative and less autocratic way of getting results.

The underlying reasoning appeared to be that the relevant unit of performance for determining bonus was a company or plant, rather than a single machine, and that improved performance (and hence bonus) presupposed cooperation across functions, and between different activities and occupational groups within functions. This cooperation, so the argument went, could only be achieved by means of the widespread disclosure of detailed company information which would then provide the basis for discussion and agreement on the appropriate action for attempting to improve performance.

Thus, in the case of the Bentley plan – a particular British variant of the VAIPS – the scheme 'is initiated through a fully representative employee management council. A structure which will establish employee involvement and participation in a wider range of problems and enable profits, productivity and earnings to be rationally discussed and improved' (Bentley Associates, 1975: 12). It is interesting to note that although the trade union response to VAIPSs was somewhat guarded, it was suggested that if unions did enter such schemes they would require, amongst other things, complete access to all the relevant data (Beddoe, 1978).

The positive value of all these changes was generally seen in terms of the improvement in industrial relations that they were said to effect. It was argued that flexible working arrangements would become more likely, and that employees would become positively motivated to cut costs and improve efficiency. As a result, there would be some amelioration in the repeated confrontation between workers and managers over working practices (Marchington, 1977; Cameron, 1977b).

It was for very similar reasons that the NBPI had earlier been so interested in productivity deals. It has been argued that the 'NBPI's recommendations on pay policy often required changes in the machinery of wage determination: in addition, the incomes policy was often used as a Trojan horse to bring about reforms in collective bargaining institutions' (Fels, 1972: 150). The productivity deal was one of the principal means whereby the NBPI sought to supplant the hold of traditional factors in income determination, and to give practical effect to its own criteria.

However, in the 1970s there occurred a significant change in the character of the discussion surrounding the intraorganizational changes associated with the reform of payment systems. The productivity deals of the NBPI period were discussed wholly in terms of the rhetoric of management control (Fels, 1972: 133).

genuine productivity agreements, for example, would have very useful side effects, such as improving management by increasing cost-consciousness, by providing new information about performance and new methods of assessing it, and by directing attention to the possibility of changing methods of work. Management negotiations were brought into closer touch with unions, and more managers became aware of the implications for industrial relations of technical and financial decisions. The experience of applying the agreements with their provisions on overtime, flexibility, manning and so on often brought a revolution in managerial control over working hours and practices. There were changes in organisation, personnel and the provision of training, and senior and other managers were better informed and organised than before the agreements.

While the discussion of VAIPSs during the second half of the 1970s still contained this thread concerned with management control and the efficiency of enterprise operations, it was also conducted according to the rhetoric of employee participation and industrial democracy. Indeed, it became possible to invert completely the normal order of presentation and use the issue of industrial democracy as a springboard for advancing the claims of VAIPSs (e.g. Marchington, 1977). The significance accorded to the participative characteristics of VAIPSs at this time was rooted in a number of parallel developments, particularly those occurring within the area of industrial relations.

### Industrial relations and information disclosure

During the 1960s, there was a significant shift in the conditions of trade union activity in the UK. The pre-existing voluntary system of 'free collective bargaining' was displaced by a system that was increasingly the object of government intervention. Collective bargaining was increasingly overlaid by a network of legal relations, and inset with a variety of new institutions concerned with the investigation, regulation and normalization of industrial relations (see Crouch, 1979).

This shift was preceded by two events of interest: in 1961, statistics concerning unofficial strikes were collected for the first time; and, in 1965, the Labour Government appointed a Royal Commission on Trade Unions and Employers' Associations, to be known as the Donovan Commission (Donovan, 1968). Thus was the production of a key statistic, one that would be read later as a sign of a 'central defect in British industrial relations' (Crouch, 1979: 264), linked to a conceptual framework for interpreting it, and for generating programmes of intervention designed to rectify this 'defect'.

'Industrial democracy' was the *leitmotif* for discussions, debates, and interventions in the field of industrial relations during the period of the 1974–79 Labour Government (Elliott, 1978). But despite its centrality to the whole field of industrial relations during this period, 'industrial democracy' is an extremely difficult concept to pin down. Indeed, according to one commentator, 'the term "industrial democracy" is incapable of definition' (Kahn-Freud, 1977). However, the equivocal character of the notion of industrial democracy was an advantage rather than a limiting factor, at least in respect to the concepts and practices of value-added. For the ambiguity of the notion made it possible for a considerable number of positions and group interests to be articulated and argued for (Pitkin, 1967).

An inquiry into industrial democracy chaired by Lord Bullock (Department of Trade, 1977a), and the enactment of the Employment Protection Act 1975, were important elements in the programme of industrial relations reform of the 1974–9 Labour Government. Irrespective of how its democratic content may be judged, this programme implied a change in the information economies of private companies. Amongst other things, it entailed the creation of new agents and bodies for the receipt and relay of information, new rights of access for certain existing bodies, and the setting up of certain national agencies to oversee and supervise the implementation and functioning of the new provisions.[1] Although the Bullock Report did not result in any legislation, parallel developments in the areas of occupational pension schemes (Lucas, 1979) and health and safety took some tentative steps towards taking workers into the sphere of management decision-making.[2]

It was in this context that there developed an enhanced interest in employee reporting. The relative status of management personnel *vis-à-vis* trade unionists came under considerable pressure, both in respect of information access and decision-making. Popular versions of companies' *Annual Reports* to shareholders were prepared in an attempt to make them understandable to employees (Hussey, 1978, 1979; Holmes, 1977). Around these corporate initiatives there grew up in turn a parallel literature of prescription and advice emanating from such bodies as the Institute of Personnel Management (IPM), the ICAEW and the CBI. In addition to the use of employee reports, this literature recommended that information be disseminated to employees by means of personal presentations by company chairmen to mass meetings, slide and video presentations, as well as small group briefing sessions. It was within this area of corporate communication with employees that value-added frequently appeared and was discussed as a preferred form of presentation (Hopkins, 1975; EEF, 1977; Smith, 1978; Hilton, 1978). The Trades Union Congress, in its statement of policy on industrial democracy, had itself suggested that companies should provide information on value-added to their employees (TUC, 1974: 33).

One final strand of interest in the industrial democracy debate is that of profit sharing. As a result of undertakings made to the Liberal Party during the formation of the 'Lib–Lab' alliance, profit sharing was encouraged by provisions introduced in the Finance Act 1978 (Elliott, 1978). This particular innovation is one that was continued under the Conservative administration which came to power in 1979. The CBI viewed financial participation schemes as a means of obtaining a 'sense of purpose, at least at company level' and 'as a useful contribution to an employee participation programme' (CBI, 1978). Of particular interest here are the changes introduced by ICI into its own profit sharing scheme. A scheme that had been running since 1953 was modified in 1976 by the introduction of a formula based on an added value concept.[3]

In the light of the above, it is perhaps no surprise that VAIPSs came into their own in the 1970s, having been introduced some two decades earlier, and having spent the 1960s in incubation. Of course, the topics of information disclosure to employees and economic performance were by no means new (see for example BIM, 1957; Searle, 1971). But they were given considerably enhanced significance by the rhetoric of industrial democracy, which tended to place in the foreground the issue of the relative status of economic agents.

It was under these conditions that profit and its associated connotations came to appear as a problem – an 'awkward term' – and that the concepts and practices of value-added came to be viewed as legitimate and possibly alternative performance indicators. Formed by the intersection of developments in the fields of setting accounting standards, the management of the national economy, and the regulation and reform of industrial relations, value-added became the focus of attention in each of these three arenas, as well as providing a link between them.

## The accounting constellation

Our concern here has been to discover the preconditions of the social space within which the value-added event took place. We have sought to understand how a calculative practice marginal to existing accounting routines was able to generate such widespread interest and debate, and in such diverse spheres. As indicated earlier, this particular social space is characterized by an intertwining of discussions concerning efficiency and productivity on the one hand, and those concerning employee participation on the other. This history of possibilities has entailed charting the ways in which the language of economic performance in the second half of the 1970s was shaped and influenced by notions of industrial representation and democracy.

In the literature of the period, administrative practices such as accounting and payment systems were diagnosed, and solutions proposed, according to the terms of a discourse organized around the notions of efficiency and democracy. However, these two ideas functioned as a pair of values the commensurability of which was far from clear. Just how was 'efficiency' to be brought into relation with 'democracy'? Value-added appeared to offer a solution to this problem. Value-added was repeatedly presented as a means of achieving a felicitous combination of participation, if not democracy, and efficiency. Within the network of statements generated by the efficiency–democracy discourse, value-added functioned as one strategic node or point of interrelation.

Our analysis of the three arenas has addressed the specific social space within which value-added emerged and developed, thereby charting a genealogy of the discourses and practices of value-added. For the value-added event was formed out of a very particular field of relations which existed between certain institutions, economic and administrative processes, bodies of knowledge, systems of norms and measurement, and classification techniques. We have called such a field an *accounting constellation*. It was in the network of intersecting practices, processes and institutions which constituted this constellation that value-added was caught, and it was this network that governed how value-added might function as a calculative, administrative and discursive practice.

We have described how developments in each of these three arenas had mutually reinforcing effects on the information economies of individual enterprises. Interventions associated with incomes policies and the management of the national economy, company and labour law and the reform of industrial relations, accounting regulation and the standardization of financial reporting, simultaneously affected a number of different aspects of the business enterprise. For example, productivity deals in general, and VAIPSs in particular, resulted in a significant elaboration of a firm's administrative apparatus. Moreover, this elaboration was aimed at increasing its pervasiveness in order to secure greater unity in the combined action of the component parts of the enterprise. Productivity deals appeared to offer workers the scope for greater involvement and participation in decision-making, giving rise to the application of wage–work rules (McKersie and Hunter, 1973: 21–3), an implication that was particularly apparent in many of the discourses that were associated with VAIPSs. Overall, there was an intensification of the regime of economic information within the enterprise, and the possibility of a move towards a reconstitution of the pattern of social relations.

But the notion of an accounting constellation, its emergence, transformation and dissolution, remains unspecified. The following observations seek to clarify certain of its more general features.

### The specificity of the constellation

It is important to note first of all that the accounting constellation discussed here has been constructed in response to a particular problem concerning the value-added event. There is no presupposition that it encompasses the entire field of relations governing the production, distribution and use of all accounting statements. An examination, for example, of the conditions of possibility of the debates surrounding accounting for depreciation, deferred taxation, or inflation accounting would no doubt reveal an accounting constellation that only partly coincided with that associated with value-added. Indeed, this might also be true if one examined an aspect of the value-added event other than the one addressed here, for instance the appearance of value-added in a particular firm. To register this point is simply to note that the analysis of a particular event is necessarily partial and specific. Its contours are neither those of a discipline, nor those of a pregiven object.

### The pursuit of interests and unintended consequences

The accounting constellation as we have described it was very much an *unintended* phenomenon. The field of action that we have outlined in relation to value-added was not designed by any single actor or agent, and no blueprint for its construction is likely to be found. It was the consequence of the intersection of a great many events, some well known and well documented, others unnoticed or only fleetingly glimpsed by observers. Most of these events were produced by people with clear views of what they were doing: negotiating a wages settlement; conforming to an Act of Parliament; fighting inflation; seeking information; informing workers of the facts of economic reality. But the effects of all these individual actions and interventions were not necessarily those that were sought. Nonetheless, they contributed to the formation of the accounting constellation charted here.

An accounting constellation is thus formed by the purposive actions of a multiplicity of different actors in diverse arenas. Each of these actors may have specific, non-overlapping, and sometimes conflicting interests in the accounting practice they are utilizing, and only partial knowledge of both its consequences and the resistance that its use will engender (Hindess, 1982). But this does not mean that outcomes are functionally related to the diverse initiatives that helped give rise to them.

### A non-monolithic constellation

One consequence of being the unintended product of a large number of different purposive actions is that the accounting constellation is non-monolithic in character. Although an accounting constellation may well govern the form of reasoning concerning certain of the decisions confronting enterprise management, such as, for example, the choice of the form of accounting and payment system to be adopted, there still remains considerable scope for conflict and disagreement. It is possible to imagine a situation in which workers and management of a firm are both agreed on the desirability of introducing a VAIPS, and yet both sides violently disagree on virtually all of the procedural and organizational details which would effectively constitute the new payment system. In an analogous way, a particular mode of reasoning and institutional milieu can be said to organize the conflictual debates that have occurred in the area of accounting standard-setting (Zeff, 1978).

In the case of value-added, we have indicated how a field of action was established by the intersection of developments in three distinct arenas. Ambiguity was central to the functioning of the various practices that made up the constellation in question. Systems such as VAIPSs, and the category of value-added itself, could thus function as the vehicle for a number of different interests and purposes. Seen in such terms, an accounting constellation is less a system or an entity governed by a single unambiguous principle, role or function, than a garbage can (Cohen *et al.*, 1972).

### Accounting's embeddedness in the organizational and the social

Our model of accounting change is still in many ways a contingency model. However, there are important differences between our approach and the more usual accounting–environment contingency model of change. For a start, we have not attempted to separate out two domains called accounting and the environment, and then to conduct the analysis in terms of this prior distinction. Instead, we have outlined a network of social relations within which there emerged a certain class of statements: value-added statements, company reports, employee reports, financial statements, statements concerning financial statements, etc. Within this network, accounting can be found providing the conditions of existence of certain social relations, such as helping to define the rights, duties and field of action of certain agents, and playing a role in the specification of both organizational boundaries and intraorganizational segments.

Seen in this way, accounting is intimately implicated in the construction and facilitation of the contexts in which it operates. It cannot be extracted from its environment like an individual organism from its habitat. Of course it is possible to discuss categories such as profit and indeed value-added in a general abstract manner without any reference to the law, organizational rules and functioning, and the rights and duties of agents. However, the added values we are interested in, the added values featuring in the value-added event, did not exist thus. To attempt to investigate them in such an abstract fashion would be to investigate a different problem. We have been concerned to capture and analyse the way value-added existed and functioned as an integral part of certain social relations.

*The accounting constellation and networks of social relations and organizational practices*

We have referred to the set of social relations that make up the value-added event as a network. Our use of this term is very similar to the way in which it is deployed in organizational theory (Aldrich, 1979). There, the idea of a network of organizations opened up research perspectives which tended to cut across the organization–environment dichotomy. Interest focused less on the intraorganizational problems of adaptation to a changing environment than on the properties of a network of interorganizational relations.

In our analysis, a particular network of social relations has been described as a means of accounting for the outbreak of value-added. But the components of this network, and the ways in which they are interrelated, differ in significant respects from the way networks are specified in organizational theory. The main components of our network are not individual organizations, but rather particular systems or processes: payment systems, financial reporting systems, information systems, and so forth. We have indicated how these systems are caught up and elaborated in networks of relations existing between various agents, agencies and the systems themselves. Moreover, these networks were uncovered by studying developments in three arenas, each of which could be characterized in terms of specific fields of action, and targets and agents of intervention, along with their means of surveillance and intervention and associated bodies of knowledge. The developments within each arena were then seen as involving the formation of relations between particular agents, agencies and administrative practices as a consequence of the various interventions taking place. Finally, the accounting constellation was itself specified as a network by noting the often unintended interdependencies between the processes and the practices in the separate arenas.

By focusing on certain administrative systems and their position within each of the arenas we have studied, we hope to have indicated how the very substance of organizations is constructed by processes which cut across any single distinction that might be made between organizational members and non-members. In a related way, Litterer (1961, 1963) has indicated how the organizational phenomenon of 'Big Business' (Chandler, 1962) was made possible by the emplacement of cost accounting, production and inventory control systems as joint effects of the systematic management movement.

In a similar manner, the developments in each of our arenas also amount to the elaboration and development of certain dimensions of those complex entities we call the economy, society and the environment (see Donzelot, 1979). The interventions within the different arenas, which are conducted according to a variety of different principles, single out and privilege certain agents and their means of action. In the process of being used to intervene in the organization, practices for the management of the social and the economic are elaborated and changed. 'The organization' thereby designates a particular site of intersection of practices conducted in the name of the social and the economic, amongst other things. It represents a common nodal point in a number of different networks, each having different objects and means of intervention. And it also represents a site where people, in attempting to draw boundaries, seek to coordinate the actions of those enclosed within them, striving to fashion out of the diverse processes and interventions at work a machine for pursuing certain goals and performing certain functions. Seen in such terms, entities such as the organization, society, and the economy are not independent realms. Rather than existing in an external relation to each other, the social and the economic pass through the organization in the course of their own formation, as we have seen in the case of the value-added event.

### On emergence and decline

The attention given to value-added waned suddenly during the early 1980s. With the election of a new Conservative Government in 1979, the three arenas of the value-added constellation were suddenly ruptured and transformed. Different policies were introduced for the management of the national economy. Industrial relations came quite quickly to be seen and conducted in fundamentally different terms. And, albeit with a lag, the specification of accounting standards was no longer seen to be subject to so real a possibility of government intervention. In these ways, the specific significances which had been attached to value-added were no longer salient. With its context so radically changed, the functioning of value-added in social relations started to approximate to its technical marginality. Value-added started to become a phenomenon of the past.

Although the state of the British economy was still such that economic performance remained a fundamental concern of government, the new administration attempted to deal with this in very different ways. Emphasis was placed on the roles that could be served by monetary policies, financial stringency and the enhancement of competitive pressures. The level of wage settlements was still seen as problematic, but incomes policies did not enter into the explicit political repertoire. Market pressures in an increasingly high unemployment economy were seen to offer more effective means for income control. Productivity and efficiency also remained important objects of government attention. Here too, however, very different interventionist strategies were used. A re-emergence of the managerial prerogative was seen as being capable of enhancing the efficiency of British industry. Gone were the days when conceptions of cooperation and participation were interwoven into the vocabulary and practice of economic management. Stress was placed on the positive roles that could be played by a re-emphasis of competitive pressures, increased training, the shedding of 'surplus' labour and increased investment, particularly in areas of high technology and capital intensity.

Related changes were taking place in the industrial relations arena. Discussions of industrial democracy, participation and the enhancement of worker rights ceased. Indeed, efforts were made to repeal or not to enforce legislative rights conveyed by the previous administration. The relevance of a relationship between democracy and efficiency was no longer seen. The vocabulary of change focused on competition, free markets, and the ending of restrictive practices and monopoly powers. Certain economic rather than more widespread social and political rights came to be emphasized. More significance was attached to decisive and entrepreneurial action rather than cooperation and persuasion. Leadership, rather than participation, was the order of the day.

The accounting profession was slow to recognize the relevance of the changes taking place. The fear of government intervention had been a very deeply felt and widely articulated one. Eventually, however, it came to realize that it was no longer subject to the same intensity of threat. Although still very much concerned with visible remnants of a past era in the form of inflation accounting, the profession in general and the Accounting Standards Committee in particular started to adjust to the new political situation. Representatives of wider industrial and financial constituencies were brought on to the Accounting Standards Committee, now that its legitimacy as a protector of the profession from an interventionist State was no longer apparent. New investments were made in the potential legitimizing roles of knowledge (see Hopwood, 1983). And the agenda of future areas of standard-setting was radically curtailed. Amongst other things, value-added was removed from the agenda for future deliberation and action.

The time for value-added was no longer. The specific constellation which had resulted in its emergence, significance and development had been ruptured. The arenas out of which value-added had emerged had been subject to significant discontinuities. The social context of value-added had mutated. Devoid of its specific social conditions of possibility, value-added was little more than a mere technical accounting possibility – perhaps something to be mentioned in the footnotes of accounting texts. The factors that had endowed it with a wider significance and momentum for development had disappeared.

Such a waning of interest in value-added was not a new phenomenon. Value-added had a period of temporary significance in the UK in the late 1940s and early 1950s. Then, as in the mid-1970s, there also was conjoined a considerable interest in employee communication and information disclosure and a concern for the performance of the British economy. It was in this context that value-added appeared in company reporting practices in a way which anticipated the practices of the late 1970s (Burchell et al., 1981). Between those two periods, there was little if any discussion of value-added, however.

The existence of such a proto-value-added enables us to reinforce the point concerning the way the functioning and very existence of accounting categories is conditioned by a complex set of circumstances. It also enables us to emphasize the highly specific and contingent nature of those circumstances. For in the early 1950s, as in the early 1980s, interest in value-added was to wane. Again with a different political context and, in this case, the emergence of relative economic prosperity rather than the use of very different policies for the continued management of adversity, the value-added constellation was ruptured and subjected to significant discontinuities. The decline of interest in value-added, just as much as its emergence and rise, further reinforces the theoretical perspective developed in this chapter.

## Conclusion

We have sought to indicate how the value-added event arose out of a complex interplay of institutions, issues and processes. The study of this particular accounting change has enabled us not only to move towards grounding accounting in the specific social contexts in which it operates, but also to address some important theoretical issues central to an understanding of the social functioning of the accounting craft.

Zeff (1978), albeit in a different way from ourselves, has pointed to the need for such richer and more contextual appreciations of accounting in action. Focusing on the setting of accounting standards, he has pointed to the myriad political factors which have intruded in the setting (and subsequent criticism) of standards. The impact of these factors is typically not registered in the accounting model which has traditionally provided the dominant frame of reference for discussing accounting practices and the reasons for adopting them. Zeff argues that the economic and social consequences of accounting practices 'may no longer be ignored as a substantive issue in the setting of accounting standards' (Zeff, 1978), and *inter alia* points to the importance of developing our theoretical resources in order to be able to adequately confront this issue.

In this chapter we have adopted a historical, genealogical approach as a device to avoid the assumption that accounting has some essential role or function. Our working principle in this has been that 'the cause of the origin of a thing and its eventual unity, its actual employment and place in a system of purposes, are worlds apart' (Nietzsche, 1969: 77 as quoted in Minson, 1980). We have suggested that the organization of our concepts and the philosophical difficulties that arise from them, have to do with their historical origins. When there occurs a transformation of ideas, whatever made the transformation possible leaves its mark on subsequent reasoning. It is as if concepts have memories (Hacking, 1981). We have attempted to indicate how the processes underlying the value-added event determined the character of discourse bearing the category 'value-added'.

NOTES

1. The Employment Protection Act 1975 gave statutory form to the Advisory, Conciliation and Arbitration Service (ACAS) which was 'charged with the general duty of promoting the improvement of industrial relations'. To this end it was empowered to issue Codes of Practice containing practical guidance for promoting the improvement of industrial relations. A Code of Practice on the disclosure of information to trade unions was issued by ACAS and came into effect on 22 August 1977. The disclosure provisions placed a general duty on an employer to disclose information to representatives of independent recognized

trade unions, '(a) without which the trade union representatives would be to a material extent impeded in carrying on with his . . . collective bargaining, and (b) which it would be in accordance with good industrial relations practice that he would disclose to them for the purposes of collective bargaining'.

2. The Health and Safety at Work Act was enacted in 1974. It provided for the appointment of employee safety representatives with functions of representation and consultation, workplace inspection and investigation and rights of access to certain documents and information. As one writer put it: 'For the first time in law, the Regulations have given trade unions decision-making rights in their workplaces' (Stuttard, 1979).

3. This scheme, introduced in 1953, covered nearly 100,000 monthly- and weekly-paid staff who received an annual profit-related share allocation. In 1976, an ICI working party report proposed that the right of the ICI board to unilaterally fix the annual bonus should be replaced by a formula based on an added value concept (Cameron, 1977a). This scheme differed from a VAIPS in that it operated at the company as opposed to the plant level, and it was not viewed as a major productivity incentive. The stated objectives were: '(1) to help encourage the cooperation and involvement of all employees in improving the business performance of the company; (2) to provide tangible evidence of the unity of interests of employees and stockholders in the continued existence of ICI as a strong and financially viable company; (3) to help focus the interest of the employees towards being part of a more effective company, by being involved as stockholders' (Wellens, 1977).

REFERENCES

*Accountant, The*, 1978. Vol. 179.

'Aims and Scope of Company Reports', *The Accountant* 1 July: 12–14

Accounting Standards Steering Committee (ASSC), 1975. *The Corporate Report*, London: ASSC

Aldrich, H.E., 1979. *Organizations and their Environments*, Englewood Cliffs, NJ: Prentice-Hall

Ball, R.J., 1968. 'The Use of Value Added in Measuring Managerial Efficiency', *Business Ratios* Summer 1978: 5–11

Beddoe, R., 1978. *Value Added and Payment Systems, Technical Notes* 42, Oxford: Trade Union Research Unit, Ruskin College

Bentley Associates, 1975. *A Dynamic Pay Policy for Growth*, Brighton: Bentley Associates

Binder, Hamlyn and Fry & Co., 1978. *Added Value as a Concept*, Binder, Hamlyn, Fry & Co.

British Institute of Management (BIM), 1957. *The Disclosure of Financial Information to Employees*, London: BIM

Burchell, S., Clubb, C. and Hopwood, A., 1981. 'A Message From Mars – and other Reminiscences From the Past', *Accountancy* October: 96, 98, 100

Cameron, S., 1977a. 'Added Value Plan for Distributing ICI's Wealth', *Financial Times* 7 January

    1977b. 'Adding Value to Britain', *Financial Times* 31 May

    1978. 'Breeding a New Type of Productivity Deal', *Financial Times* 3 April

Chandler, A.D. Jr., 1962. *Strategy and Structure*, Cambridge, MA: MIT Press

Cohen, M.D., March, J.G. and Olsen, J.P., 1972. 'A Garbage Can Model of Organizational Choice', *Administrative Science Quarterly* March: 1–25

Confederation of British Industry (CBI), 1978. *Financial Participation in Companies: An Introductory Booklet*, London: CBI

Cox, B., 1979. *Value Added: An Appreciation for the Accountant Concerned with Industry*, London: Heinemann, in association with the ICMA

Crouch, C., 1979. *The Politics of Industrial Relations*, London: Fontana

Department of Trade, 1977a. *Committee of Inquiry on Industrial Democracy* (Chairman: Lord Bullock), Cmnd 6706, London: HMSO

1977b. *The Future of Company Reports*, London: HMSO

Donovan, Lord, 1968. *Royal Commission on Trade Unions*, Cmnd 3623, London: HMSO

Donzelot, J., 1979. *The Policing of Families*, London: Pantheon

Elliot, J., 1978. 'The Liberals Make Their Point', *Financial Times* 3 February

Engineering Employers' Federation (EEF), 1972. *Business Performance and Industrial Relations: Added Value as an Instrument of Management Discipline*, London: Kogan Page

1977. *Practical Applications of Added Value*, London: Archway Press

Fanning, D., 1978. 'Banishing Confusion from the Added Value Equation', *Financial Times* 13 December: 11

Fels, A., 1972. *The British Prices and Incomes Board*, Cambridge: Cambridge University Press

Gray, S.I. and Maunders, K.T., 1980. *Value Added Reporting: Uses and Measurement*, London: ACA

Hacking, I., 1981. 'How Should we do the History of Statistics?', *Ideology and Consciousness* Spring: 15–26

Hilton, A., 1978. *Employee Reports: How to Communicate Financial Information to Employees*, Cambridge: Woodhead Faulkner

Hindess, B., 1982. 'Power, Interests and the Outcomes of Struggles', *Sociology* November: 498–511

Hird, C., 1980. 'Beware of Added Value', *New Statesman* 4 August

Holmes, G., 1977. 'How UK Companies Report Their Employees', *Accountancy* November: 64–8

Hopkins, L., 1975. 'Value Added', *Accountancy Age* 7 November

Hopwood, A.G., 1983. *Accounting Research and Accounting Practice: The Ambiguous Relationship Between the Two*, the Deloitte, Haskins and Sells Accounting Lecture at the University College of Wales, Aberystwyth

Hussey, R., 1978. *Employees and the Employment Report – A Research Paper* London: Touche Ross & Co

1979. *Who Reads Employee Reports?* London: Touche Ross & Co

Incomes Data Services (IDS), 1977. Incomes Data Report, 'New Thoughts on Profit Sharing at ICI', Report 251 February: 21

Institute of Chartered Accountants in England and Wales (ICAEW), 1969. 'Statement of Intent on Accounting Standards in the 1970s', *The Accountant* 18 December: 842–3

1978. *Survey of Published Accounts 1977*, London: ICAEW

1980. *Survey of Published Accounts 1979*, London: ICAEW

Jones, F.C., 1976. *The Economic Ingredients of Industrial Success*, James Clayton Lecture, The Institution of Mechanical Engineers

1978. 'Our Manufacturing Industry – The Missing £100,000 million', *National Westminster Bank Quarterly Review* May: 8–17

Kahn-Freud, O., 1977. 'Industrial Democracy', *Industrial Law Journal*: 75–6

Labour Party, 1974. *The Community and the Company*, London: Labour Party

Labour Research, 1978. *Value Added* February

Litterer, J., 1961. 'Systematic Management: The Search for Order and Integration', *Business History Review* 35(4): 461–76

1963. 'Systematic Management: Design for Organizational Recoupling in American Manufacturing Firms', *Business History Review* 37(4): 369–91

Low, E., 1977. 'Forget Piecework and Develop a Fair Way to Reward Employees', *Accountants Weekly* 6 May: 16–17

Lucas, R.J., 1979. *Pension Planning Within a Major Company: A Case Study of the Negotiation of the British Leyland Pension Plan for Manual Workers*, Oxford: Pergamon Press

McKersie, R.B. and Hunter, L.C., 1973. *Pay Productivity and Collective Bargaining*, London: Macmillan

McLeay, S., 1983. 'Value Added: A Comparative Study', *Accounting, Organizations and Society* 8(1): 31–56

Marchington, M.P., 1977. 'Worker Participation and Plant-wide Incentive Systems', *Personnel Review* Summer: 35–8

Minson, J., 1980. 'Strategies for Socialists? Foucault's Conception of Power', *Economy and Society* 9(1): 1–43

Morley, M.F., 1978. *The Value Added Statement*, London: for the ICAS

National Board for Prices and Incomes (NBPI), 1968. *General Report, August 1967–July 1968*, Cmnd 3715, London: HMSO

Neimark, M.D. and Tinker, A.M., 1986. 'The Social Construction of Management Control Systems', *Accounting, Organizations and Society* 11(4/5): 369–95

New, C., 1978. 'Factors in Productivity that Should Not be Overlooked', *The Times* 1 February

Nietzsche, F., 1969. *On the Genealogy of Morals*, trans. W. Kaufmann, New York: Vintage Books

Pakenham-Walsh, A.A., 1964. 'Spanners in the Growth Engine', *The Cost Accountant* July: 260–8

Pitkin, H.F., 1967. *The Concept of Representation*, Berkeley: University of California Press

Renshall, M., Allan, R. and Nicholson, K., 1979. *Added Value in External Financial Reporting*, London: ICAEW

Ruggles, R. and Ruggles, N.D., 1965. *National Income Accounts and Income Analysis*, 2nd edn., New York: McGraw-Hill

Rutherford, B.A., 1977. 'Value Added as a Focus of Attention for Financial Reporting: Some Conceptual Problems', *Accounting and Business Research* Summer: 215–20

1978. 'Examining Some Value Added Statements', *Accountancy* July: 48–52

1980. 'Published Statements of Value Added: A Survey of Three Years' Experience', *Accounting and Business Research* Winter: 15–28

Sandilands Committee, 1975. *Inflation Accounting: Report of the Inflation Accounting Committee*, Cmnd 6225, London: HMSO

Searle, G.R., 1971. *The Quest for National Efficiency*, Oxford: Basil Blackwell

Sharp, K., 1971. 'Accounting Standards After 12 Months', *Accountancy* May 1971: 239–45

Skerratt, L.C.L. and Tonkin, D.J., 1982. *Financial Reporting 1982–83: A Survey of UK Published Accounts*, London: ICAEW

Smith, G., 1978. *Wealth Creation – the Added Value Concept*, London: IPWSOM

Stolliday, I. and Attwood, M., 1978. 'Financial Inducement and Productivity Bargaining', *Industrial and Commercial Training*

Stuttard, G., 1979. 'Industrial Democracy by the Back Door', *Financial Times* 21 March

Tonkin, D.J. and Skerratt, L.C.L., 1983. *Financial Reporting 1983–84 A Survey of UK Published Accounts*, London: ICAEW

Trades Union Congress, 1974. *Industrial Democracy*, London: TUC

Turner, H.A., 1970. 'Collective Bargaining and the Eclipse of Incomes Policies: Retrospect, Prospect and Possibilities', *British Journal of Industrial Relations* July

Vickers da Costa, 1979. *Testing for Success*, London: Mimeo

Wellens, J., 1977. 'An ICI Experiment in Company-wide Communication', *Industrial and Commercial Training* July: 271–8

Whittington, G., 1983. *Inflation Accounting: An Introduction to the Debate*, Cambridge: Cambridge University Press

Woodmansay, M., 1978. *Added Value: An Introduction to Productivity Schemes*, London: BIM

Zeff, S.A., 1972. *Forging Accounting Principles in Five Countries*, London: Stipes
1978. 'The Rise of Economic Consequences', *Journal of Accountancy* December: 56–63

# 10   Management by accounting

*Brendan McSweeney*

> The operations of practice are only as good as the theory in which they are
> grounded                                                    (Bourdieu *et al.*, 1991: 63)

The Conservative Government that came to power in May 1979 described
the 'public sector' in almost exclusively pejorative terms: it was at 'the heart
of Britain's present economic difficulties' (Cmnd 7746, 1979: 1). The thrust
of policy towards public sector activities has ever since been one of
reduction, whether by abandonment, privatization, or contracting out
(Marsh, 1991; Veljanovski, 1987). What remains of the public sector has
been, and continues to be, transformed by the implantation of what is
asserted to be 'the one best way' of managing and assessing organizations:
'the management of each department can and should be informed by clear
and common principles . . . fundamental to good management and effective
use of resources' (Cmnd 8616, 1982: 7/22). This 'one best way' of management can be called *management by accounting*. Initially, Civil Service
departments were the targets of change (National Audit Office, 1986; Cmnd
8616, 1982). Subsequently, an increasing number of public sector organizations (Train, 1985; Pendlebury, 1989) have been required, or have pre-
emptively chosen, to implant what official pronouncements declare to be an
unquestionable good. The new management approach has been described
by the Prime Minister's Special Adviser on Efficiency as 'at the heart of a
change of management style in the public sector' (Ibbs, 1984: 108) and, by
the National Audit Office, to 'lie at the heart of good management'
(National Audit Office, 1986: 11). Accounting, widely defined, is characterized as a key organizing principle, as central to the changes sought (Cmnd
8616, 1982). If good management is to be the *leitmotif* of the public sector,
then this is to be defined, it would appear, as 'management by accounting'.

### Locating management by accounting: the Financial Management Initiative

One way of locating management by accounting is by reference to specific
government initiatives. The Financial Management Initiative (FMI),

launched in May 1982, might be seen as the most decisive of such initiatives, introduced as it was in the early years of the Thatcher regime. The FMI was formally launched 'with full and unqualified support of the Government and the top management of the Civil Service' (National Audit Office, 1986: 1). The initiative was described as the application of the 'three fundamental principles' of good management. 'Managers' at all levels (from the most junior to Ministers) were to have:

> (a) a clear view of their objectives and the means to assess and, whenever possible, measure outputs or performance in relation to those objectives;
> (b) well-defined responsibility for making the best use of their resources including a critical scrutiny of output and value for money; and
> (c) the information (particularly about costs), the training and the access to expert advice that they need to exercise their responsibilities effectively (Cmnd 8616, 1982: 5).

These principles, said to be 'fundamental to good management and effective use of resources' should, it was argued, 'be applied to the maximum practicable extent' (Cmnd 8616, 1982: 22). The 'ways in which the principles are applied and the form of the analytical systems might differ somewhat', the White Paper stated, 'nevertheless, the Government believes that fundamental principles of good management transcend the differences between departments: ... the management of each department can and should be informed by clear and common principles' (Cmnd 8616, 1982: 7). 'Discrete ... responsibility centres' were to be created and 'accounting', in the sense of generalizable and neutral systems, was to be comprehensively applied in order to achieve good management and efficient use of resources (Cmnd 8616, 1982: 34). Accounting was to be a central mechanism in the breaking down of a department's activity between managers, so that responsibilities might be more clearly distinguished, objectives more clearly defined, and costs and outputs more clearly assessed. Greater authority could thus be delegated to those managers who could be enjoined to choose the best way of using the resources in pursuit of the defined objectives. In a manner similar to that of an undergraduate accounting textbook, management accounting was invoked as a way of focusing attention on evaluation (costing options and activities), planning (setting objectives), and control (monitoring events quickly and taking timely action where necessary): 'The task of specifying objectives, assessing alternative means of achieving them (in terms of quantity, quality, cost, time, etc.) and monitoring results against expenditure will be helped by the application of the management accounting approach and the better information it generates' (Treasury and Management & Personnel Office, 1982: 22/29/30). The scope of the FMI's principles was considered to be 'capable of extension within the

public sector' to non-departmental bodies (Cmnd 8616, 1982: 13; Confederation of British Industry, 1985: 9).

Existing accounting methods in the Civil Service were criticized on two
related grounds. Management accounting in practice was said to measure
only some 'inputs', rather than 'relating inputs to activities or outputs'
(Cmnd 8616, 1982: 29). The focus of input calculation was described as too
narrow, in so far as it concerned only cash-flow which 'rarely gives an
adequate measure of the resources being consumed by a particular activity
and therefore a proper basis for comparison with outputs'. Good management was seen to require measurement of total costs whose components
were all assumed to be capable of recognition and measurement (Cmnd
8616, 1982: 30). Accrual accounting, and allocation of indirect costs to cost
centres or responsibility centres,[1] were proposed as the central means of
doing so. This critique of existing accounting methods was more than an
injunction to control costs, and monitor performance. Rather, the new
accounting was to be part of an attempt to transform the way in which Civil
Service Departments would be run, a means of achieving that elusive goal
of 'good management'. Accounting was seen to be a pivotal means of
achieving such a goal.

Locating the formation and emergence of management by accounting
requires consideration of wider events. The May 1979 general election is
often characterized as a major break with previous governments, a rupture
marked by radical policies of the 'New Right' (Honderich, 1990: 8). What is
described here as management by accounting has been considered to be a
consequence of such policies: 'The Thatcher Government's blows continued to rain down on the civil service; and far from petering out the quest
for "efficiency" eventually came to be translated into something akin to a
grand strategy in the form of the Financial Management Initiative' (Fry,
1984: 323). Hennessy (1989: 605) states that the FMI was 'conceived inside
the Efficiency Unit' which was established in 1979. In the government's own
view, also, it had been the originator. The necessity for change had existed,
it was said, prior to May 1979. But recognition of this, and of management
by accounting as a key part of the solution, was a result of: the 'Government's policy for good management throughout the whole of the Civil
Service as an aim to be pursued as a matter of policy in its own right' (Cmnd
8616, 1982: 2).

But we need to be wary of tracing management by accounting hastily to
the most proximate apparent cause, whether this be 'Thatcherism' or the
'New Right'. Individual initiatives such as the FMI, and management
accounting more generally, cannot adequately be treated as an event with a
single cause. A specific date, such as the Prime Minister's minute to
Ministers on the FMI in May 1982, may commemorate the launch of a

particular policy (Wilding, 1983: 39). But to take such a moment as a founding cause or an absolute beginning, or even to treat it as a relay of other more fundamental causal forces operating at that moment is to ignore the antecedent conditions of possibility (Latour, 1987; Ricoeur, 1984, 1986; Eco, 1986). Management by accounting was advocated within parliamentary arenas before the 1982 launch of the FMI, and before 1979. It was promoted as a means of achieving policies that were often indifferent to, or even hostile to the New Right, as well as those consistent with its ambitions (Honderich, 1990; HC 535-I, 1977; Cmnd 3638, 1968). The launch of the FMI was important in the implantation process, but it was neither its beginning nor its completion.

The conditions of emergence of management by accounting can be elaborated by exploring its advocacy prior to the FMI, and even before the coming to power of the Thatcher Government in 1979. Before this date, parliamentary documentation and other material shows a more complex picture of the arguments in support of management by accounting.

### The 'modernization' of the Civil Service

Some of these antecedent conditions (Foucault, 1980: 77) of management by accounting are considered here. Proposals for radical changes in management (or administration) of Civil Service Departments have been made at various times over the past centuries[2] (Robinson, 1981: 157). But the aspirations and mechanisms have differed. Whilst aspects of management by accounting can be identified at earlier times, the 1968 Fulton Committee Report (Cmnd 3638, 1968) provided the clearest example of its advocacy as a comprehensive policy of Civil Service reform. By examining the analysis and recommendations of the Fulton Report, it can be shown that management by accounting predates the 'New Right' and the Conservative Government elected in 1979, and that some of its components were set in place at least as early as the 1960s.

The Fulton Committee was appointed on 8 February 1966 to 'examine the structure, recruitment and management, including training, of the Home Civil Service' (Cmnd 3638, 1968: Appendix A). The commissioning of the Fulton Committee was the culmination of over a decade of growing and increasingly vocal criticism of the Civil Service in general, and the Administrative Class in particular. Indeed, the 'dissatisfaction was part of a wider demand ... for the modernisation of British institutions' (Garrett, 1972: 35/36). The Labour Government had already set up a Royal Commission on Local Government, another on Public Schools, and one on Trade Unions (Kellner and Crowther-Hunt, 1980: 25). The Committee's report concluded that the Civil Service was 'still fundamentally the product of the nineteenth-century Northcote–Trevelyan Report', whereas, 'the tasks it faces are those of the second half of the twentieth century' (Cmnd 3638, 1968: 9). The regulatory functions of government had 'multiplied in size and greatly broadened in scope' and it had 'taken on vast new responsibilities' (Cmnd 3638, 1968: 10). Accordingly, the Service was 'in need of fundamental change' (Cmnd 3638, 1968: 11).

The Fulton Committee's central criticism was that the Service was still based 'on a philosophy of the amateur (or generalist, or "all-rounder"), so that, "too few civil servants", were skilled managers' (Cmnd 3638, 1968: 104). Amongst its recommendations was the abolition of the 47 general classes and the 1400 departmental classes in the Service, and their replacement by a single structure. But its central proposal on the 'management' of the Civil Service was that: 'In the interests of efficiency the principles of accountable management should be applied to the organisation of the work of departments' (Cmnd 3638, 1968: 105). This, it was explained, included organization of Departments so as to:

enable responsibility and authority to be defined and allocated more clearly than they often are at present. Individuals and units could then be called to account for performance which is measured as objectively as possible.

Civil servants should have:

clear objectives and their performance should be judged by their results ... Wherever measures of achievement can be established in quantitative or financial terms, and individuals held responsible for outputs and costs, accountable units should be set up.

Costs should be 'precisely allocated to the man in charge' and 'standards of achievements by which performance can be judged' should be established (Cmnd 3638, 1968: 52). This notion of accountable management and its quantitative measurement provided the opening into which accounting would be inserted.

The similarity between these proposals of the Fulton Committee and those of the FMI are clear. For the Fulton Committee, management by accounting (or 'accountable management' as it called it) was not just reporting and monitoring performance and the monitoring of that monitoring. These monitoring procedures were considered a part, indeed an essential part, of 'accountable management'. Like the FMI 14 years later, the Fulton Committee's notion of 'accountable management' made management by accounting an integral and constitutive component of an ideal of 'best management'.

Paralleling the later arguments of the FMI, Fulton criticized accounting systems in the Civil Service. The Service's cash based accounting was declared incapable of identifying 'total and detailed costs of particular activities' and of 'allocating them to cost centres and their outputs'. Thus, it 'rarely gives an adequate measure of resources being consumed'. 'Accounting', the Fulton Committee Report said, 'is no longer a matter of bookkeeping but of financial management in its widest sense. Internal audit is no longer a matter of routine but is an important element in management services aimed at increasing the effectiveness and efficiency of an organisation'. There were, it argued, insufficient numbers of accountants: 'there are posts for only 309 qualified accountants in the entire Service out of the 25,000 qualified accountants who make up the accountancy profession in this country.' Moreover, their status was 'very low', and the range of work too limited as the Professional Accountant Class was excluded from 'responsibility for financial estimating and control, which is vested in the Administrative Class'. It should, the Report stated, be recognized 'that training and experience in accountancy can fit the right man for the highest managerial posts' (Cmnd 3638, 1968: 150).

Unlike the FMI, the Fulton Committee did not promote management by accounting as part of a programme of restricting the volume and range of government activities. Rather, it was treated as a central part of the 'modernization' of a Service without which, it said, it would be unable to expand efficiently and extend its activities (Cmnd 3638, 1968: 10/50). More efficient use of resources was treated as self-evidently desirable, rather than depicted as a necessity prompted by economic constraint.

But desires for modernization do not lead inevitably to changes in management techniques. Nor, when such changes are proposed, is management by accounting necessarily advanced. A contrasting example is the Maud Report: *Management of Local Government* (Ministry of Housing and Local Government, 1967). There were a number of similarities between the arguments and recommendations of the two reports. Like the Fulton Report, the Maud Report attributed the existing forms of administration to the nineteenth century, 'when the range of activities of local authority was limited, when government involvement in the affairs of society was minimal' (Ministry of Housing and Local Government, 1967: 35). But the Maud Report differed from Fulton in drawing attention to external financial demands. Specifically, rising current and capital expenditure meant that 'the task of ensuring that value is obtained for money' was of 'exceptional importance'. And, most importantly, whilst the Maud Report called for a 'systematic approach' to the 'process of management', including an emphasis on *ex ante* statements of goals, it did not suggest management by accounting. The 'task of ensuring that value is obtained for the money spent' was, it said, 'one of exceptional importance' but not withstanding a need for:

first class financial control . . . expert accountancy and financial measurement, [and] arrangements to induce financial awareness at the policy making level . . . accounting, costing or other numerical tests of success or failure are of only limited significance (Ministry of Housing and Local Government, 1967: 34–5).

At the time the two reports were undertaken, 1967 and 1968, local government, unlike central government departments, was already a major site of accounting (Ministry of Housing and Local Government, 1967; Cmnd 3638, 1968; Cockburn, 1977).

Management by accounting is made up of a number of diverse concepts and practices, each with its own history. Notions such as 'cost consciousness', 'effectiveness', 'efficiency', predate 1968, as do notions of accountability, responsibility centres, subsidiarity, and input–output (Holdsworth, 1888; Management Accounting Team, 1950; McKean, 1958; Cmnd 1432, 1961; Sloan, 1965; Solomons, 1965; Nairne, 1982). For example, an *Occasional Paper* issued in 1967 by the Civil Service based Centre for Administrative Studies recommended 'a technique of management accounting' which involved 'recasting governmental accounts in such a way that the costs ("inputs") are allocated as far as possible to specific objectives of policy, an attempt is then made to measure success or failure of the various activities ("programmes")[3] in attaining the objectives' (Williams, 1967). As Fry (1991: 437) notes: '*management by objectives* had become *conventional* wisdom in management theory by the time that the Fulton Committee's Management Consultancy Group was appointed, as a knowledge of the contemporary literature makes evident.' Management by objectives had been encouraged by the British Institute of Management and others since the early 1960s (Humble, 1965). And, as Garrett states (1972: 198), it had 'flourished more widely in Britain than anywhere else in the world'.

But Fry's linking of the 'conventional wisdom' of management by objectives with the Fulton Committee's advocacy of accountable management is too strong, as it implies that accountable management was considered by the Committee to be similar to, or identical with, management by objectives. For the Fulton Committee 'management by objectives' evidently meant something different from 'accountable management'. It clearly regarded management by objective(s) as a less satisfactory alternative to accountable management, to be used only when the latter could not be applied because performance could not be assessed in terms of measurable outputs. The impossibility, or difficulty, of using measurable output as the 'criterion for assessing performance' for some activities was a result, the Fulton Report stated, of their uncertainty: 'One cannot lay down in advance how long it should take to review effectively the investment programme of a nationalised industry, or to study and make sound recommendations on the acceptability of a proposed merger.' An additional uncertainty was, it was stated: 'the unpredictable demands that arise from the Minister's responsibility to Parliament, and by the fact that much of it contains a major element of new policy-making involving consultation, negotiation and the preparation of legislation' (Cmnd 3638, 1968: 52). Notwithstanding these earlier words of caution, the FMI acknowledged no exceptions to the ambit of management by accounting. It was to be applied at 'all levels' (Cmnd 8616, 1982: 5).

## Post-Fulton: the era of programmatic analysis

Some of the Fulton Committee's recommendations were acted upon, for example the establishment in 1968 of a Civil Service Department which took over responsibility for pay and management of the Civil Service from the Treasury (Hennessy, 1989). However, attempts to implant management by accounting were limited. Explanations for this differ. In its Eleventh Report (Session 1976–77), the Expenditure Committee (HC535-I, 1977: xlvii) stated that:

there has not been a determined effort to implement these [accountable management] proposals . . . We do not believe that the Fulton proposal of accountable management has been taken sufficiently seriously . . . Our evidence suggests that management accounting is being introduced in the public sector, although on a fairly haphazard and limited scale. It would appear that there is an element in the civil service opposed to the introduction of accountable management and its implications for the status quo.

Harold Wilson, who was the Prime Minister at the time of Fulton, later stated: 'I think there was an immediate burst of activity after Fulton came out and it was very much under Prime Ministerial direction. I got the impression . . . that by about 1969 it was tailing off a bit' (Wilson, 1977: 187).

Notwithstanding the view of many of the Committee's supporters that there had been insufficient attempts to implement many of the Fulton Committee's recommendations (Kellner and Crowther-Hunt, 1980), the post-Fulton period was characterized by an intensified concern with efficiency in the Civil Service from both Labour and Conservative Governments. Whilst some limited implanting of accountable management took place in parts of a few Departments (Civil Service Department, 1976; Garrett, 1972), it was not the means of change the government chose to use. Instead, attention was elsewhere – on a programmatic approach (Cmnd 4506, 1970). This was characterized by attempts to plan and control broad 'inputs' and 'outputs' in order to increase growth through avoidance of conflict and duplication. The focus was at what was called a 'strategic', 'corporate planning', or 'programmatic' level – an attempt to determine whether policies or activities were in accord with 'Government's strategic policy objectives', to prioritize current and prospective policies, and to allocate resources to the public sector on a 'rational and systematic basis' (Cmnd 4506, 1970: 14).

The first UK application of 'programmatic analysis' was probably in the Ministry of Defence as early as the mid-1960s, having been used earlier in the US Defense Department (Donnison *et al.*, 1975: 27; Townsend, 1975: 59–60; Garrett, 1972: 141). Later, the Labour Government established planning units in each Civil Service department, some of whom experimented with Programme Planning & Budgeting. Its use was endorsed in 1969 by the Select Committee on Procedure (HC 410, 1969). By the late 1960s and early 1970s a number of local authorities began introducing 'corporate planning' (Cockburn, 1977). After its defeat in 1964, the Conservative Party had hired firms of consultants to advise it on the management of the public sector, and 18 managers (or businessmen, as they were referred to) from firms such as RTZ, Shell International and Marks & Spencer were selected to work on a part-time basis in developing those policies. The Conservative Party's period in opposition coincided with the euphoria for Programme Planning & Budgeting in the US. Although 'some of the bloom had gone off the rose of the programme budgeting in the USA, nevertheless it was the only show in town, and the British businessmen modelled their original suggestion on it' (Heclo and Wildavsky, 1981). Staff from the Conservative Party's Research Department had also acquired some familiarity with Programme Planning & Budgeting in the US (Hennessy, 1989: 211).

The programmatic approach was given a particular form in the early 1970s: the new Conservative Government commenced the implantation of a variation of Programme Planning & Budgeting, titled Programme Analysis & Review, within all central government departments. Large was deemed to be beautiful and, most importantly programmable. Unlike accountable management's focus on multiple accountable units, Programme Analysis & Review was accompanied by the restructuring of existing departments into a smaller number of 'giant departments', to facilitate 'closer alignment of policies and programmes in formerly separate departments' (Garrett, 1972: 191). The White Paper *The Reorganisation of Central Government* (Cmnd 4506, 1970: 6) stated that such changes 'must be designed to remedy the major difficulty which faces government in a modern complex society, which cannot be solved by good administration and management alone'. This difficulty was held to be a matter of policy formulation and decision-taking. Without a clear definition of strategic purpose, and under the pressures of day-to-day problems (Cmnd 4506, 1970: 6/13)

governments are always at some risk of losing sight of the need to consider the totality of their current policies in relation to their longer-term objectives; and they pay too little attention to the difficult, but critical task of evaluating as objectively as possible the alternative policy options and priorities open to them.

The White Paper pledged a 'new style of government', arguing that government had been attempting too much, and as a result had placed an excessive burden on industry and 'overloaded the government machine itself'. This was in clear contrast to the Fulton Committee Report that had approved of an extended role for government, and had recommended a new 'management style' – management by accounting – for an expanded and expanding Civil Service.

### Local applications

It was the programmatic approach and its related notions of planning and central direction that received government support for use in its departments (Cmnd 4506, 1970), rather than the Fulton Committee's 'accountable management'. However, there were some localized implantations of management by accounting in parts of a few departments. The Fulton Report had recommended further inquiries into the desirability of increasing the number of activities that could be 'hived off' to non-departmental organizations (Cmnd 3638, 1968: 61), through which 'accountable management' would be introduced. Amongst the departmental agencies (Cmnd 4506, 1970: 9) hived off was the Defence Procurement Executive (established in 1970). The then head of the Civil Service, Lord Armstrong, speaking about its establishment some time later (Armstrong, 1977: 650), stated:

I came to the conclusion that the right thing to do was to try and isolate organisations within which this kind of accountable management ought to be able to apply, and to put at the head of an organisation somebody who believed in this sort of thing and who could apply it downwards and give him the right sort of relationship with Ministers and so on.

The Executive's first chief executive was Derek Rayner[4] who was to become Personal Adviser on Efficiency to the Prime Minister after 1979. He was an advocate of management by accounting (Rayner, 1977). It was under his auspices that a focus upon outputs and the inputs related to them, and breaking down of such outputs and inputs into units 'with the object of controlling what you spend in relation to what you want to get' was developed in the Defence Procurement Executive (Armstrong, 1977: 651).

In contrast with the comprehensive ambitions of those who advocated management by accounting, others argued that it had only a limited role: 'It turns out to be a very, very complicated business' although experiments showed that 'there was scope for something called accountable management in certain areas' (Armstrong, 1977: 650). According to Edward Heath, the then Prime Minister, the Executive had been established because its activities could be 'organised on a business basis'. But, he stated, it could only be applied to a very limited range of Civil Service activities (Heath, 1977: 774). Within government departments more widely, management by accounting was not used 'to any great extent' although piecemeal and more ambitious attempts were made to use it to assist in examining performance of some public sector bodies external to departments, as well as in some areas of industrial activity (Garrett and Walker, 1969).

### Expenditure and efficiency

By late 1974, the context of Civil Service reform had changed significantly. The inevitability of economic growth was no longer a widely held assumption: 'a year ago to say that Britain was in major crisis produced scandalized denial, even derision. Today, to say the same thing risks boredom' (Hudson Institute Europe, 1974: 1). The dramatic increase in oil prices following the Arab–Israeli War (Kogan and Kogan, 1982) was part of this change of assessment, but it occurred in what was increasingly to be understood as an economy undergoing deep-rooted changes (Grant, 1972; Havighurst, 1979). After 1973, whichever economic indicator was chosen – inflation, unemployment, direct tax as a proportion of income, balance of payments and so forth – indicated a worsening of conditions (Kogan and Kogan, 1982). Social conflict intensified with a significant increase in strikes (Havighurst, 1979). Towards the end of 1974, there was near complete consensus that there was an economic 'crisis', although views varied as to its nature, severity, probable duration, as well as possible remedies (Turner, 1975; Cmnd 6315, 1975; Cmnd 5710, 1974).

However, if opinions varied as to the ways of curing the underlying economic ills, there was agreement between the Conservative and Labour Governments of 1973–79 on the need to constrain public expenditure (Cmnd 6151, 1975; Hogwood, 1992). This was the end of 'policy without pain' (Rose, 1984a: 28). A 1975 White Paper, *The Attack on Inflation*, stated that the 'paramount need to move resources into exports and investment makes it essential to contain the demands on resources made by public expenditure programmes' (Cmnd 6151, 1975: 11). The following year, in another White Paper, the government declared (Cmnd 6507, 1976) that:

pay restraint and price control will not be effective in reducing the inflation rate unless other aspects of economic policy are also consistent ... failure to control public spending, or to ensure that the growth of the money supply does not stimulate inflation, would place the programme in jeopardy.

The tone of parliamentary debates about public expenditure had changed noticeably. Whilst demands for spending to be increased on specific items had not entirely disappeared, they were less frequent, and had become muted. There was more talk about 'value for money' (Hopwood, 1984; McSweeney, 1988). As Robinson (1981: 164/5) has commented:

Members of the Opposition parties were not the only ones demanding that public expenditure be controlled ... MP's from the government side were also less insistent in their demands.

Moreover, the Civil Service became the target of specific criticisms. It was depicted as 'a great bulwark against change' (*The Times*, 5 December 1977). The lives of civil servants came increasingly to be viewed as undeservedly protected (Junor, 1976: 14):

Isn't it almost beyond belief the way public servants have managed to get their greedy snouts into the public trough. Why should they, any more than the rest of us, be protected from rising prices?

Various mechanisms to constrain public expenditure in the aggregate were introduced, principally 'cash limits' on public sector spending and pay (Cmnd 6440, 1976; Cmnd 7293, 1978; Healy, 1989: 401). These constraints were reinforced by the International Monetary Fund's requirement in 1976 of further public expenditure cuts as a condition of a loan to the UK government (Donaldson and Farquhar, 1988). In this changed setting the 'programmatic analysis' was either abandoned, or what remained of it largely neglected (Heclo and Wildavsky, 1981; HC 236-I, 1982: xxiv; Gray and Jenkins, 1983; Hennessy, 1989: 591). According to the Director General of the Royal Institute of Public Administration, the Treasury's 'main concern' had become 'how to have less of what was being done' and it did not consider the programmatic approach to be 'a particularly interesting approach' to curbing government activities (HC 54, 1981: 96). There were other criticisms also which varied from suggestions that it was too ambitious, to the view that it did not go far enough. A core argument in the first position was that in political contexts decisions develop incrementally, or sequentially, in conditions of uncertainty which diminish the possibility and efficacy of comprehensive and prior analysis and planning (Kavanagh, 1985; Garrett, 1972: 147). Donnison *et al.*, (1975: 28/9) said:

We live in a society in which there can be no lasting consensus. Policies evolve piecemeal as the unforeseen outcome of decisions made in different places by different elites under pressure from different quarters. Policy-making does not call for the specification of clearly defined objectives or broader social aspirations; indeed, it rarely permits either ... supposedly rational strategies are precluded by the dizzying variety of options open to policy-makers, the profusion of unpredictable primary, secondary and subsequent consequences of their decisions, and the conflicting political pressures which must be accommodated every time something has to be done.

Those who thought that the programmatic approach did not go far enough had fully endorsed its approach, but argued that it was neither deep enough, nor detailed enough: 'it is necessary not only to specify and evaluate expenditure on a programme basis but to relate programmes to the internal management structure and its sytem of control' (Garrett, 1972: 148). Programme Analysis & Review was formally abandoned[5] in October 1979.

But the desire to transform the management of the Civil Service remained. Indeed, it received additional support from increased demands to constrain public expenditure (Kellner and Crowther-Hunt, 1980). A legacy of the programmatic approach was the search for an alternative solution to the control and management of government departments and organizations. Increasingly, these came to be viewed as 'entities' capable of analysis and improvement through the linking of 'inputs to outputs' (Donnison et al., 1975; Cockburn, 1977). There developed also a greater 'respectability' for considerations of costs (Heclo and Wildavsky, 1981), and a greater involvement of 'businessmen' and management consultants in the formulation of policy on both sides of Parliament.

In 1976, the Expenditure Committee launched a protracted inquiry into the Civil Service that lasted from May 1976 to May 1977. It was the first investigation of its kind by a select committee for 104 years (HC 535, 1977). The Committee strongly advocated management by accounting (measurement of outputs, matching costs to them, reform of and greater use of accounting, increased recruitment of accountants and so forth). It explicitly called for the implementation of the Fulton Report's recommendations on accountable management, which it said had not received sufficient commitment within the Civil Service.

Like Fulton, the Expenditure Committee condemned existing forms and methods of analysis within the Civil Service and appealed to 'accounting' as capable of providing the required data. Echoing the arguments of Fulton, the primary locus of financial analysis should, it was said, be where decisions on resource use were made and implemented. 'Where possible, expenditure plans should be the responsibility of individual accountable units, just as cash limits should coincide with accountable units' (HC 535-I,

1977: liv). This was held to require management accounting: 'The allocation of costs and quantification of benefits depends upon the general introduction of management accounting' (HC 535-I, 1977; xlviii). This, in turn, was seen to necessitate recruitment of those possessing the requisite expertise and an increased aptitude on the part of civil servants for accounting more generally: 'New systems must be designed by professional accountants and civil servants must be trained to understand them' (HC 535-I, 1977: xlviii). A statement to the Committee by the then President of the Institute of Chartered Accountants in England and Wales that 'We feel that as a profession we can offer a degree of management interest which extends well beyond the technical services' was repeated approvingly by the Committee in its Eleventh Report (HC 535-I, 1977: xlviii).

The Committee was dissatisfied with existing ways of reporting the performance of Departments to Parliament (and its committees), and with the public sector more broadly. It sought 'the accountability of the Executive to the House of Commons' and 'open government which governments have professed to have supported for the past decade' (HC 576, 1978: ix/xi). It endorsed the Fulton Committee's call for internally conducted 'efficiency audits'. But it also called for externally conducted and reported audits to satisfy accountability to Parliament, and to provide assurances that the efficiency and effectiveness it sought was being achieved. It was wholly unsatisfactory, the Committee stated (HC 576, 1978: para. 11), that:

the accounts which are presented to parliament are primarily useful for audit (i.e. verifying the proper authorization of expenditure) and not for assessing management performance or the effectiveness of policy. We therefore recommended [in its Eleventh Report, 1977] that the structure of accountable units should correspond as far as possible with the structure of accountable units within departments so that management could be examined ... we insist that Parliament cannot properly monitor policies or spending unless it is regularly supplied with information which illustrates the efficiency and effectiveness of management of government.

Support for this view included that of the trade union, the Institute of Public Civil Servants (HC 535-II, 1977): 'I think that public and parliamentary scrutiny might very well be greatly assisted if we could ensure that the parliamentary votes coincided with manageable accountable units.'

The Committee considered management by accounting not only to be the best means by which the Service would achieve efficient performance, but saw it as also a necessary condition for internal and external audits. It argued that auditing should not only address probity, but should evaluate management performance also (McSweeney, 1988). By this means Parliament would be able to determine the adequacy of management. Accountability was to be more than monitoring, or the monitoring of monitoring, it aspired to an evaluation of the management process in its entirety.

The following year, 1978, in its Fourteenth Report the Expenditure Committee repeated its calls for the establishment of 'a more rational system of accounting to the House of Commons'. The 'ideal system of public accounting should', it stated (HC 661, 1978: xvii):

provide information on:- (i) Whether expenditure had been properly authorised . . . (ii) the efficiency of the management of government. This should be organised as far as possible on the basis of identified accountable units within Departments or other public organisations . . . (iii) The effectiveness or impact of expenditure, i.e. the extent to which the spending meets its objectives and produces results . . . At present, the accounting information presented to Parliament satisfies only category (i).

The evidence submitted to the Expenditure Sub-Committee suggested that the 'economic stringency' imposed through cash limits was, of itself, insufficient to constrain expenditure. The existing division in evaluation and control arrangements, with the Treasury responsible for expenditure control (except manpower costs) and the Civil Service Department responsible for efficiency improvements and control of manpower costs, as regarded as invalid. The 'separation of control of expenditures from responsibility for efficiency' was, the Committee said (HC 535-I, 1977: para. 75):

indefensible . . . an attempt to divide a seamless garment . . . We recommend that the ultimate responsibility for monitoring the control of efficiency should be vested in the Treasury . . . the separation of control of expenditure from responsibility for efficiency is indefensible.

Efficiency was directly linked with the fiscal pressure of cash-limit squeezes. Cash-limits and issues of efficiency were coming to be considered as mutually dependent: 'The stimulus to efficiency' was 'an important benefit of the development of cash limits' (Rawlinson, 1981: 186). Such pressure was said to intensify considerations of efficiency, but it was not assumed to make efficiency improvements inevitable. That required a more active approach (HC 535-I, 1977):

cash limits . . . only make sense if the expenditure which is being controlled is necessary in the first place . . . We believe that there is considerable scope for the adoption of cash limits to our proposals . . . or management accounting and accountable units . . . efficiency audits . . . for the control of the civil service . . . Cash limits should be broken down within the Department to coincide with accountable units.

What was being advocated was a change in both the level and the type of analysis (HC 535-III, 1977). Increasingly, Civil Service activities were considered amenable to direct financial identification and evaluation.

Financial representations were considered to provide the truest and most effective means of identifying and evaluating activities. Accounting data was advocated not only for expenditure control as previously, but additionally to achieve the aspiration of 'efficiency and effectiveness' monitoring and enhancement. But this was seen to require accounting data of a type, and of a level, hitherto unavailable or insufficiently available. Belief in the supremacy and possibility of quantifying and monetarizing of inputs and outputs meant that the means of achievement and the process of evaluation were collapsed into one.

### The Conservative Government

Attempts to contain public expenditure continued in intensified form following the election of a Conservative Government in May 1979. Such attempts were buttressed by the new government's hostility to the public sector, which was contrasted with a eulogized and apparently homogeneous 'private sector' that was depicted as an ideal to which the public sector should aspire.

The 'medium-term economic strategy' adopted in 1980 set out monetary and fiscal targets for several years ahead (Cmnd 7841, 1980). Underlying the strategy was a claim that monetary expansion and inflation were usually generated by excessive government spending and borrowing. A major target, apart from the elusive money supply figure itself, was the Public Sector Borrowing Requirement (PSBR), an aggregate of the combined deficits of central and local government and the nationalized industries (Jones-Owen, 1982). Cash-limits introduced by the Labour Government in 1976 were maintained (Lewis and Harrison, 1982; HC 236-I, 1982). Measures to reduce aggregate public expenditure, already introduced by the previous government, were reinforced, with mixed results (HC 54, 1981: 46; Hogwood, 1992: 204). Spending on housing and overseas aid was consciously reduced, whilst certain activities such as 'defence' and 'law and order' were intentionally expanded. Other 'demand led' activities, such as social security, expanded because of recession rather than policy changes (Rose, 1984b). A three-month recruitment freeze on all but the most essential posts in central government Departments was imposed. These measures were considered as stop-gap arrangements whilst more detailed studies were undertaken by each Department. A target for the Civil Service of 630,000 by April 1984 – over 100,000 fewer than in May 1979 – had been announced (Cmnd 8616, 1982: 2/3; HC 236-I, 1982). Albeit less ambitiously, reduction in the number of civil servants had been a pre-1979 policy. The postwar Civil Service had peaked at 747,000 in 1976 and a Civil Service Department review completed in that year had a target of shedding 35,000 jobs by 1978–9 (Hogwood, 1992).

A series of 'scrutinies' began in 1979, under the direction of Derek Rayner. As the Prime Minister's 'Special Adviser on Efficiency', his remit was to advise on 'ways to improve efficiency and eliminate waste in government' (HC 712-II, 1980: 46). The results were given a high profile, through press releases about their findings, and other means, both within and outside the Civil Service. These scrutinies sought to go beyond the attempts of the Expenditure Committee, in 1977, to have the 'savings' which resulted from improved performance identified and disclosed. That Committee had been told by senior civil servants that it was 'rarely possible' to do so. Undeterred, the Committee asserted that such calculations should be made (HC 535-I, 1977). Now, each of the Rayner studies included a confident claim about the amounts of savings achievable. The Prime Minister stated in the House of Commons that 'Savings from firm decisions taken by Ministers on the results of scrutinies and reviews carried out in 1979, 1980, 1981 with the help of Sir Derek Rayner are around £130 million a year and £28 million once-for-all' (Official Report, 28 January 1982: col. 400). The scrutinies enhanced prior beliefs on the part of the government and others in the necessity and possibility of internal change. The solution was internal and consisted in the reduction of 'waste'. The 'enemy' was within. More could be done with less, it was said.

The Rayner scrutinies made a possibility into a necessity. Existing methods of Civil Service management were explicitly identified as responsible for wastage and inefficiency. The search for an alternative approach which would ensure 'lasting improvements' was encouraged (Cmnd 8616, 1982: 4; Hennessy, 1989: 607). The programmatic approach had lost its appeal. Management by accounting was henceforth to be widely and intensely pursued. Below, two primary sources of support for management by accounting in the 1979–82 period are considered: one of these came from a government department, the other from a parliamentary committee.

### MINIS

From about the beginning of 1980, in the Department of the Environment, a 'management planning, information and monitoring system' (Management Information System for Ministers: MINIS), was developed and promoted. 'The distinctive features of MINIS', it was said (HC 236-I, 1982: xxviii):

not normally found in systems operating in departments, are systematic annual reviews of objectives, tasks, costs and performance measures; much greater precision in the definition of tasks; much more precise performance measures; more specific attribution of costs and staff numbers to tasks and managerial functions; presentation of the results to Ministers; much greater involvement of Ministers; and publication of the results.

Initially, MINIS differed in comparison with the FMI that succeeded it in three respects: first, it was limited to senior management levels (Cmnd 8616, 1982: 8; Likierman, 1988), although an approach that would penetrate to lower levels was planned and subsequently attempted (Department of the Environment, 1981: 156); secondly, it was not regularly reviewed by audit or special studies, both of which were to become important characteristics of management by accounting (Jenkins *et al.*, 1984); and thirdly, it did not seek to attribute non-staff running costs to cost centres. The Department's aim was to 'work towards' a 'comprehensive and systematic approach to management' (Department of the Environment, 1981: 156). The first round of MINIS represented 'the first stage in the implementation of this approach (Department of the Environment, 1981: para. 1).

Accounts of the genesis of MINIS vary. According to Sir Ian Bancroft (Head of the Civil Service Department) 'He [Michael Heseltine] brought the germ of the idea in from outside and it was seized upon and developed by his civil servants' (Bancroft, 1981: 80). 'The origin of Minis', states Andrew Likierman, an adviser to the Treasury and Civil Service Committee from early 1981 to 1990 (at various times), 'was a "Rayner exercise", instigated after the present administration came into office in 1979' (Likierman, 1981: 49). Heseltine located the origin in the early 1970s: 'I think it started from my experience as Minister for Aerospace in the Government of 1970–74 ... I came from the private sector with a management idea which, when I was Minister for State, I built on dramatically with help from civil servants and Derek Rayner' (HC 236-II, 1982: 158/169/170). In evidence in 1980 to the Expenditure Committee he stated that 'the quality of public sector accountancy is abysmal ... we need a very significant improvement in the management accounting systems in the public sector' (Heseltine, 1980: 203). His desire for, and belief in efficiency through transparency is illustrated in his statement:

In May I was told that there were 52,122 people in my Department. How could I know what they all do each day? How could I take decisions, or reach informed judgements, on relative priorities? I had general advice on every policy issue – but no analysis of how each part of the machine operated, why it operated in that way, and how much it cost. I do not know. Nobody knows (*Sunday Times*, 16 December 1979).

An account combining earlier, pre-1979 changes and the influence of ministerial commitment was given by Geoffrey Chipperfield an Under-Secretary in the Department of the Environment (Chipperfield, 1983: 26):

We have taken a big jump forward more quickly with him than we would have done with other ministers. His personal contribution to MINIS must not be underestimated. But he was flowing with the tide, not against it.

Although the literature on identifying the benefits, and costs, of using specific information systems is full of pessimism about the feasibility of doing so, this did not curtail laudatory claims about MINIS' effects being made and widely publicized (Cmnd 8616, 1982: 8). Richard Wilding, Deputy Secretary, Civil Service Department, stated that: 'It [MINIS] has produced some very good results indeed' (HC 236-III, 1982: 81). In a report for the Treasury and Civil Service Committee, the Secretary of State for the Environment was reported as stating (Likierman, 1981: 51):

> that an improvement in both efficiency and effectiveness has been achieved through the operation of Minis because the tasks themselves are much more clearly defined, costs have been put on a common basis to enable comparisons to be made and the means of monitoring progress against target has become available. He has also said that Minis has directly enabled him to cut staff in a way that would not otherwise have been possible.

In common with all advocacy of management by accounting considered in this chapter, such claims were unqualified. Instead, benefits were assumed to be self-evident or indisputable.

Assertions of MINIS' benefits enhanced what for some was an already established belief in the desirability and feasibility of a MINIS-type approach (HC 236-I, 1982). MINIS became widely cited as the exemplar of what could and should be done to reform Civil Service management (Cmnd 8616, 1982: 8; HC 236-I, 1982: xxviii). In a 1982 report, the Treasury and Civil Service Committee recommended that: 'MINIS, or its clear equivalent, should be adopted in all departments and, as appropriate, in other public sector bodies' (HC 236-I, 1982: xxviii).

### Treasury and Civil Service Committee

Independently of developments in the Department of the Environment, in January 1980 the Treasury and Civil Service Committee had commenced an inquiry into 'methods of improving the efficiency of the Civil Service'. Its first report, completed in December 1980, considered the roles and effects of the central departments, namely, the Treasury and the Civil Service Department – the 'Centre' (HC 54, 1981). The Treasury was said to have the 'clout', but not to have either the direct responsibility for expenditure in Departments, nor the detailed information about what was occurring within them. The Civil Service Department, on the other hand, was said to have major responsibility for 'manpower numbers and manpower efficiency', and to have access to more information than the Treasury (albeit data that in the Committee's view was inadequate), but not to have the 'leverage' to change Departments (HC 54, 1981: ix). The Committee concluded that these Departments were only able to exercise a 'negative form of control' in the sense that departments had 'to have their prospects for expenditure and for numbers employed agreed by the centre'. As a result, the Committee stated that each Department had 'excessive independence ... in matters of internal management ... and was responsible for its own expenditure and manpower as well as the development and mode of its policies'. The departments were said by one witness in evidence to the Committee to be able to out-gun the Prime Minister, and even the Chancellor of the Exchequer, because they had a vast amount of information (HC 54, 1981: 46).

The Committee's central recommendation – that the Treasury should become responsible for ensuring the development and use of financial systems – challenged the existing separation of financial and efficiency analysis, and reiterated the 1977 and 1978 Expenditure Committees' ('seamless garment') view of the dependence of effective efficiency analysis on financial data. In evidence to the Committee, Sir Derek Rayner (who had already commenced his reviews and scrutinies) had stated that 'finance is inseparable from good policy advice and implementation, good organisation, and good management'[6] (HC 712-II, 1980). The implementation of the Committees' proposal on transfer of financial systems responsibility would, it was argued, speed the development and use of such systems in Departments and enable the Treasury to determine more readily the type of data produced. This, it was argued, would increase its capability to focus its analysis, judgements and interventions, as well as enhancing the independence of 'line managers' within the prescribed and monitored limits (HC 54, 1981). These Treasury-influenced financial systems came to be considered as essential for management by accounting (HC 236-I, 1982; Cmnd 8616, 1982; HC 494-I, 1988; National Audit Office, 1989; HC 348, 1989). The Committee's recommendation on financial systems was accepted by the Government in February 1981 (Cmnd 8170, 1981).

Having reviewed the roles of the Centre during the 1980/81 session, in the following year (1981/82) the Committee considered 'the *arrangements* that exist or are proposed to be introduced in the Civil Service to promote efficiency and effectiveness' (HC 236-I, 1982, emphasis in original). The report was written within a firm belief in the desirability of management by accounting. The commitment of some members to management by accounting was already clear from their comments in the examination of witnesses for both their 1981 and 1982 reports (HC 54, 1981; HC 236-II, 1982). Committee members were aware of the Fulton Committee report, and the 1977 and 1978 Expenditure Committee reports, as is clear from the references to those reports in the 1981 report, as well as from comments on them in the examinations of witnesses. There was also a direct membership link between all these committees. Treasury and Civil Service Committee member Robert Sheldon had also been a member of both the Expenditure Committee and the Fulton Committee, and Michael English had chaired the Expenditure Committee's sub-committee which had prepared the Committee's report recommending management by accounting (HC 535-I, 1977).

Within the framework of the measurement, matching and input–output monitoring model that exemplified management by accounting, the Treasury and Civil Service Committee's 1982 report (HC 236-I, 1982) focused especially on outputs. Clear definition of objectives and targets was considered desirable by the Committee as a way of relating 'the use of resources directly to objectives' in order to allow the achievement and evaluation of performance (HC 236-I, 1982: xxxiv). It was also considered an essential means of determining the desirability or necessity of activities.

Reducing costs by identifying eliminable activities had been tentatively proposed by the Expenditure Committee (HC 535-I, 1977), but had not been explicitly linked with its recommendation of management by accounting. The Treasury and Civil Service Committee made clear that it saw this as both possible and necessary. An increased emphasis on controlling costs was not sufficient on its own. Consideration should also be directed to 'the purpose and need for many administrative tasks whose costs have been monitored so carefully' (HC 236, 1982: xii). The Committee concluded (HC 236-I, 1982: xxiv) that:

While the broad intentions of policy are often clear enough there are too few attempts to set operational objectives and realistic targets against which to measure the outrun. Measures of output are inadequate. Consequently there are no systematic means of guiding and correcting the use of resources.

In common with the 1977 and 1978 Expenditure Committee Reports (HC 535-I, 1977; HC 661, 1978), the 1978 Procedure Committee Report (HC 588-I), and the 1981 Public Accounts Committee Report (HC 115), the Treasury and Civil Service Committee was highly critical of existing scrutiny of departments and other public sector bodies. 'Neither Parliament nor the country', it stated, 'has adequate machinery *independent of the Executive*' (HC 236-I, 1982: xli, emphasis in original). These scrutinies should be informed, it said, by internal and external audits and reviews. These should extend their considerations not only beyond probity to identify 'waste and extravagance', as the 1976 Layfield Committee on local government had urged, but to an evaluation of the activity of management itself. Already the government had indicated its commitment to such audits for some public sector activities in the proposals in Part III of the Local Government Finance (No. 2) Bill (HC 41, December 1981) which would require auditors of such authorities to verify that they had 'sound arrangements' and that they were effective (McSweeney, 1988). For the Treasury and Civil Service Committee, like other advocates of management by accounting, the means of assessment was to become the means of enactment (HC 236-I, 1982: xl).

## The Next Steps

Changes are attributed to the FMI. It is said to have brought about 'a notable advance in cost awareness' (Gray *et al.*, 1991; Colville and Tomkins, 1989; Efficiency Unit, 1988: 21); all departments have been described as having altered or introduced new financial management systems (HC 61, 1987: vi); by 1988 over 7000 line managers were said to manage budgets which accounted for about three-quarters of the Civil service's running costs, albeit the spread of budgeting into non-administrative costs (some 87 per cent of total public expenditure) was described as slow and managers' freedom 'extremely limited' (HC 61, 1987; Efficiency Unit, 1988: 23; HC 494-I, 1988). But management by accounting remains elusive, even at the level of implantation of systems and procedures. Two years after the launch of the FMI, a review in one major Department reported that outside a small group at the centre, the general understanding of the initiative was 'hazy' for the great majority of civil servants (Efficiency Unit, 1984). Three years later, the Committee of Public Accounts, in a report which firmly supported management by accounting, expressed its disappointment that departments 'had encountered difficulties in developing and installing decentralised budgetary control and informations systems' a problem which 'could undermine the FMI'. The Committee was also concerned that 'scepticism and mistrust of FMI seems to be widespread among middle and lower level management grades' (HC 61, 1987: x/xii). In July 1992, 10 years after the launch of the Initiative, the President of the Board of Trade announced that MINIS (the main exemplar for the Initiative) would shortly be introduced into that Department (Department of Trade and Industry, 1992: 2).

Dissatisfaction with the speed and range of management by accounting's implantation has encouraged further changes to Civil Service management. But these changes have both been consistent with management by accounting and have been facilitated by its cumulative 'successes to-date' (HC 61, 1987). An influential scrutiny by the Efficiency Unit, ultimately published in 1988 (Efficiency Unit, 1988: 7), stated that it had identified in the Civil Service:

First, a lack of clear and accountable management responsibility, and the self confidence that goes with it particularly among the higher ranks in departments. Second, the need for greater precision about the results expected of people and of organisations. Third, a need to focus attention on outputs as well as inputs. Fourth, the handicap of imposing a uniform system in an organisation of the size and diversity of the present Civil service. Fifth, a need for sustained pressure for improvement.

It recommended that 'agencies be established to carry out the executive functions within a policy and resources framework' set out by a government, and by a sponsoring, or core department, and central departments. The agencies should, it was said (Efficiency Unit, 1988: 9; HC 496, 1991: 124), be given

a well defined framework in which to operate, which sets out the policy, the budget, specific targets and the results to be achieved . . . The management of an agency must be held rigorously to account by their department for the results they achieve.

In the language of the FMI, and earlier advocacy of management by accounting, the agencies were conceived as strong forms of 'accountable units' or 'discrete responsibility centres'. Both the Fulton Committee and the Expenditure Committee had previously recommended that consideration be given to the possible establishment of 'hived off' agencies. They advocated management by accounting not only for Departments, but also considered it to be an essential condition for functioning of the controlled autonomy of 'hived off' activities. However, the absolute distinction between policy and execution, between formulation and implementation (Stringer and Williamson, 1987) which underlay the Efficiency Unit's recommendation had been regarded as problematic by both committees so that the range of activities they regarded as capable of being 'hived off' was far less than proposed by the Efficiency Unit.

The Unit's recommendations, subsequently named *The Next Steps Initiative*, were eventually accepted by the government and launched by the Prime Minister in February 1988 (Official Report, 18 February 1988: c.1149). With few reservations, the Initiative has been supported by the Labour Party (HC 496, 1991: ix). By late 1991, 56 agencies and 30 executive units (Employing almost 40 per cent of Civil Service employees) have been established[7] (Cm 1760, 1991: 5). By mid-1992 the number of agencies had increased to 75 and further candidates had been announced (Next Steps Team, 1992).

Identification and acceptance of an activity for establishment as an agency has been facilitated by the extent to which management by accounting is considered to be already implanted there. In its first report on the initiative, the Treasury and Civil Service Committee stated that: 'Without the FMI it would not now be possible to consider change on the scale proposed by Government' (HC 494-I, 1988). A level, judged to be sufficient, is required before approval of agency formation is given (Efficiency Unit, 1991; National Audit Office, 1989: 20; HC 348, 1989; HC

494-I, 1988: xv). The formation of agencies has intensified, not diminished, commitments to management by accounting (Efficiency Unit, 1991: 1). According to the Efficiency Unit the creation of the agencies has given 'an impetus to the introduction of financial regimes which fit business needs, while at the same time preserving overall control of public expenditure' (Efficiency Unit, 1991: 3). Agencies are required, post-establishment, to enhance their management by accounting and the extent to which they are in place is reviewed (Efficiency Unit, 1991).

### Crisis, cause and cure

From Fulton to the Next Steps Initiative, diverse issues and ways of problematizing the public sector have been involved in the advocacy of management by accounting: modernization of an expanding Civil Service; improved parliamentary surveillance; increased accountability of the Executive; enhanced transparency of Departments for Ministers; improving the Treasury's 'probing'; reviewing and culling activities, and so forth. These disparate claims and ambitions have one thing in common: an assertion of the necessity, and not simply the desirability of changing the way the public sector is to be administered and managed (Miller, 1990). The need for change is seen to derive from such failings as 'inertia' (Cmnd 3638, 1968); 'wasteful[ness] of resources' (HC 535-I, 1977); 'no clear orientation towards the achievement of efficiency' (HC 236-I, 1982); 'uneconomic activities, underutilized capacity and wastage' (Cmnd 8616, 1982), and much else besides.

A common theme is present in the solutions advanced for the alleged problems of the public sector. This theme is the imperative of performativity: optimizing input–output relationships (Lyotard, 1984: 11). This criterion of performativity is expressed in a variety of ways. It is present in the advocacy of a 'constant drive for efficiency' (Cmnd 3638, 1968), in calls for 'more efficient use and control of resources' (HC 535-I, 1977) and in appeals for 'minimising of inputs to the programme' (HC 236-I, 1982).

The norm of performativity is regarded as a reality immanent in the world, an immanence independent of human institutions, but binding upon them, yet whose achievement is not inevitable. It has to be made operational. The realization of performativity is linked to appeals to modes of accurate, quantifiable and comparable measurement. 'Accounting', taken to be an autonomous and already constituted collection of techniques capable of achieving desired ends through accurate measurements (Papineau, 1991; Miller and O'Leary, 1990), is the means through which performativity is to be enacted. But accounting, as said to be practised in the Civil Service, is always considered inadequate by the advocates of management by accounting. It is seen to require expansion, elaboration, refinement and the introduction of techniques deemed to be absent or insufficiently pervasive. But such criticisms and proposed changes do not extend to a fundamental questioning of accounting's capacities. Its capabilities are assumed to be apparent, or are explicitly said to have been preproven in the private sector[8] (Cmnd 3638, 1968; Garrett, 1982; HC 236-II, 1982; Chipperfield, 1983; Efficiency Unit, 1991). 'Accounting' in the advocacy of management by accounting functions as a discursive category. It is a designation which traverses a diversity of semantic levels, ranging from isolated calculations of costs to the wider means of achieving the advocates' reforming desires – a label that represents beliefs in the accuracy and efficacy of measurement. Aspirations are presented as a description (Hopwood, 1987).

This norm of performativity, in conjunction with the unquestioning acceptance of accounting, has led to calls for a greater intensity of accounting within the Civil Service. From Fulton to the Next Steps Initiative, and in between, every advocacy of management by accounting has sought increases in the recruitment of 'qualified accountants', that is, members of accountancy bodies, and enhancements in their status within Departments. The Fulton Report critically stated that the Civil Service employed only '309 accountants, of whom 64 are temporary' (Cmnd 3638, 1968: 17) and condemned their restricted roles (Cmnd 3638, 1968):

present practice in the Civil Service severely restricts the role of the Accountant Class and excludes its members from responsibility for financial control ... Their outlets in other kinds of work and into posts of higher management are severely limited.

The Expenditure Committee regretted that almost a decade after the Fulton Report the number of accountants had risen to only 377. It called for increased recruitment and stated that: 'new systems must be designed by professional management accountants and civil servants must be trained to understand them' (HC 576, 1978; HC 535-I, 1977). Without taking note of the increasing criticisms and doubts about the level and depth of emphasis that should be given to accounting in the management of the private sector, the Consultative Committee of Accountancy Bodies unfavourably compared the 'role of accountants in business with their role in the Civil Service'. In the former, it stated 'accountants are commonly appointed to high level management posts', but in the Civil Service, 'they are confined to executive work and excluded from policy making and their career prospects and pay compare unfavourably with the private sector and with other specialists in the government service' (HC 535-I, 1977: xlviii). The 1982 White Paper on the FMI claimed that 'action is in hand to increase the supply of qualified accountants and to improve and expand training in financial management' (Cmnd 8616, 1982: 26). Two years later, the Treasury and Civil Service Committee reported that 'The Government proposes to double the number of professional accountants as quickly as possible' (HC 227, 1984: vii).

The status, remuneration and the number of members of accountancy bodies has risen in the Civil Service since the implantation of the FMI and the emergence of the Next Steps Initiative. Whilst the comparative rise in pay and benefits no doubt has to some extent been influenced by the wider improvement in accountants' pay, what has also changed is the range and level of tasks in which accountants are regarded as significant. From 1 July 1982, members of the expanded Government Accountancy Service were included within the Administrative Group – as recommended by the Fulton Committee (Hills, 1982) – and the post of Head of the Government Accountancy Service was transferred in 1984 from the Department of Trade and Industry to the Treasury (a 'more central position') (HC 227, 1984: vi). Opportunities and facilities for training and preparation for accountancy body examinations have been significantly enhanced with a very high success rate but, of course, not all who successfully complete remain within the Service (HC 61, 1987). The number of members of accountancy bodies employed in the Civil Service has increased – from 600 in mid-1982 to 815 in mid-1992 – during a period in which the total number of civil servants has declined from 666,362 to 565,408.[9]

Whilst none of management by accounting's advocates specified a target figure, the increase is not perhaps as much as they desired given the emphasis they placed on recruitment of 'professional accountants'. Certainly, the growth is much lower than the doubling suggested by the Treasury and Civil Service Committee (HC 227, 1984). But whilst each advocacy saw increased recruitment of accountancy body members as essential, accounting for them was to be pervasive, not confined to the skills of an elite. An integral part for accounting is sought by the advocates in the activities of every manager, defined as: 'anybody who has to take ... decisions about the deployment and use of money and staff' (Cmnd 8616, 1982: 22). Everyone must become a calculator. There are echoes here of the 1964 Fabian Society tract, *The Administrators*, which argued that civil servants should be able to 'access costs, risks, interactions in quantitative terms'. As the Fulton Report stated (Cmnd 3638, 1968: 151):

In recommending a much wider role and greater responsibility for accountants, we do not wish to be understood as implying that the accountants should be regarded as having a unique claim to the work of financial management. The much-needed increase in their numbers will be no substitute for the necessity of ensuring that managers at all levels have an appropriate understanding of the importance of sound financial management especially in decision-taking and control.

But belief in the representational adequacy of accounting, assumed to be central to the successful achievement of performativity, has functioned as a principle of exclusion. It has excluded from consideration the possibility that civil servants might use a variety of frames of interpretation, that they might use data not produced by management by accounting systems, and that, regardless of its source, data is open to multiple readings, rather than a unique one. That is, a denial that the meaning of accounting (or any other) data, calculations, judgements is always contextual, and no context is ever completely closed, completely determinate (Wood, 1990: 56; Wittgenstein, 1975: 348). As a result, the problems of implementation, indeed of implantation, experienced post-1982 were not anticipated or considered. There has also been no recognition of the possibility that the consequences of management by accounting might not only be intended and desirable but could also be unintended and perverse (Hall, 1980; Merton, 1936). As Michael Heseltine has enunciated (Hardcastle, 1983: 17):

The management ethos must run right through our national life ... by management ethos I mean the process of examining what we are doing, setting realistic targets, fitting them to resources available, and monitoring performance.

At least for the present, it would appear that the norm of performativity is taken as self-evident. A notion of adapting to 'business needs' (Efficiency Unit, 1991: 3) is taken to be coterminous with management by accounting. The explicit aim is to change 'the heart of good management' (National Audit Office, 1986: 11), and yet the conception of 'good management' has itself been tightly circumscribed. Whether 'good management' may come to be conceived in broader terms in the near future is in principle an open question. However, the events charted here suggest a less than sanguine diagnosis.

NOTES

The comments of Stan Brignall, David Collinson, Sheila Duncan, Keith Hoskin, Anthony James, and especially the editors Anthony Hopwood and Peter Miller are gratefully acknowledged.

1. This was being done at the same time as the assumptions of universal effectiveness of these, and other accounting methods, in organizations generally, and in the private sector specifically, was being questioned or challenged. For a review of the concerns which had already emerged by the early 1980s in both the academic and professional literature see Cooper (1981); Hopwood (1983); Kaplan (1983).
2. For example, the Commissioners for Auditing the Public Accounts appointed in 1780 were required to consider 'in what more expeditious and effectual and less expensive manner the services can in future be regulated' (Adams, 1986: 189).
3. The description of government activities as 'programmes' indicates influences

from the US on UK proposals for public sector management change. This is considered further below.

4. Rayner came from Marks & Spencer Ltd which was in 1970, as it remains, a retail clothing and food organization which ironically made only limited use of management accounting.

5. It has been abandoned in most areas and countries where it has been applied (Jablonsky and Dirsmith, 1978).

6. See n. 4 above.

7. Examples of these agencies are the Social Security Benefits Agency, Forensic Science, Driver and Vehicle Licensing Agency, Patent Office and Historic Royal Palaces. The executive units have a transitional status between a department and an agency. The 30 executive units are HM Custom & Excise units employing about 95 per cent (27,000) of its staff (Cm 1760, 1991: 17).

8. Assertions that accounting has proven itself in the private sector are made in all the advocacy of management by accounting considered in this chapter notwithstanding the poor state of British industry, the great variations in the comparative emphasis given to accounting there (Goold and Campbell, 1989), and the growth of criticisms, or questioning, of the effects of accounting.

9. Both 1982 figures (accountants and total number of civil servants) exclude activities privatized since 1982, but include activities undertaken by Next Steps agencies. Figures provided to the author by the Government Accountancy Service Management Unit.

REFERENCES

Adams, N., 1986. 'Efficiency Auditing In The Australian Audit Office', *Australian Journal of Public Administration* 45(3)

Armstrong, Lord, 1977. Oral evidence, 24 January 1977, to the Expenditure Committee (General Sub-Committee), HC 535-II, 1977, London: HMSO

Bancroft, I., 1981. Oral evidence, 8 July 1981, to the Treasury and Civil Service Sub-Committee, HC 236-II, 1982, London: HMSO

Bourdieu, P. *et al.*, 1991. *The Craft of Sociology – Epistemological Preliminaries*, Berlin: Walter de Gruyter

Chipperfield, G., 1983. 'The MINIS and the Joubert Programmes', in *Management Information & Control in Whitehall*, London: Royal Institute of Public Administration

Civil Service Department, 1976. 'The Response to the Fulton Report', Expenditure Committee (General Sub-Committee), HC 535-II, 1977, London: HMSO

Cm 1760, 1991. *Improving Management in Government: The Next Steps Agencies – Review, 1991*, London: HMSO

Cmnd 1432, 1961. *Control of Public Expenditure*, London: HMSO

    3638, 1968. *The Civil Service*, Vol. 1, *Report of the Committee* and Vol. 2, *Report of A Management Consultancy Group*, London: HMSO

    4506, 1970. *The Reorganisation of Central Government*, London: HMSO

    5710, 1974. *The Reorganisation of British Industry*, London: HMSO

    6151, 1975. *The Attack On Inflation*, London: HMSO

    6315, 1975. *An Approach to Industrial Policy*, London: HMSO

    6440, 1976. *Cash Limits on Public Expenditure*, London: HMSO

6453, 1976. *Local Government Finance*, London: HMSO

6507, 1976. *The Attack On Inflation – The Second Year*, London: HMSO

7293, 1978. *Winning the Battle Against Inflation*, London: HMSO

7746, 1979. *The Government's Expenditure Plans (1980–81)*, London: HMSO

7841, 1980. The Government's Expenditure Plans *1980–81 to 1983–84*, London: HMSO

8170, 1981. *The Future of the Civil Service Department – Government Observations on the First Report of the Treasury and Civil Service Department, Session 1980–81*, London: HMSO

8616, 1982. *Efficiency & Effectiveness in the Civil Service*, London: HMSO

Cockburn, C., 1977. *The Local State: Management of Cities and People*, London: Pluto Press

Colville, I. and Tomkins, C., 1989. HC 348, 1989

Confederation of British Industry, 1985. *Financing the Future*, Third Report of the CBI Working Party On Government Expenditure, London: CBI

Cooper, D., 1981. 'A Social and Organizational View of Management Accounting', in M. Bromwich and A. Hopwood (eds.), *Essays In British Accounting Research*, London: Pitman

Department of the Environment, 1981. Note dated November 1981: 'Control of Departmental Running Costs', HC 236-III, 1982

Department of Trade and Industry, 1992. Text of the 'President of the Board of Trade's Video Message to Staff' – Friday 3 July 1992, Press Release P/92/440, London: DTI

Donaldson, P. and Farquhar, J., 1988. *Understanding the British Economy*, London: Penguin

Donnison, D., Chapman, V., Meacher, M., Sears, A. and Urwin, K., 1975. *Social Policy And Administration Revisited*, revised ed., London: George Allen & Unwin

Drucker, P.F., 1955. *The Practice of Management*, London: Heinemann

Eco, U., 1986. 'Language, Power, Force', in U. Eco, *Travels in Hyperreality*, London: Pan

Efficiency Unit, 1984. *Consultancy, Inspection and Review Services in Government Departments – Report to The Prime Minister*, London: HMSO

1988. *Improving Management In Government: The Next Steps – Report To The Prime Minister*, London: HMSO

1991. *Making The Most of Next Steps: The Management of Ministers' Departments and Their Agencies – Report To The Prime Minister*, London: HMSO

Foucault, M., 1980. (French edn.); reproduced with minor corrections in G. Burchell, C. Gordon and P. Miller, 1991 *The Foucault Effect – Studies In Governmentality*, Hemel Hempstead: Harvester

Fry, G.K., 1984. 'The Development of the Thatcher Government's "Grand Strategy" for the Civil Service: A Public Policy Perspective', *Public Administration* 62, Autumn: 322–35

1991. 'The Fulton Committee's Management Consultancy Group: An Assessment of Its Contribution', *Public Administration* 69(4), Winter: 423–39

Garrett, J., 1972. *The Management of Government*, Harmondsworth: Penguin

1982. 'Efficiency and Effectiveness in the Civil Service', HC 236-III, 1982: 45–8

Garrett, J. and Walker, S.D., 1969. *Management By Objectives in the Civil Service*, CAS *Occasional Paper*, London: HMSO

Goold M. and Campbell, A., 1989. *Strategies and Styles*, Oxford: Basil Blackwell

Grant, A.T.K., 1972. *The Strategy of Financial Pressure*, London: Macmillan

Gray, A. and Jenkins, B., 1983. 'The State of Policy Analysis and Evaluation in Government', in A. Gray and B. Jenkins (eds.), *Policy and Evaluation in British Government*, London: Royal Institute of Public Administration

Gray A. *et al.*, 1991. 'The Management of Change In Whitehall: The Experience of the FMI', *Public Administration* 69: 41–59

Hall, P., 1980. *Great Planning Disasters*, London: Weidenfeld & Nicolson

Hardcastle A., 1983. 'Objectives of the Seminar', in *Value for Money Audits: Proceedings of A Seminar*, London: Royal Institute of Public Administration, 1982

Havighurst, A.F., 1979. *Britain In Transition*, Chicago: University of Chicago Press

Healy, D., 1989. *The Time of My Life*, London: Michael Joseph

Heath, E., 1977. Oral evidence to Expenditure Committee (General Sub-Committee), HC 535-II, 1977

HC 410, 1969. First Report from the Select Committee On Procedure, Session 1968–69, *Scrutinies of Public Expenditure and Administration*, London: HMSO

   535-I; 535-II; 535-III, 1977. Eleventh Report from the Expenditure Committee Session 1976–77, *The Civil Service*, vols. 1,2,3, London: HMSO

   576, 1978. Twelfth Report from the Expenditure Committee, Session 1977–78, *Response to the Government's Observations on the Committee's Report on the Civil Service*, London: HMSO

   588-I, 1978. First Report from the Select Committee on Procedure, Session 1977–78, vol. 1, *Report and Minutes of Proceedings*, London: HMSO

   661, 1978. Fourteenth Report of the Expenditure Committee, Session 1977–78, *Financial Accountability to Parliament*, London: HMSO

   115-I, 115-II, 1980. First Special Report from the Committee of Public Accounts, Session 1980–81, *The Role of the Comptroller and Auditor General*, vol. 1 Report, vol. 2 Minutes of Evidence, London: HMSO

   270, 1980. Ninth Report from the Committee of Public Accounts, *Internal Audit in Central Government*, London: HMSO

   712-II, 1980. Fourth Report from the Treasury and Civil Service Committee 1979–80, *Civil Service Manpower Reductions*, vol. 2, London: HMSO

   41, 1981. *Local Government Finance (No. 2) Bill*, London: HMSO

   54, 1981. First Report from the Treasury and Civil Service Committee, Session 1980–81, *The Future of the Civil Service Department*, London: HMSO

   236-I; 236-II; 236-III, 1982. Third Report from the Treasury and Civil Service Committee, Session 1981–82, *Efficiency and Effectiveness in the Civil Service*, vol. 1 Report, vol. 2 Minutes of Evidence, vol. 3 Appendices, London: HMSO

   227, 1984. Second Report from the Treasury and Civil Service Committee, Session 1983–84, *Head of the Government Accountancy Service*, London: HMSO

   61, 1987. Thirteenth Report from the Committee of Public Accounts, Session 1986–87, *The Financial Management Initiative*, London: HMSO

   494-I, 1988. Eighth Report from the Treasury and Civil Service Committee, *Civil Service Management Reform: The Next Steps*, London: HMSO

   348, 1989. Fifth Report from the Treasury and Civil Service Committee, Session 1988–89, *Developments in The Next Steps Programme*, London: HMSO

481, 1990. Eighth Report of Session 1989–90, Treasury and Civil Service Committee *Progress In The Next Steps Initiative*, London: HMSO

496, 1991. Seventh Report from the Treasury and Civil Service Committee, Session 1990–91, *The Next Steps Initiative*, London: HMSO

Heclo and Wildavsky, 1981. *The Private Government of Public Money*, 2nd edn., London: Macmillan

Hennessey, P., 1989. *Whitehall*, Glasgow: Harper Collins

Heseltine, M., 1980. Oral evidence of 26 November 1980 to the Committee of Public Accounts, HC 115–II, 1980

1981. Oral evidence of 28 October 1981 to the Treasury and Civil Service Sub-Committee, HC 236–II, 1982

Hills, K.H., 1982. 'A Wider Role for Accountants', *Management in Government* 37(2): 83–91

HM Treasury and Civil Service Department, 1980. *The Integration of HM Treasury and the Civil Service*, London: Civil Service Department

Hodgkinson, C., 1978. *Towards A Philosophy of Administration*, Oxford: Blackwell

Hogwood, B.W., 1992. *Trends in British Public Policy*, Buckingham: Open University Press

Holdsworth, W.A., 1888. *The Local Government Act 1888*, London: George Routledge

Honderich, T., 1990. *Conservatism*, London: Penguin

Hopwood, A., 1983. 'On Trying To Understand Accounting in the Contexts in Which It Operates', *Accounting, Organizations and Society* 8(2/3): 287–305

1984. 'Accounting and the Pursuit of Efficiency', in A. Hopwood and C. Tomkins (eds.), *Issues in Public Sector Accounting*, Oxford: Philip Allan

1987. 'The Archaeology of Accounting Systems', *Accounting, Organizations and Society* 12(3): 207–34

Hudson Institute Europe, 1974. *The United Kingdom in 1980: The Hudson Report*, London: Associated Business Programmes

Humble, 1965. *Improving Management Performance*, London: British Management Institute

Ibbs, R., 1984. 'Better Services at Lower Cost', in *Papers Presented at the Annual Conference 1984*, London: CIPFA

Institute of Municipal Treasurers and Accountants, 1969. *Programme Budgeting – The Concept and Application*, London: IMTA

Jablonsky, S. and Dirsmith, M., 1978. 'The Pattern of PPB Rejection: Something About Organizations, Something About PPB', *Accounting, Organizations and Society* 3(3/4): 215–25

Jackson, D., Turner, H.A. and Wilkinson, F., 1975. *Do Trade Unions Cause Inflation?*, 2nd edn., Cambridge: Cambridge University Press

Jenkins, K., Morris, B., Caplan, C. and Metcalfe, L., 1984. *Consultancy, Inspection and Review Services in Government Departments – Efficiency Unit Report to the Prime Minister*, London: HMSO

Jones-Owen, R., 1982. 'The Public Sector', *British Economy Survey* 11(2), Spring: 11–16

Junor, J., 1976. *Sunday Express*, 25 July

Kaplan, R., 1983. 'Measuring Manufacturing Performance: A New Challenge For Managerial Accounting Research', *Accounting Review* 58(4): 686–705

Kavanagh, D., 1985. 'Whatever Happened to Consensus Politics?', *Political Studies* 33: 529–46

Kellner, P. and Crowther-Hunt, N., 1980. *The Civil Servants*, London: Macdonald Futura

Kogan, D. and Kogan, M., 1982. *The Battle For The Labour Party*, London: Kogan Page

Latour, B., 1987. *Science in Action*, Buckingham: Open University Press

Lewis, S. and Harrison, A., 1982. 'Cash Planning in The Public Sector: Theory, Practice, and Learning by Doing', *Public Money* 2(4): 46–61

Likierman, A., 1981. Memorandum: 'MINIS – Management Information Systems for Ministers', October 1981, HC 236-III, 1982: 49–61

    1988. *Public Expenditure*, London: Penguin

Lyotard, J.F., 1984. *The Postmodern Condition: A Report On Knowledge*, Manchester: Manchester University Press

McKean, R.N, 1958. *Efficiency in Government Through Systems Analysis*, New York: Wiley

McSweeney, B., 1988. 'Accounting for the Audit Commission', *The Political Quarterly* 59(1): 28–43

Management Accounting Team, 1950. *Productivity Report – Management Accounting*, London and New York: Anglo–American Council On Productivity

Marsh D., 1991. 'Privatization Under Mrs Thatcher: A Review of the Literature', *Public Administration* 69(4): 459–80

Merton, R.K., 1936. 'The Unintended Consequences of Purposive Social Action', *American Sociological Review* 1: 894–904

Miller, P., 1990. 'On the Interrelations Between Accounting and The State', *Accounting, Organizations and Society* (4): 315–33

Miller, P. and O'Leary, T., 1990. 'Making Accountancy Practical', *Accounting, Organizations and Society* 15(5): 479–98

Ministry of Housing and Local Government, 1967. Committee on the Management of Local Government, *Management of Local Government*, vol. 1, London: HMSO

Nairne, P., 1982. 'Some Reflections On Change', *Management in Government* 37(2): 71–82

National Audit Office, 1986. *The Financial Management Initiative*, London: HMSO

    1989. *The Next Steps Initiative*, London: HMSO

Next Steps Team, 1992. *Next Steps – Briefing Note*, London: Cabinet Office

Papineau, D., 1991. *Reality and Representation*, Oxford: Basil Blackwell

Pendlebury, 1989. *Management Accounting in the Public Sector*, Oxford: Heinemann

Rawlinson, A. 1981. Oral evidence, 4 November 1981, to the Treasury and Civil Service Sub-Committee, HC 236-II, 1982

Rayner, D., 1977. Oral evidence, 24 January 1977, to the Expenditure Committee (General Sub-Committee), HC 535-II, 1977

Ricoeur, 1984. *Time and Narrative*, vol. 1, Chicago: University of Chicago Press

    1986. *Lectures on Ideology and Utopia*, New York: Columbia University Press

Robinson, A., 1981. 'The House of Commons and Public Expenditure', in S. Walkland and M. Ryle (eds.), *The Commons Today*, revised edn., Glasgow: Fontana

Rose, R., 1984a. 'The Programme Approach to the Growth of Government', *British Journal of Political Science* 15(1): 1–28

1984b. *Do Parties Make A Difference?*, 2nd edn., London: Macmillan

Sloan, A., 1965. *My Years With General Motors*, London: Sidgwick & Jackson

Solomons, D., 1965. *Divisional Performance – Measurement and Control*, Homewood, 12: Irwin

Stringer, J.H. and Williamson, P., 1987. 'Policy Implementation, Policy Development and Policy Change: The Youth Training Scheme', *Public Policy and Administration* 1(3)

*The Administrators*, 1964. Fabian Tract 335, London: Fabian Society

Townsend, P., 1975. *Sociology and Social Policy*, London: Allan Lane

Train, 1985. 'Management Accountability in the Prison Service', in M. Maguire *et al., Accountability and Prisons: Opening Up a Closed World*, London: Tavistock

Treasury and Management & Personnel Office, 1982. 'Financial Management: Note by the Treasury and MPO', Appendix 3, Cmnd 8616, 1982

Turner, H.A., 1975. 'Preface of 1974', in D. Jackson, H.A. Turner and F. Wilkinson, *Do Trade Unions Cause Inflation*, 2nd edn., Cambridge: Cambridge University Press

Veljanovski, C., 1987. *Selling The State: Privatisation in Britain*, London: Weidenfeld & Nicolson

Wilding, R., 1983. 'Management Information and Control: The Role of the Centre', in *Management Information and Control in Whitehall*, London: Royal Institute of Public Administration

Williams, A. 1967. *Output Budgeting and the Contribution of Micro-Economics to Efficiency in Government*, CAS *Occasional Paper*, London: HMSO

Wilson, H., 1977. Oral evidence, 7 February 1977, to the Expenditure Committee (General Sub-Committee), HC 535-II, 1977

Wittgenstein, L., 1975. *On Certainty*, Oxford: Basil Blackwell

Wood, D., 1990. *Philosophy At The Limit*, London: Unwin Hyman

# 11    Regulating accountancy in the UK: episodes in a changing relationship between the State and the profession

*David Cooper, Tony Puxty, Keith Robson and Hugh Willmott*

These are turbulent and troubled times for the UK accounting industry.[1] At stake is the credibility and legitimacy of the members of its various occupational associations who claim the status of 'professional'. The issues that have given rise to these troubles include rapid changes in the legal framework, a quickening of competition between major players in the industry, a series of scandals that cast doubt upon established claims to independence and trustworthiness, and a sustained questioning from sceptical politicians and academics.

In this chapter, we undertake an analysis of the dynamics of these pressures on the accountancy profession. We do so through an analysis of three episodes in the regulation of accountancy: negotiations over the scope and impact of the EC 8th Directive; the positioning of the profession in relation to the Financial Services Act 1986 (FSA); and the continuing effort of the professional bodies to secure the powers of self-regulation conferred upon them by the State. What these episodes demonstrate are the changing relationships between the 'profession' and the 'State' that are at the heart of accounting regulation (Tinker, 1984; Puxty *et al.*, 1987; Miller, 1990).[2]

Common to these episodes is a struggle to manage tensions associated with the (long-term) movement of accountants into markets that have not been conventionally associated with their professional image and status (Abbott, 1988). In different ways, the EC 8th Directive and the FSA had the unintended consequence of raising the visibility of accountants' operation in arenas such as consultancy and the selling of financial services. These are operations where there is potential for the commonsense representation of their work as 'professional' – that is, 'independent' and 'expert'[3] – to be unsettled or compromised. This pressure on the credibility of accountants has been increased by a growing awareness of the material effects of accounting standards and practices upon corporate and national economic performance. The image of accountants as impartial, historical 'score-keepers' who exert little influence upon the business game is being undermined by the understanding that alternative forms of calculation – for example, in management accounting and research and development (Willmott *et al.*, 1992; Robson, 1993) – are regularly used as 'ammunition' in struggles for power and control (Burchell *et al.*, 1980; Burchell, Clubb and Hopwood, 1985), and directly affect corporate and national economic performance. In turn, this awareness induces critical questioning of whether the profession is capable of recognizing these effects or willing to devise standards and practices that take this understanding fully into account.

These developments have inadvertently exposed the extent to which the accountancy profession has become a major industry.[4] Indirectly, they have given rise to critical reflection upon the relevance and adequacy of the regulation of accounting practices and their relationship to the State (Sikka *et al.*, 1992). Consideration of the three episodes allows us to explore how accountants have sought to address and neutralize the threat to the image of themselves (and to the associated material benefits) as responsible, independent professionals. As we show later in our analysis of the episode concerned with the governance of the largest UK accounting association, accountants have not been assisted by the history of competition and rivalry between the major accountancy bodies,[5] and nor have they been assisted by the difficulties associated with regulating an increasingly fragmented membership. As one influential and laconic commentator has remarked: 'It seems that major internal reforms are only possible if the membership does not appreciate the significance of what is happening' (Davison, 1987:p.2).

The self-image of the UK accountancy profession that is at issue here is one that it shares with other professions, embracing the ideals of neutrality and independence (Goode, 1957; Greenwood, 1957; Wilensky, 1964). The language of professionalism is an important resource in the self-mobilization project of any occupation. Occupations seeking to attain or retain the status of profession affirm that their existence is the outcome of a Social Contract between themselves and the 'public' (Stacey, 1954; Worsley, 1985). In return for considerable autonomy in both organization and regulation, the occupation gains a monopoly of a certain service or services. This contract is agreed because the profession is judged the most effective guardian of the public good which it elaborates through the fostering of a body of knowledge and expertise, backed by relevant disciplinary procedures. In the UK, in the 1980s, the status of accountants as professionals has had to be constantly reproduced and modified.

Central features of the claims to professional legitimacy on the part of the UK accountancy bodies are the twin appeals to self-regulation and expert judgement. The legal construct of 'True and Fair' is deemed to reflect the expert judgement of the accounting professional, guided by professional standards, in preparing and auditing economic records. 'Regulation' is thus conceptualized as that which is 'internal' to a professional organization. Accounting practitioners proclaim 'self-regulation' as a hallmark of professional practices, and assert the independence of their 'technical' procedures from (socio-political) 'interference' by others – such as clients and State agencies.

For example, in recent decades it has become increasingly important to justify the powers and privileges of self-regulation by demonstrating the existence of statements, recommendations and guidelines on good or best practice. In this process, a professional discourse routinely assumes and privileges the regulation *by* the profession over the regulation *of* the profession. This privileging is effected by the assumption that the regulation 'of' is taken care of through the regulation 'by'. Discursive concern with the latter is limited to the framework or form set by the State within which, for example, accountants report on economic matters. The substance of those accounts has been claimed by the profession to be a matter for the judgement of the expert professional. Even if the distinction between 'of' and 'by' cannot be rigidly applied in the light of historical examination (Macdonald, 1984), it is regularly mobilized as a linguistic resource in processes of negotiation – as when, in negotiations over the EC's 4th Directive in the UK, the UK profession sought to defend itself from 'continental' accounting practices.[6]

Our concern in this chapter is to study the processes of negotiation and renegotiation of the professional status of accountancy in the UK, as these were played out between particular accountancy bodies and specific State agencies during the 1980s. Specifically, it is necessary to recall the relationship of dependency and tension between the discourse of professionalism and its attendant concepts of self-regulation, the proliferation of markets for accounting labour, and the passing of national and international State legislation. For the expansion of markets for accounting labour, and the fragmentation of the accountants' occupational practices, add to the burden of regulation for those accountancy bodies that appear uneasy, ill-prepared, and ill-equipped to carry it.

From such a perspective, the 'ideology' of professional self-regulation can be viewed not simply as a mask for the profession's activities but as implicated in the conditions that *make the practices of accountants possible*. The discourses that surround professions and are promoted by professionals form an integral part of the social practices that facilitate, maintain and promote the occupation. Accounting practitioners draw upon the professional discourse of regulation to project their practices as embodying the attributes of proper professional practice, and in so doing reproduce and legitimize their actions. This is illustrated in the connection between modern professional accounting discourses and the drive for the promotion and expansion of markets for accounting labour. For the claim that the practices of accountants help to secure the public interest in achieving an efficient allocation of resources operates to enhance and expand the services accounting practitioners can offer, whilst re-affirming the professional identity on which such a claim depends. Building on the territory first established in relation to insolvency work in the nineteenth century, the erection of the banner 'Accountancy Profession' imparted an apparent unity to a disparate set of financial, commercial, legal and managerial practices.

The accounting profession has, in common with other professional groups, articulated its practices in terms of the service ideal or 'Public Interest' that is apparently secured by its practices (in return for monopoly control). Indeed the accounting profession has not been short of narratives of its origins and development (Stacey, 1954), narratives that appeal to the image of public service and the increasing efficiency with which such functions are carried out (Kitchen and Parker, 1981). In such histories, the role of the State is typically portrayed as securing the contract between itself and the profession. It can also be seen as vouchsafing what is the public interest which the profession is supposed to satisfy. The role of the State tends to be minimized or not discussed in great detail. The professional regulatory discourse articulates the regulation *by* the profession to the relative neglect of the regulation *of* the profession. The effect is to understate, or to set limits to the possibility of the State or other mechanisms regulating accounting; the noun 'self-regulation' fixes a wide-ranging process as a bounded, natural, timeless 'thing' and attempts effectively to close off other ways of construing or accomplishing the regulation of accounting.

However, meanings are not fixed or unchanging. Nor are the institutional relations between the State and the accountancy profession. The shifting meaning of terms and their mutual interaction are especially germane to the recent events within the UK accountancy profession. An understanding of the term 'public interest' is central to the profession's self-justification, but the chain of meanings within which the term is produced has been subject to gradual transformation. Rather than referring to some political mandate that defines the public interest – the State–profession nexus – the profession in the UK has increasingly sought to define public interest in economic terms such as efficiency and value for money. Whereas *The Corporate Report* (Accounting Standards Committee, 1975) referred to the public responsibility of accountants as providing information to those with reasonable *rights* to information, accounting information is increasingly seen as a (expert) commodity which has to be *paid for*, and the public interest is held to be best achieved if accountants are profitable entrepreneurs.

It is this shifting set of meanings and institutional arrangements that we now turn to by considering three episodes in the changing relationship between the State and the profession. We begin with the regulation of auditors, in particular, the credibility of claims about their independence, sparked off by the EC 8th Directive.

## The European 8th Directive

In the past few decades accounting labour has expanded in two respects. Firstly, the core services of insolvency and audit have been supplemented by consultancy services in tax, computing systems, and management information and control systems. There has also been expansion into recruitment services and into advisory work on mergers and acquisitions. Secondly, accountancy practices have expanded their operations into far more countries, to some extent paralleling the development of the multinational corporations that they audit and advise (Jones, 1981), but also incorporating more general, geographical expansion, which now includes the economies of Eastern Europe, the countries of the former Soviet Union and China.

It is generally acknowledged that many of these more recent services are more lucrative than audit, which has increasingly suffered from competitive tendering. Audit has declined both as a proportion of the total activity of the major international accountancy firms and as a contributor to their profitability (Hopwood *et al.*, 1990). Nevertheless, most accountancy firms still see audit as a cornerstone of their business. For some firms it acts as a 'cash cow'; others argue that additional and more profitable services are prompted by the client base provided by the audit; and the monopoly of statutory audit work that is accorded the major accountancy bodies by company law feeds the reputational base of the occupation by signifying and confirming its integrity and its knowledge base.[7]

The publication of the first draft of the EC's proposed 8th Directive on Company Law in April 1978 seemed, to UK accountants, to open the possibility of new laws which could both facilitate and constrain these practices of expansion. In successive drafts the text of the Directive changed (Cooper *et al.*, forthcoming). But during its development two major themes emerged which have particular significance for the analysis here of the changing relationships between the State and the professions. First, there was the issue of auditor independence, and what conditions might be necessary to ensure that this independence existed. Second, there was the freedom of firms of accountants to set up in other member states, to undertake statutory audits, and to market other accountancy work in those states. We shall consider these issues in some detail as it affects our understanding of the changing and problematical relationship between the State and the accountancy 'profession' in the UK.

### Auditor independence and the provision of non-audit services

The probity of an audit firm's undertaking non-audit services had not prompted any major debate or conflict in the UK accountancy bodies before the 8th Directive debate.[8] The accountancy bodies in the UK seemed to rely upon the claim that 'professional' independence is a 'state of mind', as a way of justifying auditor–client relationships. The first draft of the Directive did not appear to implicate the non-audit services issue at all. It provided merely in Article 3 that 'member states shall grant approval' [to act as auditor where required under statute] 'only to persons who are of good repute and independent'. The meaning of 'independent' was not defined in the draft. Blanquet (1979)[9] wrote soon afterwards that the clause was designed to ensure there were no incompatibilities in auditors' functions, and that 'Such incompatibilities are not listed in the Directive and Member States therefore remain at liberty to identify them themselves'.

With no obvious stimulus either from the wording of the draft or from the thinking of administrators such as Blanquet, the UK accountancy bodies nevertheless anticipated possible difficulties over the provision of non-audit services, apparently on the grounds that the Directive restricted itself to legislating for the audit function only. Initially they framed their concerns in public interest terms. The 'danger' anticipated was that the provision of non-audit services might be forbidden and, of less import, that each activity might be licensed separately under EC legislation. The journal of the Institute of Chartered Accountants of Scotland commented (*Accountant's Magazine*, February 1979: 49) that,

Separate licensing of an individual activity within the range of services expected of a profession could, if too narrowly applied, undermine the unity of the profession. If that happened, its strength and influence would diminish together with the contribution which it makes to the commercial life of the whole community.

This argument appealed directly to a conception of the public interest which equates this with the range of services accountants can offer, rather than, for example, public access to reliable and full information.

In 1979, a further draft of the Directive had changed the wording of Article 3 to the following:

Member states shall grant approval only to persons who are of good repute and not carrying on any activity of such nature as to cast doubt on their independence.

The reference to 'carrying on any activity' was significant; the clause was intended to allow persons of 'good repute' (including shareholders) to act as auditors in those countries where this was then permitted, as was the case in Italy. But the focus on independence shifts to the activities and practices of the auditors themselves. To UK accountants (*Accountant's Magazine,* April 1980: 144) this was more clearly interpretable as threatening their non-audit services:

This suggests that the Commission, in accordance with the wishes of the European Parliament, might be seeking to limit or even prohibit an auditor from rendering other services to audit clients.

Similarly, a Consultative Committee of Accountancy Bodies (CCAB) memorandum to the DTI some months later noted that the provisions of the draft 'although vague, could be construed as' prohibiting non-audit services. Again translations of the public interest were invoked (*Accountant's Magazine*, February 1981: 30):

To change this system in a way that requires a company to employ one firm of accountants to audit the accounts and another to provide tax and other advisory services cannot, we think, be in the best interests of the public.

The issue was apparently laid to rest with the final wording of Article 3, which required that,

The authorities of a Member State shall grant approval only to persons of good repute who are not carrying on any activity which is incompatible, *under the law of that Member State*, with the statutory auditing of the documents referred to in Article 1(1) [emphasis added].

This Article permitted the British government to continue allowing non-audit services. The defence of accountancy's non-audit activities appeared to be successfully concluded for the present. However, the approval of the Directive by the European Council of Ministers, in 1984, left the matter open by stating that:

*The Commission* notes with regret that the rules concerning the independence of persons responsible for carrying out statutory audits have not been sufficiently harmonised by this Directive. It intends to submit further proposals in this area at a later date.

In early 1987, the DTI issued its response to the Directive, in the form of a wide-ranging consultative document, 'Regulation of Auditors: Implementation of the EC Eighth Company Law Directive' (hereafter ROA). Without expressing its own opinion, this consultative document raised the possibility of restricting the provision of non-audit services by auditors to clients they audit. ROA caused consternation in the UK accountancy Institutes in that it raised the possibility of a host of mechanisms for regulating auditors, some of which were reminiscent of those suggested earlier in the US by critics of the profession.[10]

Responses to this document were forthcoming from a number of sources, including industry, all the major multi-national accounting firms, and the accountancy Institutes.[11] Three of these bodies bolstered their submissions with surveys of business opinion.[12] All responses and all business surveys opposed blanket restrictions. However, some acknowledged that perhaps certain non-audit services might be incompatible. In their responses, some suggested a different solution to the DTI: the separate disclosure of audit and non-audit fees in the annual financial statements. This suggestion was taken up by the DTI.[13] Responses by the ICAEW and ICAS opposed disclosure on the grounds that it would not avoid conflicts of interest as such, and that it might inhibit management from appointing the best consultant for the job, if the 'best' consultant happened to be the auditor. Rutteman (1987: 14) comments,

This is really what the argument is about – auditors are afraid they will lose business in other areas if they are singled out in the disclosure requirements. Other firms of consultants believe auditors start with an unfair advantage in trying to gain the business as a result of their audit relationships.

Thus, the extent to which the accountancy bodies were justified in 'worrying' about the threat of the 8th Directive itself is uncertain. Certainly, the evidence is that they were successful in mobilizing the support of the DTI early in the discussions. The strength and vigour of the opposition to the very tentative suggestions in the ROA provides some indication of the significance that the 'profession' attached to the issue.

Equally significant is the form of rhetoric used by the 'profession' to argue for the essential harmony between its interests and those of the public. In the press commentaries that took place during the negotiations over the successive drafts, the accountancy bodies did not initially emphasize independence and integrity. Few claims to the inherent trustworthiness of the 'profession' were made as a way of countering or avoiding potential conflicts of interest. Instead, the convenience to the client was emphasized (the client, implicitly being deemed to be the company and not the shareholder), and this in turn was identified with the public interest.[14]

Towards the end of the debate, when specific responses were made to the DTI, a notion of the integrity of the 'profession' was introduced into the discourse. It had been difficult for the accountancy Institutes to introduce these terms earlier in the press and CCAB comment. This is partly because the spirit of the EC Directive was one of a formal legal based framework. This left little room for the UK model in which the 'profession' was entrusted with its own affairs, including the setting and policing of its own ethical guidelines. The reluctance was also because the accountancy bodies had, in their own perception, begun to move away in any event from a model emphasizing the professional qualities of integrity. For in the previous summer the ICAEW, prompted by the discourses surrounding this episode and the issues arising from the FSA (see below), had published a new model of self-regulation (ICAEW, 1986).

The new model of self-regulation distinguishes 'reserved' work, i.e. audit, which has special regulations, from other accounting practices. But, in both cases, regulation is expressed in the discourse of providing quality work to clients, who are seen to be agents able and entitled to choose between accountants in a free market. The language in this document draws on the wider politico-economic discourses about market quality and consumer choice (Heelas and Morris, 1992; Hindess, 1990; Keat and Abercrombie, 1990). Moreover, the new self-regulatory regime seeks to regulate account-ing *firms*, rather than individual accountants. This opens up the possibility of the ICAEW regulating non-accountants who work in accounting firms. This novel discourse of professional regulation offers the further possibility of making non-accountants partners in firms, thereby strengthening the 'non-accounting', consulting practices as an integral part of large, diversi-fied accounting firms.

But there is still an important role for the State in the new self-regulatory regime. As part of its concern to ensure the independence and accountabi-lity of each country's accounting practitioners, Article 2.2 of the 8th Directive required that the regulation of auditors should be legally enforce-able by the State. The actions of accountancy bodies would have the force of law, and they could also be challenged in the courts. This requirement necessitated a change in the law, and this was incorporated in the Companies Act 1989.

In ROA, the DTI outlined three possible mechanisms to ensure the legal regulation of accountants. The first option was to provide the accountancy Institutes with statutory powers, as provided to lawyers. The ROA indicated that this option was 'the most clear cut in terms of Community obligations' (DTI, 1987c). Without offering any explanation in the docu-ment, ROA stated that this option was 'the least desirable in all other respects'. The second option suggested was to create a new body, similar to the General Medical Council, which would have representatives both of the State and the 'profession'. This option surprised the accountancy bodies and was interpreted as a proposal to set up a quasi-SEC in the UK. To the

Chartered Association of Certified Accountants (CACA), this was an attractive option for it offered a way for the CACA to have a stronger say in the regulation of accountancy as a whole, and for it to enhance its status. For the more established accountancy bodies and the larger firms, this proposal was discussed in the terms of threatening 'professional' self-regulation and, more privately, of failing to distinguish the varying quality of different accountancy qualifications and work. The Companies Act 1989 finally incorporated the third option, whereby the government minister would approve accountancy bodies where s/he was satisfied they would only sanction audit functions to those who met the standards required.

Self-regulation could thus be rendered compatible with the operation of a free market for accountants, but one which needed to be supervised at arm's length by the State. The DTI talked about oversight by the State while not increasing the size of government. One or two civil servants would monitor a regulatory apparatus paid for and operated by 'practitioners'. This approach could still be regarded as a form of self-regulation. Moreover, the ICAEW was attracted to the fact that it would still permit the traditional mechanisms of informal influence. This could be seen as consistent with the pursuit of the public interest. As the ICAEW states in its response to ROA (1987a: para. 2.58),

one reason why the present system of self-regulation has succeeded in serving the public interest effectively has been that, when the occasion has demanded, it has been susceptible to the influence of the Secretary of State.

### The professional industry: expanding markets and mutual recognition

In the early drafts of the 8th Directive, considerable attention was paid to the issue of mutual recognition of qualifications among member states, which would allow authorized auditors in one country to conduct audits in other member countries. These discourses on mutual recognition not only articulated the 'necessary' traits to be professional, they also facilitated the expansionary desires of UK accountants to conquer new markets in member countries. Of course, the reciprocal dimension of mutual recognition was appreciated, but it was not expected to constrain the practices of UK accountants. The CCAB submission (1979) to the DTI demonstrates the concern with keeping markets as open as possible:

The UK profession fears that some other states – believing in the superiority of their own standards, and disturbed by what they believe to be the lesser standards in places like Italy – would prefer to accept none, rather than all, thus excluding the UK qualification which would otherwise have been accepted.

The concerns of the German government did indeed hold sway so that by 1983, *Accountancy*, the journal of the ICAEW, could comment that, 'this directive ... does not deal with mutual recognition of qualifications, something which the UK profession and the DTI are keen to see' (*Accountancy*, 1983: 9). The debate did not die but re-emerged, in connection with '1992', in later, and more general, EC Directives on mutual recognition.

The issue of mutual recognition is interesting in that it coincided with, and indeed helped to give form to, a more collaborative relationship between the DTI and the UK accountancy 'profession'. Thus in 1987 the minister responsible for the DTI articulated a new regulatory role for that department – the Department of Enterprise (Channon, 1987). The role of the DTI was to promote the accounting 'industry', in terms of the latter's position as a major exporter and employer of skilled knowledge workers:

Accounting as an industry is a very important industry. We don't have a huge sponsorship function because on the whole it's very competent to look after itself. And it's always a very important element in our thinking when approaching our regulatory functions as well as Company Law more generally (Civil Servant, Companies Division, DTI).

Another civil servant with duties in implementing the 8th Directive pointed out in interview: 'There are a lot more auditors than steelworkers in this country.' The expansion of markets and the issue of mutual recognition thus further transforms the issue of regulation. Regulation is reconstituted as being a resource in a competitive struggle between nations – accountants need only that degree of regulation that will convince the consumer that UK accountants are as independent, ethical, reliable, qualified, etc. as accountants from other countries. Thus with respect to the 8th Directive it was remarked by a DTI official that: 'the regulation of the profession in Europe should, to some extent, follow UK models in order to improve the competitiveness of our accountants in Europe.'

To conclude this episode, we have attempted to draw out the problems and re-alignments in the relations between the State and the accountancy 'profession' in the UK in the context of the negotiations on the EC 8th Directive. In confronting the opportunities for further expansion of the accountancy 'industry' in European markets, and the implications of this for UK exports, competing models of professional regulation have had to be addressed by both the State and by the accountancy bodies. Attempts to reconcile the existing structures of regulation with new forms of international regulation, and with differing national structures of accounting regulation, provided an arena in which the UK accountancy bodies and the State articulated the notion of professional self-regulation in order to help promote the expansion of the UK accountancy 'profession' and the full range of its 'services' in Europe.

## Accountancy as a Recognized Professional Body

The 1980s saw a 'revolution' in the regulation of the financial services industry in the UK. A DTI White Paper (1985) identified two major elements to this revolution. First, there were concerns with the competitiveness of the financial services sector, along with other changes in the market place,[15] such as the utilization of information and communications technologies, and the development of markets in unlisted securities, futures and options. A second element was introduced by the shifting political rationales of the Conservative government in building a 'climate for enterprise', through privatization, the relaxation of price, dividend, foreign exchange and lending controls, and tax changes. In this context, the White Paper addressed the issue of: 'the statutory framework of protection for investors and those who buy financial services' (DTI, 1985: 4), and sought to ensure that this was: 'not rendered obsolete by changes in the market place, either in the way a business is done or in the products on offer to investors' (DTI, 1985: 4).

The Financial Services Act 1986 (FSA) was the outcome of these varying concerns with the regulation of the financial sector. Two points are worth emphasizing here.

First, the collapse of four licensed dealers in securities in 1981, and a succession of scandals in insurance, banking and commodity markets raised considerable doubts about the efficacy of market based regulations and the maintenance of London as a leading financial centre (Clark, 1986). The international competitive position of London was also in doubt as a result of the failure of existing regulatory mechanisms in a range of financial markets. The FSA can be seen to be a response to these different forms of international pressure. Within a global system of financial markets, London was not facilitating an apparently efficient international allocation of capital, and this perception was undesirable from the perspective of maintaining the role of London as a UK invisible export earner and international banking entrepôt.

Second, the FSA was explicitly developed as a practitioner based system of regulation, albeit one that was subject to the backing and surveillance of the State in the form of the DTI and, more directly, the newly created Securities and Investment Board (SIB). As was demonstrated in the previous section, such regulatory mechanisms need to be understood as interrelated with the implementation of the EC 8th Directive. A practitioner based system of regulation means that the accountancy bodies assume the role of regulators of the investment practices of its membership. The changes to financial services regulation affected the practices of accountancy professionals operating in this market, and thus connected with the ideology of self-regulation.

Accountants were caught up in the FSA in two aspects: through their regulatory role in auditing, and as a result of being part of an industry which offers advice and sells investments (not just securities). In this section the second of these dimensions is considered in more detail: more specifically, the negotiations between the DTI and the Institutes to secure the category of Recognized Professional Body (RPB).

### Recognized Professional Bodies and the FSA

In general, the FSA is concerned to control the unscrupulous operator. Investors are to be safeguarded by means of business, monitoring and enforcement rules administered by practitioner run (self-)regulatory agencies (Radcliffe *et al.*, forthcoming; Radcliffe, 1989). The increasing concern with the crooks, rogues and incompetents in relation to investor protection reflected the desire to ensure that investors would be content to use the London market, in the context of a more rigorous and bureaucratic system in the US. Accountants became caught up in this concern as the scope of the FSA extended to investment business, defined beyond securities traders and market-makers. An efficient market in financial products was seen to require that investment *advisors* offer 'best advice' and encourage market participation.

The review of investor protection begun by Professor Gower in 1981 first proposed a system of self-regulatory agencies: practitioner groupings would administer day-to-day regulation subject to government supervision (Gower, 1982). Gower's final report endorsed the earlier suggestion: regulatory bodies should regulate their members but with government overview. A series of criteria had to be met before a regulatory agency was recognized: for example, entrance conditions ensuring that members of the regulatory agency were 'fit and proper' persons to provide investment advice.[16]

Gower recognized the involvement of certain professions (accountants, solicitors, actuaries) in advising on investment business, but his proposed regulations conferred upon them no special role or status. Within the terms of his proposals, professions were treated equally with bankers, securities dealers, insurance brokers, etc. as potential 'Recognized Self-regulatory Agencies'. This lack of division between professionals and others was to concern the accountancy bodies. But Gower reasoned that creating a hierarchy between an 'elite' and 'fringe' in investment business with differences in regulatory requirements might encourage those involved in investment business to seek registration with self-regulatory bodies whose application of the supervisory requirements was perceived as weak.[17]

The initial response to the Gower Report from the CCAB reaffirmed the importance of maintaining 'professional' self-regulation:

we [are] in no doubt about the advantages of self-regulation both in general and in the way in which it applies to the accountancy profession in particular (ICAEW, TR 543, 1984: 2).

This argument was coupled with the claim that the government must avoid direct involvement in the regulation of financial services:

We believe that the [Gower proposals] ... would open the way for unnecessarily detailed intervention by Government in to the conduct of investment business which will increase bureaucracy both in Government and in the City (ICAEW, TR 543, 1984: 2).

Public reaction to the Gower Report from the incumbent President of the ICAEW claimed that Gower failed to recognize that the majority of ICAEW members did not give investment advice.[18] However, a later President, Derek Boothman, having considered Counsel's opinion on the relevance of the FSA to the accountancy profession, was to write that the terms of the Gower Report were such that;

[The ICAEW] Council believes that most firms of Chartered Accountants are currently conducting investment business as defined in the [Financial Services] legislation (*Accountancy*, March 1987: 90).

As the accountancy bodies gradually acknowledged the implications of the regulation of financial services for their members' practices, and discussions began on transforming the Final Report by Professor Gower into a Financial Services Act, the accountancy bodies mounted an offensive on the proposals to treat professions as self-regulatory agencies in the same terms as other non-professional groupings providing investment advice. The grouping of the accountancy bodies with non-professional suppliers of investment services offended both the ideology of a 'profession' that claims to service the public interest selflessly, as well as the ideal of professional self-regulation. In their submission to the DTI on the Gower Report, the ICAEW attempted to restate the distance between themselves and other occupations with involvement in financial services and declared that the DTI: 'is wrong to view the Institute on all fours with the other City Institutions' (*Accountancy*, June 1984: 8).

Gower's Reports had considered that in addition to the Self-Regulatory Organizations (SRO) there might be a need for another regulatory category, with perhaps less restrictive requirements, the Recognized Professional Body (RPB). Gower had rejected such an option. However, one year later the government published its White Paper *Financial Services in the United Kingdom. A new framework for Investor Protection* (DTI, 1985). This confirmed the view that professions such as lawyers, accountants, and actuaries could not be exempted from the regulation of their investment business; however, the form of regulation for professional bodies was to be similar, but not identical, to that of the SROs for brokerage, insurance and investment management.

The RPB concept was reintroduced: for two years following the publication of the Gower Report the chartered accountancy bodies lobbied for a differential mode of regulation that would recognize their *status* as professionals. From a position of seeming to deny that financial services were of any importance to their memberships, the accountancy bodies gradually recognized the implications of the practitioner based regulation of financial services for their membership, a slow recognition that was possibly borne out of an ignorance of the extent of members' involvement in such markets.

The RPB option allowed the Secretary of State (for Trade and Industry) to exempt from the requirement to seek authorization those members of a professional body 'recognised for the purposes of other statutes' (DTI, 1985: para. 4.12). RPBs would register and regulate their own membership with regard to investment advice, and accounting practitioners could no longer act as 'tied agents'. The RPB section of the White Paper did not escape criticism in the British Parliament (Radcliffe, 1989). Although the front bench spokesman for the Opposition condoned the RPB status for accountancy, one backbench Labour member denounced the accountancy profession as a mere trade association, and argued for the removal of the RPB clause (Hansard, Standing Committee E, Financial Services Bill, Seventh Sitting, col. 248). The Consumers' Association and the National Consumer Council also opposed the less stringent regulation of investment advice for the accountancy bodies.

Although the accountancy bodies appeared gratified by their victory in securing an RPB clause in the FSA, such an achievement needs to be set against the views of SIB. The apparent entrepreneurial success of accountants in widening their fields of activity was clearly recognized, but SIB retained some reservations about the overall competence of the accountants in the domain of investment advice. As one senior regulator in SIB expressed it:

Everybody takes the line that regulation is for those villains down the road but not for them ... You will appreciate that the 'lesser breeds' [non-professional providers of financial services] don't look with a benevolent eye on the members of the professions ... There are some insurance brokers who see some accountants as amateur, part-time bunglers in the field of selling assurance and unit trusts.

The supervisory rules and requirements for RPBs were substantially the same as for the SROs. In submissions and discussions with SIB, the four accountancy bodies reiterated their professional claims and the confidence regulators could have that accountants are 'fit and proper' persons to provide investment advice. However, whilst the exemption of professional bodies from having to register with an SRO reaffirmed a commitment to the self-regulation of the profession, little was conceded in terms of the rules and regulations RPBs would have to enforce as distinct from the SRO equivalents. The response from the ICAEW was predictable:

It is ... difficult to see what purpose exemption would serve if complete identity of rules with those of recognised self-regulatory organisations were to be required (ICAEW, TR 577, 1985).

The attempt to secure institutional and legal recognition for the principle of professional self-regulation was thus limited. The RPB route for regulating accountants giving investment advice was a concession to the professional ideal, but one that was of limited import. The accountancy bodies were thus subject to external monitoring, albeit directly via the SIB rules, rather than through an SRO.

This episode is indicative of the success of accountancy in colonizing non-accounting markets, even if it indicates a possible failure on the part of those accountancy bodies, responsible for regulating their members, fully to recognize this success. However, it also shows how the discourse of professional regulation was mobilized in defence of their existing regulatory structures. Whilst this strategy was only partially successful, it needs to be understood in relation to the territory gained. The 'entrepreneurial profession' extended and secured its activities in non-accounting/auditing domains, unrelated to the education and training of the professional accountant, and in so doing became caught in regulations for the provision of financial services. Yet it still managed to secure a distinctive regulatory mechanism, one that is likely to have far-reaching consequences for the professionalization project of accountancy, and the commitment of the membership to their professional identity.

One consequence of the pursuit of RPB status has been to reinforce tendencies toward consolidation and coordination between the accountancy bodies. The ICAEW, ICAI and ICAS (with the position of CACA, the fourth professional body recognized in the Companies Act 1989 in relation to audit, still unclear) set up a Joint Chartered Accountants Financial Services Monitoring Unit: to act as their agent in ascertaining the information on which each individual Institute, as an RPB, can make its authorization and enforcement decisions (ICAEW, 1987b: 17).

The form of information obtained by the Monitoring Unit will significantly affect the relation between the accounting bodies and their membership. The RPBs will be involved in 'passive' and 'active' monitoring. Whatever the vigour of their monitoring and enforcement, accountants see the accountancy Institutes no longer predominantly as professional associations protecting their mark and interests, but as regulatory agencies concerned with surveillance, monitoring and bureaucratic rules.

The nature of this 'self'-regulation is distinguished by its object. In contrast to the ideal of self-regulation of the professional *person*, passive monitoring will involve scrutiny of a *firm*'s not a *member*'s:

annual returns including information about the accounting records which firms will be required to keep and declarations that they continue to comply with the regulations [i.e. in relation to conduct of business and financial regulations] (ICAEW, 1987b: 15).

Accounting firms conducting investment business other than the most basic kind (e.g. offering advice and arranging deals but not holding clients' money) will be subject to an independent accounts report. This form of *passive* scrutiny is, however, supplemented by more proactive investigations. *Active* monitoring will involve visits to firms to review compliance once every two years (except again for the most basic investment businesses where the visit will be every five years). This move to active monitoring is a significant break from the distant form of regulation accountants have received from their Institutes.

   This outline of the effects of the pursuit of RPB status for accountancy suggests that accountants, in their pursuit of investment business, became involved in the governmental concern to improve the 'efficiency' of the UK financial services industry. The new regulatory regime in the financial services sector incorporated the accountants in their role as providers of financial services and offered a challenge to their received notions of professional regulation and status.

   In the third episode we explore how the issues raised by the changing nature of the regulation *of* the profession have passed into the professional bodies themselves. Problems of maintaining the image of professional self-regulation in the face of national and international regulation, and the expansion of the accountancy industry into new markets, have had parallels in, and effects upon, the problematical relationships between the membership of the accountancy bodies and their professional regulatory institutions. We shall explore how the entrepreneurial practices of the accountancy profession have created concerns for the self-identity of accountants in the UK, their relationship to the professional bodies in the UK, and how the ICAEW has attempted to resolve the problem of maintaining the cohesiveness of the occupational organization of accountancy in response to diminishing professional commitment and identity amongst the membership.

### Governing the ICAEW

In this section, we explore the efforts of the major accountancy body in the UK, the Institute of Chartered Accountants in England and Wales (ICAEW, hereafter the Institute), to develop a new form of organization and sense of purpose in the face of changes that undermined its capacity to retain the powers and privileges of self-regulation. Two reports, commissioned by the Institute, on its governance mechanisms provide the focus for our discussion (Willmott et al., forthcoming).

The commissioning of the Tricker (1983) and Worsley (1985) Reports followed a series of episodes during the 1970s and early 1980s which placed in question the capacity of 'the accountancy profession' to discharge its dual responsibility to its membership and to the 'public interest'. Inter alia, these included the members' rejection of proposals to integrate the accountancy bodies, a number of highly visible auditing scandals, complaints about the imprecision of accounting standards, and the failure to develop an acceptable inflation accounting standard. At issue also was the role of the Institute in regulating the financial services activities of members and the perceived growth of State regulation in prospect from, for example, the 8th Directive considered above. Conceived initially as an assessment of Tricker's recommendations, the Worsley Report became a vehicle for presenting a different diagnosis of the challenges facing the Institute, together with the presentation of an alternative set of prescriptions for organizational change expressed through a re-interpretation of the principle of professional self-regulation. The broadening of its terms of reference was indicative of a growing anxiety, at least in some quarters of the Institute, that the implementation of the Tricker proposals would weaken and divide its organization at the very time when changes in the economic and political context required a more unified stance in defence of the powers and privileges of self-regulation.

The focus of the Tricker Report was upon the internal segmentation of the membership of the Institute, highlighting the presence of deep divisions between members employed within different sites (and operating in different markets), and revealing considerable disaffection with activities undertaken in their name. In general, the small practitioners and members employed in industry were reported to be suspicious and resentful of an Institute which they perceived to offer them little or no representation (Tricker, 1983: 20–1). In contrast, those interviewed from the big firms expressed an elitist concern about the calibre of Council and the ineffectiveness of its leadership in relating to influential forces in its environment. Having considered a range of alternative forms of governance, Tricker proposed a structure founded upon the establishment of a number of 'Subject Conferences' – such as those concerned with taxation, with management accounting, and with insolvency – to reflect the specialist interests and concerns of different members; and the recomposition of Council to represent this diversity. Tricker situated his proposals in an analysis of what he provocatively termed the 'post-professional world' (1983: 1–38).

The reorganization of the Institute's structures of governance is commended by Tricker because it would assist recognition that 'members no longer all face similar issues in their work' (1983: 14) yet allegedly re-affirms:

the essential community of interest shared by members of the Institute, the underlying values, the underpinning common knowledge and the unifying sense of purpose and commitment.

It is this claim that the Worsley Report assessed and rejected. Tricker's proposals for a change of governance structure were criticized on the grounds that they would aggravate, rather than legitimate, the segmentation of the Institute's membership. It was acknowledged that the opportunity to join 'Subject Conferences' might encourage greater identification with the Institute amongst some of its members (e.g. those working in industry). But such a reform was seen to institutionalize and deepen these divisions and risk the loss of segments of the membership to other, more specialist professional bodies – such as the Association of Corporate Treasurers. Most especially, Tricker's analysis of the 'post-professional world' was premised upon a rejection of the professional ideals that the Worsley Report wished strategically to re-affirm.

Central to the Worsley Report was the view that effective governance of the Institute depended upon identifying and appreciating the compatibility of its purpose for the individual member and its collective purpose for the membership as a whole. The former is associated with providing, and securing the value of, 'a prestigious qualification' (Worsley, 1985: 16); the latter is associated with fulfilling its responsibilities to 'the public interest' by maintaining professional standards (1985: 22):

In short the Working Party believes that the present purpose of the Institute could be stated very simply as the maintenance of standards in the public interest and hence in the interests of individual members, linked with efforts to help members in their professional activities.

Although the purpose of the Report was ostensibly to provide a framework for discussion of the problems between the Institute and its members, the Report had a more strategic role in attempting to rationalize and legitimize the movement of accountants into non-accounting domains.

In particular, the first object as set out in the ICAEW's Royal Charter (Supplemental Charter 1948) read 'to advance the theory and practice of accountancy in all its aspects, including in particular auditing, financial management and taxation'. The Worsley Committee suggested this be changed to the less specific 'to advance the theory and practice of accountancy in all its aspects'. The Report noted the 'explosion of services which members in practice offer' (1985: 18), and suggested that 'members would not want to pursue excellence in the abstract but also as a way of promoting their individual interests' (1985: 21). Accordingly, the Institute now had further 'related' purposes, the first of which was: 'to ensure that members maintained a leading position in the contribution made by financial services to national prosperity' (1985: 21). The Report attempted to redefine accounting, partly for external consumption, as what account-ants do, rather than limiting it to specific functions such as accounting, auditing, etc. Furthermore, the 'interests' of accountants in pursuing their wide-ranging activities is still held to be (in principle) in the public interest. Thus, in response to the perception of alienation from the Institute among certain members, the Report recognized that new representational struc-tures were needed to accommodate the variety of functional specialisms now practised by accountants. Nevertheless, the members also must apparently recognize their 'interests' in accepting regulation of their practices by the Institute. As the Report put it: 'Democracy must in short, be reconciled with the need to maintain high professional standards' (1985: 30). These 'professional' standards the Institute alone can ensure, to the advantage of its members and the public.

The possibility of a conflict between the notion of 'self-interest' and a duty to the 'public interest' was acknowledged in the Report, but it was argued that the potential for conflict is not realized so long as 'the balance is constantly reassessed and the two elements clearly distinguished' (1985: 22). According to this argument, the guardians of the Institute have a responsibility to protect elements of the membership from their own miscalculated desire to strengthen the trade association role of the Institute, at the expense of its professional role. The absence of real cohesion and consistency in the views of the membership was acknowledged, yet only in order to stress the need to present a united front. Instead of changing the structure of the Institute in a way which institutionalized division, the recommendation of the Worsley Report was for improved communica-tions with the membership in order to educate them about their latent professional interests (1985: 22):

The goal of greater participation cannot be divorced from the goals of better communication and greater readiness on the part of members to think hard and constructively about the affairs of the Institute. These goals presuppose a continued sense of identity among members, from the background either of their professional education and training or of the subject with which they deal in their professional lives.

The value of increased participation in the affairs of the Institute was questioned on the grounds that it was likely to expose divisions between the Institute and active sections of the membership, and thereby undermine its credibility in the eyes of those able to circumscribe its powers and privileges. The capacity 'to show that collectively its members can take a longer-term view *and* reconcile self-interest with the public interest' (Worsley, 1985: 30, emphasis added) was understood to depend upon the Institute's ability to persuade its members that their individual professional interests would be best served by nurturing the perception that the activities of the Institute are motivated by concerns other than self-interest (1985: 20):

a higher level of participation without cohesion or consistency is unlikely to add to the standing of the Institute. It is self-evident that if Council is seen too often not to be supported by members at Annual and Special Meetings, the Institute will not be taken as a credible source of professional advice.

In emphasizing the need to improve communications with the membership, the Worsley Report recommended (1985: 58) that the Institute should adopt:

a more open style to administration, to greater readiness to discuss issues openly and ... to the practice of serving members in a way which makes them feel that it is *their* Institute [emphasis added].

Although critical of Tricker's proposals, the analysis presented in the Worsley Report accepted that the development of more commercial orientations was influencing the processes of self-regulation and the claim to 'professional independence'. However, this was interpreted less as a weakness of professional self-discipline than as an indicator of the importance of maintaining professional standards so as 'to safeguard the public in matters when the claims of individuals could not easily be verified' (1985: 20). Worsley alluded to the material significance of the claims of independence and impartiality for those who purchase the skills of accounting labour: without the certification provided by the Institute, the buyers of accounting labour would encounter greater uncertainty about its quality and dependability. In this regard, the reputation of the Institute is seen as a condition of exchange in markets for accounting labour.

Accordingly, the Worsley Report advanced the argument that the opportunity to penetrate new markets for accounting labour depends upon resisting pressures from the membership to play a stronger role as a trade association or trade union. This is because the perception of the Institute as a trade association undermines the claim to serve the public interest, and thereby weakens the claim to retain the material and symbolic privileges which accompany self-regulation. At the same time, it argued that the Institute must preserve a form of governance which enables its members 'to promote publicly the services which the Institute's members can provide' (1985: 20). The paradox of private regulation in the public interest must be accepted, the Worsley Report asserted, because the effectiveness of the discourses developed by Council on behalf of the members rests upon 'the fact that they are perceived as authoritative expressions of opinion by those with specialist expertise' (1985: 20).

In sum, the Worsley Report argued that retaining the confidence of the patrons of accountancy could best be achieved by articulating and demonstrating its strength and unity, and by accepting the role of 'professional' self-regulation in both 'public' and 'private' interests. Instead of indulging the diverse concerns of the membership in a way that fails to appreciate how such reforms are likely to be interpreted by their patrons, it favoured a re-affirmation of existing 'professional' structures of regulation combined with greater sensitivity to the style of communications with the membership. The intention was that greater participation in the electoral processes would serve to curtail the disruptive, unrepresentative influence of vocal minorities. The Tricker Report had diagnosed dissatisfaction with the Institute primarily in terms of the lack of sufficiently representative and democratic structures and procedures. In contrast, the Worsley Report emphasized the need for a less remote form of governance which would clarify and fulfil more effectively its purpose in serving the individual interests of its members, and their collective 'professional' interest in securing the standing of the Institute, by articulating the public interest.

The significance of the Worsley Report is that it presented an explicit re-affirmation of the value (to self-interest) of minimizing the visibility of the trade association role by privileging its 'professional' guardianship of the standards of accounting practice. Relatedly, because the pursuit of the private interests of individual members is identified with the guardianship of the public interest, there is a new rationale for maintaining a 'professional' ideology and organization to retain control over accounting policy in the context of increased state regulation and the growing segmentation of markets for accounting labour. Maintaining the collective purpose of the profession, the Worsley Report argued, would do more to promote the interests of individual members than would a reform of the governance structure. For the latter would have the consequence of weakening its capacity to secure the material and symbolic privileges associated with its self-regulating, professional status.

### Conclusion

Through the analysis of three recent episodes in the history of the accountancy bodies this chapter has given some indication of the changing nature of the relationships between the State and the profession in the UK. Our analysis is centred upon the interplay between two processes present in the accountancy bodies in the UK during the 1980s. The first is the ideal of professional self-regulation that professionals project to others to help legitimate their monopoly control of particular occupational territories. The second is the expansion of accountants into markets where their expertise has no necessary authority, and where alternative regimes of regulation hold sway. Each of the three episodes considered above illustrates that the recent 'worries' about the regulation of the accountancy bodies in the face of new national and international regulations can be interpreted as maintaining self-regulation in the context of the expansion of accounting labour.

First, in the case of the 8th Directive, the expansion of the multi-national auditing firms into Europe, and the range of non-auditing services they have provided to 'clients', have confronted concerns as to the independence of UK auditors in the context of the harmonization of company law in the EC. Appeals to independence as a 'state of mind' have had to give way to forms of State regulation, albeit weak ones, with the language of self-regulation providing a significant residue from previous understandings of professional regulation. The ROA was an intriguing instance of the DTI's awareness that the regulatory arrangements in the UK might be insufficient legitimation for the promotion of the UK accounting 'industry' in European markets.

Second, the RPB episode, an unanticipated consequence of accountants' moves into the markets for financial services, has had a major impact on conceptions of both what it means to be a professional, and on what the roles of a professional body are. Moreover, in providing the regulatory and institutional framework for financial services, the SIB has been faced with regulating the activities of market players (accountants) who have attempted to defend and to differentiate themselves by asserting their 'self-regulatory' status. The introduction of the RPB status for the accountancy bodies reflects the persuasive power of the notion of professional self-regulation in attempts to resist external regulation. However, the movement of entrepreneurial accountants into the financial services sector has enmeshed accountancy within forms of regulation that are equivalent to those applied to non-professional suppliers of financial services, forms of regulation that one might have expected their claims to professional status to have successfully withstood.

Third, it is important to recognize the interconnected nature of the discourses in the three episodes. At the most trivial level, many of the debates and many of the documents were produced around the same time. More significantly, the discourses concerning the governance of the ICAEW need to be interpreted in the light of the circumstances and events examined in the other two episodes passing into the professional bodies. These events have presented considerable difficulties for institutional organization and for the control of the membership – a membership exploring a diversity of commercial markets and with varying, and increasingly unstable, interest in the semblance of a 'professional' order in what they may perceive as a 'post-professional' world. The tensions between the membership and the institutional leadership have been heightened by the requirement that the accountancy Institutes administer new forms of regulation negotiated by them with the State that seem to undermine the tacit notions of professional self-regulation. This has raised severe doubts about whether the accountancy bodies can unify and control the membership in the manner that 'professional' self-regulation implies. The Worsley Report is an illuminating example of the manner in which the notion of professional regulation can be invoked and reformed in order to legitimate the new regulations that accountancy in the UK has been forced to accept.

Each episode signifies the changing nature of the relationships between the profession and the State in the UK. While the accounting 'industry' (an industry whose value to the UK economy is appreciated by the State) attempts to re-affirm the concept of professional self-regulation in order to legitimize involvement in new markets, the accountancy bodies have in turn had to accept new, proactive regulatory structures between themselves and the State. In this way, the internal cohesiveness and 'professional' identity of the membership has been eroded. This continues to create difficulties for accountancy in asserting the concept of self-regulation – a concept central to the ideals of neutrality and independence and to the success of the professionalization project.

NOTES

1. This chapter draws heavily upon presentations made at the Policy Studies Institute, London (January 1988), the Interdisciplinary Perspectives on Accounting Conference, Manchester (July 1988) and a seminar at the University of Lancaster. We appreciate the helpful comments of Anthony Hopwood, Sten Jonsson, David Knights, Cheryl Lehman, Anne Loft, Peter Miller, Stephen Parsons and Tony Tinker. The research assistance of Vaughan Radcliffe is gratefully acknowledged. The authors wish to acknowledge the financial assistance of the UK Economic and Social Research Council (award EO4250007), the Francis Winspear Fellowship of the Faculty of Business, University of Alberta and the Research Board of the Institute of Chartered Accountants in England and Wales.

2. Scare quotes around 'profession' and 'State' are used to highlight the dangers of (1) uncritically ascribing and thereby endorsing the status of profession to the numerous associations of accounting labour and (2) referring to the institutions of the State as if they formed a unity. In the history of the regulation of the accounting industry, there is considerable evidence to show the presence of tensions between different ministeries and offices of the State – notably between the Treasury, the DTI, and the Office of Fair Trading.

3. The expansion of the accounting profession in the UK and its success in penetrating 'non-accounting' domains has not necessarily been the result of a conscious strategy by the accounting 'profession', although at least since the

mid-1980s the large accounting firms and the accountancy bodies have carried out strategic exercises involving expansion (Greenwood *et al.*, 1990; Hopwood *et al.*, 1990). Much of accountancy's growth could be put down to the consequences of state regulation of productive and financial practices in the UK. Much of the content of accountancy work is externally defined. In addition the relative lack, in the UK, of alternative managerial qualifications, such as MBA or Civil Economist, has assisted the rise of accountants to a higher relative position in the corporate hierarchy (Armstrong, 1987; Whitley, 1986). Unlike some countries, accountants in the UK can move out of public practice and still remain members of their profession.

4. Accountancy in the UK has secured a monopoly of audit not only of large enterprises but also of a million companies in the private sector. From this 'base' it has expanded to become involved in the provision of an extensive range of services to business (Jones, 1981; Armstrong, 1987) and, more recently, to local government (McSweeney and Sherer, 1990), the health and education sectors (Bourn and Ezzamel, 1987), nationalized industries (Hopper *et al.*, 1986) and central government administration (National Audit Office, 1986).

5. There are six major accountancy bodies with rights to operate in the UK. The Institute of Chartered Accountants in England and Wales (ICAEW), Institute of Chartered Accountants of Scotland (ICAS), Institute of Chartered Accountants of Ireland (ICAI), and Chartered Association of Certified Accountants (CACA) all have the right to act as auditors under UK company law. The Chartered Institute of Management Accountants (CIMA) is composed, as the name indicates, largely of management (company) accountants, although management accountants can be members of the other bodies. The Chartered Institute of Public Finance Accountants (CIPFA) is the body for local authority and other public sector accountants. Of the six accountancy bodies the ICAS is the oldest and the ICAEW has the most status with respect to links with UK government.

6. This 'professional' discourse does not exhaust the possible ways of understanding the question of professional regulation. More critical perspectives on professional regulation have emerged partly out of the inadequacy of this image of the 'Ideal Profession' promoted by professional institutions. Theorists have challenged the claims to the service of the public good. Thus Watts and Zimmerman (1986), and those influenced by economic models of professions, have emphasized the self-interested behaviour of professionals in attempting to restrain competition and thereby enhance their wealth (Pilcher, 1974). Other theoretical positions emphasize that the practices of professions such as accountancy depend upon the patronage of an elite social group whose 'interests' they are obliged to secure or that the professions serve to maintain structured patterns of social inequalities (Parkin, 1979; Johnson, 1972). In this latter formulation the claims associated with professional self-regulation are presented as little more than an illusion. Professional practices and policies are interpreted as the outcome of the domination of the profession by other social groups. In the Marxian variant this refers to either capital or some fraction of capital (Johnson, 1977; Tinker, 1985). The discourses of professions on their own identity, functions and organization are presented as a form of ideological

mask that obscures the 'true' nature of professional practices and their regulation by 'private interests'. What accountants do and what they say they do are regarded as unattached, except to the extent that the ideological mask serves a legitimating function for the activities of professionals, obfuscating their 'true' nature.

7. The public spectacle of audit failures may also serve to undermine this reputational base.

8. This refers only to the UK. In the US, the Metcalf Committee of the Senate had in 1976 argued that the 'Big Eight' auditing firms had 'used their designated reputation for independence to market a variety of non-accounting services' which 'impair their ability to act as independent auditors for the vast majority of the Nation's large corporations' (US Senate Report, 1978: 50). This was not followed up immediately by action to curb these services, and does not seem to have stimulated any debate in the UK at the time. There is little doubt that the UK partners of the international firms of accountants were well aware of these developments. In response to the Senate deliberations, the American Institute of Certified Public Accountants set up the Commission on Auditors' Responsibilities (Cohen Commission, 1978). This concluded that there was no substantive evidence that provision of non-audit services affected auditors' independence. The Commission was quoted approvingly by the ICAEW in its submission to the DTI (see ICAEW, 1987a).

9. Magistrate, and Principal Administrator to the Commission of the European Community.

10. It also raised a further possibility: compulsory rotation of auditors at regular intervals.

11. The relevant accountancy bodies were the ICAEW, ICAS and CACA.

12. Two were major international accounting firms, Ernst & Whinney (quoting a survey by the 100 Group of senior industrialists), and Price Waterhouse. ICAS also conducted a survey.

13. Letter from the Department of Trade and Industry to the accountancy bodies dated 28 July 1987.

14. It is notable that the quotation given earlier from the *Accountant's Magazine* of February 1981 takes the individual company's interest and the public interest to be identical.

15. For example, 'the action brought by the Director General of Fair Trading against anti-competitive aspects of the Stock Exchange rules and the subsequent agreement between the Secretary of State for Trade and Industry and the Chairman of The Stock Exchange in July 1983' (DTI, 1985: 3).

16. Self-regulatory agencies had also to demonstrate a measure of independence from members.

17. Gower also pointed in the Green Paper to the practical problems of assigning responsibility to the 'plethora' of accountancy bodies.

18. 'We told Professor Gower that at least twice' (Hardcastle, ICAEW President, quoted in *Accountancy*, March 1984: 6). There is a certain irony here. In an interview with the authors it was clear that *before* starting his Report Gower conceded he was unaware just how much the accountancy 'profession' was involved in the provision of investment advice! There is a possibility that the

Institute itself was not fully aware of the extent to which its members were involved in the provision of financial services. The Memorandum from the ICAEW to the DTI in response to the 1985 DTI White Paper (ICAEW, TR 577, 1985) stated:

> We are conducting a survey which will give us a clearer indication of the extent to which our practising firms are involved in investment business as defined.

REFERENCES

Abbott, A., 1988. *The System of Professions: An Essay on the Division of Expert Labor*, Chicago: Chicago University Press
*Accountancy*, various issues
*Accountant's Magazine*, various issues
Accounting Standards Committee, 1975. *The Corporate Report*, London: ASC
Armstrong, P., 1987. 'The Rise of Accounting Controls in British Capitalist Enterprises', *Accounting, Organizations and Society* 12(5): 415–36
Blanquet, F., 1979. 'Proposed Eighth Directive concerning the approval of persons responsible for carrying out statutory audits of the annual financial statements of Limited Liability Companies', translated, *Journal UEC*: 302–26
Bourn, M. and Ezzamel, M., 1987. 'Budgetary Revolution in the National Health Service (NHS) and Universities in the UK', *Financial Accountability and Management* 3(4): 29–46
Burchell, S., Clubb, C. and Hopwood, A.G., 1985. 'Accounting in its Social Context: Towards a History of Value Added in the UK', *Accounting, Organizations and Society* 10(4): 381–414
Burchell, S., Clubb, C., Hopwood, A.G, Hughes, J. and Nahapiet, J., 1980. 'The Roles of Accounting in Organizations and Society', *Accounting, Organizations and Society* 5(1): 1–25
CCAB submission to DTI, 1979. Reported in *Accountancy*, 'Accountants say Eighth Directive on qualifications goes too far', February: 4–5
Channon, P., 1987. 'Why is there a DTI?', *Journal of the Royal Society of Arts, Proceedings*: 819–30
Clark, M., 1986. *Regulating the City: Competition, Scandal and Reform*, Buckingham: Open University Press
Cohen, M., 1978. *Commission on Auditors' Responsibilities, Report, Conclusions and Recommendations*, New York: AICPA
Consultative Committee of Accountancy Bodies (CCAB), 1984. *Response to the Gower Report*, TR 543, London: ICAEW
Cooper, D.J., Puxty, T., Lowe, T., Robson, K. and Willmott, H., forthcoming. '(In)stalling European standards in the UK: The Case of the Eighth Directive on the Regulation of Auditors'
(Council of) European Communities, 1984. Eighth Council Directive based on Article 54(3)(g), *Official Journal of the European Communities* L126/20, 12 May
Davison, I.H., 1987. 'The Twilight of the Profession?', paper presented to the Conservative Accountants Group, published, London: Arthur Andersen
Department of Trade and Industry (DTI), 1985. *Financial Services in the United Kingdom. A New Framework for Investor Protection*, Cmnd 9432, London: HMSO

(Companies Division), 1987a. Letter (unsigned) sent to Accountancy Bodies: Regulation of Auditors: Implementation of the Eighth Directive, May, London: DTI

(Companies Division), 1987b. Letter (unsigned) sent to Accountancy Bodies: Regulation of Auditors: Implementation of the Eighth Directive, July, London: DTI

1987c. *Regulation of Auditors: Implementation of the EC Eighth Company Law Directive. A Consultative Document*, London: DTI

Goode, W.E., 1957. 'Community within a community: the professions', *American Sociological Review* 22(1): 194–200

Gower, L.C.B., 1982. *Review of Investor Protection: A Discussion Document*, London: HMSO

1984. *Review of Investor Protection Report Part I*, Cmnd 9125, London: HMSO

Greenwood, E., 1957. 'Attributes of a Profession', *Social Work* 2(1): 44–55

Greenwood, R., Hinings, C.R., and Brown, J., 1990. 'The P² Form of Strategic Management', *Academy of Management Review* 33: 725–55

Heelas, P. and Morris, P., 1992. *The Values of the Enterprise Culture: The Moral Debate*, London: Routledge

Hindess, B., 1990. *Reactions to the Right*, London: Routledge

Hopper, T., Cooper, D., Lowe, T., Capps, T. and Mouritsen, J., 1986. 'Management Control and Worker Resistance in the National Coal Board', in D. Knights and H. Willmott (eds.). *Managing the Labour Process*, Aldershot: Gower: 109–41

Hopwood, A., Page, M. and Turley, S., 1990. *Understanding a Changing Environment*, London: Prentice-Hall/ICAEW

Institute of Chartered Accountants in England and Wales (ICAEW), 1985. *Response to Financial Services in the United Kingdom*, TR 577, London: ICAEW

1986. 'Self Regulation and the Quality of Professional Service: A Proposed Framework', *Accountancy*, August: 141

1987a. *Regulation of Auditors: Implementation of the EC Eighth Company Law Directive: Response of the ICAEW*, February, London: ICAEW

1987b. *Authorization of Investment Business*, London: ICAEW

Johnson, T.J., 1972. *Professions and Power*, London: Macmillan

1977. 'The Professions in the Class Structure', in R. Scase (ed.), *Industrial Society: Class, Cleavage and Control*, London: George Allen & Unwin

Jones, E., 1981. *Accountancy and the British Economy 1840–1980*, London: Batsford

Keat, R. and Abercrombie, N., 1990. *Enterprise Culture*, London: Routledge

Kitchen. J. and Parker, R.H., 1981. *Accounting & Education: Six English Pioneers*, London: ICAEW

McSweeney, B. and Sherer, M., 1990. 'Value for Money Auditing: Some Observations on its Origins and Theory', in D.J. Cooper and T.M. Hopper (eds.), *Critical Accounts*, London: Macmillan

Macdonald, K.M., 1984. 'Professional Formation: the Case of Scottish Accountants', *The British Journal of Sociology* 35(2): 174–89

Miller, P., 1990. 'On the Interrelations Between Accounting and the State', *Accounting, Organizations and Society* 15(4): 315–38

National Audit Office, 1986. *The Financial Management Initiative*, London: HMSO

Parkin, F., 1979. *Marxism and Class Theory*, London: Tavistock

Pilcher, J.A., 1974. 'An Economic Analysis of Accounting Power', in R.R. Sterling (ed.), *Institutional Issues in Public Accounting*, Houston, TX: Scholars Book Co.

Puxty, A.G., Willmott, H.C., Cooper, D.J. and Lowe, E.A., 1987. 'Modes of Accounting Regulation in Advanced Capitalism: Locating Accountancy in Four Countries', *Accounting, Organizations and Society* 12(3): 273–91

Radcliffe, V., 1989. *The UK Accountancy Profession and the Financial Services Act 1986*, unpublished MSc. ms., UMIST

Radcliffe, V., Cooper, D.J. and Robson, K., forthcoming. 'The Management of Professional Enterprises and Regulatory Change', *Accounting, Organizations and Society*

Robson, K., 1993. 'Accounting Policy Making and "Interests": Accounting for Research and Development', *Critical Perspectives on Accounting* 4(1): 1–27

Rutteman, P., 1987. 'De wijze waarop in het verenigd koninkrijk de Ae rightlijn in de wetgeving wordt ingevoerd', *VERA najaarsconferentie*, November

Sikka, P., Puxty, T., Willmott, H. and Cooper, C., 1992. *Eliminating the Expectations Gap?*, London: ACCA

Stacey, N., 1954. *English Accountancy, A Study in Social and Economic History 1800–1954*, London: Gee

Tinker, T., 1984. 'Theories of the State and the State of Accounting', *Journal of Accounting and Public Policy* 3(1): 55–74

1985. *Paper Prophets*, New York: Praeger

Tricker, R.I., 1983. *Governing the Institute*, London: ICAEW

US Senate Report of the Sub-committee on Reports, 1978. 'Accounting and Management of the Committee on Governmental Affairs, Improving the Accountability of Publicly Owned Corporations and their Auditors', *Journal of Accounting* 145, January: 88–96

Watts, R.L. and Zimmerman, J., 1986. *Positive Accounting*, Englewood Cliffs, NJ: Prentice-Hall

Whitley, R., 1986. 'The Transformation of Business Finance into Financial Economics', *Accounting, Organizations and Society* 11(1): 171–92

Wilensky, H.J., 1964. 'The Professionalization of Everyone', *American Journal of Sociology* 70(2): 138–58

Willmott, H.C., Cooper, D.J. and Puxty, T., 1993. 'Maintaining Self Regulation: Making "Interests" Coincide in Discourses on the Governance of the ICAEW', *Accounting, Auditing and Accountability Journal* 6(4): 68–93

Willmott, H.C., Puxty, A.G., Robson, K., Cooper, D.J. and Lowe, E.A., 1992. 'Regulation of Accountancy and Accountants: A Comparative Analysis of Accounting for Research and Development', *Accounting, Auditing and Accountability Journal* 5(2): 32–56

Worsley, F.E., 1985. *Governing the Institute*, London: ICAEW

# 12 The audit society

*Michael Power*

There is little doubt that the word 'audit' is being used, in the UK at least, with growing frequency. In addition to financial audits we now hear of environmental audits, value for money audits, management audits, quality audits, forensic audits, data audits, intellectual property audits, medical audits and many others besides. The words on this page have themselves come to be viewed as a 'product' that can be subjected to academic research audit. But does the proliferating usage of a single word signify any systematic relationship between the diverse contexts within which it is invoked? Indeed, can it be argued that audit is becoming a constitutive principle of social organization to such an extent that we can talk of an 'audit society'?

If the linkages between the practices listed above are more than superficial, then some consistency should be evident between them over and above the sharing of a common terminology. For it could be argued that 'audit' practices are in fact diverse, that they instantiate very different bodies of knowledge, that they are only imperfectly linked by the concept of audit and that the descriptive utility of the concept itself is even doubted by practitioners.[1] And yet the durability of the word is not so easily dismissed. Despite the fact that many practices can be differentiated and defined according to whether they are, for example, 'assessment', 'review' or 'verification' activities, the concept of audit has resisted attempts to displace it in favour of technically less ambiguous labels. Why is this?

The answer to this question has much to do with the distinctive managerial rationality which audit has come to represent. As a basis for reconfiguring social and organizational relations, almost regardless of any demonstrable technical efficacy, audit functions as a norm or 'rationality of government' in Rose and Miller's (1992) sense. Accordingly, the significance of audit is not anchored in a 'definition' of its role. Indeed, it matters less what different audit practices 'really' are in some operational sense than how the idea of audit is appropriated and mobilized. Audit is a particular manner of *(re)presenting* administrative problems and their solutions, one that is becoming universal.

299

As these problems have grown in scale and complexity, audit sustains traditional hopes of control by a subtle translation: impossibly costly technologies of inspection are displaced by something more distant which acts upon local sub-systems of control. Audit has thereby become the 'control of control' and the constitutive principle of the audit society exemplifies certain postmodern motifs of the 'loss of reference'. In this sense audit must be differentiated from more traditional logics of managerial control. In place of a proximity and directness of control, such as in supervisory practices of real time inspection, audits function at a temporal and often spatial distance from the organizational processes to which they are applied.

The 'audit explosion', at least in the UK, has its conditions of emergence in transformations in the organization of state activity. These transformations cannot be understood merely at the level of a quantitative intensification of 'audit practices'. The growth of audit as a distinctive administrative rationality also embodies three interrelated 'problematics' of control: the invisibility of audit; the politics of 'regulatory failure'; the construction of auditees. First, despite the rhetorics of transparency which have accompanied the growth of audit, the audit process itself remains publicly invisible. Second, audit practices are part of a politics of regulatory failure within which they constantly reproduce and re-intensify themselves. Third, audit actively constructs the contexts in which it operates. In this respect the audit society is characterized by active processes of making environments auditable, structuring them to conform to the need to be monitored rather than to what may be regarded as their own primary logic. The relations between these modalities of the audit society are undoubtedly complex, but they are linked by a pervasive rhetoric of accountability which gives to audit its almost unassailable moral density. It is this that we must address at the outset.

### Auditing and the rhetoric of accountability

The genealogy of the word 'audit', which is derived from the Latin 'audire' to hear, seems to indicate a disjunction.[2] Early characterizations of the audit process consisted in the accountable party defending his actions in person to a relevant audience. The auditee was often 'visible' throughout this process of defence but it is the aural, rather than the perceptual, intimacy which informs characterizations of the practice, no doubt related to specifically judicial conceptions of the 'hearing'. Today this imagery of aural intimacy has been displaced as modern audit practice has largely disengaged itself from its quasi-judicial origins.[3] In the work of Mautz and Sharaf (1961) audit emerges as a protoscientific observational practice and, according to Flint (1988), arises from relations of accountability between two parties and from a certain complexity or distance in this relation such that one cannot easily and directly verify the relevant activities of the other. While law has undoubtedly influenced the demand for financial audits, the knowledge base of audit and the claims to expertise of its practitioners are increasingly shaped outside the law.

Traditional accounts of the institutional preconditions of audit are usually expressed in terms of an emergent demand to generate assurances that accountability has been discharged between parties. In certain, very recent, economic literatures it is argued that it will be rational for the auditee to contract voluntarily to undergo an independent audit in order to make good offices visible. On this view audits are costly monitoring technologies which arise 'naturally' under conditions where 'agents' expose 'principals' to 'moral hazards', because they may act against the principal's interests, and 'information asymmetries', because they know more than the principals. Audit is therefore a risk reduction technology which inhibits the 'deviant' actions of agents. According to Perrow (1990: 123), this 'agency' view implies that 'Four people performing a cooperative task, say loading trucks, find that the risk of any one of them slacking is such that they hire a fifth to monitor their work'.

This widely accepted characterization of the source of demand for audit expresses and reproduces a particular model of social relations. Indeed, an appeal to the categories of 'principal' and 'agent' makes possible the very problems of accountability which demand to be solved by audit. In other words, far from being a natural response to problems of accountability, audit only makes sense within particular *representations* of social arrangements, representations which are reinforced by the imperatives of audit. Thus financial audit has its origins in specific ways of problematizing the relationship between management and providers of finance,[4] ways which are reflected and reinforced by economic theories of the corporation (Jensen and Meckling, 1976). Indeed, particular economic rationales of audit represent a social world in which action can no longer be coordinated by trust alone.

Accordingly, auditing can be regarded as a technology of mistrust (Armstrong, 1991) in which independent 'outsiders' must be summoned to restore that trust. Expert auditing invests heavily in the image of restoring credibility, a strategy designed to reproduce trust in its efficacy and thereby sustain demand. Of course the audit society is one which must disguise this 'regress of mistrust', a regress which requires that the performances of auditors are themselves subjected to audit but which cannot in practical terms be infinite and must therefore terminate in further acts of trust. The audit society is therefore one that trusts auditors before operatives (Armstrong, 1991) and values the symbolic capital of their perceived independence as much as any technical expertise that they may possess.

The potential for Perrow's fifth monitor to become a dominant element of the accountability structure is one of the key conditions of possibility of the audit society. For here the fifth monitor is valued to such an extent that the work of the four auditees is to be transformed in order to make it conform to ideals of auditability. Thus, in contrast to the image of audit as a *derived* activity, audit increasingly influences the institutional context within which it is demanded. Indeed, at its most extreme, audit creates and sustains the very structures of accountability from which its demand is supposed to flow (Power, 1991). 'Principals' and 'agents' become fully visible only via the audit process.

Traditional representations of financial accountability suggest that audit is a control over the 'quality' of the account given by the auditee and that this makes the auditee visible by means of periodic *ex post* inspection of books and records by an independent party. Yet financial auditors have had a decisive influence on the standards of performance to which the auditee is subjected. Indeed, to the extent that standards of financial performance make accountability visible in highly specific ways, then auditors are far from being neutral relays in an exogenously given accountability system. Not only do they construct and reproduce the values of that system but they also export them to new arenas. An important dimension of the audit explosion is the diffusion and generalization of the financial accountability model, particularly in the public sector where the 'new public management' (Hood, 1991) embodies new receptivities to private sector images of management and reframes public accountability in relation to concepts of goal definition, efficient resource allocation, financial performance and competition.

This realignment of public management styles and objectives is informed by two forces which tend to pull in opposite directions. On the one hand, centrifugal pressures for the decentralization and devolution of welfare services represent an 'enterprization' of state functions. On the other hand, centripetal pressures to retain control over newly autonomized services inform a new governmental rationality in which intervention can be accomplished by indirect means. Audit is a decisive political technology (Rose and Miller, 1992) in which these mutually constitutive forces are reconciled and ensures that the displacement of organizational hierarchies by market structures is never complete; audit is the shadow of hierarchy which saves the appearance of central control.

As a political technology audit represents a distinctive modality of government, one that can be distinguished from more direct methods of control, such as inspection. Audits attempt to act indirectly upon systems of control rather than directly upon first-order activities. Audits therefore have less to do with control in a traditional sense and more to do with the allocation of responsibility (Brunsson, 1990). Thus, audits are 'responsibilizing' technologies (Miller, 1992) in which being subjected to independent audit, being represented as an auditee, comes to be more significant than the operational detail of the *particular* audit.

The audit society expresses an emergent organizational logic in which 'auditability' is an uncontestable value. Audit is also expressive of a particular managerial rationality which does not simply value a form of 'first-order' hierarchical control which can be assessed for its instrumental efficacy. Rather, certain 'rituals of inspection' (Meyer and Rowan, 1977) have much to do with the establishment and renewal of accountability relations and with the affirmation of particular patterns of responsibility. Hence, the audit society is not simply the surveillance society and auditing is not a form of disciplinary 'superpanopticon' (Poster, 1990: 85–98). Rather, the tendency of the audit society is to shift monitoring practices from direct inspection towards the control of control. This is a move which is internally paradoxical because it expresses a recognition of both the economic and epistemic impossibility of direct control at the same time as it reaffirms the appearance of control.

The audit society is not simply a 'control' society in a purely functional sense. Indeed, the growth of audit practices represents a radical departure from a certain industrial preoccupation with inspection and quality control. Financial audit emerged as a regulatory by-product of financial capitalism (Montagna, 1986) and was relatively remote from managerial preoccupations with product quality. Indeed, the rise of the financial audit model as a mobile technology can be attributed to its lack of organizational specificity as compared with other more direct control technologies. 'Philosophies' of audit have invested the practice with abstract principles which are portable across diverse organizational contexts. Furthermore, the role and function of financial audits have been subject to greater public scrutiny than have operational technologies of control because of their role in regulatory programmes. By appearing to link the internal workings of organizations to macroeconomic goals, such as the smooth functioning of capital markets, audit has secured a role in the economic system almost independently of its operational potential.

The financial audit model has been an enduring conceptual resource for the audit explosion precisely because of, rather than despite, its operational ambiguity and variability. Its very abstraction from organizational specifics has allowed it to become central to a particular liberal 'political rationality' (Rose and Miller, 1992). In the context of changes in public management, audit represents the means by which newly autonomized service providers are linked to newly constructed consuming publics. In this way the concept of audit has begun to assume the status of a 'cultural logic' which is greater than the sum of practices which it unites; audit has become more than its official statutory and economic meanings. It has moved to the very centre of administrative discourses as the practical embodiment and enforcement of the values of accountability and transparency of process. Audit has become an all-purpose enabling technology which makes diverse regulatory programmes possible. The force of its logic is such that to be against audit appears to be to support non-accountability.

To summarize: core values of organizational transparency, quality and accountability give the audit society its distinctive form. Audit has become an important technology of government by virtue of a special versatility in which submission to audit establishes legitimacy regardless of the operational substance of audit. Not only is audit implicated in the 'enterprization' of service provision by the State, it also figures prominently in the 'politicization' of the private sector. In other words, audit is both an instrument by which newly created markets are linked to regulatory centres and also the basis by which a newly problematized corporate governance can be reprogrammed. This mobility and diversity of application is the great appeal of audit; it can be invoked by markets and hierarchies, entrepreneurs and regulators, citizens and states.

### Auditing and the new obscurity

Audit can be represented as a substitute for democracy. This may seem strange, especially given that audit practices are publicly represented within extensive rhetorics of accountability and transparency. And yet auditing practice denies the very ideals which mobilize it. This paradox lies at the centre of the audit society and arises because of a principle which is constitutive of the audit society: *how* an audit is done is less important than *that* it is done. In other words, considerable symbolic and financial capital is invested in the activity of audit without a corresponding publicity of process and results. As a consequence, the rhetorics of communication and disclosure through which audits are traditionally promoted are hollow.[5]

The audit society is characterized by audits without publicity and by processes which restore the appearance of external control. In this way audit is both 'politicized', as an organ of regulatory processes which extend their reach into new organizational settings, and 'depoliticized' as an expert practice which is shrouded from the mythical target publics it is intended to serve. Another way of putting this is to suggest that auditing is a black box on the shiny surface of which the aspirations of regulatory programmes are reflected and made possible. From this point of view, it is actually undesirable to look beneath the surface of audit practice into the box. For example, the Bingham Report (HC 198, 1992) on the collapse of BCCI notably did not concern itself with the audit *process*, preferring instead to deal with the nature of the requirement for auditors to report directly to bank supervisors. This is not simply because process is a matter for the experts themselves. Rather, audit has become a condition of possibility for banking supervisory practices which can no longer function on the basis of trust. It is a practice whose *general* effectiveness must always be presupposed.

Much has been written in the US and the UK about the audit 'expectations gap'. This gap is usually articulated as a difference between how auditors are perceived (responsible for the detection of fraud) and how auditors see themselves (primarily responsible for forming a professional opinion on the financial statements). This 'problem' has been addressed in terms of the need to 'educate' user publics on the one hand and the need to change the audit product on the other. But while such expectations gaps are a problem when viewed in these terms, there is little appreciation that such gaps are also political resources which preserve a discretionary space for professional action. If the public expects that an audit provides a certain kind of assurance, whereas in fact it provides much less, then such an expectations gap can be managed as a resource for both parties as follows: auditors can help themselves to the high fees that correspond to high expectations and regulatory publics can help themselves to the appearance of high levels of assurance necessary to legitimate regulatory programmes. In short, the audit society routinely *requires* expectation gaps about the nature of audit, an imperative which is disturbed by crises where the gap becomes politically visible.

Another instance of the invisibility and ambiguity of audit is evident in the case of UK 'environmental audits'. The corporate sector has lobbied both for voluntary, rather than statutorily imposed, audits and for non-disclosure of results on the grounds of confidentiality. Both moves serve to retain environmental audit firmly within the orbit of the definition proposed by the International Chamber of Commerce (ICC): it is to be regarded primarily as a 'management tool' (ICC, 1991). In this way, companies obtain the perceived marketing advantages of being seen to conduct environmental audits, yet without having to disclose either the results of these audits or any remedial action which they may require. While it seems unlikely that non-disclosure of audit results can be sustained against extensive European legislation, the general point of this example remains valid: the public perception *that* an activity is performed, while remaining in substance invisible, is an important strategy of legitimacy in the audit society.

In terms of democratic aspirations, audits are in fact a dead end of accountability, a process which terminates in the necessity of trusting experts rather than providing a basis for rational public deliberation (Day and Klein, 1987). While the public discourse of audit is conducted in the name of a new visibility of the inner workings of organizations, audit is itself an increasingly private and invisible 'expert' activity, an expertise which has historically been sponsored by State regulatory initiatives which require audit as the basis for their enforcement. The audit society idealizes 'independent validation' without public transparency. That internal control systems of auditees have been subject to expert scrutiny is valued, without a corresponding public transparency of those systems themselves.

The democratic content of the accountability concept is also articulated in terms of an ideal of transparency which empowers a 'relevant' public to exercise the control to which they are institutionally entitled, be they shareholders or a more generally conceived public. Audit is often expressed in terms of serving and empowering popular governance (APB 1992; Cadbury Committee, 1992). For example, corporate financial audits are formally intended to serve the goal of shareholder control by linking the operations of corporate boardrooms to the decision-making calculus of distant financiers. In this way, audit expresses the promise of external visibility of internal processes and functions as a technology of government which assures regulatory bodies about the internal control culture of diverse organizations.

However, this promise of visibility is ambiguous. The political technology of audit has expanded with only limited public exposure of the auditee; and the audit society is an increasingly closed society, albeit one whose declared operative principle is that of openness. Accordingly, communication is terminated rather than enabled by the audit process. Indeed the factual density of audit practices which have become tightly interwoven in regulatory programmes is indicative more of the 'new obscurity' (Habermas, 1992) than the 'transparent society' (Vattimo, 1992).

### Auditing and the politics of regulatory failure

The audit society is characterized by institutionalized patterns of trust and mistrust. The type of individual or entity subject to audit – i.e. not trusted – is as important as the nature of audit. In the audit society, the set of auditees is increasing and structures of organizational time and the periodicity of audits express a new intensity for existing auditees. However, the production of trust from mistrust via auditing is not automatically effective. Indeed, the production of trust is constantly threatened and constantly exposed by the continuing visibility of 'healthy' companies which fail, the accumulation of ecological risks, the decline of educational standards, the wastage of public revenues and so on. Ideals of accountability, transparency and control which are undermined must continually re-affirm themselves in a politics of failure which allocates blame and reconstitutes 'failed' practices.

The audit society is the *anxious* society in which perceived regulatory failure must be continually overcome and the mission of regulation re-affirmed. In the context of this permanent dialectic, audit is a crucial political technology. The 'fact of audit' reduces anxiety or, more positively, produces comfort (Pentland, 1993). And yet, paradoxically, the audit society is also one in which visible failure of audit is the norm and in which there are extensive investments in audit activity irrespective of their demonstrated substantive effectiveness.

It could be said that the 'audit explosion' has occurred at the threshold between the traditional structures of industrial society and an emerging 'risk society' (Beck, 1992b). From this point of view the audit society is necessarily a transitional form in which audit functions to reconcile contradictory forces: it is both a radical continuation of control philosophies and also an expression of their failure. For example, environmental audit practices have evolved as a 'remanagerialization' of risks which constantly threaten to escape their representations within systems of insurance. Audit, far from being simply a 'management tool', is a symptom of the limitation of those tools to engender control by other means, such as through solidarity, social responsibility and so on.

The audit society is one in which managerial practices can be re-represented in such a way as to reconcile the production of wealth (goods) with the production of risk (bads) (Beck, 1992a, 1992b), whether financial, environmental or otherwise. In this sense, the practice of audit embodies a certain cultural hope for control in the face of increasing evidence of its absence. While perceptions of audit 'failure' can be represented as an official crisis of political control, this should not be taken to mean that the success and failure of audit can be determined unequivocally. Audit success or failure is never a public fact but is rather an object of persistent dispute. The audit society is characterized by a pervasive discourse of regulatory failure in which there is a continual re-intensification of its available instruments of control. Accordingly, the audit society is one in which audit cannot be permitted to fail systemically.

The regulatory politics of the audit society attempts to control the definition of success and failure of the audit function. In particular, strategies of 'particularization' allow the failure 'event' to be reconciled to a re-intensification of the audit function itself. This is reflected in the litigation process where questions of negligence relate to the actions of particular auditors. A defence of practice is normally conducted in terms of adherence to generally accepted practice. In this institutional setting, the investigation of auditor failure is already highly particularized and only in very exceptional cases takes issue with the system of auditing practice in general. Additionally, criteria of success are withdrawn from public discourse and become a matter for expert determination. Such strategies attempt to immunize the system of audit knowledge from radical doubt (Power, 1993). The audit society offers the 'promise of security' (Beck, 1992b: 20) via the remanagerialization of risk and the construction of responsible auditees. Accordingly, any perceived technical failure of audit is overshadowed by its durability as a 'political rationality' and as a norm which demands that 'auditee' organizations must be represented in terms which make the audit process possible. It is to this role of audit as a technology of representation that we now turn.

### Auditing and the construction of the auditable object

Audit is to a large extent a question of 'making organizations auditable', a process which requires the active construction of forms of receptivity to audit. Far from being exogenous or environmental features of audit practice, modes of accountability and standards of performance are emergent features of audit arrangements. While audit may initially be mobilized by programmatic claims for 'improved' accountability, it reconstructs these claims in specific ways, effectively creating specific patterns of visibility and performativity (Power, 1991; ch. 10 in this volume).

The traditional 'technical' conception of the audit process is that it depends for its efficacy upon the collection of evidence of the appropriate quality to support conclusions as to the 'performance' of the auditee. On this view, audit can be modelled as a quasi-scientific practice and derives its rationality from a certain instrumental neutrality in its mode of operation. This official story also requires that standards can be set for the performance of the auditee. Audit then assumes the simple character of verifying or assessing performance *qua* compliance with such standards. In the case of financial audits, these standards are expressed by the rules of financial accounting. At the centre of this conception of audit is the regulatory ideal of compliance with standards, the visibility of which is a cornerstone of governmental legitimacy. Officially, audit is neutral with regard to such standards. However, this disguises the fact that it is active in constructing them within a 'politics of best practice' in which the audit functions as much to impose definitions of quality on the local auditee environment as to monitor it.

Against the traditional image of the audit process it is necessary to consider auditing as a system of knowledge in its own right to which the audit society gives a particular priority. Auditing 'represents' the auditee and thereby creates the condition of its own functioning. It does not 'passively' observe the auditee but constructs and inscribes it with the material basis upon which audit can operate. In many instances, these inscriptions are required by legislation, e.g. company law requirements for financial reporting and the maintenance of proper books and records, or by other arrangements such as the pronouncements of the British Standards Institute (BSI).

Recent transformations in the public sector (Hood, 1991; ch. 10 in this volume) are also indicative of the manner in which the audit society functions. Public sector audit practices, undertaken by the UK National Audit Office and the Audit Commission, enable State bodies to observe themselves in the service of initiatives in public financial management and policy accountability. However, 'value for money' (VFM) audit, which lies at the heart of these changes, is much more than a monitoring 'technique' and functions as the normative basis for a transformation of administration itself (McSweeney, 1988). Procedural ideals of performance around notions of economy, efficiency and effectiveness express a new basis for the organization of the efficient society and a new knowledge system for these changes. In many service sectors the notion of effectiveness is not easily reducible to measurable variables (Hopwood, 1984; McSweeney, 1988). Under such conditions of uncertainty VFM necessarily prioritizes that which can be measured and audited – efficiency and economy – over that which is more ambiguous and local – effectiveness. This makes possible a new organization of public life around the audit process.

Another example is apparent in the recent academic audit initiatives in the UK. 'Performance' is difficult to assess in contexts which are traditionally unaccustomed to thinking in such terms and where different, highly localized but less easily quantifiable standards of 'quality' control have been evident. Audit demands something standardizable to audit. Despite a rhetoric of attentiveness to quality, a 'reductionism' is visible in education where there is widespread use of standardized student course questionnaires as a basis for assessment. In the audit society everyone knows about the crudity of such measures, but the imperative of auditability overrides these doubts and qualifications, such is its irresistible logic. Thus, not only do audits create and reinforce the conditions for their own functioning, but they seek to do so by creating a new bureaucratic 'surface' or social reality which is highly standardized and which represents the auditee for the purpose of the audit.

The construction of auditability is also evident in the BSI initiatives on quality generally and on environmental management systems in particular (BS 5750 and BS 7750 respectively). Both standards emphasize the development of systems which enable quality and environmental audits. Such systems are also essential to the accreditation process for companies who wish to gain a marketing advantage from being seen to comply with the standards. More generally, the establishment of a 'system' whose operations can be verified is more important than the operations themselves. This may seem to be a strange claim but it follows from the capacity of the norm of auditability to eclipse others. For example, BS 7750 articulates the structure of an environmental management system but not the standards of performance themselves (which are always controversial). At first glance this can be understood quite innocently as an efficient division of labour; standards will be addressed in other documents. But the high profile of BS 7750 is such that the significance of these standards is displaced by the imperative of an auditable system. When audit becomes the dominant medium of administration, the 'performance' of the auditee is reduced to the possibility of being audited. In a bizarre fashion, subjection to audit tends to become the sole basis of administrative legitimacy.

An important principle which underlies these examples is that audit aspires to a form of second-order control, a control of control. This idea is given paradigmatically by the concept of the 'systems audit', whereby it is the auditee's own system for self-monitoring that is subject to inspection, rather than the real time practices of the auditee. In this way, the existence of a system is more significant for audit purposes than what the system is; audit is simply a formal 'loop' by which the system observes itself. While there is a sense in which this immunizes the auditee from the audit process, the necessity of having an 'auditable system' nevertheless impacts upon real time practices. Auditable systems require subjects to represent themselves primarily as auditees.

Ironically, financial auditors promote the 'systems audit' as one of the higher stages in the 'evolution' of the practice. But this 'progressivist' interpretation also corresponds to the decline of informed direct inspection. Economic and epistemic arguments have been used to rationalize a shift in audit philosophy away from direct contact with auditee practices, and the idea of the 'systems' audit reconciles cost efficiency with required 'levels of assurance'. The operations of the system in real time compensate for the increasingly *ex post* nature of audit because they leave 'residues' for the purpose of making audits possible. It is not so much that direct inspection has become literally impossible in the audit society, but that it no longer corresponds to the standardized logic of audit practice. Organizational specificities are mediated by systems to create an auditable product and in this way a certain kind of failure, the loss of direct control, can be represented as 'progress'. In this way, doubts about the very possibility of audit are accompanied by active transformations of the auditee domain in order to make it 'auditable'.

The concept of 'auditability' points to the increasingly self-referential nature of the 'system of auditing knowledge' which, in building up its own organizational representations, is a simulacrum (Francis, 1994) which nevertheless reinforces its normative exclusivity. Ironically, this is apparent in the responses to the regulatory arrangements for financial auditors in the UK. Fearnley and Page (1993) observe that audit practitioners subjected to audit needed to standardize their audit approach in order to demonstrate technical competence. By doing so they tended to 'equate better files with better audits'. This is a consequence of the norm of auditability where even the 'audit of audit' requires that it be standardized. While audit decouples itself from underlying organizational processes, the abstract representations which it promotes nevertheless force the auditee to become isomorphic with the audit process.

There is nothing conspiratorial about this. Audit, as the 'self observation of the economic system' (Luhmann, 1989) is a system in its own right. It functions by virtue of an 'auditing logic' which demands auditable auditees as the condition of possibility of its own functioning. The auditing system of knowledge 'productively misunderstands' (Teubner, 1992) the auditee in order to make it auditable. In turn, auditees are potentially alien disturbances to this system which reacts by rendering them familiar and auditable. But, if auditing is an 'autopoietic' practice in this sense, it is itself the disturbing environment for auditees who may adapt their practices in the name of ideals of verifiability, calculability and responsible control (Miller and O'Leary, 1987).

The system of audit knowledge consists primarily in a network of dense procedure, and the compliance checklist is paradigmatic of its operations. This image of audit knowledge would be disputed by financial audit practitioners for whom checklists impose too much structure on the audit process and thereby inhibit professional judgement. However, the checklist remains a norm even if it is not formally encoded in audit procedure. The ideal checklist inscribes 'best practice' and establishes the completeness and visibility of audit work. In addition, by insulating the particular practitioner from the knowledge foundation of the checklist it provides him or her with a defence against critics. Over time, audit practice has attempted to establish linkages between this procedural knowledge base and 'higher', abstract (Abbott, 1988) bodies of knowledge. However, the latter have been invoked as much to confer a certain scientific credibility upon the practice as to provide instrumental guidance. Hopes were expressed that statistical sampling could place auditing on a scientific footing (Power, 1992), and the importance of sampling technologies to the scientific image of audit cannot be underestimated. Indeed, the symbolic importance of statistical sampling is relatively unaffected by its actual (mis)applications. As a way of talking,

writing and justifying, sampling makes possible certain rational representations of the audit process, and of the auditee.

More recently, these representations have taken 'risk' as their organizing
concept, and have promoted the image of audit practice in terms of risk
reduction as well as quality enhancement (Power, 1994). Audit can be
described in Beck's (1992b: 45) terms as an instrument of definitional risk
management, effectively subsuming those risks which are open to social
definition and construction within a new managerialism with its own
esoteric risk knowledges. In this sense, the 'new obscurity' of the audit
society represents a 'loss of social thinking', and the allocation of problems
to a particular class of experts who may profit from its own abuses (Beck,
1992b: 56):

demands, and thus markets, of a completely new type can be created by varying the
definition of risk, especially the demand for the avoidance of risk ... in risk
production, developed capitalism has absorbed, generalised and normalised.

The explosive growth in the UK of environmental consultants offering
auditing services is an example of 'risk normalization' in Beck's sense and is
closely linked to professionalization processes in an emergent market for
environmental advice. More generally, audits are mechanisms by which
risk is represented for managerial purposes. Auditees are constructed with
particular classes of risk, and their likely management in the form of
'improved systems', in view. As Ewald has put it (1991: 199):

Nothing is a risk in itself: there is no risk in reality. But on the other hand, anything
*can* be a risk; it all depends on how one analyses the danger, considers the event
[emphasis in original].

Risks are therefore knowledge dependent and the audit society can be
characterized by its systems for the social 'recognition' of risks. The
recognition capabilities of audit are always relative to an overriding
managerial logic of auditability. Thus, just as auditing consists of specific
technologies for representing the auditee as an auditable object, it necessarily fails to recognize precisely those risks which escape the norm of
auditability. This is suggested by Beck's (1992b: 22) claims that the routine
calculation of risk collapses in the face of a certain non-corroboration of
risks which exist at the limits of any formal verifiability.[6] In other words,
the profound irony of the audit society is that where auditing may be most
desirable, it is least possible.

### Conclusion

Audit is as much a distinctive principle of social and economic organization
as it is a technical practice. But in these interrelated respects it has escaped

serious sociological attention. In those countries where auditing is a relatively unimportant practice – one might characterize them as 'high trust' cultures – this neglect is unsurprising. Elsewhere, a different explanation is required. This neglect can be partly attributed to the dominance of existing audit research by functional commitments within the framework of cognitive psychology. Preoccupations with 'improving' the judgements of individual, atomistically conceived auditors prohibits enquiry into the mobilization of audit in new settings and its function as an institutional norm (Kirkham, 1992; Power, 1994).

Another reason for the intellectual neglect of audit as social practice is that, in the system of knowledge, academic status often mirrors that of the target professional culture itself (Abbott, 1988). Thus, if practitioners of financial audit suffer from public perceptions that they are boring and unimaginative, then research into audit is similarly condemned. Even within the community of academic accountants, audit research remains unfashionable. And yet, Foucault's work on practices of government (Burchell *et al.*, 1991) and the 'new institutionalism' in organizational analysis (Powell and DiMaggio, 1991) give a distinctive intellectual credibility to the examination of the routines of social and economic life, routines which enact significant normative commitments by virtue of a certain 'moral density' in the manner of their operation (DiMaggio and Powell, 1991).

In this chapter I have suggested that audit is an emerging principle of social organization which can be discerned in the UK. The idea of the 'audit society', which describes systematic potentials as much as identifiable practices, draws attention to the function of audit as a 'rational norm' which is greater than the apparently diverse technical practices which are conducted in its name. Many of these practices have their conditions of emergence in transformations in public sector management and newly prominent ideals of quality, governance and accountability. And yet paradoxically, while audit technologies have contributed to managerial discourses of 'performance', the performance of audit itself is far from being unambiguous and free from public dispute.

I have argued that the audit society can be theorized in relation to four primary themes: new rhetorics of accountability and control; new obscurities in the name of transparency; a politics of regulatory failure; and the construction of auditees. In an important sense all these themes are invisible within official discourses of the nature and role of audit. Audit is part of the new 'cosmetics of risks' (Beck, 1992b: 57) in which newly perceived difficulties and dangers can be ritually purified and reconciled to existing managerial and economic practice. It is conservative not in the sense of a conspiracy of vested interests, but in the sense of a knowledge system which filters and appropriates environmental disturbance under the norm of auditability. In the process of 'responsibilizing' subjects, structures of trust are displaced. But in the audit society a reduction in audit intensity, and the possibility of leaving groups and individuals to themselves, is literally unthinkable.

NOTES

An earlier version of this chapter was presented at the *History of Present* workshop, London School of Economics and Political Science, 4 November 1992. The author is grateful for the helpful comments of Andrew Barry, Nils Brunsson, Anthony Hopwood, John Law, Brendan McSweeney, John Meyer, Peter Miller, Christopher Napier and Nikolas Rose.

1. The varied practices which describe themselves as audit can be distinguished on the basis of their temporal relation to the auditee. Thus, 'impact assessments' are usually prior to the activities of the auditee whereas 'verification' and 'performance assessment' are usually *ex post*. Between these extremes, regimes of 'monitoring' are often coterminous with the actions of the auditee.

2. The *Concise Oxford Dictionary* (7th ed., 1982) provides a narrow definition of audit in terms of the 'official examination of accounts'. In addition those who 'attend class without intending to obtain credits' also engage in audit. (See Hoskin and Macve, ch. 3 in this volume, for an early conception of audit.)

3. A notable exception to this is the European Court of Auditors. The idea of such an auditing court is alien to UK and US traditions of audit.

4. Despite the fact that traditional histories of financial audit describe its emergence in terms of the separation of ownership and control, the demands of capital markets and the varied forms of regulating the enterprise (Chatfield, 1977; Edwards, 1989), its precise role has never been uncontested. Questions of auditor liability and shifting public expectations, usually in the light of perceived audit failure, have been more or less continuous pressures for modification and change.

5. For example, recent concerns in the UK with the wording of financial audit reports, the only aspect of audit work which is publicly visible as a truncated and coded report, have been conducted in the name of improving communication (APB, 1991). However, a close reading of these proposals suggests a different view; an attempt to limit the *de facto* expansion of audit responsibilities.

6. It is important to contrast Beck's realism (1992a, 1992b) about certain environmental dangers with Ewald's constructivism (1991), in which risk categories are relative to insurance technologies.

REFERENCES

Abbott, A., 1988. *The System of Professions: An Essay on the Expert Division of Labor*, Chicago: Chicago University Press

Armstrong, P., 1991. 'Contradiction and Social Dynamics in the Capitalist Agency Relationship', *Accounting, Organizations and Society* 16(1): 1–25

Auditing Practices Board (APB), 1991. *Proposals for an Expanded Audit Report*, October, London: APB

1992. *The Future Development of Auditing: A Paper to Promote Debate*, November, London: APB

Beck, U., 1992a. 'From Industrial Society to the Risk Society: Questions of survival, social structure and ecological enlightenment', *Theory, Culture & Society* 9: 97–123

1992b. *Risk Society*, London: Sage

Brunsson, N., 1990. 'Deciding for Responsibility and Legitimation: Alternative Interpretations of Organizational Decision Making', *Accounting, Organizations and Society* 15(1/2): 47–59

Burchell, G., Gordon, C. and Miller, P., 1991. *The Foucault Effect: Studies in Governmentality*, Hemel Hempstead: Harvester Wheatsheaf

Cadbury Committee, 1992. *The Financial Aspects of Corporate Governance*, London

Chatfield, M., 1977. *A History of Accounting Thought*, 2nd edn., Huntingdon, NY: Robert E. Krieger

Day, P. and Klein, R., 1987. *Accountabilities: Five Public Services*, London: Tavistock

DiMaggio, P.J. and Powell, W.W., 1991. 'Introduction', in W.W. Powell and P.J. DiMaggio (eds.), *The New Institutionalism in Organizational Analysis*, Chicago: Chicago University Press: 1–38

Edwards, J.R., 1989. *A History of Financial Accounting*, London: Routledge

Ewald, F., 1991. 'Insurance and Risk', in G. Burchell, C. Gordon and P. Miller, *The Foucault Effect: Studies in Governmentality*, Hemel Hempstead: Harvester Wheatsheaf: 197–210

Fearnley, S. and Page, M., 1993. 'Audit regulation – one year on', *Accountancy*, January 59–60

Flint, D., 1988. *Philosophy and Principles of Auditing*, London: Macmillan

Francis, J., 1994. 'Auditing and Hermeneutics', *Accounting, Organizations and Society*, forthcoming

Habermas, J., 1992. 'The New Obscurity: The Crisis of the Welfare State and the Exhaustion of Utopian Energies', in J. Habermas, *The New Conservatism: Cultural Criticism and the Historian's Debate*, ed. and trans. Shierry Weber Nicholsen, Cambridge, MA: MIT: 48–70

HC 198, 1992. House of Commons, *Inquiry into the Supervision of the Bank of Credit and Commerce International*, London: HMSO

Hood, C., 1991. 'A Public Management for all Seasons', *Public Administration*, 69, Spring: 3–19

Hopwood, A.G., 1984. 'Accounting and the Pursuit of Efficiency', in A.G. Hopwood and C. Tomkins, *Issues in Public Sector Accounting*, Oxford: Phillip Allan: 167–87

International Chamber of Commerce (ICC), 1991. *Effective Environmental Auditing*, Paris: ICC

Jensen, M. and Meckling, W., 1976. 'Theory of the Firm: Managerial Behaviour, Agency Costs and Ownership Structure', *Journal of Financial Economics* 3: 305–60

Kirkham, L.M., 1992. 'Putting Auditing Practices in Context: Deciphering the Message in Auditor Responses to Selected Environmental Cues', *Critical Perspectives on Accounting* 3: 291–314

Luhmann, N., 1989. *Ecological Communication*, trans. J. Bednarz, Cambridge: Polity Press

McSweeney, B., 1988. 'Accounting for the Audit Commission', *Political Quarterly*, Spring: 28–43

Mautz, R.K. and Sharaf, H.A., 1961. *The Philosophy of Auditing*, Sarasota, FL: American Accounting Association

Meyer, J. and Rowan, B., 1977. 'Institutionalised Organizations: Formal Structure as Myth and Ceremony', *American Journal of Sociology* 83(2): 340–63

Miller, P., 1992. 'Accounting and Objectivity: The Invention of Calculating Selves and Calculable Spaces', *Annals of Scholarship* 9(1/2): 61–86

Miller, P. and O'Leary, T., 1987. 'Accounting and the Construction of the Governable Person', *Accounting, Organizations and Society* 12(3): 235–65

Montagna, P., 1986. 'Accounting Rationality and Financial Legitimation', *Theory and Society* 15: 103–38

Pentland, B.T., 1993. 'Getting Comfortable with the Numbers: The Micro production of Macro Order', *Accounting, Organizations and Society* 18(7/8): 605–20

Perrow, C., 1990. 'Economic theories of organization', in S. Zukin, and P. DiMaggio, *Structures of Capital: The Social Organization of the Economy*, Cambridge: Cambridge University Press: 121–52

Poster, M., 1990. *The Mode of Information*, Cambridge: Polity Press

Powell, W.W. and DiMaggio, P.J. (eds.), 1991. *The New Institutionalism in Organizational Analysis*, Chicago: Chicago University Press

Power, M., 1991. 'Auditing and Environmental Expertise: Between Protest and Professionalisation', *Accounting, Auditing & Accountability* 4(3): 30–42

　　1992. 'From Common Sense to Expertise: Reflections on the Pre-History of Audit Sampling', *Accounting, Organizations and Society* 17(1): 37–62

　　1993. 'Auditing and the Politics of Regulatory Control in the UK Financial Services Sector', in S. Picciotto, J. McCahery and C. Scott (eds.), *Corporate Control and Accountability*, Oxford: Oxford University Press: 187–202

　　1994. 'Auditing, Expertise and the Sociology of Technique', *Critical Perspectives on Accounting*

Rose, N. and Miller, P., 1992. 'Political Power beyond the State: Problematics of Government', *British Journal of Sociology* 43(2): 173–205

Teubner, G., 1992. 'The Two Faces of Janus: Rethinking Legal Pluralism', *Cardozo Law Review* 13(5), March: 1443–62

Vattimo, G., 1992. *The Transparent Society*, Cambridge: Polity Press

Zukin, S. and DiMaggio, P., 1990. *Structures of Capital: The Social Organization of the Economy*, Cambridge: Cambridge University Press

# Index

*Cambridge Studies in Management*